East of Kingston
South of Here

About the Cover

 John Wesley Mincy family; ca 1900

 John Wesley Mincy Family; ca 1925

 Homer F. Mincy Family; 1938

 Virgil Mincy Family; 1975

 Virgil, Mouse & daughters; 2001

 The next generation; 2003

Cover Design: Jenette Nijak

East of Kingston South of Here

Virgil Mincy

iUniverse, Inc.
New York Lincoln Shanghai

East of Kingston South of Here

Copyright © 2006 by Virgil Mincy

All rights reserved. No part of this book may be used or reproduced by any means, graphic, electronic, or mechanical, including photocopying, recording, taping or by any information storage retrieval system without the written permission of the publisher except in the case of brief quotations embodied in critical articles and reviews.

iUniverse books may be ordered through booksellers or by contacting:

iUniverse
2021 Pine Lake Road, Suite 100
Lincoln, NE 68512
www.iuniverse.com
1-800-Authors (1-800-288-4677)

ISBN-13: 978-0-595-40474-2 (pbk)
ISBN-13: 978-0-595-67805-1 (cloth)
ISBN-13: 978-0-595-84844-7 (ebk)
ISBN-10: 0-595-40474-X (pbk)
ISBN-10: 0-595-67805-X (cloth)
ISBN-10: 0-595-84844-3 (ebk)

Printed in the United States of America

In Special Memory of
Robin D. Pierce Esq. 1949–2000
Jurist, husband, father, enthusiastic hobbyist, neighbor, and friend.

A few years ago, during a most casual neighborhood gathering, Rob described his current passion-genealogy; I was interested but going nowhere; he was hooked and on a roll. He shared how, where, and what. He proudly exhibited the results of his efforts. He kicked me off the fence and started me moving.

Without Rob's advice and encouragement, this effort may have eventually started, but not then. His memory directs a light of support and enthusiasm on each page; I can only express my appreciation with a heart-felt "thank you." He is a contributor to all that follows.

Contents

Prologue 1
The Hedgecocks and Roberts 7
Mincys, Harts and Marneys 43
The Canupps, Farners and Runions 83
Homer F. Mincy Sr. 115
Eva Estelle Hedgecock Mincy 149
Early Days, School and the Learning Years 187
4-H Days 227
"Hail, Hail the Working Man..." 263
Picking, Grinning and Other Non-Essentials 321
Family, Those Mincy Girls, Mouse and More 337
"My Faith Looks Up to Thee" 367
Epilogue 377
Index 383

Acknowledgements

Most works of fiction start, tell a story, and then ride off down the trail; most autobiographies, personal works, or historical novels seem to contain almost as many words of appreciation, bibliographies, permissions, and footnotes as the stories themselves. I noted some mammoth works by the big guys that must have benefited from the efforts of a platoon of researchers and support staff, with nary a peep of thanks to anyone. So what are the rules?

One can thumb through *Southern Living* and find pages of beautiful pictures illustrating where to place nine pieces of silver, six items of crystal, festive plates, or colorful napkins; I tend to think that is more for show than to know. If half one's meals are taken at a counter in a service station containing a Subway, and one's source of "service" is a stand containing paper and plastic, yet, you want to make your Mamma proud, how do the "rules" come into play?

Perhaps Mamma would just say, "Son, be honest about what has been inspired by or contributed to by others, and be gracious showing your appreciation to those who have helped." My heartfelt thanks follow.

My work on the Mincys was, first, aided by several professional genealogists who made some breakthroughs, helped search out the blind alleys, and, collectively, amassed valuable and interesting information. In no order of importance but with thanks to all, those include: Gale Bamman, Marjory Watts, and Linda Walker. Cousins who were discovered in this process and who graciously shared their memories and knowledge include: Kyle Smith, Ann Chory, Connie Watters, Sheila Rodrigue, Stacy Sanchez, Nancy Dill, and Linda Skinner. The shared e-mails with Linda could almost source another book.

Material relative to the Civil War experience of the Mincys, as well as all my family branches, was greatly enhanced by Robert K. Cannon's work: *Volunteers for Union and Liberty; History of the 5th Tennessee Infantry,*

U.S.A. 1862-1865. Robert assisted further by providing insight regarding specific issues of that time. Also, *The Sultana Tragedy,* by Jerry O. Potter, was beneficial to a better understanding of that tragic accident. This chapter and others benefited from web sites dealing with the specific period, or, in some instances, specific information shared through family forums.

I began the Hedgecock story, armed with family memories and a better sense of its history; cousins Lester Smith and Billy Hedgecock Wyatt are appreciated for spending their lives helping to preserve it. Several years ago, cousin Wayne Hedgecock Treece prepared a simple, but accurate and meaningful, family story and chart. In 1988, Lieutenant Colonel, USAF Retired, Byron E. Battershell published his first edition of *Willis Edward Hedgecock, 1813-1895: His Ancestors and Descendants.* I was fortunate to discover Robert E. Hedgecock's *The Hitchcock, Hedgecock, Hedgcock Family in Maryland and North Carolina and Their Descendants.* A few questions of Bob led to Cousin Jim Hedgcoke, in Oklahoma, who filled in other voids. Snyder D. Roberts' *Roots of Roane County, Tennessee 1792* proved to be a useful source, and Robert Bailey (related to the Roberts) was a courteous and helpful host during a few visits to the Roane County Heritage Library. Helpful employees in the Register of Deeds Offices at the McMinn County and Roane County Courthouses are thanked for pointing me to the correct corners, where all the old, yellowed, and moldy secrets are kept. All those resources were used, with respect and appreciation, to make what was written, as accurate and meaningful as possible.

I was fortunate to find Robert Canup, who, throughout his life, has collected material about the Canupps. He was able to supply the lineage, down to Joseph Taft Canupp and, hence, to my family. I certainly am grateful for his help. (Sister) Betty and Ed Axley assisted with specific projects; Frankie Benton, Kathy Stanfield, June Waggoner, and, perhaps unknowingly, a few of my children contributed to stories of the Canupps and Farners.

Friends Ben Tyler, Earl Melton, Bill Casteel, Tom Nicholas, and Sam Wyrosdick have read parts of this narrative, from time to time; their advice and support was always of value.

Brother Homer read every word and served as chief editor; we came to describe the returned work as, "The Passion of Homer" due to the dripping, red ink. Mary Anne Ciotti added encouragement, editing, and format work. Jenny Nijak is the picture genius and assisted with cover design; the enhancements are theirs; the glitches, alas, mine.

I have referred throughout these stories to Betty and Homer; they have shared this life with me, supported me in trying to describe it, and are very close members of a family of which I am proud. Mouse always encouraged and provided big-time cheerleading…often when it was greatly needed.

Now, I think Mother would say, "That about says it."

Prologue

Somewhere in or near La Rochelle, France, Robert Brasseur, a Huguenot, born about 1597, begat a son, Benjamine. Benjamine also begat a son, Robert, who begat Samuel, who begat Robert, who begat Nancy Brashears Roberts, who gave birth to Brashears Roberts, who begat Thomas, who begat Sarah Alice Hedgecock, who gave birth to Eva Estelle Hedgecock Mincy, who gave birth to Virgil, who begat Pamela, who gave birth to Cristina Helen Clapp. Cris, my oldest granddaughter, graduated from Mary Washington College in 2005.

Cris is also a direct descendant of John Alden, [of, "Prithee, John, why do you not speak for yourself?" fame] who, in September 1620, joined 99 other adventurous souls on the Mayflower to begin a new life. In the process, they helped open a New World.

About 1670 in Scotland, Amos Marney also begat a son, Amos, who migrated to Ireland. From there, the Marney family voyaged to the colonies where, generations later, one Letitia Marney wed John Sawyer Hart whose father, Henry, was born in London. Their granddaughter, Elizabeth Hart, later met and married John Wesley Mincy. John's son, my father, Homer Franklin Mincy, is the great grandfather of my youngest grandchild, Joseph Michael Hartnett. I would love to survive and be able to enjoy *his* last day in college.

Along the way these Marneys, Hedgecocks, Mincys, and Brasseurs did meet Nicks, Rausins, Ladds, Roberts, Staleys, Harts, Selvidges, Martins, and Byrums; wedding, bedding and breeding as they went. Thus, today, if we all gathered two by two, we would most surely sink an ark and, probably, the Titanic.

Until a few years ago, I had no clue about this and much, much more (except that I had grandchildren).

At this point you may say, with good reason, *so what?*

Let me recall a couple of stories: in September 1958, my wife, June, and I, with three year old Pam, had recently moved to 18 Lee Street, Nixon, New Jersey. This was my fifth work assignment in two years, following school, and certainly my deepest penetration into the *North*. June soon had an interesting experience with our apartment complex neighbors, as she and other mothers strolled, with their children, up and down the street. These women mentioned being either "Italian" or "Jewish" or "Greek" or "Polish" or "Catholic" and wanted to know what she was. June was somewhat embarrassed and, not knowing what else to say, retorted, "I am just an American, I guess."

I always gave her high marks for this response because it complimented a viewpoint that nurtured for years. It is that my immediate relatives' ancestors had been here so long that what they did (farmer, merchant, lawyer, preacher) and who their immediate relatives were, was more important than where their distant ancestors originated. Most of them had long forgotten if, in fact, they ever knew.

I grew up, like most, caring little about what tales were told and, for whatever reasons, my father told few. The years went by; I had questions and there was no one to answer them. Who was I? (Other than *Virgil Mincy, American*)

It is my observation concerning genealogy that the normal bell curve of distribution applies: a few are rabidly interested, a few could not care less or are turned off, and the rest (a majority) may show mild curiosity if struck over the head with a family bible or album. I rested comfortably in this *sans* coat of arms majority. For whatever reason, perhaps genes, sense of mortality, or wanting to know the origin of Mincy, I developed a strong desire to know more and, through a series of circumstances, set out to do something about it.

This effort was, admittedly, a somewhat selfish one. I wanted answers to questions about my past and finding some of them has been well worth the search. More importantly, some nephew, grandchild, great granddaughter, or cousin will someday have the same longing to *know about us*; so, for them too, I made this effort. I found information about "who I was." However, finding facts only created the desire for more facts. I became interested in adding to what was known about my mother's family. In fairness to my children and my grandchildren, I wanted to find what I could about their maternal families, the Canupps and Farners. This activity dredged up all the memories of my lifetime and the desire to tell some of it. What to do?

Write a book? Me? I have struggled to write a memo, letter, or a concise sentence throughout my life. Any volunteers? (Silence). There being none, I seriously considered this project: Could I? Should I? Would I? The answer came from "Little Engine that Could": "*I think I can; I think I can*".... So, I shall.

This will not be a tell all. While it may, in fact or by implication, be about war, mystery, excitement, and love, it will not, in fact or by implication, say anything that would belittle, hurt, or malign anyone, living or dead. It will stray on the side of blandness rather than charge straight toward controversy.

In genealogy, the professionals remind us, as a teacher would by tapping you on the wrist, that "You must have three verification sources" for authenticity. Much of this work includes the results of professional efforts. More is from family sources, and it all is, or is believed to be, accurate. Most I just know to be true. I may not have, in every case, documents in triplicate to support a premise. For example, if every reference gleaned from "the Internet" was downloaded and copied, the paper left for someone to throw out someday would be staggering. Generous acknowledgement will be given later to those whose work and support made this possible.

There are gaps and mysteries that may never be filled or resolved about some family links. In some cases, conclusions may be drawn or hypotheses formed as to who did what and why but, if so, it will be evident.

Today, we see ourselves in mirrors, photo prints, film, and video. We are in color, often moving, and always real. The grass is green, the sky blue, blood is red, a dress is yellow, and pink lips smile to reveal perfect teeth that are usually white. We take all this for granted.

Move back a few generations, however, and the pictures that exist are black and white or sepia toned. The subjects they preserve for us are always stern, posed, and look "old worldly." We usually identify no more with those ancient, framed portraits hanging in an obscure attic than we do similar artifacts displayed in T G.I. Fridays or Cracker Barrel.

They deserve something more.

Those distant relatives of mine helped found a nation, fought its battles, taught their children, tilled the soil, ministered to lost souls, and lived real lives. Their blood was as red as ours, their love as deep, their passion as strong, and their belief in tomorrow perhaps clearer. Their stories warrant telling.

That is what I intend to do: tell some of their stories. This cannot be **the history of** Mincy ancestors and descendants, for that would truly be another *War and Peace*. What I shall do is tell **about these people**, trying to abstract and preserve small bits of their lives so we can better understand ours. If you find some of it pathetic, share our pathos. If it seems mildly amusing, chuckle slightly. Sad? Tears are in order. If you happen to be a grandchild, eight or 10 generations removed from Jacob Knupp, Amos Marney, Robert Brasseur, or one of the Hitchcocks, maybe you will look at it this way: these are only a few footlights along the path from them to you.

Then, of course, I have my own tales to tell. It is interesting to note how family lore, long buried or passed down as gospel, turns out to be quite different when the facts are revealed. Society surely will benefit if the truth about me can be, and is, told. You also need to know I have an older brother, Homer, and a younger sister, Elizabeth Alice (Betty) Axley. I could not do justice to a story of their lives; however, each has contributed to this work and when events include them, please accept them as characters in that plot who are near and dear to me. More importantly, their insights make descriptions about our parents *our story*, not just mine.

My first marriage lasted *only* 27 years. For the most part, I always considered that relationship to be better than any others I observed. I do, and always did, credit June with being an untiring and giving mother to our five daughters. I shall never forget or fail to appreciate the support she gave me and the companionship we shared. For the fact that it ended, I assess no blame but accept my share.

Unmerited, I have been blessed with a new relationship. My present wife and best friend, Dorothy Jean Ciotti (Mouse), and I are enjoying our twentieth year of wedded bliss. I did nothing worthy of deserving her. If I were to write a separate book about our life together, it would truly be a fairy tale.

The point of bringing this up now is to alert you that, if history involved June, I shall just say June, and when it involves Mouse,…. well, you get the picture.

I think this is going to be a hoot. Perhaps someday, someone will find it touching them a little, too.

On with the story!

The Hedgecocks and Roberts

The presumption of taking on the task of finding, describing the lives of, and telling stories about an ancestral line certainly risks challenge. On the one hand, if not much is known, what does one tell? If, on the other hand, one is trying to present for generations yet unborn, stories about historically significant, tradition-rich, and relationship-inspiring people, what formula does one use? Two pages per generation? Two paragraphs per person? Three lines per child? Just tell all you know and cut out the "fat" later? Perhaps unspoken, but nonetheless felt, this is the dilemma that lurks for me as I take on the "duty" of telling about my mother's "people." Those "people," those Hedgecocks and Roberts, whose blood flows through my very veins and whose gene pool contributed to the shape of my nose, the color of my eyes, and the thoughts that emanate from my somewhat inadequate brain, are worthy of my very best. They will certainly get that.

I was blessed that my mother was born into an outstanding family; I remember aunts and uncles, remember my grandmother, although the visits with her were really very few, and remember the pride and respect she (mom) always displayed as she recounted her ancestral anecdotes. I had a starting point. I have sort of sloughed off most of the digging efforts to uncover more than what seemed to be known, as so much has been collected over the years by cousins far and near. I was challenged somewhat to prove or disprove some aspects of those "stories" because a few seemed suspect. Perhaps I can succeed in that endeavor, in a minor instance or two, and add to factual knowledge of those many families. Again, at least, I shall give my best. In doing so, I simply flipped a coin and the Hedgecocks won the toss; they get to be up first.

Mom never really talked a lot about the origin of the Hedgecocks that I recall; she would make reference to our perhaps **being** "Dutch" or "Black

Dutch" with no explanation of either. Other relatives, when quizzed, have related to me that the Hedgecocks went all the way back to South Carolina....Virginia, maybe, without the next logical question being answered: how far back do we really have facts and where do they evidence our origin? Garden of Eden? Europe? England? Any or all the above? What I shall set about doing is relate what is known and if, or when, I break new ground or add a different conclusion than that previously assumed, you will be the next to know. This simple compilation will be from all I have seen about the Hedgecocks, what I was able to sort out that fit my purpose, and a little I was able to dig up, or add to, from my own efforts. This purpose, again, is to relate what is known of the "earliest Hedgecocks" and bring the line straight down to me; the side trips will be only for the sake of interest. The Hedgecocks were prolific, and, today, the direct offspring of William Hitchcock of England must number in the tens of thousands. At three lines per child, I just cannot get them all; we shall look at a few.

First, let's get the name out of the way. Mom was a Hedgecock, of course, but this name, both now and in the past, has always had many variants: Hedgecock, Hedgcock, Hedgcoke, Hickock, Hitchcock, to name just a few. Where did it start? Who knows, but let me offer some insight from the work of Robert E. Hedgcock, who authored *The Hitchcock, Hedgecock, Hedgcock Family in Maryland and North Carolina and their Descendants*. In Appendix XI, he shared this: "In 1933 Dr. Dudley Rossiter of Fort Wayne, IN noticed that Frank Arthur Hedgcock appeared in the "English Who's Who" and wrote him a letter inquiring about the origins of the Family. The response follows:

Camelot, Madeira Ave, Bromley Park, Kent 30, IX, 1933

Dear Dr. Rossiter,

...........I have always looked upon them (Hedgcocks) as a very humble, though very ancient family, probably attached to the soil for centuries; and until my older brother, Walter, who died last year, made the name known to some extent, I do not believe there had ever been a Hedgcock known to a wide public.

I have always understood that the H's were a Kentish stock, though there are, I believe, some few in Yorkshire. My father's family came from Hoo, at the mouth of the Medway, a desolate looking, sheep rearing county on the mud-flats of the Thames Estuary. There are many Hedgcocks buried there……..

My idea always has been that the Hedgcocks came over with Hengert and Horsa in their invasion of Kent, AD 449 (they landed near Hoo) and that being slow and easily-contented folk they settled down there-stopped there for centuries!

Certainly, the name is Low German. The talk about "little Isaac" (we aren't Jews) or "little Richard" is all nonsense. The name comes from "edj" or "ecdg" (as in "edge" meaning something that cuts, a knife, a dagger.) The "cock" is diminutive as in "haycock, hillcock." So the name probably means "the little dagger" and our original ancestor was some disreputable pirate whose "little dagger" had an unenviable reputation.

The present forms Hedg (e) cock or Hitchcock are corruptions-people thinking in joke or in earnest that the name had something to do with a cock on a hedge! You speak of some of the family being buried in the cemetery where Ruskin is interred; and also with Dickens. I do not remember where Ruskin is buried; I thought it was in the Lake District and there are no H's there. But Dickens is buried in Westminster Abbey and I guarantee there are none of us in that noble pile!

Yours very truly
Signed
Frank A. Hedgcock"

A few lines omitted.

So there! Is this the whole truth and final word? Unlikely. From research I have done, it is clear there were many, many of this clan that migrated from England to America in the 17th and 18th centuries; several forms of this name were in use even then and our line, which was apparently Hitchcock upon arrival, is just the luck of the name draw. It started (in America) as Hitchcock and evolved into various other forms for a variety of common reasons: spelling, pronunciations, illiteracy, record keeping, and, perhaps, many others. No mystery, no scandals; it just happened. Here we are; case closed. As to ethnicity, the "Hengert (Hengist) and Horsa" referred to were Anglo-Saxons (Jutes), who, the story has it, came to Kent to support (as mercenaries) the existing ruler, Vortigern. Soon, being good business men, they literally "cut out" the "middle man" and founded the Jutish kingdom of Kent. Were they really our "kind of folks?" Again, historical facts are not clear; "brother-warrior" myths abound and whether or not these two really existed is questioned by historians. The movement of peoples from northern Europe to the Isles is not and, after 1,600 years, does it matter? I have proudly worn my "Hedgecock nose," wherever its source.

William Hitchcock (I) was born in England, presumably Kent; he arrived in the Colonies in 1670 and, that same year, married Mary Gerves, the sister of a close friend. They settled in Calvert County, Maryland, near the town of Joppa. As of this writing, I have been unable to identify the ship on which William left kith and kin to seek his fortune in the new world; one can only speculate as to his financial status upon arrival. It is my guess he had the means to obtain land. There are other possibilities.

William lived a relatively short time, dying from "the Fever" in 1684 at age 35 (ca). His will, which was probated in 1685, seemed to indicate his primary estate was a tract of land called "Hitchcock's Fortune" (100 acres) in the Province of Ye Clifts of Calvert County, Maryland. While this was a solid base of existence, it was no large tract and seemed to have been acquired rather than granted. On the one hand, many came to the Colonies as bonded or indentured servants and were able, under the terms of their situation, to become independent and acquire property. However, whether this would have been likely in fourteen years, before his death, is open to conjecture; it could have been either way. Until specific facts are determined, we know he came, he obtained, and he died, leaving his estate to his sons, William (II) and Christopher, both younger than 17 years of age. Richard Stallings and Robert Gerves were appointed as guardians for his children. William Jones Sr. is mentioned as the one taking an inventory of the estate after William's death. It is apparent that the younger son, Christopher, died near the same time his father had; they were buried beside each other. Mary and William (II) went to live with Mary's brother, Robert, although shortly thereafter, Mary married the same William Jones, who was involved in settling the estate.

William II learned to be a blacksmith and probably worked in the mill his uncle operated near a small creek. After his twentieth birthday, he went to live with his mother and Mr. Jones; after Jones died, he cared for his mother until she died in 1705. Upon her death, he (William II) apparently inherited his father's estate; tradition has it that family members living in Cecil County had harbored "ill feelings" against Mary and William, possibly because of their (Mary and William) being sent to live with Mr. Gerves. In any event, William supposedly returned to Cecil County after his mother's death and asked those relatives if they needed anything. They reportedly concluded he was a fair man and normal relations were established at that time among the Maryland Hitchcocks.

William Jr., (II) the second generation Hitchcock of our line, became very prosperous, although perhaps by circumstances as much as by planning and effort. He did make some aggressive moves, land-wise, that, due to location and the economy of that time, resulted in business success.

William decided to convey Hitchcock's Fortune, the land his father had willed to him, to Ed Reynolds, of Calvert County, for a tract of land in Baltimore County, called Turkey Hill, which appears to have contained 262 acres. Nine years later, Lord Baltimore granted an additional 100 acres called Bednell Green and, in 1721, William purchased Richardson Reserve (214 acres) for 5500 pounds of tobacco; in 1729 he was granted another land patent for Timber Hall by Lord Baltimore. This land lay on the east side of the Little Falls of Gunpowder River and totaled almost 600 acres. All this property was near the port of Joppa, which, from 1724 until about 1768, was the leading port for the Province of Maryland, as well as the county seat of Baltimore County.

Tobacco and corn were the primary products of this agricultural community and soon were shipped through this active port to many other parts of the world. William, through contacts in England, traded agricultural products for manufactured goods for use on his properties or in other merchandising ventures. He was known as a "planter" and certainly prospered.

When William's mother, Mary, died in 1705, he moved to Baltimore County and, in 1707, married Mary Jones; Mary was a niece of Williams' step-father, William Jones Sr. Mary had been a frequent visitor in the home of her uncle, and William II would certainly have known her. Interestingly, however, William was probably 36 years old before this marriage occurred.

William and Mary had five children; one died at birth; Mary died in 1715 in Baltimore County. Their children were: infant (died at birth), Phillis Anna, 1708; William III, 1710; John, August 30, 1712, and Mary, 1714.

In 1716, William married Mary's younger sister, Anne Jones. Anne was several years younger than William, and, after his death in 1738, married Peter Carroll in Baltimore County, March 23, 1739. William and Anne had six children: infant, died at birth in 1717; Asel, April 26, 1719; Elizabeth, 1721; Ann, 1722; Amelia (Emelia), 1724, and Jemima, born 1726.

Hartford County was formed out of Baltimore County in 1773; at that time, no Hitchcocks were noted on the Baltimore County tax records, implying that the family had remained mostly in Hartford County. In 1768, most of the county records were moved to Baltimore, which became the county seat; its port also replaced Joppa in importance during this period. While Joppa was still enjoying success at the time of William's death, gradual erosion of soil resulted in mud and silt from the river flowing into the tidewater, rendering it useless as a port. The upstart, "Baltimore," took over this role as the port of choice. Disease, poor farm practices, the county's seat moving to Baltimore, and the loss in prominence of its port caused Joppa to become but a footnote in the history of Maryland and Baltimore County.

Within five years of his (William II) death, most of his lands had been sold. The decline of Joppa as a port, poor use of the land, and mismanagement, among other factors, caused many of this family to begin movement to the Carolinas and other places, North and South. A not unique lesson that could be William's legacy: it is sometimes easier to "get" than it is to "keep."

John Hitchcock, the fourth child of William II and Mary Jones, born August 12, 1712, in Baltimore County, Maryland is perhaps one of the most influential links in our family; between William I and Willis (my gggrandfather), it is John who most affected the location of and circumstances of, not only his children, but others of the family, who migrated from Maryland.

It should be acknowledged that family tradition and other recorded sources credit Isaac, the son of William III (John's nephew) and Nancy Horne with being the parents of Thomas, the father of Willis. Some factors reasonably call into question whether or not "two Johns" may have existed, but the preponderance of evidence indicate that John, son of William II and father of Thomas (who was born November 1, 1755) is the actual link between William I and II and Thomas/Willis. A careful review of the known facts can be found in a narrative by the late Byron Battershell as well as in Robert L. Hedgecock's *The Hitchcock, Hedgecock....;* I have concluded the evidence, both traditional and actual, as researched by Robert L., confirms that John is the father of our Thomas, which is the most important fact to be considered. From my perspective, I have been more interested in who fathered whom, than who owned what. To add credence to John's importance, the birth date of his son, Thomas, November 1, 1755 is the same date used by sources that indicate Thomas was the son of Isaac and Nancy Horne. Further, the birth date of Thomas, the son of Isaac and Nancy Horne is also known to have been ca 1771. The Thomas born 1771 married a "Rebecca" and his life facts are known, yet different, from those pertaining to the father of Willis. What follows, then, about John, is from the perspective of accepting him as father of Thomas, father of Willis.

Family tradition that relates happenings from the period of William I, II and John indicate that John appears to have been very strong willed and at odds in many ways with his father, William II. Paramount among these differences may have been religion; although he may not have "belonged," John appears to have been influenced by the Quaker Movement and, for whatever accumulated reasons, was disowned by his father. About 1732, John left his home in Baltimore County and went to Cecil County, where he lived for a short period with his uncles, Thomas and Christopher Hitchcock. Tradition has it that William I had paid to transport his brothers, Thomas and Christopher, to the Colonies and that he had named his second son, Christopher, after his brother, who had just arrived.

Having no land of his own, and not likely to inherit any from his father, John, with his cousin William, a descendant of Thomas, joined a Quaker wagon train in 1735 and left Cecil County for Virginia. It is significant that these two were the first family members to leave Maryland and John was probably the first Hitchcock in the Carolinas. John and William stopped in what is now Albermarle County, Virginia, and remained for a short time, during which he helped William get established. John had heard of land being available for the taking, plus a small tax to the King and, growing tired of waiting for a Lord Fairfax grant, gave the few acres he had to William and set out in 1738 for the wild lands of North Carolina, an area called Bath. It was there, in 1739, he married Mary Ruth Millikin, 16, the daughter of Will Millikin; she was a Quaker, born about 1722, in Albermarle County, Virginia.

William Millikin and John were close friends and helped each other during the Revolutionary War; William, being a good Quaker, did not fight the British, but hid and fed many who did. John had, perhaps, served in the war as a spy or scout; after his death, his son, William, applied for his father's land grant for Revolutionary Service, as a legal heir, and was granted 640 acres in the Tennessee Valley. (He sold it immediately)

Soon after John and Mary were married, they went to Bladen County, North Carolina, and, in 1741, John received the first of many land grants he would receive. The records of his land acquisitions and grants are numerous and impressive. From 1741 until his death, about 1788, he amassed holdings of approximately 3,420 acres. Much of this property was along what are now both sides of the border between North and South Carolina but also included property in what are now Orange, Rowan, and Guilford Counties (NC). Records of the many transactions by which John acquired this property, as well as how most of it was settled on his heirs, has been researched and validates the traditional stories of his activities.

In an unusual twist to the "Prodigal Son" story, three of John's nephews from Maryland arrived in North Carolina about the time the Revolutionary War began; the family had fallen on hard times in Maryland, and the outcast from the Maryland Hitchcocks, who had become wealthy in North Carolina, took them in. Isaac, William IV and Joshua, sons of William III, were offered the use of lands in what was then Rowan County; John gave them a home, and for a small share of the crops and taxes during the War, provided for them until they could get their own land.

After the war, John offered all his relatives who had come to North Carolina title to the lands they had farmed, if they paid the taxes. Predictably, after John's death, some of his heirs, led by his son, William, wanted to fight the cousins to avoid their retaining this land, but to no avail; John had given them this land "right out." These cousins had used the land and kept it from the Tories during the war; John was still wealthy after the war, and had always been generous to his relatives. This situation was further worsened when some of the relatives soon sold the land that had been given them; other than hard feelings, not much resulted from those controversies.

John and Mary had the following children: Robert; William, 1741; Matthias, 1743; Josiah, 1745; Susannah, 1747; Asahel, 1749; Thomas, November 1, 1755; Mary, 1761; Jesse, 1763; Moses, 1763; Margaret, 1765; Jesse 1768, and Ruth, 1770. The records of John's disposal of his properties and his wills cause some confusion as to whether John had more than one wife; it is generally conceded that his children were all born of Mary.

John's story surely equals any success saga that we could imagine, even today. He was born into wealth, disowned, ventured into the unknown, accumulated great wealth, survived a war that shaped and defined a new nation, shared his wealth with those in his family who had fallen upon bad times, and forged a legacy that influences thousands today, who proudly remember him as "an ancestor." John died in 1788 in Anson County, North Carolina, and his wife, Mary Ruth died in 1783; it is believed they were buried beside each other on property near their home

Thomas Hitchcock, the seventh child of John and Mary, was born November 1, 1755, in the Marlboro District, South Carolina. He was married July 10, 1783 in Rowan County, North Carolina to Elizabeth Wood; it is not known when or why this relationship ended. He married Martha Patsy Earle Edwards in Lincoln County, North Carolina, January 3, 1811. Thomas and Martha were the parents of: David, 1811; Willis Edward, December 21, 1813; Melitta, 1815; Minter, August 25, 1817 and Martha, 1825. Thomas was ca 56 years old when his first child was born.

Thomas is not specifically mentioned in any of John's wills that have been researched; however, his occupation was a farmer and it is likely he possessed land in his own right or worked that owned by his father. He lived in the Marlborough District during the Revolutionary War; shortly thereafter, he moved to Rowan County, North Carolina, lived there a short time and then moved to Lincoln County, North Carolina, where he lived for about 14 years. He later moved to Cocke County, Tennessee and finally, to Macon County, North Carolina (now Swain), which was his home when he died. He was buried in the Brush Creek Cemetery, in Swain County, North Carolina. The spelling on the grave marker is "Hedgcock," however, this marker was placed shortly after WWII by a group that did not know the family; Thomas used "Hedgecock" in his pension application, for land transactions, and in his last will and testament. Thus, insofar as my line is concerned, Thomas is the bridge between "Hitchcock" and "Hedgecock."

After Thomas died, Martha crossed the Smokies into Monroe County, Tennessee, to live with her daughter, Martha, who was married to a gentleman named Mull. Mr. Mull was later killed on Ball Park Road, in Monroe County, during a Civil War battle. Martha is buried in the DeHart Cemetery in Monroe County, TN, not far across the state line from where Thomas was buried. Coincidently, her oldest son, David, rests in this same cemetery.

It is interesting to note records of Thomas' service in the Revolutionary War. He may or may not have received a land grant for service; however, when he was 81 years old, he applied for a pension or whatever specific benefit was applicable under an act of Congress, passed in 1832. Portions of the testimony taken before the Macon County, North Carolina, Court of Pleas and Quarter Session, are historically significant and revealing; all young maidens aspiring to become DARs should listen up and remember this source. It should be all you need.

Taken the 15th day of April, 1836:

Q. How were you called into service; were you drafted? Did you volunteer or were you a substitute? A. "I enlisted in the State troops of South Carolina." Q. State the names of some of the regular officers who were with the troops where you served, such Continental and Militia Regiments as you can recollect and the general circumstances of your service. A. "I enlisted and marched to the 4 Hole Swamp under General Marion, then to the fork of Wateree; there, crossed the Waccammas, fought the British Col. Watson and the Tories; then crossed the Pee Dee; met the British and Tories at

Goose Creek Bridge; they were foraging-tried to take the forage from the British. We were defeated. Then, went to Black Creek and to Black Mingo and encamped, scouting there; the enemy had about 1200 NC Militia prisoners; placed our blankets on the bridge to prevent the enemy hearing the horses feet............scouting about in the neighborhood on a scout within a few miles of Camden; met the British and were defeated-joined Greens at Pine Tree Creek, went to Sand Hill Creek; there fought and were whipped.......... I was off below Ancrams old fields with 50 other men on a scout under Captain Snipes as a scout when the battle of Evitaw (Eutaw) was fought; heard the guns distinctly; battle fought about the 8th of September, 1782; a memorable day. Continued to serve for three months after my term of a year was out because the times were hot and the country in such state our officers would not discharge a man, even when his time was out if they could possibly induce one to serve."..........

To put this into historical context, the General Marion mentioned was Brigadier General Francis Marion, nicknamed "The Swamp Fox" by British Colonel Banastre Tarleton, who complained that it was impossible to catch the "swamp fox." Near the end of the war, Marion and American General Nathaniel Green (mentioned) joined forces, and, in 1781, successfully fought at the Battle of Eutaw Springs, forcing the British retreat into North Carolina.

The Court, in it's summary report, stated,..."and that he was discharged in the spring of 1783; this would fit with the wedding in Rowan Co. which is copied from the records of that county....." This corresponds with the traditional date given for his first marriage to Elizabeth Wood. Thomas, in his testimony, indicated he had lost his discharge papers long ago, but thought they had been signed by General Marion.

Many years ago, my mother participated in a college project with her granddaughter, Karen Axley; it was an inter-generational effort, and Mom completed a rather lengthy questionnaire relating to her ancestors, life, experiences, and values. Question 10 was: What do you remember hearing about your great-grandparents? Mom: "Nothing." Question 12: Did your great-grandparents....come to the United States from a foreign country? Mom: "My great-grandfather, Willis Hedgecock, was **Dutch,**

from Holland. He lived in Knox County." (My Uncle Ernest, Mom's brother, is quoted as remembering his grandfather, Thomas, stated his (Thomas') father was Dutch, from Holland)

Sorry, Mom, everybody.... but Willis Edward Hedgecock was born December 21, 1813, in Lincoln County, North Carolina. Various birth dates appear but this date was entered by him in a diary he kept during his Civil War experiences; it seems a reasonable source to me.

Several references to Willis' early years indicate he grew into adulthood in North Carolina. There is record, however, that his father, Thomas, was in Cocke County, Tennessee, as early as 1819, at which time Willis would have been only six years old; it is more likely Willis actually grew up in East Tennessee. We know he married Mary Ann Rausin April 18th, 1833; again, references give her age at that time as 14, however, in Willis' diary, he lists her birth date as September 12, 1816, which makes her almost 17—a little more respectable.

There are references to Willis living in Blount County, and the inference is furthered by the fact most members of the Company he directed in the (Civil) War were volunteers from Blount County. He did pay (poll) taxes in Blount County from 1847 until 1853; the earliest record of his purchasing land was in 1855 and was property located on the Clinch River, in Knox County, in or near the Hickory Creek Community. He added to that property in 1865, and he is remembered as being a tobacco farmer in that area. After Mary Ann died, he married Margaret J. Fox in Knox Count, Tennessee, May 11, 1878. Both wives are buried in the Hickory Creek Cemetery, in West Knox County, as is Willis. Willis and Mary Ann were the parents of twelve children: Mary Jane, January 19, 1834; Angeline, February 18, 1835; Thomas, May 27, 1837; Martha, July 8, 1839; Elizabeth, August 24, 1841; Caroline, September 17, 1842; John Rausin, February 2, 1847; Henry Willis, December 3, 1849; Julia, February 19, 1852; Talitha, March 26, 1854; Margaret Malissa, August 26, 1856, and William Leroy, January 28, 1860.

Other than his fine family, of course, and the legacy of the generations that followed, Willis is often remembered for his Civil War experiences, particularly because he documented them in diary form, preserving those times and his thoughts for us all. Those were traumatic times for our nation, and we often take for granted the sacrifices, hardships, tragedies, and family rending circumstances this time forced upon individuals. Historians, through books, movies, and early pictures, tell interesting tales of "brother" against "brother" and the upheaval of family life in that period. It cannot be forgotten that our families, the Hedgecocks, Roberts, Marneys, Mincys, and many others, were certainly caught up in this great struggle and endured a circumstance that was unique to Tennessee.

Tennessee was a "border state" and among the last to secede from the Union. East Tennessee was predominantly Republican—therefore, for Lincoln, for the Union, and mostly, against slavery. When the war began, volunteers by the thousands from Tennessee moved north, joining Union forces in Kentucky or Ohio. Of course, there was "brother against brother" in many states, both North and South, but no state experienced the significance of such numbers leaving their homes, joining the "enemy," an enemy that often occupied, captured or ravaged the homes they had left, then, having to endure the knowledge or uncertainty of circumstances back home. The battles at Antietam and Gettysburg were fought in Northern territory, but those areas did not actually endure occupation, and the enemy (Confederate) forces promptly withdrew. East Tennessee was largely a Confederate occupied territory, with the men folks off fighting that enemy. The magnitude of Tennessee "Volunteers" can best be expressed by noting there were at least 14 Calvary Regiments, eight Mounted Infantry Regiments, seven Artillery Regiments, 24 Infantry Regiments, and countless units of Home Guards, Militia, or National Guards serving the cause of the Union. Let Captain Willis E. Hedgecock, 5th Tennessee Infantry, USA, Company H, relate bits of this experience:

Civil War Diary of W. E. Hedgecock
Transcribed July 15, 1892
Which I kept while in the Army, against the Rebellion, 1861

(As written, with no corrections) "*I left my house in Knox Co. Tennessee on the evening of the 11th of August 1861. Traveled at night by Scarbro town on the Clinton road then turned and passed through Frosts bottom and across*

to New River wearing my summer goods. This was the 2nd night. It rained upon us all night. Some took shelter in a Rock house. Some around a fire standing or lying, taking the rain; next morning we overtook our comrades who set out on the 10th. We were delighted to procure a guide consulted and determined the safest route to proceed upon........March 14th set out under a new pilot, traveled that day down Brimstone Creek leaving Huntsville to our right hand about three miles crossed the line separating Kentucky from Tenn. Stayed at Chitwoods, met up there with Sam Williams' Co., Ky. Where we arrived on the 16. Here we alighted with other Tennesseans and remained until the 18. Here we were received as a company and went on to Barbourville about the time of leaving the former place I experienced the first attack of bad feeling derangement of bowels inside which caused me some uneasiness from the effects. I did not recover until nearly ready to leave for Camp Dick Robinson.

(30th)....Drew our clothing and gun the 1st of September; First E. Tenn. Reg. was organized on the 1st. Col R. K. Byrd, Lieut. Col J.G. Spears, Maj. J.F. Shelley. Here many of the Tenn. boys were attacked with measles which proved fatal to some. Here I witnessed such attention and kindness shown to our sick, suffering and dying soldiers as sympathizing hearts and Angel hands above can administer. (July 12th).....traveled all day and lay at night at big Creek gap. Myself and company out on picket. 13th set out at 4 o'clock to hunt the rebels; march all night cross Clinch River. At breakfast time next morning march about 4 miles; come on the rebel Calvary in their encampment at 12 o'clock at Wallace X Roads, Anderson Co. Rout them killing some and taking 17 prisoners 29 horses 4 mules, guns, swords, blankets, chickens etc. etc.

(February 10th, 1863) This is now 19 months since I left Home. No letter rec'd since Sept. 17th, 1862. ½ after 8 o'clock continues to rain. Thomas (his son) not much better yet in health, is still with me at my qtrs. Some indications of other cases of smallpox in the company. No news yet today from the front............(11th) Roar of artillery about 12 o'clock; we suppose to be an omen of good news. Thomas no better but seems to grow weaker. 12th. Thomas seems a little better today; weather continues fine. Thomas received a letter from home today, all well. News from my family given by her is that all is well.

(June10th, 1863)...Next morning separation; some bound for Kingston, others for their houses upon the Clinch and others for Blount Co. Their houses.

We waded Clinch River about ten o'clock in the night and in an hour more I found myself once more at home, to the great joy of myself and family."

Robert K. Cannon's work, **Volunteers for Union and Liberty, History of the 5th Tennessee Infantry, U.S.A. 1862-1865,** details an engagement that we can parallel with Willis' diary. It reads:

"On September 6, Colonel James Cooper began an expedition to drive the Confederate forces out of Camp Pine Knot. (Near Cumberland Gap) Included in his troops were one hundred men of the 5th Tennessee, Company H, under the command of Captain Hedgecock. On the morning of the 8th, a detachment engaged one hundred and twenty of the enemy. Five of the Rebels were killed while retreating. "The principal part of the fighting and effective fire were done by the force of the 3rd and 5th Regiments, respectively, under the command of Captains Ledgerwood and Hedgecock, and the main body of the enemy (seventy or seventy five) were captured by Lt. Crudgington and his command at Camp Pine Knot." Lieutenant Crudgington was in the 5th Tennessee, Company H. Two men of the 5th Tennessee deserted during the expedition. In Cooper's report on the expedition, he stated, "The officers and men all underwent the fatigue and exposure with marked fortitude. Too much praise cannot be bestowed on the officers and men."

Covering the same period, from Willis' diary:

"Nothing more of importance occurred till Sept. 5th. Orders were given to raise out of Spears Brigade, 400 men out of Shelley's Regiment, one hundred, all under Col. Cooper at 5 oclock the following day. 6th set out, Shelleys 100 men under my command, stayed at night on clear fork of Cumberland river, set out early next morning, stayed at night on hickory creek next morning set out for camp pine knot 26 detailed under Lieut. Crudgington with orders to search the house of Archie at Camp Pine Knot. 26 detailed under Lieut. Crudgington with orders to search the house of Archie at Camp Pine knot for rebels and rebel property, myself was ordered to post my one hundred men somewhere near the top of the mountain. This I done choosing my own position some others were ordered to repair to the top of the mountain another sqad was sent further along the road in the direction of Big Creek Gap. This was

Thomas Hedgecock Family

Front (left to right): Jane, Martha
Middle (left to right): Thomas Hedgecock, Martha Ladd Hedgecock, Henry Marion Hedgecock
Back (left to right)) William Thomas, Jr., Cordelia, Bertha

Alice and Henry Marion Hedgecock
Burton and Hugh Hedgecock

Thomas Hedgcock Family Reunion 1907

Front (left to right): Eva, Ada, Pearl Hedgecock; Wilbur, Oscar Guettner
Middle (left to right): Alice Hedgecock (holding Virgil), Mattie Guettner (holding Carlos), Thomas Hedgecock, Almeda Kreis Hedgecock, Delia (holding Floyd), Bob Eblen
Back (left to right): Henry Marion Hedgecock, John Guettner, Hugh Hedgecock, Verna Hedgecock, Bertha Smith, Marion Smith, Ernest Hedgecock, Frank Hedgecock.

My grandmother
Sarah Alice Roberts Hedgecock

Great grandfather
Thomas L. Roberts

done in order to blockade the road while we were thus posted. A company of Rebel Cavalry came along at double quick speed. They were fired upon at each post at the one held by myself. They passed with all speed on fleet horses and quick as the rough nature of the road and good riders could make it. A full volley was fired into them and reloaded and continued to fire as they passed killing some and wounding others & literally piling horses after which they passed on to Lieut. Crudgington who had drawn up his little command on an eminence at Camp Pine Knot and who ordered them to halt. Three or four disobeyed and passed on one being killed in the attempt, the rest were taken prisoner by the Lieut. who brought them back about 75 in No. and the whole of the killed and wounded about 9 the prisoners 96 horses 88. the road was Blockaded and the return march taken up the same day; six days was allotted for this expedition. It was made in five back to Cumberland gap with not a man injured on our part."...(as written by Willis)

These are but samples of the daily entries Willis made during his almost 20 months of service. The 5th Tennessee Infantry campaigned from Barbourville, Kentucky, to Big Gap, Cumberland Gap, Tennessee, Manchester, Kentucky, Wheelersburg/Sciotoville, Ohio, Gallipolis, Ohio, Cincinnati, Ohio, Louisville, Kentucky, Nashville, Tennessee, and Carthage, Tennessee, during this period. On May 2, 1863, Willis wrote a letter of resignation to HQ near Carthage complaining of chronic bronchitis and corals (?) of the femur. (This probably was caries, a necrosis or death of a bone) He also claimed to have suffered for over 30 years from scroffa (likely "scrofula," or tuberculosis in the lymph glands, neck, or other bone areas); he immediately received an honorable discharge. During much of the last year or so of his service, he cared for his son, Thomas, who stayed with him (or in hospitals); however, Thomas was not in the 5th. Most likely, Thomas suffered from smallpox.

Family lore has long held that Willis' brothers, David and Minter, both served the Confederacy; it was further reported they both likely spent time in Andersonville Prison, and David probably perished there. How such mis-information started will never be known, although it is entirely possible those brothers did not contact each other after the war; they had fought each other for four years and possibly did so for the rest of their lives. The fact is, however, Minter moved to Texas in 1853 and served in a Confederate unit there, although he saw no action. He lived a full life, sired a fine family, and was buried there.

David may have joined a Confederate Unit in North Carolina, but never served. (There is record of a David Hedgecock joining the NC 39th Inf. Co. F, February 15, 1862; he was listed from Cherokee Co. and was 18. He failed to report for duty and was dropped from the rolls. This age does not match "our" David, who would have been 51 years old in 1862.) "Our" David was a non-combatant and actually lived his life in Monroe County, (but a few miles from Willis) where he married, raised a family, and was buried (in the same cemetery with his mother, Martha). Did Willis know the facts regarding his brothers? If so, why did his descendents believe they suffered in Andersonville—possibly dying there? Such is the stuff of legend; families fight, brothers fall out, grudges remain, and reasons for estrangement abound. Before the war, this family must have been close; both Minter and David named sons, Willis. More than likely, as in other areas of my family, these facts got skewed because no one asked....therefore, no one told.

Thomas Hedgecock, the third child and the first of four sons born to Willis and Mary Ann Rausin Hedgecock, was born May 27, 1837 in Blount County, Tennessee. It is likely he lived there with his parents until 1854, which was the last year Willis paid taxes in Blount County. Willis first purchased property in Knox County in 1855. Thomas married Martha Ladd, of Roane County, March 4, 1858.

It is not known precisely when Thomas moved to Roane County; his first child, Henry Marion (my grandfather) was born in 1861, presumably in Roane County. The first record I have of Thomas purchasing property in Roane County is the purchase of 200 acres from John W. Pyott, in 1867, near what then was the land of the Ladd heirs, John Crowder et. al, and near "Patterson Creek." This farm began a few hundred yards northeast of the Young's Chapel CP church, on what is now Lawnville Road. Since Martha was from Roane County, this couple could have rented in the area or on property belonging to her parents.

Thomas, as did his father, marched north into Kentucky and joined the Union forces in August, 1861; his service was with Company G, 1st Tennessee Infantry Regiment. He served until September 17, 1864. There is not much specific information regarding his service; however, we know from Willis' diary that Thomas was very ill during the first several months of his service (probably with smallpox). He stayed with the unit until its original members were mustered out in September, 1864; during this time, the 1st Infantry saw extensive duty in East Tennessee, including some action in and around Kingston. It has been interesting to note that, in addition to Thomas, my Great Grandfathers, Roberts and Mincy, also served in actions that took place near or around Kingston, Athens, Philadelphia, Riceville, and other locations significant to my early memories. I often ponder that those grandparents could have slept in the same tent(s) and buttons from their uniforms and bullets from their rifles could have been among those we have plowed up, at various locations. Thomas served as a 2nd Lieutenant, and his tales, along with those of Thomas Roberts, were those my mother heard as a child and retold to her children.

Thomas and Martha Ladd Hedgecock were the parents of seven children: Henry Marion, January 2, 1861; Talitha Ann, April 10, 1866; Cordelia, May 28, 1872; Jane Isabel, November 8, 1874; William Thomas, April 6, 1876; Bertha Amelia, June 7, 1878, and Martha Resign, March 12, 1880. Thomas acquired many pieces of property in his life, including, in a series of land transactions, a portion of the Brashears Roberts/Thomas Roberts properties, part of which later became the "home place" of my grandparents. Martha died in 1899, and Thomas married Almeda S. Kreis in 1901. My mother often related that everyone thought grandmother Almeda was a fine person and enjoyed visiting their home. She (Ms. Kreis) had been married to a member of the Kreis family, who were leading industrialists in the Harriman/Rockwood area; they were among early pioneers in iron and coal businesses. It was remembered and noted, that, when Ms. Kreis married Thomas and came to live with him, "she had many nice things, and several wagons were required to move those things." Thomas, Martha and Ameda are buried in the Lawnville Cemetery, near the Young's Chapel Church.

I have always suffered from the handicap of moving away from Roane County at an early age and being denied an opportunity to know any of my many Roberts relatives; our "line" of Roberts was important to the early settlement of Roane County and contributed to the growth of that area. I had, and have, Hedgecock "first cousins" and have known many of them well; the Roberts are all further removed, I grew up not knowing or being around any of them, and simply missed out on the opportunity to have a first hand experience sharing the legacy of this important link to my past. In tracing family history, many (including myself) ignore certain family lines....usually the maternal....because of the greater desire to emphasize the "family name" and, of equal importance, conserve time and space. When many generations are recognized and documented, to give equal time to each would pose an overwhelming task; it rarely is or can be done. However, much is known about the Roberts and other families into which the Roberts married. I wish I had known them better; however, my grandmother's family certainly merits being remembered. I shall try to belatedly introduce some of them to you; those families are certainly equal partners in forming the heritage of all who follow.

The first documented records of my grandmother's line (of Roberts) place them in South Carolina in the late 1700s; historically, it is believed this family was Welch and, if moving to South Carolina from Virginia, probably had been in America since the early 1600s; if from Pennsylvania, the family was still likely of Welch origin, but probably came into this country in the mid-1700s. We know Zaccheus Roberts was born ca.1753, reportedly in Pennsylvania, and died in 1826 in Roane County, Tennessee. There is some documentary reference to Edward Roberts, as the father of Zaccheus, indicating Edward was born in 1729 and died in 1789. Other references call into question a

Hezekiah Roberts, as perhaps being the father of Zaccheus (and his brother, Elias).

Zaccheus, our first link that is certain, was a Revolutionary War Veteran; his widow, stated (or claimed in pension documentation) that he served from 1776 until "peace was made" in 1783. She believed he had volunteered and that he served either as a scout, or on the line in actions principally in South Carolina. While it would be strictly supposition, one can imagine that he served in the same actions under Generals Marion and Greene, as had Thomas Hedgecock, whose great-grandson, Henry Marion would one day marry Zaccheus' great-granddaughter, Sarah Alice. Of course, the same claim, from a generational concept, could be made of most participants in that early struggle; these were "fathers of our country."

In 1788, Zaccheus married Nancy Brashear, at a location near the mouth of George's Creek on the Saluda River near Greenville, South Carolina. Present at the wedding was Nancy's older sister, Rebecca, who was married to Elias Roberts, presumably a brother of Zaccheus. This is an appropriate place to simply step aside and pay homage to the family from which Zaccheus chose a bride.

The Brashears are a storied and important family that not only has a distinguished past, but, paralleling the Roberts, moved into Tennessee and were among the first settlers of what is now Roane County (Tennessee). The known lineage of this family dates to Robert Brasseur/Brashear/Brassieur, of France (possible near La Rochelle) b. ca 1597. Nancy was sixth generation, from Robert.

The "Brassieur" families were originally Huguenots; the history of this religious group is a story unto itself. They began in England, were persecuted, resettled in France and, ultimately, Robert and his large family voyaged to America. Volumes have been written tracing the lineage of this family, its movements and recording the history of their accomplishments. With due respect to the validity of their achievements, I shall simply acknowledge each generation to the point they merge with the Roberts.

Robert Brasseur obviously came to America early in the development of the Virginia Colony. The establishment of Jamestown was in 1608 and

Robert is assumed to have been here as early as 1637. To put this into perspective: the population of Virginia would have been only a few thousand; George Washington's great grandfather was only four years old; and, the Declaration of Independence would not be signed for another 139 years.

The confirmation of Robert's arrival date is documented by a land-lease contract filed in Virginia for another individual, indicating the land was "bounded....West on land of Robert Brasheare." That contract date was November 24, 1637; Robert was there, then, at the latest. It is not known if Robert owned this specific land; however, within three months, he filed a patent registered as "Robert Brassure and Peter Rey on the Warrisquicke Creeke and butting upon the *Nanzemond* River." Satisfying interest in antiquated verbiage, the patent read:

"To all to whom these presents shall come, I Sr (Sir) John Harvey, Kt(Knight), Gorvenor, & c., send, &c now know yee that I, the said Sr John Harvey, Kt, doe with consent of the Councell of State accordingly give and grant unto Robert Brassure and Peter Rey six hundred acres of land seituate, lying and being in the upper Countie of New Norfolke (land now in Nansemond County, Virginia) lying north east and south west along the south side of Creeke upon the head of said Creeke and butting upon Nansemund river, alias Matrebers River. The said six hundred acres of land being due unto them, the said Robert Brassure and Peter Rey, by assignment from Peter Johnson to have and to hold &c. dated 24th of February 1638." (VA Land Patents, Book 1, p 622/Backp 7)

On April 12, 1653 another patent was issued to Robert for twelve hundred Acres "in the County Nanzemond at the head of the southern branch of Nanzemond river." Those patents were given as reimbursement to the colonist for the cost of their passage; each person who paid his own way, or for another, was given 50 acres. Robert's patent was for 24 persons, including his wife, Florence (this is questioned) and other family members.

On this same date, a patent was issued to Benjamin Brasseur (Robert's son) for three hundred acres on "a creeke called Indian Creeke being a branch of Nansemum river for the cost of transporting six persons into the colony." Whether Robert Sr. was in the colonies before Robert Jr. and Benjamine, or if they traveled together is subject to some conjecture; the patents are fact and their presence at the time of those patents is not contested. I find it interesting that those land grants were specifically tied to reimbursement for passage to the colonies; only seventeen years later, the Hitchcocks (Hedgecocks) arrived in Maryland and no mention in later patents/grants to this family is made regarding reimbursement for passage. Was Virginia practice different than Maryland's? Did the time difference matter? Did the Hitchcocks pay their own passage? Perhaps others can sort this out; however, it appears the Brasseurs were able to transport themselves to the colonies and were awarded land for their efforts.

At the time of their arrival, the Brasseurs were "subjects of the Crowne of France." That being acknowledged, it is also interesting reading to review Benjamin's Citizenship papers, apparently recorded in Maryland:

"..Whereas Benojs Brafseuir late of Virginia and subject of the Crowne of France having transported himselfe his wife and Children into this Crownes hereto inhabite hath besought us to grant him and the said Benojs Brafseuir leave here to inhabite and as a free Dennizen freedome and to hime and his hieres to purchase Known ye that wee willing to give due encouragement to other subject of that Crowne doe hereby declare them the said Benois Brafseuir his wife & children as well those already borne as state hereafter to bee born to bee free Dennizens of this our Province of Maryland..." signed Charles Calvert, December 4, 1662. (Hall of Records of Maryland, Council Proceedings, Liber HH,ff. 157, 158).

This was one step, among many, on the path that allowed all of us who followed, to be. Benjamine had moved from Virginia to Maryland in the late1650s, possibly because of Maryland's more liberal laws on religious freedom. It is recorded he was called for jury duty in 1660, was selected to be Justice of the Peace in 1661, made application for citizenship in 1662, and died in Calvert County in late 1662 or early 1663. He left three sons and five daughters whose ages ranged from about two to 17 years.

After Benjamine died, his wife, Mary, married a Thomas Sterling; upon her death in 1667, her son, Robert, the descendent of our line, was left some 300 acres and other property, leaving him reasonably well off. His step-father, however, assumed no responsibility for Mary's other children, and it is believed Robert took over the care of his younger brothers and sisters. Over the years, he apparently sold most of his land, piece meal and, upon his death, had little to leave his heirs.

Robert's second child, Samuel, and the next descendent in our line, was born 1673 in Queen Anne Parish, Maryland and died in 1740 in Prince George's County Virginia. He married Ann Jones and they were the parents of 10 children. Samuel was a successful land owner and planter, and seemed to be a skilled carpenter and builder; there are several references to his constructing "mills," repairing or completing work at the St. Barnabas Church of England, among other activities. During their lives, he and Ann deeded several pieces of property to their children, in such a manner to ensure the property passed to them. At his death, his carefully prepared will distributed a great deal of personal property to his heirs; in addition to his construction skills, he had been known also as "a planter" and "slave owner."

Samuel's fifth child, Robert, born February 19, 1704 in Prince George's County, Maryland, is next in line (toward us); he married Charity Dowell, who bore him seven children; Samuel died after 1782, presumably in Guilford, North Carolina. Samuel was left at least 250 acres of land in Maryland by his father, as well as other personal property; however, by 1732, it appears Robert began to sell his personal property and divest his interests in the land. Apparently in an effort to start over, by the late 1740s, he had migrated to the Indian-infested areas of North Carolina; he appears in an Orange County tax list in 1755, but had probably been there for some time. In 1761, he was issued a grant for land in Orange County that contained 640 acres; it was located "on Reedy Fork of Haw River and Buffalo." This area of Orange County became part of Guilford County in 1770.

During the Revolutionary war, Robert offered aid and supplies to the Revolutionary Army. At least one son, Asa, did serve in the Army. Validation exists supporting the claim that Robert did support the Revolutionary efforts.

The third child of Robert and Charity, Robert Samuel Brashears, came to be referred to as "The Rolling Stone" and for good reason; born August 20, 1731, in Maryland, he moved with his parents to Orange County,

North Carolina, then to Eastern Tennessee, later to an area near the Saluda River in South Carolina, and, finally, back to Roane County, Tennessee. He acquired property, married Phoebe Nicks and raised nine children. His seventh, daughter Nancy, born May 11, 1773, became the wife of Zaccheus Roberts.

Robert Samuel Brashear is important to the history of East Tennessee in that he may have been the first to settle in present-day Roane County. On August 11, 1794 he registered a deed from "Reed and Swagerty for 640 acres on Poplar Creek and Clinch River, in a section of Knox County" (that would later become Roane County). The deed was witnessed by Phillip Brashear (son), Robert Gilliland (son-in-law), and Elias Roberts (son-in-law). The land was on the west side of the Clinch River and their nearest neighbors would have been the troops at Fort South West Point, five miles away. The nearest neighbor to the northeast would have been Thomas Frost Sr., the first known settler in Anderson County.

Zaccheus Roberts and Nancy Brashears Roberts, though married in South Carolina, moved into East Tennessee soon thereafter, settling in what is now Roane County. They were parents of 11 children, the sixth being Brashears Roberts, born February 19, 1795. Brashears Roberts married Peggy Rogers in 1828, and, together, they had four children. Brashears bought property and lived with his family on land that ultimately became my mother's "home place."

The third child of Zaccheus and Nancy, Thomas L, born May 12 1834 (100 years before me) married Mary Jane Adkisson June 18, 1857; they were the parents of 10 children. Thomas, my great grandfather, becomes the first of this line to seem "real" because it was he whom I heard my mother describe, and it was his exploits, family and accomplishments that were the repeated stories told 'round our table' in my early days.

Thomas was a contributing citizen to his community, was an Elder and charter member of the Cumberland Presbyterian Church in Lawnville, a successful farmer, and obviously, a prolific parent. He is perhaps best remembered for his Civil War service, as that great "event" was a life defining one for the hundreds of thousands who served. Thomas was no exception.

Thomas had marched into Kentucky and joined the Union Army; he was mustered in at Barbourville, Kentucky, August 31, 1862. He originally was a member of Company "B" although he was promoted to Sgt., in 1864, and served in Companies F & S. Thomas was with those companies throughout the war, serving in all campaigns until the unit was disbanded and he was mustered out, in 1865.

Although I do not remember my mother mentioning it, legend has it that "his face was scarred by a shell." The pictures I have of him as a young man and also, when he was "up in years" are inconclusive, either way. Robert Cannon's *History of the 5th Tennessee Infantry* does not include Thomas among the wounded, although it is acknowledged that all those wounded did not report their injuries nor become part of the official record. Either way, he was involved in all activities of the Tennessee 5th, including the Battle of Resaca (Georgia), which was the most significant action this regiment experienced. The government of the United States of America, when asked in 1880, indicated "there was no record of (Thomas) suffering from kidney or heart disease, as alleged."

Interestingly, in Cannon's *History of the 5th..*, Thomas L. Roberts is listed among those taken prisoner during the conflict; the listing indicates he was captured October 31, 1862. During this time, the Tennessee 5th was actually in or near Gallipolis, Ohio, having retreated there from earlier action in the Cumberland Gap area. Thomas' statement of service from the Adjutant General's Office, April 26, 1880 is unclear (rather, illegible) on this matter: there are comments relative to "4 months" followed by "left sick at Cumberland Gap September 14, 1862; rejoined Regiment December 1, 1862...." Cannon made no remark relative to Thomas' imprisonment nor is there anything further we can add; however, this inclusion was from official war records. A likely explanation is that he was missing on subsequent muster rolls and was presumed captured. Current record keeping would not have been a high priority when his Regiment was on the run through Kentucky. At Cumberland Gap, he probably was left in the home of sympathizers—either side—and rejoined his outfit when able.

His fifth child, Sarah Alice became my grandmother. I can still picture mom referring to "Uncle Ab," "Aunt Dixie", "Aunt Mattie," or "Uncle Yerb." I am sure she mentioned others, but those stand out. An interesting (to me) bit of trivia concerning this family was the marriage of Thomas's sixth child, Laura Ann to George M. Graham. This was Graham's second marriage, his first wife having died. His daughter, Mrytle Mae Graham, by his first wife later married Yerb Roberts. It could be, and was, said, "she married her uncle-in-law."

Yerb, and the Grahams had moved to and lived in the Northwest (Washington, Oregon, Idaho); a daughter of Yerb and Mrytle, Mary Ola, who was a first cousin to my mother, became one of mom's favorite "pen pals." I do not know if they ever actually met in early life. Ola could have visited; however, in my life I know they never had contact. But write they did and those letters always lent an air of adventure and mystery, being from so far away and describing a life far different than ours. For instance, in my memory, Ola and her husband, George Dunsmoor, raised chinchillas—how exotic! They probably raised potatoes, (since they lived in Idaho) too, but that did not seem exciting. After retiring, George and Ola traveled back to Tennessee, living in a small camper. I recall meeting them during a visit with mom; again, I am not certain, but this may have been their first actual meeting.

Back to Thomas—after his wife died, he would stay for periods of time with some of his children; he, also, faithfully kept a daily diary. During the time my grandparents were building their house, these were some of the scintillating entries:

October 1908

    18th Began house this morning

        ****

    26th Putting in window frames and fixing for covering

        ****

30th They are working on house. Covering the kitchen today. Marion and his boys and two carpenters, Mr. Martin and Mr. Burns.

November 1908

10th Marion got back from Harriman about dark; brought three loads of brick

****

23rd Mr. Babb and son came this morning to build Marion's chimneys. Got chimneys well under way.

****

26th Thanksgiving Day. Dark cloudy morning. They are building kitchen flue while it rains. Weather not favorable to finish brick work. They finished chimneys and stove chimney today and drove for home this eve. Marion and family moved in their new house this eve. They have a good house.

Indeed, they did.

My grandparents, Henry Marion Hedgecock, the first child of Thomas and Martha Ladd Hedgecock and Sarah Alice Roberts, the fifth child of Thomas L. and Mary Jane Adkisson Roberts, grew up on nearby farms, may have been childhood sweethearts, and lived their entire lives in the Lawnville Community. They were married October 6th, 1887, and became parents of 10 children: my mother, aunts, and uncles. I never met nor knew my grandfather Hedgecock; he died, of course, before I was born. I well remember my grandmother, although when I was old enough to begin to know her, we had moved to McMinn County and, for all practical purposes, may as well have lived in California. My visits to "grandmother's" (that is what we called her home) were all too few, but always memorable.

Of my grandparent's 21 grandchildren, Homer, Betty, and I are the only ones who did not grow up either across the road, or, at most, a few miles away; I have forever been saddened and jealous of this lack of opportunity. My cousins were and are such loving, interesting people and our grandparent's home a place of such warmth and wonder that to have missed out on this added "growing up" experience only magnifies the tragedy of our being forced to leave that area. More about that later.

Talk about my grandparents generally focuses on Mr. Hedgecock, "Popa," as I believe he was called. Grandmother was a housewife, typical of the day, who devoted her life to filling the role of mother, homemaker, dutiful wife, and example to her children, as to how that role should be filled. My memories of her seem to be the same as those shared by cousins who were frequent visitors: her cooking, her warmth, the friendliness of her home, the mystique of the entire home place, and the respect for her that just came naturally to those of us who ever experienced being around her. She was in her seventies at the time of visits that I recall. I remember her moving around; remember the relationship between her "approval" and a reward from an always abundant supply of cookies, pies, or other goodies kept in the "table drawer" in the dining room. I have always described the visual memory I have of her sitting in her room (front left, as you entered the house) in a regal, dignified manner, sort of holding court for those who would pass through, as might the "Queen Mother," herself. She seemed to exhibit an air of formality, yet, was warm and tolerant of the never ending parade of grandchildren who seemed to be present. Those cousins or neighbors who were around her often, or knew her when she was much younger are, I am sure, privileged to remember more of her true personality and presence.

"Popa," Grandfather, on the other hand, is memorable for many reasons—the leadership and strength he gave his large family, of course, but also the entrepreneurial spirit he displayed in the variety of enterprises he undertook during his life. I do not know the "land arrangements" that existed when he was a young man or when he was married; both he and Grandmother grew up on nearby farms, and he may have worked on property adjacent to where Grandmother lived. What is known is that he and his sons, Hugh, Frank and Ernest bought 100 acres of what had been his father's farm; he bought the remaining 56 acres in his own name. This constituted what his children and grandchildren always call the "home place."

He was a farmer, obviously; what are of interest are the other ventures he undertook to support his large family. Part of his farm lay on the Clinch River and its rich bottom land was suitable for crops of corn, wheat and other food items. Local mills turned the corn into meal, the wheat into flour and the straw wound up in the mattresses under the featherbeds that were standard in the Hedgecock bedrooms. For several years, he and his son, Burton, ran a general merchandise store at Lawnville; he operated a "cannery" on the farm, packaging both produce raised on the farm as well as that supplied or canned for "toll" from neighboring farms. He raised and marketed peaches during the "peach boom" in the mid to late 1920s. He had a blacksmith shop and was skilled at performing the work normally done there.

Cotton was grown and used for making quilts; geese provided feathers for the "featherbeds," and chickens, hogs and cows served their intended purpose. The Hedgecock home was in an area of hills and ridges typical in East Tennessee; the house itself sits on the top of a small hill and across a small valley from a higher ridge; the land drops off steeply behind the house, falling to a ravine that contained a spring (still in existence) which, other than cisterns, was the primary water source. Grandfather, early on, rigged a pump at the spring and piped the water to the top of the opposite hill into a tank, from which it flowed by gravity to the house, providing "running water" long before such systems would have been widely in use. Every grandchild remembers those slipping, sliding trips down the hill to that spring; it was cool, shaded, deep in the woods, and offered an aura of mystery and enchantment that was enjoyed by anyone ever visiting that site. Young legs even endured the climb back to the house…perhaps with a bucket of water or two; I would love another look, but like climbing Mount Everest, a man must admit his own limitations, so, my distant memory must remain the lasting one.

Sickness and disease, prevalent in that time and place, did not spare my grandparents. My eldest uncle, Hugh, died of tuberculosis in 1926 at the age of 37; Uncle Burton, the second son, died from the same cause in 1916, when he was 26. Neither ever married. In addition to involvement in the other family enterprises, Burton was a professional photographer; he and Uncle Hugh also taught school. My uncle Virgil, the next-to youngest child, also contracted tuberculosis and moved to California where he fought the disease for many years; he overcame this illness, remained in California, and worked for the state, managing a vocational rehabilitation unit. He lived in Acton until his death at age 65.

Other than Hugh and Burton, I remember all my aunts and uncles. There were many similarities: family features, voice timbre and modulation, manner of speaking, humor, dignity, friendliness, and manners...many, many positive traits. I can imagine, and Mom often described, her father as rather stern and a strict disciplinarian; I can envision Grandmother not countenancing much mischief. However, I cannot dream up any criticism to level at a single aunt or uncle; no neurosis, no moral lapses that I ever knew, no lack of love and support for each other, and for such, I must comment that my grandparents...whatever their techniques...should have left a "how to" book for all generations to follow in the art of raising children; theirs are examples that I have never known to be equaled or surpassed.

My Aunt Verna (third child) probably elicits the fewest memories because I was around her less; she married Walton Smith and they lived their lives in the Shady Grove community, in the general area where my father lived. They had two daughters, Helen and Edith, who were favorites of my mother as they were almost as near to Mom's age, as would have been her older brothers. I believe Uncle Walton loaned Dad some money that he invested in his Watkins Products venture; I doubt very much it was ever repaid. More on that later, also.

Uncle Frank was perhaps the uncle we all remember most, as he and Aunt Ada never left their home; life's circumstances determined that they become the keepers of the farm and the caretaker of their mother until her death. He (Uncle Frank) served in the Army during WW I, as did Uncle

Hugh; they both spent most of their active duty time in Alabama. Interestingly, Uncle Frank received a small disability pension, although I do not know the nature of his complaint. I have seen a copy of an application Uncle Hugh submitted, although it does not seem complete. The only problem he mentioned on the application, relative to his service, was "having the mumps." I do not know if Hugh was granted disability compensation. Uncle Frank died in a VA hospital, in upper East Tennessee, in 1962.

Uncle Frank and Aunt Ada were always the hosts for visits to "Grandmother's." Every grandchild can recite memories of helping Uncle Frank around the farm or Aunt Ada in the house. Each grandchild has probably slept in one of the upstairs bedrooms, with its table, wash basin, treasure of interesting artifacts, and air of refreshing comfort. Trips to town with Uncle Frank in his late thirties Dodge, helping with the tobacco, gathering produce, eggs, or flowers…; hanging around Aunt Ada who always seemed to have a sugar cookie or other morsel of sweetness….; paying homage to or having a private word with Grandmother…all these experiences provide a richness that has enhanced dozens of lives.

Uncle Ernest, a minister and teacher, was the father of 10 children. He and Aunt Nettie lived in front of and on the left side of the road into Grandmother's place. These many cousins were playmates and acquaintances whom I encountered during those all too few visits; many were older and some younger; we never had a fight and their companionship contributed to great childhood memories. Aunt Nettie, after serving in a support role to Uncle Ernest in his endeavors, worked for years in department stores in Knoxville, Oak Ridge, Harriman and Kingston, until she finally opened her own store in Kingston, managing it until she retired, in 1964.

Of my five Hedgecock uncles, I only remembered Ernest, Frank and Virgil. Ernest was, by far, the most outgoing, gregarious and engaging. He was humorous, would readily engage in conversations and was an avid story teller. I never recall anything bawdy or course, but he would tell jokes; down to earth stories that were funny and to the point. Mixing his skills and training as a teacher, minister and experienced businessman, he could capture one's attention by his command of a variety of subjects. Uncle Frank and Uncle Virgil were more reserved and conservative.

Uncle Virgil was almost a mythical figure to me. As previously mentioned, he was afflicted with tuberculosis when he was a teenager; he met a family, the Torrys, when attending a Cumberland Presbyterian Synod in Knoxville, and returned to California with them. I believe they befriended him, and maintained a close relationship with him while he was in a state sanatorium, trying to overcome his illness. Later, Uncle Virgil cared for and remained friends with them until their deaths; I can recall mention of this family in correspondence between Uncle Virgil and my mother.

Living in California, he existed only through Mom's comments and the infrequent letters that were exchanged between her and him. She loved him dearly and hung on to any shred of information he shared. For several years, we would receive the January 2nd edition of the Los Angeles Times; it would include reports of the Rose Bowl Parade as well as the game and was an effort by Uncle Virgil to keep us informed. When, in the mid-forties, he was able to return home for a visit, the excitement of meeting him was difficult to contain; I was his namesake and certainly felt that special bond. I was fortunate to see him on another visit or two and retain to this day a wrist watch of his that was given to me after his death.

It would be impossible to pick or have a favorite aunt or uncle from the Hedgecocks; my vote for Ms. Congeniality, however, would have to be Aunt Pearl. First, judging from the many pictures that exist, all the Hedgecock girls were very attractive; no exceptions. Aunt Pearl just stands out as *very, very* attractive. By the time I began remembering her, she looked like everyone else's mom; when one is a child, everyone in their forties looks like everyone else, and is old. What always stood out was her smile, her cheerfulness, her bubbly, outgoing personality. On the surface, I cannot imagine Aunt Pearl ever having a bad day, as she always seemed "up," interested in what everyone was doing or had to say, and was a delight to be around. She married Roy Norman and they, with their four sons, lived in the Buck Creek Community, near Kingston. Roy spent his life in law enforcement and automobile businesses, with most of his sons following suit.

Aunt Ruby, the other "jewel" and baby of the family, was the only daughter to attend high school and, in fact, completed college. She enjoyed an outstanding career as a teacher, musician, community leader, great wife, mom, and aunt. As of this writing, at 95, she is the surviving member of this family. (Ruby Alice Hedgecock Smith, 97, died April 5, 2006) Aunt Ruby married Tom Smith in 1933 and has lived since in a house behind the Young's Chapel church; this property was bought from Uncle Ernest. (Ruby's brother) Their two children, Lester and Dixie are very close in age to Betty and me, and we seemed to share more time together in the early years, and even since, than we perhaps enjoyed with other cousins. Lester has invested much time and effort toward preserving bits of family history, as have Billie Hedgecock Wyatt and many others. Of interest, when Burton died and H.M. sold the seven acres of property (that had been the family "store"), four acres and the store were sold to D. P. Roberts; the remaining three were sold to the Roane County Board of Education for the Lawnville School. Later, after the school was moved, the youth group of the church bought this property and gave it to the church. Around 1915, Henry Marion Hedgecock purchased an acre and donated it to the church cemetery and, in 1928, purchased another piece of land, deeding it to the church; both were obtained from J.M. Smith. The land around this little church has the footprints of my grandfather all over it, and Aunt Ruby has lived her long and productive life standing watch, with her front porch being about 30 yards from the back of the church.

There is no better way to get a flavor of the legacy the Hedgecock and Roberts families have left the Lawnville community than to visit the Lawnville Cemetery and the Young's Chapel CP Church; to stroll among the well kept stones, noting names and dates, is to stroll down memory lane past generations of those great families. While I am in no rush, I am comfortable with the thought I shall one day rejoin those dear family members in this most serene resting place.

To visit the church on Sunday morning is to witness a spirit of friendliness and fellowship that echoes, as does the sound of the old time hymns, across the ages; the legacy is that generations later, beliefs, values, and convictions are still intact and honored. What more could any family ever ask?

The eighth child of Henry Marion and Sarah Alice, Eva Estelle Hedgecock, born December 9, 1901, was my very special mother; her story will be told, later.

Mincys, Harts and Marneys

What you have read thus far and all that follows originated from a simple, perhaps primal, urge to know "who I am," where my clan originated, or what they might have accomplished. That urge, that curiosity nudged me into looking under stones in history's rock piles, hoping to find answers. Everything else between these covers has been dug up, looked over, and written before this particular section was even started; the problem has been that my prime objective has turned out to be the most elusive. While my first evolutionary digs were directed toward uncovering "Mincys" and a few bones turned up rather quickly, I never got to the point I felt I had it all and could begin to tell our story. I have concluded I never will, and must go with what I have.

This search has been more than gratifying. It led, of course, to other family branches and much time was spent before I was able to return to the Mincys. All my other relatives are viewed with equal respect and appreciation. However, there is just something that seems traditional, although it may be an acquired taste, concerning the wish to know more about or proclaim the greatness of "the family name." This "something" is what started this effort and has sustained its pace. I am a Mincy and wanted to know what that means.

Many others have, too. During the past few years, I have stumbled across several distant cousins, or, they me; most had worked their way toward the common goal of determining where we started, and most had arrived at the same successes or dead ends. Finding one would have made this trip worth the effort; getting to know many is a reward unto itself.

Having reached the point along the trail where it is time to pull over, rest awhile, and describe what I have seen thus far, it is tempting to spend an unwarranted amount of time talking about what I have *not seen*. Professional researchers, cousins, other family branches, and I have poked, prodded, pursued, and persevered; we have tried to take this family name back into antiquity and learn more about who we were and are. Therefore, there are just more data available about what *does not fit* than there is about where it all started. One bit of rather intriguing evidence turned up from an unexpected source: National Geographic's *Genographic Project*.

The summary of this effort is that National Geographic, attempting to trace the movement of man from his/her origin, has, through DNA analysis, been able to plot our movement from that origin in central-east Africa to every corner of the earth. The premise is the established fact that the very widely dispersed M168 marker can be traced to a single individual "Eurasian Adam"; this African man, who lived some 31,000-79,000 years ago, is the common ancestor of every non-African person living today. His descendants migrated out of Africa and became the only lineage to survive away from humanity's home continent. I shall add that (from National Geographic's findings) all persons on earth share this marker; conversely, certain people still living in that area share no other markers from any other people on earth today. In my personal quest, I scraped certain body parts, sent off my DNA kit, and have evidence of my distant relative's early movements.

My Y chromosome identifies me as a member of haplogroup R1b, a lineage defined by the genetic marker M343; this group is the final destination of the journey beginning some 60,000 years ago from the ancient M168. There are, roughly, four further markers chronicling the movement of (my) group from Africa, to the Middle East, to Central Asia: Markers M89, M9, M45, M173 and finally, M343. My group journeyed from Central Asia, north to the northern steppes of Asia, west toward Europe, through the Balkans, ending in Spain, Italy, and the west coast of Europe; today, some 70 percent of men in southern England are R1b. In parts of Spain and Ireland that number exceeds 90 percent. (Authors note: although not appreciating the political labels and intrusive approach, I believe in an original, creative or Devine intelligence; I also believe in science and the results of scientific methods applied by intelligent human beings; I believe the results of those methods do not refute but, rather, only reveal the wonders of the creation story.)

So, we have the Mincys pegged from 70,000 years ago through about 30,000 years ago, give or take 10,000 here or there. It was the next 30,000 that gave me trouble. It is a given we came from Western Europe, Spain or Portugal, England, or Ireland; from exactly where or under what name identity is still unknown.

For instance: the first known reference to my most distant, direct Mincy ancestor is an entry in the 1820 census (to move forward, slightly) from Wilkes County, North Carolina, which listed a Samuel Minsey and his then family members. This family was next found to exist in Grainger County, upper East Tennessee. While not one shred of information has been uncovered about the Wilkes County experiences of this family, all that follows is from Grainger County, forward. Efforts to fill in the dots before Wilkes County have led to the accumulation of reams upon reams of paper detailing what does not work, while describing the activities or examining the possibilities of finding something that would. Interesting stuff, but these are mostly pieces of a puzzle that do not fit.

The most logical conclusion supported by the most factual evidence is that we were not always Mincys. I mention the origin of Sam, the patriarch of our line; other Mincys trace their ancestry to a Jesse Mincy, born about 1800 in Green County, North Carolina. This Jesse, in the 1830 Macon County, North Carolina census was using the surname of Minshew; he does not appear in the 1840 census and by 1850 he had become Jesse Mincey. This family migrated to South Carolina and spread west through Georgia, Alabama and Mississippi; family members of this branch have performed their own searches and although arriving at a close common source, can find no factual, verified connection to our Sam.

Further, I happened upon a genealogy report detailing the family of a Richard Minshew, born about 1650 in Nansemond County, Virginia; his grandson, Jacob, born 1730, was referred to as "Mincy." Interestingly, some of Jacob's brothers were known as Mincy, others, Minchew; go figure. A great grandson of Richard, Jesse Minshew, was born about 1750. This would seem too far back to be the Jesse of Greene County, North Carolina, however, could this be the same line? The family of Richard all migrated south and west and, in fact, the report I have shows most of the later generations to be in Mississippi. They have become, almost entirely, Mincys. Yet, the descendents of Jesse of Greene County have made no connection with Jesse, descendant of Richard of Virginia, and I know many have worked diligently in the effort. Finding treasure is not an exact science.

I have pages of data detailing the examination of neighbors, business associates, census groupings, or other possibilities, trying to link Samuel of Grainger County to those Minchews/Mincys/Anybody from Greene or Wayne County, North Carolina. Nothing.

Extensive data exist of Munsey families that originated in New England and migrated to Virginia; since Samuel, on occasion, is shown in census records as having been born in Virginia, this possibility must be considered. No evidence is known that would corroborate this thesis, and no connection to the many Munsey family members has been established.

Let's make our peace, then, with these facts and conclusions:

1. Our name was likely, at one time, something other than Mincy; possibilities include Minchie, Minchew, Minshew, or variations thereof. This would not begin to address more difficult, ethnic sounds.

2. No one, to date, has established our particular line beyond Samuel, b. ca. 1790, in North Carolina; that he was a descendant of one of the other "Ms" seems logical but is unproven. The search must be continued.

So, we begin with Samuel Minsey; we begin with the assumption that he is, indeed, our man. Many searchers and many family members cite the common mantra: "Samuel Minsey, b.ca.1790 North Carolina; m. Mary about 1810. She was born about 1777 in North Carolina. and died before 1860, in Tennessee." Those facts are the stated ones; as indicated in the beginning of this chapter, they are unverified and, in fact, I have never seen the source of this "source information." The 1820 census, if reviewed carefully, could be easily nit-picked: it lists Samuel as "Head of Family" and further, lists two males; one 0-10 years of age and one 16-26. Under females, three are listed; two 0-10 and one 16-26.

The historical birth date of Samuel's known children (before 1820) are: 1811, 1815, 1818 and 1820. This is not an exact fit with the census information or later, anecdotal information; further, the listing of one male and one female (16-26) neither corresponds with the supposed age of Sam and Mary nor matches the ages of known children. Was this really our Sam? Most likely.

Census records are notoriously suspect regarding exact dates or other information. Many times, the census taker is receiving information from a neighbor and, even if the source is correct, illiterate, uneducated citizens could, understandably, not know exact birth dates or places of birth. Who could remember it all, if one were not able to write it down? Later census records of this family *generally* are consistent regarding number of family members, where they were born, and age range. The 1830 Grainger County (Tennessee) census recorded this family with similar information, and they are not present in the Wilkes County (North Carolina) census. It is comfortably accepted by most who are interested that the 1820 Samuel Minsey and the later Samuel Mincey/Mincy are one and the same; that said, from a biblical perspective, I am comfortable, also, that my thousands of cousins and I are, indeed, seeds of his loins.

Little, really, is known of Samuel. What is known includes Mary and his being the parents of eight children: Sarah, b. 1811, North Carolina, married Robert Martin September 23, 1829, Grainger County, Tennessee (It is possible Robert was a brother of Martha Martin who married David, Sam's third child); William Jesse, b. 1815, North Carolina, m. Martha Boyd, August 5, 1835, Grainger County, Tennessee; David Mincy, b. 1818, North Carolina, d. July 28, 1896; Baby Mincy, b. before 1820; died before 1830; Major Merideth Mincy, b. about 1821, North Carolina, d. November 29, 1864; James M. Mincy, b. about 1828, Grainger County, Tennessee; John M. Mincy, b. 1829, Grainger County, Tennessee, m. Mary McElhaney, October 21, 1851, McMinn County, Tennessee, and Elizabeth Mincy, b. ca. 1831 in Grainger County, Tennessee. This was his family and from them, came us.

There are a few deed records in Grainger County listing Sam; further, there are some references to his having offered security for his son, James, who seemed to differ with the law for one reason or another. When a search is mounted in vast genealogical reference sites, Sam turns up as having filed a claim with the U.S. Commissioner of claims in 1872, attempting to recover the value of "1 gray mare, 7 years old, 15 hands high, and valued at $150.00." Sam's claim indicated he lived at Blains Cross Roads, Grainger County, Tennessee, and that in September, 1863, members of the 3rd Regiment, Tennessee Volunteers, which he believed to have been stationed in Knoxville, took his property for government use. The petition was filed by a John A. McKinney, Attorney, who witnessed Sam's "X." The claim was "barred" in 1875. The copy of the application received from Tennessee Archives Department is not legible enough to discern the reasons for not accepting it; the most common reason was that proof of a claimants disloyalty to the Union was discovered; in that at least two, possibly three of Samuel's sons were serving the Union, this seems unlikely; however, Sam never received anything for his mare. Upon review, it appears this was actually Sam's grandson, Samuel, son of Major. There is not much on record to tell about the original Sam.

Samuel does not appear in any known 1840 census records; he is shown in 1850 living in Roane County Tennessee and in 1860 is listed as living with his daughter, Elizabeth Mincy Colquitt. His wife Mary is not shown in this census, and is presumed to have died before 1860.

It is not known when Samuel died or where he was buried; it is believed he could have been buried in the Philadelphia (Tennessee) cemetery. A death notice for Elizabeth Colquitt indicated she would be "buried in Philadelphia." We shall revisit the historical significance of this little village; however, in absence of any other information or cemetery records, a logical place for him to be laid to rest would have been where the family keeping him intended to be buried later.

It is time to introduce some perspective: as oft stated, a few years ago I did not know another Mincy direct relative existed; of Samuel's eight children, I only have lineage information on four. From these four (others may or may not have had children; some most likely did), the "descendant report" of Samuel Minsey numbers 73 small type pages and is most certainly growing. I am not alone.

My line is from David, the third child, and we shall get to him in a moment; with due respect, the other distant aunts and uncles will be mentioned.

The oldest, Sarah Mincy, was born ca. 1811, presumably in North Carolina, and married Robert Martin, September 23, 1829; Robert may (or may not) have been related to Martha Martin who married Sarah's brother David. Nothing more is known of Sarah, nor of the fourth child, "baby Mincy" who was born before 1820 but apparently died before 1830. The second child, William Jesse, born ca. 1815 in North Carolina, married Martha Boyd, August 5, 1836 in Grainger County, Tennessee.

The third child, David, is being bypassed for the time being; the fifth child and third (known) son, Major Merideth (Henry) Mincy seems well known. First, in historical records and references, the Henry is usually shown in parenthesis, but the reasons are not known or apparent to me. I cannot suggest the significance of these three "given" names. Major seems to have been the name he used, and it was not a title, as the only rank (we know) he obtained was Private, Company L of the 9th Tennessee Volunteer Calvary. Further, Major is engraved on his marker stone; his last name is spelled "Mince."

Major was married three times; his first marriage to Rachel Morgan was in Grainger County, Tennessee, March 24, 1839, and resulted in three children. The first two were either stillborn or died in infancy; the third, Samuel, born 1834, is the "presumed" Samuel of the confiscated mare story and the Samuel who served, also, in the Union Calvary. He died in 1916 in Cleveland, Tennessee

The union of Major, and his second wife, Elizabeth "Polly" Mynatt, March 6, 1843, occurred in Granger County, Tennessee and resulted in three children: William, b. 1845; James, b. 1848 and Lewis Francis, b. 1852 In 1852, Major married Mary Ann Culverhouse (also in Grainger County) and this marriage resulted in five children: Louis Lafayette, b. 1853; Franklin Pierce, b. 1854; Margaret Elizabeth, b. 1856; Nancy Jane, b. 1862, and Harmon Lee, b. 1863. The death date of Rachel or the circumstances of the marriage ending is unknown; Elizabeth died before

1852, and Mary lived until 1922. These eleven children were all born before the Civil War.

Major served in the Civil War, with the 9th Tennessee Calvary Volunteers; his sons William and Samuel served in the 8th; the military adventures of both these units were primarily in East Tennessee and many members of these units were from East Tennessee. The gray mare for which Samuel (with Major as a witness) submitted a "war claim" just may have been ridden off to war by one of those family members.

Major succumbed to diarrhea, of all things, and died in a Knoxville army hospital, November 27, 1864; his marker, in a military cemetery, exists and is still very legible; he is listed as "Major Mince (Sickness, disease and infection probably killed as many soldiers from both sides, as instant death on the battlefield)

The descendents of this family certainly number in the hundreds, if not thousands; one distant cousin, a direct descendent of Major, Sheila Rodrigue, of Louisiana was discovered on the Internet and was the first person to reveal to me the identity of our mutual great-great-great grandfather, Samuel.

James M. Mincy married Emaline Harless, December 28, 1851, in Grainger County Tennessee; they became the parents of six children: Alfred, Andrew Jackson, b. 1852; Mary Catherine, b. 1853; Elizabeth, b. 1854; Martha, b. 1857; Frank, b. 1864 and Thomas, b. 1866

Little is known of John M. Mincy; born 1829 in Grainger County, Tennessee, he married Mary McElhaney, October 21, 1851 in McMinn County; the marriage record is spelled Minsey. Interestingly, I have seen no record of this family in McMinn County nor stumbled across any burial records; I do vaguely remember the McElhaney name among other McMinn County families during my sojourn there

Samuel's youngest child, Elizabeth, b. ca. 1831 in Grainger County, Tennessee married William H. Coliquitt, May 9, 1852 in Philadelphia, (then) Roane County, Tennessee. They became the parents of eight children. I mentioned previously that evidence indicates Elizabeth was buried in the Philadelphia cemetery and suggested Samuel may be there also; there is no marker for William, Elizabeth or Samuel. Although stones exist for David and other relatives, there is no specific evidence concerning the Coliquitts or Sam. Perhaps one of those stones will turn over some day.

My great-great grandfather, David, the second son and third child of Samuel, was born ca. 1818 in North Carolina; an ordinary, uneducated farmer, he was the father of 15 children, born of two wives; he served more than three years in the Civil War and left for us interesting stories, the legacy of hundreds of other Mincys, and unanswered questions concerning who, where and why.

David's first marriage was to Martha Martin, June 6, 1839, (This date is in Bryon Sistler's *Early East Tennessee Marriages*; it would appear at odds with the birth date of his first natural son, Robert and, perhaps, his adopted son, John Wesley; it is what we have and should be noted, as well as subsequent dates relating to David, with reservations) and took place in Grainger County, Tennessee; he is shown in the 1840 census living in Grainger County. By 1850, David and his family were living in Roane County, Tennessee; apparently, he, his father, and perhaps others of this family, had moved. Reasons for this migration are unknown; it does not appear that immediate family members acquired much land, but the move was likely work related; they were primarily farmers and perhaps the opportunities, real or imagined, appeared greater in Roane County.

This marriage resulted in eight children, born between 1835 and 1857. There are some interesting aspects to many of these family members.

While working on this family history and gathering information from cousins or interested parties, it sort of jumped out that the first child, John Wesley, was shown as being born in 1835, four years before the listed marriage date of David and Martha. A cousin, Linda Skinner, who has done extensive research on the Mincys, came across a publication by Alan N. Miller, *East Tennessee's Forgotten Children; Apprentices from 1778-1911*, which indicates that a John Wesley Martin, age 9 in 1844 and apprenticed to Master James Trott was rescinded May 4, 1846 to David Mincy. How interesting! Was this a child from another marriage of Martha's? An illegitimate child of Martha's? We likely will never know, but the fact seems evident that David's relationship with this John Wesley Martin was such that he adopted him and, further, John Wesley must have influenced other family members in a positive way; his nearest brother, Robert, named his first child John Wesley; that John Wesley was my grandfather. Of course, the evangelist, John Wesley probably influenced more name decisions than my great uncle, but I prefer this familial thought than believing the founder of Methodism influenced my good Baptist ancestors.

Other of John and Robert's brothers and sisters are the ancestors of many cousins discovered in this search; Elizabeth (Bettie) Mincy married a Bradshaw, and her family graves are in the same cemetery (Philadelphia) with David, Mary Jane (Petty) and other family members.

It is apparent David left Grainger County, moved to Roane County, raised a large family and left his mark, primarily because of his many offspring. We must thank early government bureaucracy for the fact we know much more about David and are able to piece together other aspects of his ordinary, yet interesting, life. He served in the Civil War, and his application for a simple pension of $12 per month resulted in more than 100 pages of documented information, information that reveals more about his life than all else we know put together.

We described earlier, the mood in East Tennessee prior to the beginning of hostilities. On February 9, 1861, an election was held to determine if the people wanted to participate in a convention on the issue of secession. The state voted overwhelmingly for "no convention." Tennesseans were not ready to secede from the Union. That changed with the "firing on Fort Sumter" and, subsequently, in an election held in June, 1861, Tennesseans voted to secede. While Middle and West Tennessee citizens were in the majority, two-thirds of East Tennesseans voted to remain loyal to the Union. The stage was set.

Throughout the remaining months of 1861 and early in 1862, several prominent East Tennesseans, loyal to the Union, began organizing military units from Tennessee, mostly at Camp Dick Robinson, in Kentucky. Thousands begin moving north, to join in the effort. Acts of "bridge burning" in several areas of East Tennessee, in November, inflamed Confederate forces, resulting in harsh retaliation and forcing those moving north toward Kentucky to do so by stealth and secrecy. Not to elaborate upon this lesson in history, but one must try to imagine the emotions of leaving family, friends, and property....in an area mostly occupied by the "enemy" and under severe circumstances, to join a cause that was mostly political in nature. To keep this in perspective, around 51,000 Tennesseans joined the Union cause; however, more than 187,000 Tennessee citizens fought for the Confederacy. After Virginia, more battles were fought on Tennessee soil than that of any other state.

Many from the same family were split in their loyalties. David Mincy, father of eight, husband and farmer, chose the Union. With his son, Robert, and many other neighbors or relatives, he enrolled in the Union Forces at Barboursville, Kentucky, February 25, 1862; they were mustered into Company B, 5th Tennessee Infantry, March 6, 1862.

During the remainder of 1862, this regiment (which served during the war as part of several different Brigades, Divisions and Corps) saw operations that included Cumberland Gap, Pine Mountain, Tennessee, Manchester, Kentucky, Gallipolis, Ohio, Cincinnati, Ohio, Louisville, and ended the year in Nashville, Tennessee. 1863 presented actions in Murfreesboro, Tennessee; Carthage, Tennessee; Jasper, Tennessee; Lookout Mountain, Tennessee; Sale Creek, Tennessee, and Kingston, Tennessee. The year ended with the 5th located near Strawberry Plains, Tennessee. One can but imagine the experience, problems, and emotions as these soldiers moved through their home communities on many of these maneuvers.

The year 1864 began with this regiment beginning a move southwest, toward Chattanooga, in pursuit of Confederate forces retreating from Chattanooga and beginning a defense of Atlanta and northern Georgia; this resulted in the major battle of the war in which the 5th played an important role: the Battle at Resaca, Georgia, May 14, 1864. Seventy-three soldiers from the 5th were wounded; several died, more from infection and resulting disease than instantly on the battlefield. Other, smaller, engagements in north Georgia followed, and the regiment detached during the summer in Marietta, Georgia. In November, the unit was moved to the Nashville, Tennessee area, in response to Confederate movements toward Nashville; after the first of the year, in early 1865, this unit began a journey that ended in Annapolis, Maryland. From that point they moved toward Wilmington, North Carolina, and participated in the capture of that Confederate base. That was the last action of the War for the 5th; its members were transported back to Nashville, where most of the troops, including David Mincy, were mustered out March 30, 1865.

Before the War and after moving to Roane County, it appears David farmed on land owned by others, including James Roberson and possibly Michael Wrinn, among others. While I do not know exact sites, this was in the general vicinity of the little town of Philadelphia. Philadelphia now sits along side old US route 11, which runs from Champlain, New York to New Orleans, Louisiana; in my childhood, this was the major northeast-mid south highway; now, it (US 11) has been bypassed by bypasses and I-75; it, now, is little more than a rural, farm, paved road. In David's time, Philadelphia was part of Roane County; it now is in Loudon County, between the small towns of Loudon and Sweetwater.

No infantry soldier spent three or more years in the Civil War without his life and/or health probably being dramatically affected; hundreds of thousands of stories certainly parallel those of David's. David is my great-great grandfather, however, and my sadness and sympathy must be directed toward him; it extends to all who suffered similar experiences….on both sides.

David was present and participated in all activities involving the Tennessee 5th Volunteer Infantry Regiment; probably every day of the duration of this experience brought some hardship, misery, tragedy or discomfort. David always emphasized two.

In late December, 1862, the Tennessee 5th was in the vicinity of Nashville; the first special Order of the new year was written to Colonel Shelly from Nashville on January 2nd, which shows that the 5th Tennessee was in Nashville at that time. Quoted from Robert Cannon's *Volunteers for Union and Liberty*....

"Col. Shelley comdg. 5th Regt will send out a sufficient picket to relieve the picket of Col Byrd's Regt now on duty between the Pike and Cumberland River on this day. They will report to Major Gamble Field Officer of the Day. The pickets will be placed under a commissioned officer and provided with two days rations."

Accounts written by members of the 5th Tennessee verify that they arrived in Murfreesboro after (that) battle. In his answer to the Tennessee Civil War Veteran Questionnaires, Private Marion Finger of Company H stated that "we were ordered to Murfreesboro Tenn, but the battle had ended just as we arrived." Lieutenant G. H. Tipton of Company I stated in his pension application that "my command was compelled to wade the Stone River when there was snow on the ground which caused the mumps to fall on me and left me in bad condition." In Tipton's pension records, a letter from: Private J. C. Vernon of Company I stated, "Said Gilbert H. Tipton had measles while we were encamped at Murfreesboro, Tenn. This was just after the battle…"

The pension records of Benjamine F. Roberts, 1st Lieutenant of Company B (David's Company) contain statement from members of the 5th Tennessee that around the last day of December, 1862, they were ordered by General Mitchell on the "Dog Creek Raid" to intercept General Nathan Bedford Forrest. During the two day raid in the extremely cold weather, the men were without food, blankets and constantly exposed to the elements. Captain Monroe Masterson would call the Dog Creek Raid the "worst night I ever put over my head." Masterson went on to say, "when we came back to Nashville the snow was about knee deep and the weather desperately cold, frozen & bad." Colonel Shelley would later write, "this march used up my men more than any other cause."

David simply stated over and over that "while in the line of his duty at or near Murfreesboro, Tennessee on or about the month of January, 1863, he contracted a severe cold resulting in disease of head, eyes and deafness caused from exposure, wading streams, and sleeping on the cold and frozen ground." Witnesses in David's subsequent claim for disability aid testified to similar conditions and to David's complaining of various ailments after this exposure. There was to be more.

After the battle at Resaca, Georgia, May 14, 1864, the 5th was engaged in several other, smaller skirmishes, then retired to Marietta, Georgia for the summer and early fall. After attempting several attacks on General Sherman's forces in northern Georgia, Confederate General John Bell Hood swung north in an attempt to interrupt the supply lines between

Chattanooga and Georgia and, while at it, tempt Sherman to pull away from his assault toward Atlanta; after this strategy failed, Hood decided to move into Tennessee, and perhaps even Kentucky and Virginia, in a bold attempt to alter the results of the war. The XXIII Corps, which included the 5th Tennessee, was ordered to Nashville; the 5th began moving, by rail, November 5, 1864.

While not of major military significance, David reported that, "I got stove up after that (the Murfreesboro experience) near Chattanooga by a rail road rack(wreck); my legs have been in a terrible bad condition..." Other witness and fellow soldiers confirmed that several cars derailed near Chattanooga, November 11, 1864 and reported seeing David Mincy, "all scratched and bruised." David specifically complained that he "badly hurt his back and left side."

He returned home to his family and to farm life able to do "not much more than half" what he could do before, according to neighbors and, later, witnesses to his war claim. His first wife died, in 1862, while he was away. David married again, in 1865, this time to Margaret A. Byrum; a Mary A. Paul later stated that, "this was a run away marriage; the said David Mincy and Margaret Byrum came to my father's home at night and was married by my father, then a J P of Roane County, July 20, 1865."

Ailments and disabilities aside, David and Margaret were able to become the parents of seven more children between 1866 and 1880; perhaps love conquers all. During this time, it appears David worked for others on their farm(s), mostly in the Philadelphia area. March 15, 1888, John Grayson and wife, of Monroe "sold to David Mincy of Loudon, land in counties of Loudon and Monroe is the north quarter of section 11, twp1, range 2nd east of Meridian:.....containing 160 acres, for $480 in three installments." It is interesting, considering the claimed state of David's health and inability to work, where he got the money for this purchase. It seems that David, Margaret and their youngest child, Sarah Tennessee, were living on this property from about that date.

Further, July 3, 1890, "David Minsey and Margaret, his wife, of Loudon Co., (sold) to W.G. Lenoir of Loudon...for $100 land in D#4, it being 1/9 interest to a reversion in 195 acres of land owned by T.J.

Byrum, now deceased, who was the father of said Margaret Minsey and on which lands her mother now has homestead and dower...said land lies west of the farm of E. S. Adkins now owned by W.G. Lenoir...." Apparently, David and Margaret were selling Margaret's interest in her late father's property.

An Act of Congress, 1890, offered benefits to Civil War veterans, for disability, and would seem to have been retroactive; David was awarded $10 per month, beginning in 1889; his application had to be revisited in 1892 but, subsequently, in November, 1892, he was awarded $12 per month for 10/18 disability.

Medical records seem to confirm that, by the time of his application, he suffered from deafness, diminished eyesight, congestion, blood in urine, general muscle soreness and a noticeable scar on his back; he was about 5'10" and weighed around 150; his neighbors testified that he was, generally, unable to work, poverty stricken, and in great need; in 1890, he was "only" 72 years old.

In 1895, David and Margaret gave a note to one John B. Grayson, of Monroe County, for $245; their land was put into trust, as security for payment of the note. These transactions were probably for the purpose of simply meeting living expenses. David died July 28, 1896.

Margaret's fortunes appeared not to improve with David's death; she immediately applied for a window's pension. The debt on the farm appeared to be more than it was worth, she had few assets and no means to earn income other than her own labors. The same friends and neighbors were affiants to her applications: Joel Byrum (likely a relative), Michael Wrinn, James Roberson and fellow soldiers of David's, James E.Schrimpsher and William Thacker. Schrimspher and Thacker both stated they were on the train that "racked" near Chattanooga.

Margaret received a small pension in 1896; it is likely she lost the farm although that is not confirmed. By 1915, she was living in Etowah, Tennessee, with her daughter, Sarah Tennessee, "Tennie," where she died in 1919; Tennie applied for reimbursement of funeral expenses, claiming the family was unable to pay them.

David, by some distant relatives and fellow researchers, was christened "War Dave," I suppose, to distinguish him from his son, David, or other David Mincys in the chain. He lived most of his adult life in the area of Philadelphia, Tennessee; he farmed and worked around there; he and his first wife, Martha died and were buried there; his legacy must be related to that location; **tuck this away in your memory, as it will be revisited**.

My great-grandfather, Robert Mincy, David's second son (perhaps his first natural child), was born January, 1836 (other dates are used; his military records seem to indicate an 1838 date) in Roane County; he is with this family in the 1850 census but not included in the 1860. His first child, John Wesley (my grandfather), was born July 28, 1857; therefore, Robert's marriage to Martha Selvedge is presumed to be before that date.

Some interesting facts have emerged regarding Martha; first, there were many Selvedge families in Roane County during this period and, while I have no facts regarding her lineage, she was from a local family. To confirm the approximate date of her marriage to Robert, there is an entry in the minutes of the Prospect (Baptist) Church for the Third Saturday in May, 1857, which reads: "…..By motion and second, a charge is taken up against Sister Martha Mincy for playing in plays and disobeying the calls of the Church." Indeed! Further, that Sister Mary Edwards was admonished to "…see and cite her to the next Church meeting." A couple of others members were also cited for "playing" which would imply that we had a troop of Shakespearian thespians traipsing around the county, titillating and exciting the natives. This matter did not die a quick death.

The Third Saturday in June, 1857, one of the "players," Richard Turnbill was deemed to "be no more of us," or, in other words, was kicked out. Martha did not show, and Sister Edwards was requested to "see and cite her to the next meeting." Sister Josephine Edwards (was Sister Josephine sister of Sister Mary??), who had been also charged with "playing at plays of mirth and disobeying the calls of the Church" was present at this meeting and gave the "Church satisfaction and the Church forgave her and received her in fellowship." Martha seemed not to give in so easily; perhaps Sister Martha, Sister Josephine and Brother Richard had been operating a "house of mirth" down on the Tennessee River.

In July (1857) her case was brought up again; Brother John W. Taliaferro was to see and notify her of that fact. The Man had been brought into the case. In August, Brother Taliaferro reported that he was satisfied, agreeable to his information that she was not able to attend, (my grandfather had just been born; I guess there were no plays that month) and the case was laid over until called for. It seemed not to have been "called for" until February, 1859, at which meeting "the Sister gave satisfaction to the Church, and she in act says she forgives the Sister." Which sister did what to whose sister will remain for time to tell; interestingly, on the second Saturday in November, 1859, the Church of Prospect met and, after preaching, opened the door of the Church for the reception of members; received by experience and Baptism were Robert Mincy and John Selvidge, among others.

I have often stated, as I uncovered and contemplated the events in Robert's life, that there should have been a movie about them starring John Wayne. Not because of fame, fortune or notoriety he gained, but by the simple fact the odds of him surviving and being able to relate them were so slim. Robert was married, had two children and, presumably, was farming for someone else at the outbreak of the Civil War. He marched (or snuck and slithered) off to Kentucky with his father, friends, and neighbors to join the Union forces in 1862 and, to a point, his experiences were the same as David's and other members of the 5th Tennessee. We will not repeat them here.

Earlier, we described the name situation with Mincys; some of Robert's official War Department records show his name as "Mintyz" or "Mintzy." I often marvel that by now, I am not "Mintzovitch" or such; name changes, once struck, seem difficult to erase but, happily, our ethnic heritage, whatever it is, survived. Further, I have often conjectured that up (or down) in Barbourville in 1852, when these raw farm boys from Tennessee lined up and yelled out their name, it was no wonder an army clerk from, say Brooklyn, would record it thusly. Such was life in the name game.

The first I knew of Robert's existence were the findings of a genealogist I had asked to trace our family. Included in various documents were some of his service records. They read, in part, as follows:

"June 30-October 31, 1863: absent; "absent without authority, October 24, 1863." He was on a list of deserters, dated in the field, 31 May 1864: "Deserted 3 May 1864, Charlestown, Tennessee.

On muster-out roll dated Hartsville, Tennessee, March 30, 1865, age 24; under Remarks: "deserted May 3, 1864." On muster-out roll dated Nashville, Tennessee June 30, 1865, age 24; under Remarks: "Deserted Co. B. May 3, 1864. Returned since Muster out of Co B."

Notation by War Department on Robert Mintzy, dated, Washington, March 18, 1887: "Was absent without authority from about October 10, 1863, when he left his command to go home until about April 21, 1865, when paroled."

Notation by War Department, Washington, June 13, 1885: "Charge of desertion of May 3, 1864 is removed. He was captured at Philadelphia, Tennessee October 20, 1863 whilst absent from his command without authority; was confined at Richmond, Virginia, November of 1863. Went to Andersonville, Georgia February 5, 1864. Date of arrival and subsequent whereabouts to April 21, 1865 is not shown by records. He was paroled at Vicksburg, Mississippi about April 21, 1865, reported at Camp Chase, Ohio May 3, 1865, was sent to Provost Marshal Columbus, Ohio and rejoined regiment...

On prisoner of war record: "Captured at Philadelphia, Tennessee October 20, 1863, while absent from his command without authority; Confd. Richd. November 7, 1863. Sent to Andersonville, Ga. February 15, 1864 where he was confined-date not given. Paroled at Vicksburg, Miss about April 21, 1865. Survived the Sultana disaster April 27, 1865."

Whew! Cameras! Lights! Action! Get Big John on his mark! When I first received this, I had no idea of the Tennessee 5th Infantry Regiment, its war service, or any information about where, when, what, or why. Where had Robert deserted **from**? Texas? North Dakota? What did we have here: The Odyssey? Cold Mountain? What was the rest of the story? Since David's records include notation that he was "absent: sick at Loudon, Tennessee..." and since I found David's first wife, Martha, had died sometime in the mid-sixties (before I determined the actual date) I conjured up the romantic notion that this father and son snuck off to Philadelphia to visit a dying mother and wife; made for sentimental pondering.

The actual facts are just as interesting and compelling:

In October, 1863, the 2nd Division of the Army of the Cumberland was near Sale Creek, Tennessee; this is just north of Chattanooga, about 57 miles or so, as the horse would meander, from Philadelphia. This was the route of movement ending in Upper East Tennessee and involving previously described actions there. Why Robert was in Philadelphia October 20th, if that were the correct date, will never be known, but some things can be surmised; first, an "army" involves a little more than can be seen in one picture, a frame on a movie screen or, perhaps, even imagined. The Army of the Cumberland consisted of several thousand soldiers and the assorted support organization that kept it going. Perhaps Robert took off one night to ride up and see Martha and little John Wesley; perhaps he was on a spy errand; perhaps he and others were on a foraging run; perhaps he was sick; perhaps, as implied (I believe) he asked permission but was denied. Fact is, he was in Philadelphia. Often, soldiers were sent home to protect their property from the Confederates or drifters; many historians have exclaimed, "Hey, if I had been there and my family was threatened, I would have taken off, too."

Let's look at another historical event that occurred in October of that year: (From *Loudon County and the Civil War*, Loudon County TNGEN Web page)

"Following the Battle of Chickamauga on September 19-20, 1863, CSA General James Longstreet moved from Chattanooga to Knoxville in an attempt to recapture Knoxville. During this time, General Burnside (Union Commander in Knoxville area) sent a detachment of men to the Loudon area. They set up headquarters in the Wiley Blair Home, which was located between Loudon and Lenoir city. Down the road, Colonel Frank G. Wolford, commander of the Union troops currently stationed in Philadelphia, had set up headquarters in the **Walter Franklin Lenoir Home** (remember this!). On **October 20, 1863**, two Confederate Cavalries, one commanded by Colonel George. Dibrell (of the Tennessee 8th Cavalry) and the other by Colonel John J. Morrison surrounded and attacked Wolford's forces. Colonel Morrison had marched his men 50 miles in 15 hours to place them between Loudon and Philadelphia. He sent part of his troops to Loudon to hold Wolford's troops and sent the remaining troops to Philadelphia to join the fighting with Dribell's troops. The Union troops were severely beaten. Seven men were killed and **447 captured**. Wagon trains, supplies, and other equipment were also captured."

Robert was captured in uniform, in action, and recognized by the Confederate forces as a prisoner of war. Not a spy, not a deserter, but a prisoner of war. Of course, his company did not know that, until he turned up almost two years later.

My great-grandfather was marched off (or hauled) from Philadelphia to the Richmond, Virginia area and, subsequently, the Belle Island prisoner of war camp. Much has been written about the tragedy of POW camps….on both sides. We shall not attempt to travel there. It needs to be understood, however, that early on, prisoners were exchanged by both sides, and an informal system existed whereby the exchange occurred in an organized way; e.g.; 10 privates for one captain; two captains for one colonel, etc; perhaps not accurate but true in principle. As the war developed, however, Union forces observed that the soldiers they exchanged were being captured repeatedly and concluded they were just feeding a revolving door; they (the Union) unofficially ceased prisoner exchanges. Prisons on each side were not built nor prepared for the vast influx of prisoners that ensued. While the abuses at Belle Island, Andersonville, and other sites became famous (after all, the North won and, therefore, held the tribunals), conditions at many Union prisons were hardly better, and many Confederate soldiers perished in those, also. Robert lived through Belle Island and Andersonville; that he did is one of the miracles few others shared. How he did, we will never know. What his survival entailed, we, perhaps, would not want to know.

As the war drew to a close, prisoner exchanges lurched into existence again. As the records indicate, Robert was "paroled" at Vicksburg, Mississippi, April 21, 1865. This did not mean he was "paroled" from his desertion charges, as the term would imply today; it meant he was paroled from

Confederate prison, as part of general prisoner exchange. That the exchange was in Vicksburg is significant, as that was the direction of existing transportation routes to the North; rail to the Mississippi River, up the Mississippi to the Ohio at Cairo, and on to destination points. Circuitous, yes; practical…..well, that was the only way. Sherman had torn up rail lines in Georgia, South Carolina and parts of Tennessee, and most of these poor souls were not capable of marching, even if the means had existed for Confederate guards to effectively escort them. To Vicksburg, Robert was hauled.

Again, the next chapter in Robert's story was a major, historical event; it has been written about, investigated, mourned and questioned. It is the "Sultana" chapter of history.

Put simply, the transportation for these "paroled" POWs from Vicksburg was by steamboat; this involved government personnel being transported, for fee, by private enterprise, i.e. vessel owners. No stranger to the nineteenth century, avarice, greed, bribery, and gross neglect was present in great supply. Military procurement officers were responsible for purchasing passage on available steamboats for the troops; steamboat owners and/or captains sought cargo for their vessels. Obtaining a high paying cargo was the desired goal for each leg of a steamboat's passage up or down the river. Thus, on the 21st of April, 1865, many sick, diseased, and debilitated ex-prisoners of war were in Vicksburg and various vessels were in the port, seeking "cargo."

Among them was the Sultana; this vessel had made a voyage down the Mississippi and had developed problems with her boilers that necessitated repairs at Vicksburg. These repairs, suffice it to say, were ultimately deemed questionable; there was pressure to finished the task quickly and, at best, the repairs were probably not sufficient to withstand excessive stress.

There was pressure on the military to move the prisoners north as quickly as possible; there was pressure on the boat owners to obtain cargo…as much cargo as possible…as quickly as possible. In this chaos, fate dealt hundreds of poor Union soldiers the hand of being loaded onto the Sultana…..approximately 2500 of them…notwithstanding the fact the Sultana was designed to carry at maximum, 376.

My grandparents

Elizabeth and John W. Mincy
Elizabeth Alice, Homer, Virgil

My uncle
George Leonard Mincy
He always called me "Leonard"

Mincys, Harts and Marneys 65

Aunts Olive (right) and Sophia

Front: Homer Mincy
Back: George, John Wesley, Olive, Elizabeth, Sophia ca. 1900

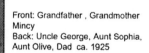

Front: Grandfather , Grandmother Mincy
Back: Uncle George, Aunt Sophia, Aunt Olive, Dad ca. 1925

The process of procuring this vessel and loading these soldiers can best be described as a combination of confusion, carelessness, collusion, and crass disregard for the welfare of the soldiers. Even while the Sultana was still undergoing repairs in Vicksburg, her agents and officers were threatening to leave if they did not get "a good load of prisoners." They insisted they could "carry them all." The military procedure for making lists, identifying and accounting for every soldier, and determining the exact number to be transported was, basically, waived at the insistence of the Sultana's owners, with the acquiescence of Quartermaster Corp officers. The soldiers were "to be listed as they came on board," which actually did not happen. In absence of lists, no one really knew how many prisoners were present or how many actually boarded the Sultana. Further, a voucher for $10,000 was prepared and quickly cashed; this was for 2,000 passengers at the going rate of $5 per head; $3 actually went to the Sultana, however, with the implication the difference stayed with Quartermaster officers, as a bribe.

The Sultana also carried a large store of freight; 250 hogsheads of sugar, 97 cases of wine, 70 to 100 mules and horses, and 100 hogs. Strangest of all, in a crate was a crew member's pet—a large alligator. The soldiers were packed solid on every available inch of space in both decks, forward and aft; while this boat was loaded in such a manner, empty or partially loaded boats lay on each side of the Sultana, not being utilized. April 24th, 1865, the Sultana steamed north. Notwithstanding the conditions on this boat and the physical state of most of the passengers, not one physician was provided by either the military or the boat owners; one private physician had removed some of his patients from the Sultana before it departed Vicksburg, likely saving their lives in the process.

Up stream, as the vessel passed Helena, Arkansas, the sight of so many crowded onto this one boat created such a curiosity that photographers gathered to take pictures. When word spread throughout the boat that "they were going to have their picture taken," soldiers moving to the land side almost capsized the Sultana. In Memphis, a few passengers disembarked and some cargo unloaded, but others were added. On the 27th, the Sultana was struggling upstream, heading toward Cairo and fighting swift currents resulting from spring flooding throughout the Mississippi River system when, at approximately 2 A.M., the boilers blew. Volumes have been written describing this carnage but, put simply, the blast ripped through the central section of the vessel, throwing passengers, wood, hot cinders, boiler parts, steaming water, cargo, and body parts up, out, and into the cold waters of the Mississippi, creating a horrible, chaotic, tragic, and fatal circumstance. The total passenger list, often debated and never exactly determined, renders an exact fatality list unknown; at best, it is believed over 1800 perished…the largest single naval disaster in our nation's history. Why was this event not more widely known or remembered?

The war had ended, Lincoln had been assassinated, and the news was filled with these stories; the facts of this disaster were both time consuming to accumulate and somewhat suspect, as efforts to "cover-up" or avoid acceptance of responsibility ruled the day. An inquiry was held, of course, and despite the fact the Quartermaster officer responsible for procurement of transportation had previously been charged with accepting bribes, no actual finding of blame resulted nor was anyone convicted of wrong doing. The innocent died, and the guilty went unpunished.

Robert was a survivor. We do not know the facts, but it is likely he was thrown overboard and held on to debris until he was rescued; he later testified that occurred after five or six hours.. Most others were not so fortunate.

It almost defies comprehension that by May 3rd, at Camp Chase, Ohio, Robert had somehow arrived, had been sent to the Provost Marshall in Columbus, Ohio and had been mustered out; Robert was headed home.

As a footnote to this horrifying episode, years later Robert stated in a pension deposition for the wife of one William Davis, of Hamilton County, that he had witnessed Davis' last words: "I cannot swim." No one could make this stuff up; I deem this a fitting epitaph for those hundreds caught up in the same circumstance.

Robert Mincy returned to Roane County and his family, in 1865; a daughter, Julie A. had been born in 1859, before the war, and a second daughter, Sarah Josie, was born in 1868. It appears from anecdotal evidence that, when Robert returned, he was living on a farm owned by E. D. Robinson; this farm was in the vicinity of a village known as Adolphus, which now is in Loudon County. This area is a scant mile or so from the south side of a south-north loop in the Tennessee River, and south of an area in Roane County known then and now as Dogwood. (On the north side of the river) Further, this is on County Road 72, which runs east-west from US highway 11, through Adolphus, then south to Stockton Valley before turning west-northwest and intersecting with state route 58, south of Kingston. This area is near the Prospect community and the Prospect Baptist Church. Robinson later testified that Robert had worked for him before the war, and seemed to live on the farm, or work for him intermittently, long after the war.

Robert's wife, Martha, died March 6, (or 1st, according to church records) 1882; she was 48. It was stated she suffered from liver trouble and derangement of the mind. Robert was married to Sophronia Jay Jackson by W.S. Davis, a minister of the gospel, March 18, 1883.

The state of Robert's health, and his efforts to obtain a pension parallel those of his father, David. Witnesses reported that Robert was not able to work continuously from the time he returned from the war; "he was constantly complaining" from his various ailments. I have occasionally stated that if one were prone to feel sorry for himself, he should remember my poor great-grandfather: "one tooth, suffering from scurvy, piles, diarrhea, heart disease, partial deafness and shortness of breath." This man, at the time of filing his pension claim in 1990, was 5'7", 160 lbs. and 54 to 59 years old, depending on which of the many offered dates one uses.

Robert first filed for disability in 1889, seemed to have expected it to start at any time, but refiled in 1892 and was awarded $12 monthly, starting February 6, 1892. Robert and Sophronia had purchased a small tract of land in 1888, comprised of 15 acres, a log cabin and barn, somewhere near the Prospect Church and in the general area where he had lived most of his life. They had purchased this property from a John W. Clendening for $150. I find it interesting that both David and Robert made purchases of land within six months time, in the same year; this during a time when both claimed disabilities, both claimed being unable to work, and neither seemed to have accumulated very much. Notwithstanding their relatively short lives and the obvious justification for their disability claims, just perhaps, those disability claims did not accurately portray the actual efforts both Robert and David exerted to support themselves.

In 1902, he and Sophronia deeded the land to Robert Jackson, (Sophronia's son) who lived with them, for $1.00 and for further consideration that "I and my wife (Sophronia) shall be cared for during life and at our death, given a decent burial…" Robert Mincy died either December 13 or 14, 1903; the coffin dealer was unsure. He was buried in the Prospect Cemetery, where his military marker still exists; Martha is buried nearby, and Sophronia was buried beside him.

Sophronia Jackson was an interesting lady; born in Habersham County, Georgia, March 1, 1848, she married Levi Jackson "a couple of years after the war of the rebellion, in White County, Georgia." (Habersham County is the northeastern most county in Georgia, bordering Tennessee, to the north; White County is immediately west). Levi had been married previously and had at least two sons by that marriage. Levi and Sophronia soon left Georgia and moved to McMinn County, Tennessee; they lived about six miles east of Athens in the Liberty Community near Piney Grove Academy. They were the parents of one son, Robert, and two daughters, Victoria and Allie. Levi died *about the year 1876* and was buried, allegedly, in the Liberty Methodist Church cemetery. How this family of Confederate sympathizers blended in with ex-Union soldiers in McMinn and Loudon County is a good question; apparently, they were able to work it out.

Shortly thereafter, Sophronia appears to have been living in the Loudon County area….near Adolphus, and where Robert Mincy lived. In 1904, E. D. Robinson, who had been deposed in Robert's pension application, also served as witness to Sophronia's widow's claim; he stated he had known her for "about 30 years." In any event, Sophronia was married January 23, 1876 to a William Smith, and the two reportedly lived on Robinson's farm; Smith deserted her soon thereafter, never to be heard from again. This marriage date is specific and brings into question the death date of Levi Jackson; no one claimed to know exactly when it (Levi's death) occurred. (Records exist that indicate Levi died in 1874; this is more likely near the actual date.)

In Sophronia's first statement supporting her "widow's claim," she neglected to mention this second marriage; most of the testimony and reason for such lengthy statement gathering usually centered around the marriage records of the applicants, to assure they were not eligible for, receiving, or had been denied pensions from other qualifying factors. She, later, issued a corrected statement, indicating this marriage had been of such short duration and having ended as it did, she had "just forgotten about it; she had not wanted to think about it." "She had been abandoned and forced to care for herself until such time as she filed for a divorce in 1883." Further, Sophronia testified that a child had been born of this union in April, 1877; her name was Margaret Smith, and I have seen no mention of her other than the deposition.

Sophronia continued living in her home with her son, Robert (Jackson), until her death January 19, 1919. Robert Jackson apparently never married. Surviving descriptive comments include that "she was a large woman," "fierce looking," "was called, Big Mamma," among others. Perhaps Robert had chosen wisely, when he selected Sophronia to be his bride; she was probably capable of doing more work than he was. E.D. Robinson testified that Sophronia had "a good reputation for truth and chastity, yet she is wholly deficient in memory as to dates (or) cannot even approximate time; incidents and circumstances, she relates clearly and accurately; her general intelligence is fairly good except she has no conception of time as measured by months and years." As had every Mincy in my line, including my grandfather, Sophronia dutifully signed her "X" and was apparently capable of no more.

At the time of her death, she was described as having "no property (the home had been "sold" to Robert Jackson), except one sow and one cow and a few pieces of household goods, all worth probably no more than $100."

Robert's oldest daughter Julie, married William Clark, December 24, 1885; the oldest of their four children, Cora Ethel Clark, born September 29, 1886, married Thomas Pete "Tom" Mincy, July 01, 1906. Tom was a grandson of "War" Dave, and a second cousin of Cora's. The reason I mention this union (other than the questions asked by some relatives when they notice a "Mincy marrying a Mincy") is that Tom, who would have been a first cousin to my father and Uncle George, is the only "Mincy" relative either my brother or I remember our family mentioning. With, as it turns out, cousins by the dozen hanging around, one would think we would have been surrounded by them, but, that is not the way it was....for whatever reasons.

Robert's second daughter, Sarah Josie, born 1868, basically, vanished; little, factually, is known of her. By the rarest of chance, I happened to be reading a book by a grade school classmate, Mabel Norwood Boylston, *New Hopewell Baptist Church; the Little White Church in the Dale,* which details the minutes of this church from as far back as records exist. This church is in a community where I lived for a few years, and what caught my eye was a short sentence in the January minutes, 1894: "Josie Minsie.....received by experience." Hmm. A summary of the church rolls, from 1880 until 1903, lists a Josie Mincey, received January 1894, "by experience" and further, shows her as "deceased" (by 1903).

I later noted that in 1898, this church met to consider the matter of a heresy charge against one "Brother Lane"; at this meeting was R. A. Mincy, who stated he was not legally sent by his church; he was voted upon and received as a councilor (?). It would be nice to think this was Robert, Josie's father.

In all existing records I have seen, or that are known by others, Robert never used initials nor is a middle name shown; further, no records of an "R.A. Mincy" in McMinn County can be found. A rather thorough search seemed to indicate this last name was something else, and that the original, hand-written notes of this meeting were simply illegible. Considering his health, where he lived and financial status, I rather doubt Robert was traveling around as a church "councilor." No additional records of Josie's life or death have turned up, to date. One would think my father, aunts or uncle would have mentioned "Aunt Josie" at one time or another, but that just did not happen.

John Wesley, Robert's son and first born, was living with Robert into the early eighties; we just presume wherever Robert farmed, John W. farmed. He married Susan Elizabeth Hart, my grandmother, June 3, 1888 in Roane County. Again, only as an assumption, John and Susan Elizabeth probably started life together living on the south side of the Tennessee River, in (what was then) Roane County, near the Adolphus community.

Grandmother, and I shall usually refer to her as that, was a Hart, of course, but was also from a long line of Marneys, among other in-laws. Before I relate what little I remember of my grandparents, I do want to visit a spell with the Marneys and Harts.

Many years ago, at the funeral of one of my Mincy aunts, a distant cousin from the Hart side gave my brother a "family tree" listing of the Marneys. I think we ran off copies, put them away, and lived on, smug in the knowledge we had the history of our "family line." I only wish!

A few years ago, I pulled out my copy, dusted it off, and prepared to write the family history, looking forward to this being the cornerstone of an epic work. On second look, I came to add others to the list of ancient relatives who should be shot for their negligence in not preserving what was known of kith and kin. This "tree" did list some names, coming down the line, but was totally void of dates, places, or most of the tree branches. Over the years, I have been able to add some confirmation and related information.

As with Samuel "Minsey" the stated family tradition of the Marneys usually reads: "Amos Marney, b. ca. 1670 in Scotland, m. Rebecca_____; their son, Amos, b. ca 1700 in County Cork, Ireland, m. Betsy_____ (by Rev. Simeon Wade; it is interesting to note references are made to Amos' {perhaps} grandson, Amos, being married to Sarah Vance by a Rev. Simon Ware; coincidence? Other references show the Amos/Sarah minister, as Simon Harr. Just examples of how lineages get distorted.)" My original legend jumped forward to a third Amos in Virginia. However, numerous other sources list the next Marney as Robert R, b. ca 1730 in Ireland, who, supposedly, was the first Marney immigrant to America. Robert Marney was of record in Frederick County, Virginia on the 1749-50 Rent Rolls, LDS data. A Robert "Merney" was listed as head of household in the census list of Samuel Porter in 1785 Shenandoah County, Virginia. A Robert Marney was listed as head of household in the 1783 Shenandoah County, Virginia census. He was married to Mary_____ . The will of Robert Marney, Bourbon County, Kentucky Will Book B, pg 264 was dated 24 January, 1805 and probated March, 1805. The executors were James Drummond and Mordecai Batson. The will listed grandchildren John Batson and Mary Drummond and seven children, including the third son, Amos (no "numbers" or 'juniors"; just another Amos), b. 1 September, 1760 Frederick County, Virginia. Amos married Sarah Vance, b. 8 May, 1764. Both Sarah and Amos moved to and died in Roane County, Tennessee.

Quite often, more attention is given to Sarah's father, Samuel Vance, for his documented service in the Revolutionary War: he served as Lieutenant in the battle of Point Pleasant, October 10, 1774; he was made Captain 1777 and Colonel in 1781. He participated in the siege of Yorktown and was present at the surrender of Yorktown. Samuel, later, was a Lieutenant in the militia of District 14 of Dunmore County.

Amos, in his own right, participated in the War of American Independence; in his pension application at Roane County, Tennessee, July 23, 1833, he stated that, "He was born at Frederick County, Virginia, September 1760 and that he enlisted while living at Shenandoah County, Virginia, 1779. He served two months under Captain Denton's Virginia Company and marched to Staunton against the Indians; he enlisted again in April or May following and served three months. He had forgotten the names of his officers and was stationed the greater part of the time at Albermarle County, Virginia. He again enlisted, names of officers not given, and marched to Richmond and was one of a party of riflemen and had an engagement, place not given. He went to Yorktown and was in the siege of that place and was discharged three days before Cornwallis surrendered, having served his three months. In the winter following, he volunteered again in Capt. Benjamin Frey's Company and guarded prisoners at the barracks in Frederick County for one month. After the Revolution, he lived in Shenandoah County, Rockbridge County, for 10 years, thence to

Roane County, Tennessee." Among the references he gave was Sawyer Hart....his son-in-law.

In Sarah's Pension Claim W1046 (allowed), she claimed Amos (and she) had "moved to Tennessee in 1798 and settled on the Clinch River; purchased 500 acres on north side of the Tennessee River adjoining Zaccheus Ayers for $1000 on 11 June, 1803, from John Stone. On 15 November, 1833, Amos purchased a sorrel horse, 5 sheep, 3 plows and many other items for $1 as part of a complicated three way transaction. Amos died in Roane County, TN and was buried in Marney Cemetery near Tennessee Baptist Church and Riley's Creek, near Kingston, Tennessee. (The) cemetery moved to area behind church when Watts Bar Lake was flooded....." I have visited his grave in the Tennessee Church cemetery; it is still very visible and clearly reads: "Amos Marney; Denton's VA.CO; Rev. War."

Amos and Sarah were the parents of thirteen children; again, that first "family tree" I received listed Letitia first, implying she was the eldest; other references lists dates of birth, to the extent they were known, and show Letitia as the ninth child, born ca 1806. Letitia married John Sawyer Hart March 27, 1823.

This is a timely moment to insert a bit of information that illustrates the difficulty of accurately portraying family history; it involves the Marneys. My father and his family always proudly claimed being related to Samuel T. Rayburn, distinguished Speaker of the House of Representatives from Texas; actually, my mother made similar claims based on some (unknown) connection to her family.

The source of the Mincy claim, or at least confirmation of the legend, is perhaps shown in the "Marney genealogy report" given us by the distant Hart cousin; it list Polly Marney and Joseph Rayburn being the parents of a William Rayburn, and further, indicates William married a Martha Waller and became the father of Samuel Rayburn. A search into the factual background of Sam Rayburn indicates that William, father of Samuel, was not the son of Polly and Joseph, but of John and Lucinda Amos Rayburn; John and Lucinda migrated to East Tennessee from Virginia; Joseph Rayburn from North Carolina. Various sources indicate these branches of

Rayburns often referred to each other as cousins, but an actual link between these two lines of Rayburns has not been established. Alas, our family claim to fame has been exposed and we must live on, Rayburnless.

Anyway, the Harts were apparently English; an unverified Web responder stated, "He had traced back (his) Harts to Henry Hart, b. 1761, London, England who ended up in Roane County, Tennessee." Other reports list Henry as being born in Charleston, South Carolina, and married to an (unknown) Sawyer. They had nine children, the first two being Eli, b. ca 1793 and John Sawyer Sr., b May 20, 1796. Eli married Nancy Littleton November 2, 1816 in Roane County, Tennessee.

Much has been recorded about Eli, most of it negative. We will simply refrain from specifics; although involved in various business deals and property transactions, he was the subject of several lawsuits, prosecutions and, in the end, was declared "a lunatic and had not capacity sufficient for the government of himself and property."

John Sawyer and Letitia Marney became the parents of eleven children; the fifth, Amos M. Hart, b. July 19, 1835, married Mary Ann Staley (or Stanley) May 10, 1866, in Roane County; they were the parents of six children, the second being Susannah Elizabeth, born October 19, 1868——my grandmother. Amos died January 20, 1880, and was buried in the Tennessee Missionary Baptist Church Cemetery; I have visited this site, and viewed Amos' stone which is still in good condition.

Growing up, we occasionally visited the families of Dad's first cousins, the Bowmans and Bowdens, in Lenoir City, Tennessee; I remember mention of Aunt Sallie (Allen), the Hines, Harts, Prestons, Littletons, and perhaps others long forgotten; sadly, I grew up not knowing the scope of the Harts, Marneys, and their descendents. These families, among many others, were founding settlers in Roane County; they fought and died in every war in which this country was involved; their remains fill graves in cemeteries all over Roane County. I wish I had known some of them better and could have grown up sharing the heritage of their lives.

I also wish I knew more about my grandparents, John Wesley and Susan Elizabeth Mincy. They both died when I was six, and my memories are brief and vague. There are a few pictures of me in their presence. I was born and lived up the road from them until I was four, and remember a visit or two with them shortly before they died. I do not remember a specific conversation or lasting memories of their personalities.

There is little point is creating scenarios about their lives that I cannot verify; I believe they lived either on one side of the Tennessee River or other, either in or around the Dogwood Community (now in Roane County) or the Adolphus Community (now in Loudon County). He farmed, she housewifed and they were the parents of seven children. Three were stillborn or died in infancy. Those surviving were: Olive E., b. March 24, 1890; George Leonard, b. November 15, 1892; Sophia M., b. December 2, 1894, and my father, Homer Franklin, b. January 28, 1897. This was my family and, other than the brief memory (and reference) of my grandparents, was all I knew of the line I have traced, until I started tracing it, a few years ago.

I shall relate my grandfather's land ownership stories later, in describing my father; suffice it to say now, I believe he was able to work up to greater "farm" responsibilities and get to a point that he was able to acquire land, in a somewhat more skilled manner than his parents or grandparents, although I know he was illiterate, as were they. He, with his sons, came to farm on a large operation in the Dogwood Community and, later, acquired land and a home near where I was born and where I first remember them. My brother, Homer, recalls him better than I, and his memories of grandfather are only that "he was an old man, complained that George and Homer did not take care of their tools and did not farm right." Further, Homer remembers Grandfather discussing, at great length, the merits of "shallow plowing vs. deep plowing" as advocated by the federally funded County Farm Agent. Although illiterate, he latched onto the thoughts of educated people.

Grandmother is simply remembered as being kind, friendly and supportive, although a common family trait would have to be described as, at times, they could be rough around the edges.

Aunt Sophia married Henry Littleton in 1921; I always wondered where names (such as) Sophia originated, not knowing any other family existed. Hardly a mystery; Susannah Elizabeth had a younger sister, Sophie

E. and, of course, there was step-great grandmother, Sophronia. Aunt Olive never married and she and Uncle George lived with their parents until they (my grandparents) died; my father married in 1929. Again, this will be discussed later, but, in 1934, these Mincys lost all the property they owned in a foreclosure and were evicted from that property in 1939. Uncle George, Aunt Olive and my grandparents moved into a small, brick house in Philadelphia; this is where our story gets interesting.

Think back to earlier references where you were admonished to take notes and remember; now comes the test. The small brick house in Philadelphia had actually been the "slave quarters" next to the large mansion described as the "W.F. Lenoir" house, vintage 1848-1853 and later, during Civil War times, the home of Henry Lenoir; this was in the Lenoir family until 1930. Remember? This was the house which served as Headquarters for Union Colonel Frank G. Wolford, who fought a losing battle against General Longstreet's troops, who were in the area in their campaign against Knoxville. It was at or near where my great grandfather was captured by the Confederate forces; it is less than a mile, as the crow would fly, to where my great-great grandfather, David, and other family members are buried. Why did my uncle, aunt and grandparents end up there? I will never have a clue; it defies logic, as there must have been nearer places to rent, beg, or borrow near Kingston and where they had lived for over 20 years.

The house was owned at that time by the Frew family, and I have never seen a reference in any form between my family and the Frews; it is a fact they moved there and there must have been some connection; whatever it was, it will remain a mystery.

I recall visiting this location; I would have been five or so, and I was taken to Athens, put on a (Tennessee Coach Company) bus which took me to Philadelphia, on its route to Knoxville, letting me off along side US Highway 11. I would be met by my Uncle George; it was a short walk to this dwelling. I do have vague memories of the two large rooms in this "church looking" brick structure and of the presence of my grandparents. This structure, as well as the "mansion," still stands.

What still blows me away is having no memories of any mention why they were there, the history of that area, the fact their great grandfather and mother were buried a short walk to the other side of the tracks, or any trace of the path that must have caused them to be there. My always lingering questions: (also directed at my father) did they know of happenings from this area? Did they actually know the burial place of War Dave? For that matter, did they know where Robert had lived and been buried? Uncle George and Aunt Olive would have been eleven and thirteen, when their grandfather, Robert, died; should they not have known about that? If not, why not? Was there some estrangement or reasons these relatives seemed to vanish from my immediate family's recollection or, as is most likely, did it just seem to them there was nothing to talk about? On the one hand, reticence, particularly if negativism is involved, is a distinct family trait of all my relatives of that era; on the other, my Uncle George was an outgoing, friendly and gregarious person; he, as well as Aunt Olive, would brag about any subject, that seemed to enhance their worth, at the drop of a suggestion. They were loyal, visited graveyards, attended funerals, worked in churches, and were characteristic of people who would enhance and embellish, if possible, the accomplishments of any relative (Sam Rayburn being a good example). Why I never remember a peep about their direct ancestors will remain the mystery for the ages; however, had they talked, had I listened, and had I known all this, it perhaps would have never been written; maybe, just maybe, it was meant to be.

Uncle George, Aunt Olive, and my grandparents moved from Philadelphia, sometime in 1940, to a house west of Lenoir City, near Eaton's Crossroads. My Grandfather died December 4, 1941, and Grandmother died February 17, 1942; they were buried in the Lawnville Cemetery, near Kingston, Tennessee. I remember, from a couple of visits to the Philadelphia location, Uncle George working in a mill there and specifically remember getting up about 4:00 A.M. one morning to view the first diesel locomotive I had witnessed. The Southern Railway tracks ran in front and to the west of the old Lenoir Mansion; when these trains began being powered by diesels, it was a sight to behold versus the old steam engines that had served for more than 100 years. Called "streamliners" (who knows why), I doubt these trains moved faster than had the steam engines; after all, track conditions, traffic, location and number of cars dictated speed more than engine power, however, the different sound and ambiance of the experience made this an exciting event

Aunt Olive never married; never even dated that I remember witnessing or hearing mentioned. She just continued her life as a housekeeper for Uncle George. A heavy, plodding woman, she, at times, could adopt the short, curt, even rude tendencies of this family. It is only fair to extol her many virtues, also; she was a great (country) cook, had a touch for raising and cultivating flowers, read constantly and was kind, loving and supportive to Homer, Betty and me throughout her life. We were the closest to having her own children she would ever know; sometimes, she could be demanding. Mother, later, would lament Aunt Olive (and other family members) "taking over" Homer Franklin. Aunt Olive made every effort to play the hand dealt her, without complaint.

After Philadelphia, Uncle George continued to work in mills for a short time, farmed, raised gardens and, in the mid-forties, went to work in Oak Ridge, Tennessee, at the huge Manhattan project; later, he became a fireman there and worked in that capacity until he retired. In his spare time, he raised tobacco, worked as janitor and in cemetery maintenance for his church and stayed busy. Uncle George was always an energetic, industrious man and was constantly busy doing something or looking after someone.

Visits to their home were, generally, fun; there was more to eat, car trips to take and attention given that, at the very least, was different than home. They would buy cereal, in a box, which was a treat; Aunt Olive would get small "transfers" out of the cereal boxes and press them onto handkerchiefs for me. Uncle George always called me "Leonard" (his middle name) in a possessive way; I suppose, early on, it had been a battle of wills to see which of my uncle's names would stick. The middle name seemed to win out, but, in the computer/data entry era, that is no blessing. First initials do not work.

Later, Homer stayed with Uncle George and Aunt Olive while attending the University of Tennessee; Uncle George helped me a time or two, also, when I came up a "little short" while attending UT.

Uncle George usually seemed to have some lady he was "seeing" or, at least, gave that impression; nothing serious seemed to develop from these relationships. He was certainly always interested in whatever affairs Homer, Betty or I seemed to be enjoying and would usually voice his approval, disapproval or opinion regarding the appearance of our selected mate. In 1967, that changed when he married his friend of that time, Octavia Greenwell Lancaster of Lenoir City. Aunt "Ocky" was a widow and retired school principal who had taught for 56 years in the Lenoir City system; her reputation was that of a stern disciplinarian and forceful teacher. Uncle George moved into her house on West Broadway in Lenoir City.

Needless to say, this caused some problems within the family; Aunt Olive was left alone and between her and Aunt Sophia, who was also widowed, this union of their dear brother was not welcomed with open arms. Uncle George secured a house in Lenoir City and persuaded Aunt Olive and Aunt Sophia to move there; he continued as their basic care giver. Unfortunately, Uncle George died suddenly, November 20, 1975 (this I very well remember; I was in Chicago on a business trip), leaving my aunts pretty much on their own. Octavia had not bargained for this, but she continued to offer assistance and support for my aunts for a short while; health issues soon dictated they both move into a rest home in that area.

I mentioned that Aunt Sophia had married Henry Littleton in 1921; this was not her first marriage. A short time previous to that date, she had married a William Flannigan; the facts of the beginning of this relationship or the circumstance of it ending are not known; remember, Mincys don't talk or tell. I know it was short lived and I have seen the entry for this marriage in a "family bible" that had been obliterated. Nevertheless, end it did.

Henry Marshall Littleton was a relative of both the Harts and Marneys but, insofar as I can examine, several distant cousins removed from Sophia; they never had children. Uncle Henry, born October 9, 1882, was the sixth of eight children born to George P. (Pres) and Margaret (Polly) Ann Huffine Littleton; the Littletons were another old line Roane County family, having been in the area from its earliest days; their many branches were mixed with Prestons, Hines, Harts, Marneys, and these combined family trees, if possible to collect, would fill a gymnasium floor. Henry farmed and, later, was a livestock trader. When I first remembered him, he and Aunt Sophia lived on a small farm west of Lenoir City, and a couple of miles from where Uncle George lived. Visiting Uncle George always involved the obligatory visit to Aunt Sophia, or she would get her feeling hurt; sometimes that was a problem as either Uncle George had to take me or Uncle Henry had to come and get me and that was not always convenient. The visits were always enjoyable, however.

Aunt Sophia, at her best, was a sweet, loving woman. Later, my children would always shudder at Aunt Sophia wanting to "kiss on them" with her (perceived) whiskers, snuff smell and, they would say, her "strange eye." The fact is, she was affectionate and only wanted attention and affection in return. She was a gracious host, although she and Aunt Olive were usually in competition over who cooked the best whatever or what one had said about the other. That was just part of the equation. Aunt Sophia had, actually, been very attractive in her younger days.

Uncle Henry was really a solid citizen. He certainly seemed old to us, although, during my period of childhood visits, he would probably have been in his early sixties. A thin, droll man, he seemed very serious and restrictive; yet, he had a wry sense of humor, would talk, and would usually excuse Aunt Sophia's occasional hysterics by stating, "don't pay any attention to Sofie; she is just high strung," or, "Now Sofie!" Trips with Uncle Henry on his animal buying or trading runs around Lenoir City were always interesting. Homer and I would often amuse ourselves trying to imitate Uncle Henry's voice: he spoke in a low, raspy manner that sounded as if he was breathing in through his mouth, as he talked; at least, that is the way we tried to do it. We respected him, and thought he was successful and supportive. He died November 9, 1954 and is buried in Lenoir City with Aunt Sophia, who died in 1982. Aunt Olive had died in 1978 and was buried in the Lawnville Cemetery alongside her parents.

An interesting note about Aunt Sophia: in the late seventies, she had fallen and injured her hip. This was one immediate reason she and Aunt Olive had to enter a rest home and I remember, during this time, visiting them there. I did not recognize Aunt Sophia; she was in the hall, strapped into a wheelchair and weighing probably no more than 90 pounds; she was "totally out of it" and I never expected to see her alive, again.

She recovered, however, and the last few years of her life seemed more peaceful and serene than we ever remembered. She was pleasant, sweet, and a joy to visit. In addition, guess what: William Flannigan, her husband of long ago, appears to have been a resident in the same "home" and renewed his friendship with Aunt Sophia; for the brief period she remained alive, I believe he "called on her" and I think she enjoyed those visits. Of course, he may have lived in the neighborhood and been known by the Mincys all their lives; again, that was not to be talked about. Whatever that past, show up he did, talk they did and both seemed to mutually enjoy this renewed opportunity.

Uncle George, Aunt Olive and Aunt Sophia all died from sudden heart attacks; Uncle George at his home in Lenoir City, and my aunts, in their sleep, at the rest home. They lived uneventful but giving lives, enjoyed few extravagant creature comforts, but, in the end, were spared most of life's many sad ways of leaving it. While they were with us, they were my only, known, Mincy relatives; I am blessed by their memories.

My Dad, Homer F., will be visited later.

The Canupps, Farners and Runions

Family histories are, more often than not, arbitrarily limited; either one runs out of paper, forgets some of the stories, dislikes some family members, and, thereby, shuns them, or the task just finally overwhelms the author. Churchill's *A History of the English Speaking Peoples* comes to mind; although considered a definitive work, it certainly does not include me and rather vaguely slides over vast stretches of historical happenings. Although a multi-volume work, of necessity, its scope is limited. This little effort will not cause old Winston to turn over but suffers some of the same restriction; too many, too much.

However, my goal being to acquaint grandchildren or other interested friends and relatives with their kith and kin, an omission that could not be tolerated would be to bypass June's line, the Canupps and Farners. That was never a consideration; I remember my in-laws well, cannot forget the kindness and friendship shown me, and I proudly consider them "family." I wish I knew more about them. I must respectfully admonish/encourage my genetic contributions to always honor and be eternally curious about their mother's (June) ancestral line. That DNA is worthy of pride in descendent ownership.

Tracing the Canupp line was difficult for the same reasons that limited my success with the Mincys; spelling, lack of immediate family "lore," no one around to ask, and, of course, no interest in asking when there was. Eventually, I was fortunate to stumble across distant relatives who had been interested in this family and had worked to put pieces of their genealogical story together. As least some information can be shared.

The "spelling" bit can best be explained by stating the first family member arriving in this country was Jacob Knupp, born ca. 1714 in Germany, who disembarked through the Port of Philadelphia. This name is known to have been spelled, at various times: Knop, Knup, Kanupp, Kenupp, Kunuip, Keneipp, among other spellings. Those just include the "K" sounds. The same genesis applied when "C" words began to be used. But, we think it started as "Knupp." Whatever the case, Jacob did arrive, did work his way into the Carolinas, did marry, and did raise a family. Few, if any, actual facts are known of his life, and I shall not attempt to manufacture any. Jacob and wife (name unknown) were the parents of five children, the oldest being Thomas Canup Sr. (note the name change of the first born in this family), who was born about 1756 near the Trent River, in Craven, North Carolina.

Thomas married an "Ester," and they were the parents of eight children. Family notes suggest most were born in North Carolina; however, both Thomas and Ester died and were buried in Habersham, Georgia. (An interesting note: this location is also common to the early Farners as well as the early Jacksons/Sophronia Mincy; my first wife, in theory, may very well have been my 18th cousin-in-law) Ester is assumed to have been an Indian; family history and the fact her grandsons were in an Indian regiment during the Civil War, suggest this. No proof will be found, as it was illegal for a white person to marry an Indian, in North Carolina, during that time. While the information is somewhat conflicting, the youngest child of Thomas and Ester, Jacob, may have married a Margaret (Mary) Crow and, to do so, special dispensation would have been given for this interracial marriage. In all probability, Margaret was a Christianized Indian.

Their first child, Fredrick Canupp (note the addition of an extra "p") was born about 1798 in Lincoln, North Carolina, and also died in Georgia; he married Mary Ammons, and they were the parents of five children. The oldest, Henry Jackson Canupp, born May, 1829 in Habersham, Georgia, married, first, Eleanor Gibson, then, Elizabeth C. Smith, and, finally, Charity Bullard. Henry Jackson died in White, Georgia. Hold on to your hats as I tell you that Henry was the father of nine children by Eleanor, five by Elizabeth, and six by Charity. Our line continued through the third child of Eleanor Gibson Canupp, Susan Canupp, born September 1854, in Habersham, Georgia.

David Amos Canupp was born of Susan and an unknown father about 1878 in Cherokee, North Carolina, and died February 8, 1948, in Athens, Tennessee. (All else being equal, we might imagine that had "father unknown" been known, David Amos would not have been a Canupp and, subsequently, neither would any who followed; June, in theory, might have entered North Athens Elementary as Sylvia June Wrestled with Bear) Susan later married Newton Frankum, born January 1858, in Habersham, Georgia; they became the parents of six Frankums. David Amos married Eliza Wright, who was born August 2, 1878 in Cherokee, North Carolina, and died November 16, 1953; she is buried in the McMahan Calvary Baptist Church Cemetery in Athens, Tennessee. David Amos and Eliza were the parents of eight children.

These children were: Claude A., born ca. 1898, Nora, born ca. 1900, Verdie Louise, born November 22, 1900, Floyd Amons, born September 22, 1902, Everet Allen, born ca. 1905, Joseph Taft, born October 15, 1910, Infant Canupp, born ca. 1913, and Velda, born May 17, 1914. Verdie, Everet, and Velda are buried in Tennessee (McMahan Calvary Cemetery); Claude is believed to have been buried in East Tennessee; Floyd lived and is believed to have been buried in California, and nothing is known of Nora.

To relate the known, all these children appear to have been born in the Murphy, North Carolina, area; David Amos and Eliza, along with Claude, Verdie, Everet, Joseph Taft, and Velda migrated to Athens, Tennessee, in the early 1900s and, for the most part, lived their lives there. David Amos and Eliza separated at some time (it is not known when) and David A. married an Elizabeth Yates (again, dates unknown). Certain facts indicate that by the mid to late thirties, at the latest, David Amos was married to Elizabeth Yates.

David Amos appears to have owned a few acres of land in "North" Athens, and, in a series of land transactions, either sold or transferred, as lots, this property to his children, then living in Athens; subsequently, these lots were transferred or exchanged between some of these family members or to others, outside the family. David lived his later years in McMinn County, farmed, made molasses but, generally, had little to do with other members of his family. He and Elizabeth Yates Canupp were the parents of at least one child, William "Billy" Canupp; June remembers a few contacts with him, but no relationship subsequently developed. Claude, who married Ola McNabb, was involved in several property transactions during the mid-forties.

(I remember Claude and Ola very well; this moves ahead, but they lived next door to Bess, June and Kathy, when June and I were married. Claude did not work. He hung around the house, considered world events, and expressed his opinion about them. Perhaps his real estate ventures had enabled his independence; however, at that time, Ola still worked in a hosiery mill, full time, and seemed less than pleased with Claude's leisure). Verdie married Riley Reynolds in 1920, with Riley spending most of his life in law enforcement in McMinn County. Joseph Taft married Bess Farner in 1933.

What he (Joe) might have done before that time is anyone's guess; I can personally vouch for having heard him "talk about" working "out west," being a "gigolo," shooting someone, and, mischievously, describe periods of tough life. All that may very well be, as when Joe would casually refer to some of those exploits, he would get a certain twinkle in his eyes that would indicate there was at least some element of truth. For certain, however, he worked in the hosiery business most of his life. The mills in and around Athens may have been what drew members of this family to that area, and Joe was in the mills as far back as June can remember.

Joe was about 43, give or take, when I first met him. I knew him and was around him on an intermittent basis, for the next 30 years, or so. The Joe I knew was probably different from the Joe of earlier years, but some of the temperament, traits, and habits, I believe, were consistent. He was a piece of work.

It would probably help to provide the canvass for a portrait of him, by just laying out some of the baggage he carried throughout his life; it influenced what he did and how he lived.

Joe was not well educated; I have no clue how far in school he went, but his literacy was rather limited. Yet, he was aware of and interested in events around him; world happenings, political viewpoints....he would expound upon them. He drank...probably had from a very early age. It would be trite and misdirected to just say "that was the Indian in him" as, while it may be commonly assumed the Red Man cannot handle his firewater, it is equally true poverty, hopelessness, and lack of opportunity provide the breeding grounds for abuses of many types in all races of people. Are there not also a few persons of means who succumb to weaknesses of the flesh? Joe perhaps was hooked before he had a chance to consider alternative lifestyles maturely.

June, and others of his family document the tragic consequences of his drinking and his temperament when doing so; he would become belligerent, abusive, and other than a model citizen. It is not for me to try to describe a situation that I did not witness; his first marriage failed, he left a wife and child who were victims of his excesses and who carried throughout their lives the scars of those years. I believe Joe forever regretted those days and his failures. I have seen him drunk, and although he usually had his beer around and might have been in a good mood, I must also say in the later years, I never saw him "under the influence." He may or may not have been, technically, an alcoholic, but as he matured, I would say he made an effort to live responsibly.

Having introduced this element, we can go on to say he was always a hard worker. Other than whatever he may have done (or not) in his wild, younger days, he was a machinist, and a very skilled one, in the "half-hose" or men's hosiery business. He was certainly working in mills during the earliest of June's memory. She recalls, probably when she was 10 or eleven, preparing "supper" and walking to deliver it, from their home in North Athens to the Vestal Mill, where Joe and Bess worked the second shift. This is a good time to mention the hierarchy of hosiery mill workers: "knitters" attended a group of machines, assured each was running properly, cut (or separated) each sock as it came from the machine, and accumulated them into bundles, accounting for the production of each machine. They were usually paid "production wages" or a minimum, plus premium if they produced more than the "standard."

A "fixer" generally rose from the ranks of knitters, but was usually male in those days. Fixers performed minor maintenance on the machines, would assist in changing yarns or the set-up for different style hosiery, and were the floor mechanics for a group of machines.

A "machinist" (in the hosiery business) was capable of complete assembly or disassembly of knitting machines; he would be responsible for major maintenance, changeover to different dies or patterns, and any other action beyond the competence of a fixer. Joe was a machinist, at least during the time I knew him.

June was born in 1934, and a son, Donnie, was born in 1943; he lived less than one month. A daughter, Jeanette, was born around 1945 and also died. It was at this time that the situation with Joe became untenable, and he and Bess parted for good. He may have remained around Athens for a time; however, it seems he left for the High Point/Lexington North Carolina area soon thereafter and lived there the rest of his life. June recalls visiting him at least once, possibly in the late forties, when he was living in High Point with his mother. Or, she could have been living with him. In any event, around 1948, Joe married Ida Mae Watson, who had been married to one of his close friends; again, most of their life together was spent in North Carolina.

It was during the summer of 1952, after June and I had graduated from McMinn High, that Joe turned up, contacted June, and I met him for the first time. The specific memory that lasted was that he and Mae sported a new Frazier automobile, offered June and me a trip to Lake Winnepesaukah, in Chattanooga, and let me drive, while he and Mae chilled in the back seat, enjoying the beverage of their choice. We had a fine time, and I was in high cotton steering that big car around. What is a Frazier, you say?

After World War II, industrialist Henry J. Kaiser, who had operated a variety of vast industrial enterprises during the war, began production of passenger cars; his first two products were the Kaiser and an upgraded series, the Frazier. Later, as an innovative offering to the masses, he marketed the Henry J, a compact that, alas, did not become the Volkswagen of the world. The company soon folded, in spite of the fact the Henry J was briefly offered in the Sears, Roebuck & Co. catalogue (I believe under the Allstate name). Anyway, I enjoyed driving Joe's Frazier, and we (Joe and I) seemed to get along fine.

I do not recall being around him again for a year or so; however, around 1952 or 1953, June and my sister, Betty, went to Mrytle Beach with Joe and Mae for a vacation; I think Joe had begun to make an effort to establish some type of relationship with June. A step in the wrong direction occurred when Pam was born, in August, 1955; I remember it well, and, sadly, June probably wishes she could forget it. It occurred while June was still in the Epperson Hospital, in Athens.

Joe had learned of Pam's birth; I may have called him, although I do not remember having done so. This was his first grandchild, and I think Joe was rightfully proud of his "accomplishment." Whatever his reaction, he headed over from North Carolina, with a buddy to help him drive, and arrived in Athens, and the hospital, somewhat the worse for wear (and tear). He staggered in, demanding that he see his daughter, June **CANUPP**. When he was told, of course, that no such person was a patient, he rather loudly and belligerently begged to differ and created quite a commotion. He had slightly overlooked the fact that his daughter's name was now, Mincy.

Either we heard him from wherever we were, or, somehow, he got through to the reception personnel, as he did get a brief hearing. He was so far "out of it," however, that he probably never remembered the occasion. I think he was asked to leave, and I know June was terribly embarrassed. Perhaps I am giving too much credit, but I have always cut him a little slack for that occasion, recognizing that he cared enough to be there.

Another factor that explains part of the hospital story is that Joe was quite "loud," as are most people who work very long in textile mills. A large area with hundreds of knitting machines running, plus the power equipment driving them to do so, creates a substantial noise. (Nothing compared to the weaving room, in a textile plant) Anyone working in this environment not only gains the habit of yelling to be heard, but, in many cases, suffers substantial hearing loss. Joe, (Bess, too, for that matter) and many others simply talked loudly and, if agitated, even louder. At his best, Joe was animated, loud, and somewhat boisterous when communicating. When working, however, he was serious and attentive to the task at hand.

I do not recall seeing Joe again, until after I finished school. Immediately after I escaped the University of Tennessee, I traveled to Burlington,

North Carolina, to begin work with Burlington Industries, Inc. June had to wait in Knoxville, until I could draw my first check, in order that we complete the move with our meager possessions. By this time, Joe (and Mae) was working at the Silver Knit Hosiery Mill, in Lexington, North Carolina, and, on the side, he and Mae were operating "Shep's Boat Dock" on High Rock Lake, off North Carolina Route 8, about eight or nine miles south of Lexington. This was a modest operation, with an area to launch small boats, gasoline facilities, a small store, and a few cabins for people desiring to stay near the lake, for whatever reasons. Joe and Mae lived in one of the cabins; the first weekend I was in Burlington, I got directions and went down to spend that time with them.

Then, as always, they were gracious hosts. My own cabin, use of his boat, and all the junk items from the store that my hungry heart desired were there for the taking. I actually pitched in and worked the cash register, as needed. I do recall trying to get up on water skis; I do not recall long periods of time gracefully gliding over the lake, flexing my buffed up freight handler's body. I do recall getting the worst sun burn of my life. Although there may be no medical precedent, I know a little of my hair line receded at the front corners, as the peeling took its inevitable course. June, little Pam, and I probably visited this location a weekend or two, during the brief time we were in Burlington.

That first weekend, Joe and Mae treated me to a big steak dinner at the American Legion Club, in Lexington; I was grateful, as my rations had been rather sparse, waiting for that first check. I vividly remember Joe and Mae gracefully dancing around the floor, as the juke box intoned the current jitter bug ditty of the day. He seemed a natural, and I could imagine then, and to this day, that he would certainly have been an interesting and charismatic figure in his time. Years of bending over machines resulted in his being somewhat "slump shouldered;" however, he was probably over six feet, with a quick smile (when in a good mood), an outgoing personality, and one could surmise his having no problem with the ladies. I always thought of Mae and Joe waltzing around the floor, that Saturday night in 1956, when later, I would listen to the late Lewis Gizzard, the noted author and humorist, recount his story of a troubled childhood. His father, returning from Korea and suffering from war traumas, lapsed into alcoholism and drifted apart from his family. Lewis would say his happiest times had been when his father, who dearly loved his mother, would waltz with her around the kitchen; he later penned and performed a song, "Dad's Tennessee Waltz," describing those emotions.

This is not the end of Joe's story, but perhaps a good place to insert my belief that he always regretted having succumbed to the demons that drove him from Bess and June.

It was 1962 before we moved back to North Carolina and had regular contact with Joe. I have no specific memory of visits with him, or his visiting us during that time, although that may have happened. Our all too brief vacations during this period were taken driving back to Athens from either Memphis, Chattanooga, Columbus, Ohio or New Jersey and splitting time between June's or my family. I am sure Joe kept in touch; he was certainly interested in the new grandchildren that came along. When we did move into our home in Graham, Joe and Mae visited us frequently. He was usually in a good mood, would arrive with every imaginable piece of candy or junk for his grandchildren, and took great delight in parent's angst over his selections. In fact, some of my most distinct memories of him, instances that, to me, defined his humor and view of life, grew from occasions of "gifts."

Christmas, 1962, Joe and Mae rode in on their sleigh loaded with trinkets, candy, small things for one and all and, at a climatic moment, Joe went outside and started unloading from his vehicle ominous bundles that he stacked in our carport. He proudly announced his gift of an outdoor swing set, fully unassembled and there for my erecting pleasure. The memory, again, is of that gleam in his eye as he acknowledged the fun I was going to have putting it together. Mr. Machinist first grade made no offer to belt on his tools and lend me a hand. Nope, he just mounted his sleigh, and with a nod, away he did fly. I bet he laughed all the way back to High Point. You see, there were two factors: one, I am somewhat mechanically impaired what with having no role model growing up nor, for that matter, any machinery or implements around on which to work. Two, at that time, I might have owned a screwdriver and pair of pliers. To properly erect the monster slide/

swing set left in my garage would have required a complete set of tools in that big, red box from Craftsman. The swing set had an attached slide to be constructed of the sheet metal parts, bent to curve and made to align, fitting precisely the screw holes that seemed to number in the thousands. I hung Joe in effigy hourly for the week or two it took me to get that thing together. It was a great swing, lasted for years, and probably entertained all five of Joe's granddaughters. I hope they were grateful.

Then, there was the car caper. Sometime around 1976, Joe and Mae showed up for a routine visit and, unannounced, Joe proceeded to hand me the keys to an old car he had parked in front of our house (I do not recall the transportation arrangements getting it there). I want to give this to you, Virgil; good luck! Again, as he rode off into the sunset, he had that malevolent grin and look in his eyes that said, "Gotcha"!

What he had left was an old (probably 1964-5) two door Ford, V-8 engine, with "busted" muffler; the gift of the car and the model, itself, were not the issue. The condition was the issue. First, this car had been outside all its life, and cars then were not what they are today; it was faded, body parts of various colors, loud, and, the worst part, had been used as a "truck" to haul his dog, tools, junk…you name it…and then, left on my doorstep for me to deal with. I worked a week trying to vacuum dog hair, dirt, junk stains, all in an effort to use the car without starting an epidemic. Actually, I think some of my girls drove it for a short while. I got the last laugh, however.

Probably within that year, I took the car to the local Ford dealer for routine service. I explained when I left it that I was going on vacation and would not pick the car up for several days. When I returned, no car; it had been stolen from the dealer's lot. Had they humored me and laid some nice on me, I would probably have thought, "Good riddance," and called it a day; I felt guilty for leaving the car in their care, that long. However, the wise officials at the Firm chose to "stonewall" me, claiming no responsibility and did not show an inclination to discuss the issue. I felt offended that, while in their care and custody, this prized and beloved family heirloom had been allowed to disappear, so I sued them in Small Claims

Court; lawyer and all. We won, and, after the lawyer's share, I was left with more than the value of the car, by any stretch. Thank you, Joe.

The last, lasting insults, that my children remember better than I, were occasions, usually at Easter, when Joe would arrive with a box of live chickens, or ducks, and joyfully celebrate that Holy Holiday by laughing at my concern regarding these newly acquired flocks. Of course, they outgrew the box; of course, they outgrew any pen, outside; of course they, later, graced the dinner table of our friend, Willie Hadley, who always agreed to solve our "problem." Got me, again, Joe!

A couple of business ventures fashioned the last stages of Joe's work life. First, Joe was always kidding about, "What he was going to do when that black bag of cash fell out of the sky at his feet." He would daydream, and I am sure he always had hopes, as he, and Mae, worked hard and enjoyed a rather meager, hard-earned existence. He thought it had arrived sometime in the early seventies.

The knitting machines of Joe's day were predominantly Banner (although other machines were in use); the Banner Co. held most of the patents on those machines, and sold parts and supplies for their operation. One key feature of those machines was the fact it was an expensive and time consuming chore to change the pattern from one specific sock to another. Each machine had to be changed, and this not only entailed the cost of the new die or part but the cost of lost production during the change.

As Joe described it, he developed a new methodology to speed up and simplify those changes. I believe he sought and obtained a patent for his work and I know he enlisted the aid of partners and intended to market the innovation. He thought the black bag had fallen. I have no doubt that he, in fact, did develop something that would have worked. Alas, his hopes never reached fruition.

Joe claimed he was double-crossed by his partners, and I remember his always believing they had "sold out" to Banner, who, of course, would have wanted to protect their monopoly on the status-quo. I cannot vouch for the specifics of the case, but he was greatly disappointed. It is very likely Joe just did not understand or take the necessary precautions to protect himself.

Also, in the late sixties-early seventies, Joe and Mae opened their own small mill; he bought some machines, rented a small building, put the machines on one floor, and he and Mae moved into and lived in the basement. He was in business. I would observe that Joe always had an entrepreneurial spirit and wanted to be his own boss. This seemed the right opportunity. I never fully understood or have forgotten the specifics of the deal; I believe he had help financing the machines; further, that he bought his yarn from, and had an agreement to manufacture socks for, the same firm. There did seem to be a close tie with this much larger mill, similar to owing one's soul to the company store. In any event, he and Mae ran those machines, made socks, and actually hired another knitter or two. Our visits during that period were to "the mill," and I remember all my children helping themselves to the pop and candy from whatever vending machine or ice cream freezer Joe left open for them.

In the final analysis, this did not work, either. I have no reason to suspect they were flimflammed again, although contracts with only one supplier and customer could have certainly set the stage for that to happen. I rather suspect their lack of business acumen did them in. It always seemed they struggled to maintain control of yarn purchased versus product produced, and lack of satisfactory cash flow overwhelmed them. It was not for lack of effort that the plan failed; in the end, Joe had at least the small satisfaction of knowing "He did it his way."

Time and wear took their toll on Joe's health, and, I suppose, in the end, gradually deteriorating heart disease completed the job. He died in High Point August 31, 1982. Mae lived until 1991; she was always a kind, supportive and loyal partner to Joe; both are buried in Guilford County, North Carolina.

Joe made mistakes; he hurt people; he chose, at times, directions for his life that resulted in some wrong turns. Haven't we all? He was always kind and helpful to me; he was always proud of and loving to my children. Deep down, I think he always felt the same toward his. At the very least, he was an interesting man.

Bess, my first mother-in-law and the grandmother of my children, started life as a Farner. She was a member of a large family; I remember most of them. I am reminded of something I often heard Bess recount, as I attempt to describe what is known of her relatives:

"My papa didn't have no papa."

That fact, and Bess described it as well as many flowing words could, puts a limit on how far back we can go; we will have to make do with the anecdotal information at hand. Obviously, the Farners (and Runions) were early pioneering settlers in East Tennessee; we just do not know, at present, any facts about this family before 1850….give or take.

"Papa," William Issac "Will" Farner, was born August 23, 1877 in Polk County, Tennessee, in or near the little town of "Farner." Farner is a common name, Farners abound, have for a few hundred years, and there certainly were several in Polk County at the turn of the last century. The Village of Farner was supposedly named after Will's grandfather. Although Will kept the name of his mother, Agnes Farner, there are some interesting family connections: an Issac Farner was born July 25, 1848 and died June 2, 1911; he was buried in the Zion Hill Cemetery, in Polk County. Also, a William Issac Farner, born November 17, 1867, died September 30, 1931 and is buried in the Mount Isabill Missionary Baptist Church Cemetery, in Monroe County, (Tennessee). Further, an Issac Farner, from Polk County, served with Company F, 19th TN Infantry, CSA and died in the Battle of Shiloh in April, 1862. It would seem too coincidental for our Will to not be somehow related to those Williams or Issacs. However, I have no factual information to tie Will's mother, Agnes, to other specific Farners in that area.

What is known is that he lived in childhood with a Maru Runion; the relationship between Maru and Will's Mother, Agnes Farner is unknown, if, in fact, one existed. Will had two half-sisters, Alice and Elsie Runion. The story understood by Will's children, oft repeated and passed down, is that Maru was cruel and abusive to Will. Among other occurrences, Will would state he had often been, "Tied to a tree and whipped with a plow line." The inference was that it was undeserved, but, in any event, Will left (that) home at an early age.

What Will did after leaving the home of Maru and before his marriage is not known; what is known is that he did marry Nancy Jane Runion, in 1900. This marriage likely occurred in Polk County, either in or near Farner or Turtletown. While the inference certainly arouses curiosity, there is no known connection between Maru Runion and Nancy Jane; she was the daughter of George Runion and Rachel Kirkland Runion, who were both born and lived in Farner. She (Nancy Jane) had four brothers and three sisters. Again, these were common names, likely connected at some distant point, but not, to our knowledge, insofar as Will and Nancy Jane are concerned.

Will and Jane started their life together in the Farner/Turtletown area; I have no information regarding their actual home place, therefore, shall not guess. These two small towns are only three miles apart; therefore, they could have lived near one and received mail through the other. Some family information indicates Fred, their first child, was born in Turtletown; other anecdotal references indicate, "All Will's children were born in Farner, except the last two, who were born in either Etowah or Athens."

Early on, Will worked for the L & N railroad, gathering "crossties" for railway road bed from the forest in the area; whether he was actually employed by the railway company, or worked as a contractor, is unknown. At some point, he moved his family to Etowah. Whether some of his children went first or he led the migration, move he did. It was most likely work related, as, in fact, the L & N only ran a spur into the Farner area; however, Etowah was on the main line and perhaps offered additional opportunities for his cross-tie work. At some point, work related opportunities apparently prompted a move to Athens, where, either prior to or eventually, all his children settled. He worked for years at the Athens Planing Mill and seemed to have continued in the cross-tie business; it is known he was involved in processing ties by "burning" them, or at least the outer layer, which repelled insects and decay. Such ties are known to have remained in service for almost a century. This type operation was before high pressure creosoting or use of other materials.

Reportedly, he was also skilled at woodworking and was known to be a "casket maker." He built the casket in which his mother, Agnes, was buried.

The known facts of Will's life can perhaps best be summarized by simply observing his obituary: "Mr. Farner was a native of Polk County and was of a pioneer family. The little Village of Farner, which became widely known when the Bachman Memorial School was established there several years ago, derived its name from his grandfather.

Mr. Farner was converted early in life and joined the Baptist Church of Turtletown. After locating in Athens, he became a member of the church in North Athens. He was an employee of the Athens Planing Mill and worked all day Friday and appeared as well as usual. On his way home, he purchased a bag of apples and was eating some of the fruit, when he fell dead from his chair. He succumbed to a heart attack, physicians say." This was January 28th, (my father's, and, coincidentally, Bess' birthday) 1938, and Will was 61. (Another interesting coincidence: my first wife, June, Will's granddaughter, was sitting in his lap when he collapsed and died.)

His wife, Nancy Jane, lived until January 23, 1959. In their later years, Will and Nancy lived on Astrid Street in Athens, a short distance from the Athens Hosiery Mill and the North Athens Elementary School.

I either knew fairly well, or at least met, the eleven surviving children of Will and Jane. During the brief time I lived in Athens, before graduating from college and on visits thereafter, those were my extended family members. My sister, Betty, married into this family. The relationships are forever entwined. It is only appropriate that we honor them by sharing some of the memories that remain (while they still do), as this side of June's family is a storehouse of cousins by the dozen, and my children would do well to always remember it.

James Lester, or, Lester as he was known, married Della McKeehan O'Daniel (Irish blood, there!) and were the parents of six children. They lived on the east (down hill) side of Anton Street, between Bess' and her sister, Monnie's home; it was within a stone's throw of the house where Joe and Bess last lived together. Lester worked a good period of his life at the Hoback Planing mill, then, later, for Webb Brothers Construction Company, as a cabinet/window builder. While this term will be applied to many

Left to right: Rachael Kirkland Runion, Will Farner, Jane Runion Farner; Rachael was Jane's mother.

Sylvia June Canupp

Bessie Farner Stanton Canupp Hamilton Dockins Melton

The Canupps, Farners and Runions 99

Joe, Bess and June

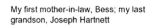

My first mother-in-law, Bess; my last grandson, Joseph Hartnett

Mae and Joseph Taft Canupp at Pam's wedding, Los Colinas, TX 1981

of the Farners, Lester was rather quiet, modest, but friendly, and it was always a pleasure to run into him and Della or any of their children, at either their home or when they would visit other family members.

By circumstance, I came to know Monnie Mae, "Monnie," perhaps better than any of the others; she became my sister, Betty's, mother-in-law. Monnie had married Jim Axley August 4, 1923, and they were the parents of three sons: Odine Curtiss, Grayson, and James Edwin. Later, they adopted Eula Dean Farner, the natural daughter of Monnie's brother, Hayden. Eula Dean used the Axley name and became a regular member of this family.

Jim, as were his sons, was a talented and skilled machinist; he spent most of his work career in hosiery mills around Athens, the latest one being the Athens Hosiery Mill, near their home in North Athens. Jim was not only a professional machinist at the mill, but could repair anything else. He started life on his own, as his mother died when he was eight, and his father could not care for his children. His father later remarried, but his wife did not want the children, then. Jim simply existed by working on farms, staying wherever he could find work, and a place to stay. Later, he worked in sawmills, and it was in Etowah where he met and married Monnie. Their first son, Odine, was born in Etowah.

Odine was as mechanically skilled as Jim, but after World War II, pursued further education and applied his skills to designing, installing and maintaining various precision instruments for the medical and other professions. Grayson followed his father into the mills and Ed, after the Korean War, spent his work career with two firms: the Park Avenue Laundry, where he did everything: then, later, with Westinghouse/White Industries/Electrolux (same plant), designing, hand assembling, and testing prototype electric motors. It is unfair that one family should receive all the blessings of being able to fix anything.

Monnie was perhaps the best "country" cook I ever knew. To put this into perspective, let me explain that, during the time Jim, Grayson, and Ed were all working, Monnie served lunch each day, Monday through Friday, for them, their wives, nieces, nephews, boyfriends, and assorted grandchildren. Including Monnie, that could be from a minimum of four to a house full, on a routine basis. I know because my feet were stuck under her table many the days during the time from 1952 until 1955. The fare was not a bologna sandwich or can of soup, either. Each day, Monnie would have a variety of fresh vegetables (in season), a meat, freshly baked bread, and desserts to kill for. It was just her job, and she pulled it off in style. She was the best, and if there seemed to be any doubt, she would settle the issue by declaring herself so. As Dizzy Dean was quoted saying, "If you can do it, you ain't bragging." Actually, I cannot attest, in memory, to the cooking exploits of any of the other Farner ladies, except Bess; in my book, she was skilled also, and some of her desserts certainly rivaled Monnie's. However, Monnie had an edge in variety, as she turned out the pies, cakes, turnovers, puddings, etc., in style and quantities, with quality unsurpassed.

And, lest you drool for a mother-in-law like her, keep looking; Monnie could sew, also, and turned out beautiful clothes for Betty and others in her favor. She certainly was a skilled lady.

Jim was always one of my favorites; he in many ways reminded me of my father. He was about the same size, similar demeanor, quiet, unassuming, and you would never much notice he was around. He just listened, but did not miss much; when asked, he had an answer, and if he heard more than enough, he would let it be known. He was a kind, friendly, and remarkable individual.

I shall revisit the Axleys, but to move on, the next child of Will and Jane was Goldman Hayden Farner, who was born February 25, 1908 and died January 18, 1967. He first married Dorothy Goins; they were the parents of two children, Bobby Gene and Eula Dean. Dorothy developed some emotional problems and died, after which Hayden married Gladys Boyd, with three children resulting from this union. I believe Hayden also worked in one of the planning mills in North Athens.

The fifth child was Nola Marie Farner Ellis, who was born February 16, 1910, and died June 20, 1967. She married Howard Ellis, who died unexpectedly in 1935; they had three children, Susan, Robert Lee (Euppie) and Betty Ross (Penny). Susan was not Howard's daughter, but lived in this family, was adopted, and always used the Farner name. Nola's home was my most frequently visited destination, until Ed, hence Monnie, came into the picture. When Nola's husband died, she moved in with her parents and sister, Hattie Hazel, "Jack," as she was known. Jack, as a result of childhood illness, was emotionally disadvantaged; she functioned, could reason, but was just slow and could be temperamental, if stressed. She was, however, part of the family and was treated as such, with kindness and respect.

I mentioned Nola's home being a frequent Sunday afternoon visit after I met June; other family members were also constantly dropping by. As was the case with my Grandmother Hedgecock, people of that generation just respected and showed concern for their "mothers" and Nola's home was where "mother" was; therefore, it was just logical for her many children (and grandchildren) to "drop by." It was a warm and jovial place to visit; lively conversation, families gathering, and shared friendship. My naïve eyes never caught it, but I would guess Nola, grandmother, and perhaps others might have slipped a nip or two on occasion, just to ease the tension, of course. They were kind to me, and I enjoyed becoming a part of that group. They all worked, had their homes, were industrious, and certainly earned my respect.

"Jack" I mentioned, and I shall by-pass Bessie Alice for the time being.

The eighth child, daughter Jessie Janet, was born March 25, 1916 and lived until January 8, 1996; she married Robert Wayne Winder and they were the parents of four children. Their home was on Tellico Avenue, east of the Athens Hosiery Mill, and across the road from an intermittent, small stream known as "dye branch." I recall hearing people identify where they lived as "dye branch" rather than the actual street. This stream was so named, I suppose, because at times, it served as the means to dispose of dyes and other liquids from the finishing department at the mill. This was before environmental protection issues, and, perhaps, even sewer systems. The Winder house, like most others on this street was simple but pleasant; all the homes nearby were well cared for, mostly family owned and housed the Claytons, Erwins, and other long-time, fine, North Athens families. Since only a block to the south was Woodward Avenue, where much finer homes existed, it was only poetic that the L & N Railway spur ran between the two streets; the good folks up on Woodward could geologically "look down their noses" at the folks "down on dye branch" which truly was on the "other side of the tracks." I later worked in a mill with other families living there, and remember them all as fine folks.

"Dude" (as Jessie was known) and Wayne's children were Frankie Sue, Daniel Paul, David Claude and Evelyn Janet. Frankie Sue was my age, and we shared the high school experience. She married a classmate and friend from Mouse Creek days, Kenneth Benton, and they have lived in the same area since. I remember Daniel somewhat, although he was five years younger. My sister Betty's best friend through grade and high school was Virginia Benton, Kenneth's sister. This relationship remained strong through the years, with the East Athens Baptist Church being a common denominator for Frankie, Kenneth, Virginia, Betty and Ed. The Axleys and Winders attended the North Athens Baptist, down the street from their home.

Frankie has been invaluable rounding up, keeping, researching, and showing interest in family history information. Her contribution to these stories about the Farners has been big time.

After "Dude," along came Maggie Lee, born March 4, 1918; Maggie always seemed to be everyone's favorite, and I was no exception; she was cheerful, possessed a great sense of humor, was outgoing and always reminded me of my Aunt Pearl. It also never hurt that she was surrounded by those four lovely daughters, who were followed by two sons. She married Ray Ferguson; it is not my place to comment on Maggie and Ray's relationship, as I did and do not know the facts or issues. There just seemed to be a perpetual strain there and Ray was not very involved with other members of the family. He drove a taxi in Athens and many evenings was my ride home from visiting June, long after the moon was up. For Ray, the trip from his cab stand to Bess' house, to my home, then, back to town, was probably six miles; the fare was usually 75 cents and I cannot remember offering many tips. Whatever the truth about Ray, I do remember early in my marriage that if, or when, I would get grumpy or have my lip pooched out over something, I would be called, "Ray Ferguson."

Maggie was the last surviving Farner. It was my good fortune to visit her, with Betty and Ed, at a rest home in Athens a couple of years before she died, and she, though not in the best of health, seemed as I remembered her 40 years earlier—friendly, interested and engaging. A couple of the "daughters" were there and they turned out well, too.

Continuing this countdown, number 10 was Alvillia Edna Farner, born March 14, 1920, who married Joffery Matthews. They seemed a nice couple, and Joffery was certainly adored by everyone—tall, dark and handsome with a pleasant personality as a bonus. They should have lived happily ever after. I remember their small children, Renda and Warren Allen. Alas, it was not to be, as shortly after I became acquainted with this family, Joffrey, who worked the second shift at the Williamson Hosiery Mill (he was a "fixer," also) was smitten by a co-worker there and a relationship developed. This most assuredly was not taken lightly by the Farner family. Alvillia was understandably distraught, and I seem to remember other Farners wanting to tar and feather the scarlet lady who was blamed for this calamity. That was long ago, but in memory, I do not think Joffery intended to break up with his family; it happened, a mistake was made, and the deed(s) could not be undone.

They divorced, of course, and Alvillia re-married twice; another son was born with her second husband, John Calhoun. Alvillia died February 10, 1968. Joff, with his "lady," left town for awhile; he married her and, to my knowledge, they were together the rest of Joff's life. Joff and his wife returned to Athens, and he was one of the first employees at the Westinghouse plant, when it opened; this, of course, was the same plant where Ed Axley went to work when he left the laundry.

Number eleven was Warren G. Farner, born February 2, 1922. Warren G., and that is what he was called, seemed the darling of his older brothers and sisters, and I cannot identify the reason other than his absence. Warren lost a leg in World War II and, upon his return, spent time in a VA hospital in Richmond, Virginia; he met his first wife there, where she worked as a volunteer; he lived in Richmond the remainder of his life. Perhaps, as with my Uncle Virgil, absence makes the heart grow fonder, because I think I heard Bess, and perhaps others, talk more about Warren

G., and hang onto every shred of news regarding his coming and going, than all the nearby relatives put together. I remember meeting him a time or two; tall and handsome, he was deservedly impressive. He became an electrical engineer and was very gracious in speech and manner. I can understand the pride bestowed upon him by his distant family. I think he enjoyed a successful life in Richmond; married twice, he had two children by his first wife, Ann Carpenter.

Whew! Finally, there was Harvey William Farner, who was always called "Junior." Born June 28, 1926, in a relative sense, he was not that much older than I. When I first met June, Junior and his wife, Violet Clayton, lived next door to Bess. Violet was only three years older than me and although they worked, they seemed like just another young couple, similar to our high school friends, who were pairing up. I well remember several times, on Saturday nights, Junior and Violet, with Grayson and Winnie Axley, would drop in on June, or Bess, and me, if I were there, to complete their night out, just "chilling" and passing the time.

When I first met Nancy Jane Farner, mother of this clan, she was "only" 69, although she seemed much older; she died at 76, which is rather young, by today's longevity standards. However, bearing twelve children and surviving seems a miracle, and like my Grandmother Hedgecock (10) or Great-Great Grandmother Mincy (8), these numbers took a natural toll. None lived to what we today would call "old age." What gifts they left us, though, in the time they were given!

Bessie Alice Farner, June's mother and my first mother-in-law, was born January 28, 1914; I have mentioned the coincidence of this date with my father's birth date and her father's death date. Bess' story is rather hard to put in a box, neatly, or get one's arms around: first, most records list her name as Bessie Alice; however, her application for marriage to Art Shield Dockins, in 1956, states her name as, "Bess Ressie Hamilton" (her third husband's name). Her surviving relatives can quibble over which is correct. Of her eleven siblings, she was certainly the most often married, lived as long as any, except Jack, possibly traveled the most, and in spite of her many trials and troubles, likely had the most fun. She was a unique individual, and there was more to her than first met the eye. I knew her for 47 years, a major hunk of my life and a sizeable portion of hers; what I shall say about her is what I know and I shall not dwell too long on what I do not. I loved her and respected her; she always made me feel she felt the same about me. I have observed the same depth of feeling from a vast number of her extended family. She "left her mark."

Bess, as had been all her siblings, was born into a challenging existence; in the hills and ridges of Polk County, this large family certainly struggled to exist. Including Fred, the firstborn, there were, ultimately, fourteen mouths to feed in this family unit. Regardless of how enterprising Will was in his cross tie business, it was likely a struggle to pay rent and put food on the table. Everyone went to work as soon as they could find it, doing whatever was available. Monnie worked as a house servant; Junior falsified his age to get work in the mills; while I have no factual information, I doubt many finished the eighth grade. Most members of this family talked in a grammatically-challenged manner; those who worked in mills, talked loudly. They were working people.

I have no doubt Bess went to work in a mill as soon as she could; I do not know of other (public) work she ever did. Whether or not she dated a lot is questionable; she simply seemed to marry whoever caught her eye or seemed practical. I mean this as a compliment, as I think she preferred stability and permanence rather than meeting different people.

In any event, she married Elmer Stanton, August 6, 1929 (the date of the marriage license application; dates for other marriages are similarly shown); she was 19 and had no children by Mr. Stanton. Obviously, her family knew of this at the time, however, information concerning this union was not discussed in later years. June was unaware of this marriage until I informed her during research of this family. Where they lived, why the relationship ended, or what Elmer did for a living is unknown. The termination was before March 18, 1933, as that is the date of her second marriage, to Joseph Taft Canupp.

It is likely they both worked in hosiery mills at that time, and it is conceivable that is where they met. It is also likely they lived with some of Bess' family early on, but, in any event, June was born August 13, 1934.

June does not know where they were living at that time; Joe split about the time she was born and did not turn up for a couple of years, or more.

June's first memory was living in a house on "Happy Top," an area/street so called because it was on a hill next to, and on the north side of, the Athens Hosiery Mill; June remembers this as anything but a "Happy Top" because they were living with other family members, possible the Axleys, but, in any event, in crowded conditions which still left her feeling alone and threatened. From that point, Bess moved to three or four other locations, obviously rented and not memorable. Joe was not a factor during this time, and any memory of his being around was that he was usually drunk and abusive to both June and Bess; Bess certainly was working, as, until 1956, her only support was what she was able to earn on her own..

Sometime around 1943, Joe and Bess built a small house at the end of Knoxville Avenue, which was near and between where Lester Farner and Jim Axley lived; a son, Donald Joe was born, October 20, 1943. (This was on the lot Joe had acquired from his father, David Amos.) He lived less than a month; in 1945, a daughter, Sonya Jeanette, was born and lived only a few days. During that time, Joe and Bess parted for good.

Between 1945 and 1949, Bess married Roy Hamilton. I have been unable to find a record of this marriage and my guess is that they were married in a county other than McMinn; that they were married is evidenced by the granting of a divorce in 1955. Roy had several children, and they all moved into the house on Knoxville Avenue. June remembers this as not a good period; the conditions were crowded, the families seemed incompatible, and Roy was not around long. May 5, 1949 a daughter, Kathy Sandra Hamilton was born. Soon thereafter, Bess left the house on Knoxville Avenue (which is now a small church) and bought a house on E. Fisher Street; this was on "the other side of the hill" from the Knoxville Avenue home.

Roy Hamilton was not Kathy's father; this was not known by Kathy, until Bess told her around 1975. There must have been some knowledge "going around" as I recall, after I started dating June, a high school classmate blurted to me, "You know June's sister is illegitimate." This was never discussed with me by any family members, nor did I ever initiate a conversation about it. The memory lingered, however, and I had an opportunity to discuss the situation at length with Kathy in 2002; she was open and comfortable talking about it, and related several aspects of the situation.

She recalled meeting people who looked familiar, and having a strange feeling about such contacts; further, she had received comments at various times by those who would say she, "looked just like so-and-so." Kathy never met her biological father, but came to know of him and members of his family.

It was in 1952 when I first met Bess and began to appreciate her. As I indicated, she and June lived on East Fisher Street. She was working at the Athens Hosiery Mill and she immediately made me feel welcome. I enjoyed visiting their home. Although it was a small, two-bedroom home, it was neat, had indoor plumbing, running water, and amenities I had not, to that date, enjoyed. It did not take long to find a way to be there at meal time, as Bess' servings of fresh vegetables, meat and dessert were always offered and rarely refused. Bess was not judgmental of me and did not seem suspicious nor questioning of my motives concerning her daughter; rather, I think she allowed me some space and trusted our better judgments. What she did was talk to me. We joined in good natured ribbing and joking back and forth that continued for 47 years. I have already described the fact that being around Bess and June involved soon being around all other family members, as they visited, talked, and shared family time. This was especially true regarding Bess' mother, Jane and, to some extent, Monnie and the Axleys; those two locations seemed the most common destinations. I do not recall Bess ever being "on the outs" with any of her brothers or sisters, and they all shared a warm relationship with each other, at least, insofar as I noticed.

Kathy, who was less than three when I first met her, became another "little sister," a relationship that continued throughout her life. Basically, Bess, Kathy and June only had each other (except the support of other Farner family members, of course) which made them very "close." Bess was the only stable factor in June's childhood, and I suspect Kathy always felt the same. I would observe that Bess was always supportive and certainly worked hard to provide for them as best as she could.

When I first met Bess, I do not recall her "dating" in the normal sense or having any gentlemen friends or callers; she would "go out" on Saturday nights with Junior or other of her brothers or sisters who might be so inclined, but I do not recall late hours or anything other than conservative behavior. Bess was friendly, did have an eye for "a good looking man," and was not bashful about meeting people or making conversation. She was just not "on the prowl."

In 1955, Bess was "called upon" and pursued by Artis, "Art" Dockins, a Calhoun area farmer. Art's second wife had died; he was divorced from his first wife, who lived, with other family members, a few houses out Fisher Street from Bess; they (Art's family) were certainly neighbors and acquaintances. Art was fourteen years older than Bess and made every effort to be courtly and generous in his pursuit of Bess; he was a small, wiry gentleman, definitely "country" but warm and attentive to Bess. I remember his leaving the impression he was interested in and proud of his association with Bess.

Most of his family members were less so; sometime during 1955, a couple of his brave, adult sons caught Bess in front of her house and worked her over with blackjacks; certainly, a low experience. Bess' friendship with Joe's brother-in-law, Riley Reynolds, a county deputy, came in handy, as he took the necessary action to ensure these fine citizens swung their clubs no more. Bess did prosecute them, and they received some small, official sanction. Interestingly, the attorney who represented Bess, Tom Taylor, attended Carson-Newman College at the same time my father was there. Bess and Art were married February 16, 1956. Bess and Kathy moved from East Fisher to Art's farm, below Riceville, and Bess was able to quit work in the mill for the first time, I suppose, in her adult life. She was 42, Art, 56.

Art was active on his farm, which probably included a couple hundred acres; he raised corn, hay, tobacco and sold some pine pulp wood to the Bowater paper mill, which had just opened a short distance away. It was to this location that June and my children traveled for several years when we had opportunity to return for vacation or holidays. Art's home was a white, frame "farm house," two stories, with a porch on the front. It was neat, well maintained, and his farm was skillfully worked and productive. Bess settled into being a "farmer's wife," pitched in with the house work, quilted, raised a garden, cultivated flowers, and created a warm, comfortable environment. A daughter, Mary Jane Dockins, was born in November, 1962.

I recall a couple of years when June, Pam, and I spent our week or so of vacation with Bess and Art; I would "farm" the entire time. I distinctly remember going almost stir crazy for a day or two (after life in New Jersey, for instance); however, in a few days, the routine of hard work, quiet nights, crickets, frogs, and whip-o-wills created such a calm and restful environment that the week went all too fast; it was truly a relaxing time. Kathy became a teenager, Mary Jane grew, and life was good.

Sometime in the late sixties-early seventies, Art sold part of his farm and built a modest, brick home near the paved road that ran west from US 11 past his farm; Bess' sister, Nola, died, and Jack came to live with Bess and Art.

In 1968, Kathy married Carl Dewain McCaslin; their first child, Carrie Ann, was born in May, 1969. Early in 1970, Kathy, Carrie Ann and Dewain moved to Graham, North Carolina, where June and I lived. I was able to arrange a job for him at the Burlington Industries trucking terminal, for which I had responsibility. We enjoyed their company for the brief time they lived near us and were pleased to become "aunt and uncle" to twins, Ivan and Vince, born December 13, 1970. Soon thereafter, they left Graham and Dewain joined the Air Force.

While it was a gradual process, I observed Art growing older, Jack becoming more dependent, and Bess becoming the head of the household and the driving force in getting things done. Her life was still one of work: gardening, canning, growing flowers, loving and helping family, always quilting, and, increasingly, caring for Art and Jack. There were aspects that, at times, were rather sad. In the new home they had built, as Art's health deteriorated, he retreated to the basement and did not interact much with anyone (such as my growing family) when they would visit. He would try to remain a part of what was going on but was generally ignored and stayed out of sight. The same was somewhat true of Jack. At times, it was as if they were not even there. While it may not have been the warmest of family situations, Bess steadfastly provided for their care, managed the home, nurtured Mary Jane, and maintained interest in her grandchildren and other family members. Art died in 1977.

In 1984, Bess was wooed and gave in, again; she married Henry Melton, an Athens native who became her fifth husband. During this time, Bess moved from the Riceville property to Henry's home, in East Athens, and remained there until after 1988, the year he died. Before Bess married Henry, Kathy had built a house on the hill above the "brick house" and moved into it, after she and Dewain divorced. Bess stayed in Henry's home for a few years, but in the 1990s built another house behind Kathy's and lived there (between visits elsewhere) until she died. Both of those houses were on the site where I had tilled their garden, when we would visit Art and Bess during the "brick home" years.

When June and I separated and after her marriage to Larry Waggoner, June remained loyal and supportive of all her immediate family members: particularly Kathy, Mary Jane, and, of course, Bess. Bess came to be a frequent visitor to wherever June and Larry were living, a companion on their many travels, and a constant in their lives, as well as my many children and grandchildren, who lived in proximity to June or visited her. During all of Bess' life, if I let it be known I would be visiting, Bess would almost take orders for whichever of her famous baking products my sugarholic taste desired; fried pies, her famous stacked fruit cake, or, the ultimate, her fresh coconut cake. She never let me down. She created quilts, almost on order, for all my children and was a regular companion during summers to Larry's mother, Ann. Soon after Larry and June married, Winnie Axley (Grayson's wife) moved to Texas and served as a special friend, helper, and child care giver to June and some of my grandchildren. Winnie and Bess would, of course, spend time together for the almost 20 years or so that Winnie was with them.

Bess seemed to be happy and content during her last years; she was around family and friends who appreciated her, contributed her skills and personality to the joy of others, and always exuded cheerfulness and warmth to those around her. At least, when I was in her company, I felt that way. She died October 22, 1999 and was buried in Athens, next to Art Dockins; in the end, she would claim Art was the best husband she had, and her respect for him was such that she wanted to share the rest of time and that space with him.

On my flight to her funeral, I could not help but reflect upon my memories of her and my appreciation for her kindnesses to me. Never knowing what need might arise, I jotted down some notes that summarized my thoughts; I could end no better than to repeat them:

"I knew her for over half of her life; she knew me more than two thirds of mine. When I first met her, I was a "teen-ager" and I was still one when she became my first mother-in-law. She was always that for 47 years.

In those early years, I thought I knew it all, and she probably was not really aware of much that went on. Through almost a half-century of learning the hard way, I have come to realize that what I may have mistaken for ignorance was really tolerance, love, and wisdom.

She had the wisdom not to sweat the little stuff. She had the wisdom and tolerance to allow young people to grow, while she tried to head them in the right direction. She had the wisdom and love to understand that people can make mistakes and still be GOOD people. She allowed those around her to grow and profit from experiences (good and bad). I wish I had been better able to do that, when my children and I were young together.

Bess was knocked down many times (both literally and figuratively)

- She always got up
- She never lost her spirit
- She never lost her sense of humor
- She never lost her joy of life and of having fun
- She continued to put it all into perspective and never gave up on other people.

I miss her.

We lose the lesson of her life, however, if it stops there. The life of Christ was for naught if it has no bearing on the way we live. The influence of other memorable people are noteworthy, usually because they continue to affect our way of life, our freedoms, our beliefs, our comforts, or our thinking. Bess' life ends here if we do not allow our memories of her to influence how we live.

How can, for example, we honor her tolerance, if we do not allow our children "room" to grow, as we try to guide their general direction?

How can we remember all that she has given us if we fail to share our time, our love, our support, and our friendship with those who could use it?

How could we be comfortable under one of her quilts, if we fail to find a way, any way, to comfort some other soul yearning for some human warmth?

The answer is that we cannot; we must not.

I am grateful that I knew Bess; I miss her but I shall never forget her."

Homer F. Mincy Sr.

I last saw Dad in the summer of 1984. It was the year after Mom died, and I was passing through on one of my all too infrequent trips, triangulating business connections with a little pleasure. I had been in Pittsburgh a couple of years; I guess it was about this time that it began to dawn on me parents are not around forever, and that I should bring to closure some things that were or would be important. After Mom died, suddenly, in August of the previous year, I started the process of facing life without parents. One would think it should not take 50 years for this mortality trip to start, but that is usually the way it is; we expect parents to live forever. We know, intellectually, that they will not, but we just do not face the fact that, on a specific date or year, they will be gone. Consequently, we do not ask about things not known, reveal things kept personal, share things of mutual importance, or just visit enough. We will always do that next time.

So, by the time of this visit, it had started to dawn on me that I did not know much about Dad's relatives, very early life, or facts about his early homes, and I wanted to get into some of this. He still lived in his little house on the hill west of Athens that had been home since 1949. When Mom passed away, he had insisted on staying there. At 87, he was getting pretty slow, did not drive anymore, but managed to do some food preparation and got by. Betty and Ed remained the primary caregivers and had to provide all transportation and shopping. This home was where he wanted to be and remained the way he wanted it to be.

He had survived a heart attack in 1967 that was perhaps a blessing; he had been persuaded to stop smoking, probably changed very little of his diet, considering the environment and times, but walked regularly, and though increasingly frail, was in pretty good shape, all things considered. I had looked forward to this visit and Betty was with me as we drove up and went in. Dad was in the living room, reading, and looked up slowly, acknowledging my presence with an expression seeming to convey that my visit occurred every day.

"Well…where did you come from…?" he asked slowly, speaking in the halting manner that was his trademark. Talking was always a problem with Dad and for those communicating with him. All his adult life, he was slow, deliberate, and irregular with his speech patterns, requiring patience if you really wanted to share thoughts. With children, particularly argumentative, abrasive children wanting their particular way, or arguing their particular viewpoint, he had a difficult time countering the mindless chatter he had to endure. In normal conversation, he was prone to start a sentence and pause at any time; all too often, someone would interrupt him before the next word or thought would be expressed. However, with patience, and a sincere interest in what he had to say, conversation could be just fine. Children and young adults all too often possessed neither.

"Oh, just passing by, and thought I would drop in," I replied. "How you doing"?

"Tolerable well, I recon….; you by yourself"? He always wanted or expected some of his grandchildren (now grown) to be along, insinuating that my company alone was not enough.

"Yep." I sat down, and we chatted about the weather, what I was doing, and his health, going through the litany of stuff that was usual between us. We got to a pause and I thought I would get into some of the things that were on my mind.

"Dad, I want to ask you about some things that I have been fuzzy about for a long time. I apologize for not paying attention when you probably talked about them, long ago, but I sure am interested now. Can you tell me exactly where you were born"?

Long pause. "Down on the river…we lived on the Brabson place, then."

"Where, exactly"?

"You know…." Dad had never gotten away from his habit of answering a question, by often stating that you knew the answer; it was his way of stalling for time while he collected his thoughts, or equally, his way of soliciting your help in formulating the answer, particularly if it involved roads, directions, names or geography.

"No, Dad, I don't. I have never been down there and have no idea where it is."

"Well, it was down in Dogwood....it was off what we called the Cave Creek Road. I...., I don't know what they call it now."

"What can you tell me about your grandfather, Robert, or Aunt Josie"?

He listened to my question, thought for a moment, then looked at me with the strangest expression. I remember it yet. It seemed a mix between something he did not want to talk about or something he did not know, or remember, but wanted to.

"I..., I....," he started,...

Then, I awoke from my night dream, daydream, imagination, reverie, or that profound, never ending hunger to know what his answer might have been. Of course, this conversation ***never happened!*** The heart attack in '67 was not only his first, but also his last. He was taken from us suddenly, unexpectedly, long before I became very curious about details of his early life, or the families before him. After all, I had my own life to live.

Now I am left to try to piece it together, to try to recreate Dad's part of the Mincy trail, when all required long ago would have been a simple question or two. A lesson too late for the learning, as the song goes. With love and respect, I want to tell his story, to the extent it can be told.

Homer Franklin Mincy, born January 28, 1897, was the fourth child to bless the union of John Wesley and Sarah Elizabeth Hart Mincy. Three other children were born, two stillborn after Dad, with dates on the third not clearly known. This was a time when the nineteenth century was drawing to a close, when William McKinley was president, when the Klondike Gold Rush was in full swing, and the 25th Infantry would stage a bike-a-thon by riding from Ft. Missoula, Montana, all the way to St. Louis. Digging started on the Boston subway system, and John P. Sousa wrote the *Stars and Strips Forever*. Most of this never raised much fuss in the hills and valleys of Roane County, East Tennessee.

Dad was born into an agricultural life. Most of the Mincy neighbors farmed, and most of the Mincy relatives farmed and had done so for the last 100 years. At the time of Dad's birth, his father, John Wesley, was working on a large farm belonging to J.M. "Colonel" Brabson, an absentee landlord, who lived in Greeneville, Tennessee, 100 miles to the Northeast. Col. Brabson had accumulated over 2000 acres of land, in a period from 1895 until 1905, and had contracted with the Mincys to till the rich bottom land along the river; Dad's uncles, the Allens, Harts, and Bowmans may have been involved also, as they lived nearby. The river meanders in snake-like bends, generally heading southwest. At the point of the Brabson Farm, the river is turning more northwest, before it curves back into a south-north loop. Farming, then, could be on the northeast, north, northwest, or west side of the river, within a mile or two.

To understand life in such surroundings, one almost has to live it; the Mincys had to be, like their relatives and neighbors, self-sufficient. They grew their food and many of the raw materials for other of life's necessities. Surplus crops were often bartered for "store bought" items, or "tolled." Corn, for example, would be taken to a mill, where it would be ground into meal, with the miller keeping a percentage of the meal for sale, in settlement for his services. General merchandise stores bartered hard goods for eggs, butter, produce, meats, hides, or whatever was useful in the commerce of the area. Timber was taken to a sawmill and reduced to whatever was needed for the project at hand; again, the sawmill operator took his payment in lumber. Often, larger farms included their own sawmill, operated on an as needed basis.

Dad, as much as anything else, seemed born to plow. The Brabson farm was large, successful, and, as such, used the latest tools and techniques. Grandad, Uncle George, and Dad soaked all this up, and, at the very least, throughout their lives, were skilled at tilling and working the soil. Corn, tobacco, grains, "truck" crops, or whatever else was grown in the area, was produced in the rich soil along the river. Crops constituted the foundation of the way of life for young Homer. He often recounted life along the river: his use of a "skiff" (a flat bottomed canoe) that he would row across the river, exploration of caves along the bluffs of the river, and visits with cousins: the Allens, Prestons, Bowmans, and others. Always, however, it was plowing, harvesting, raising, butchering, and doing the work things that provoked the most conversation and memories. He was skilled and certainly taught Homer (Jr.) and me all we ever knew about farming....usually, more than we really desired to know.

Dad and Uncle George often referred to companionship with Tom Brabson, the Colonel's son, who would frequent the farm in the summer; Tom later became President of a bank in Greeneville, Tennessee. Homer (Jr.) met and became acquainted with Tom while serving as Superintendent of Schools in Greeneville; Tom remembered Dad fondly.

Homer and his siblings attended the Dogwood School, a one-room affair with grades 1-8. This school was built in 1892 and had 17 double desks. It had been built on one half acre of land obtained from the Doughty Farm. There is some indication that, in the beginning, only grades one through six were taught, but there probably were more when Dad attended. I have no evidence Uncle George, Aunt Olive, or Aunt Sophia completed the eight grades; I believe Dad did. Interestingly, several years later, my Aunt Ruby taught there (perhaps one of her first assignments), and Mom's friend and mentor, Verna Briggs, was also one of the teachers in the 20s.

Other than farming and family, religion was the prominent influence in Dad's family, as well as most of the families living in the Dogwood, New Midway, and Cave Creek communities. Most of the churches nearby were Baptist, either Missionary or Primitive. The Mincys were Missionary Baptist and attended the Cave Creek Church, although there were Baptist churches nearby at both Dogwood and Tennessee (community). The Dogwood Baptist Church (and school) was in "Dogwood," on the Wolf Creek road, which runs east west between Cate Road and Dogwood Valley Road, north of the river. Cave Creek Baptist Church was in Cave Creek, on the Cave Creek Road, which runs north-south from the river to what is now US 70. These places and boundaries marked the perimeters of Dad's life of church, school, and farming, in his early years.

I do not know if Granddad owned property at the time Dad was born, as there is no record of land transfers either to or from him. In 1903, the property known as the "Amos Hart Place" was sold to Col. Brabson by all the heirs, who included Grandmother Mincy; this comprised some 215 acres, so, there had been land in the family. In 1916, he (Granddad) bought approximately 292 acres at New Midway, which is north of the river, along the Kingston Highway. This property included a house, and I presume the family moved there at that time (not to get ahead, but this house was around a curve, and west of the site where I would be born some eighteen years later). These land issues did not change the life styles within the Mincy family enterprise.

These were seemingly good years for the Mincys. Farm life went well, a good living was made, and a little money could be saved. As previously mentioned, in August 1916 Granddad consummated the purchase of the 292 acres from B.V. Ottinger for the sum of $4,500, part as down payment, the balance in two notes payable in 1917 and 1918, respectively.

In 1913, Dad had bought (or been sold) a life insurance policy from the Equitable Life Assurance Company of New York. The family had cash flow, was self sufficient, and seemed to be accumulating modest assets.

Sometime in his late teen years, Dad felt a call to the ministry. This experience, at the most basic level, was and is no different from that emotional and spiritual revelation that occurs to anyone who feels compelled to do God's work. It would be consistent with the times, however, to believe Dad was greatly influenced by the ministers, lay leaders, and revival experiences in the churches of the area. Whenever the occasion and whatever the circumstances, in 1921, Dad went off to Carson-Newman College, in Jefferson City, Tennessee, to study for the ministry. Why there? This school was affiliated with the Southern Baptist Convention and is where Baptist, then and now, go to study in preparation for church work. So, with his calling, the need for study, and at least the acquiescence of his family, to Carson-Newman he did go.

Actually, he enrolled in the "preparatory" department. This was more like high school which, to my knowledge, Dad never attended. Jefferson City is about 20 miles northeast of Knoxville, and perhaps 70 miles from his home, but may have seemed another world to Dad at that time. I do know this: all his life, he was proud of his Carson-Newman experiences. He seemed to have enjoyed it immensely, developed the sermon organizational skills he possessed and used during his life, and made friends whom he remembered with respect and fondness.

He attended Carson-Newman 1921, 1922 and 1923. He seemed active in many religious related organizations and activities: the Philomathean Literary Society, the B.Y.P.U., the Young Men's Sunday school Class, and the Bible Department. From notes and autographs in his 1923 yearbook, a picture can be drawn of his personality: shy, quiet, tobacco chewing, did not date much, seemingly had many friends. He never complained, later, when his circumstances were not the best and old classmates like W.D. Hudgins, Tom Taylor, Clay Kyker, and others rose to the top of their professions. He remained proud of his association with them.

He often talked of the intramural football games, life in Davis Hall, the fire brigade, time with his friends, and would endlessly recall anecdotes of those days.

I do not know, specifically, why he did not go on, although the road would have entailed at least five more years. There were probably several circumstances. Sometime in his late teen-early twenties, Dad suffered from typhoid fever that seemed to have been quite serious. We know from pictures and his comments that he lost sections of his hair, and that small patches turned white (temporarily). There was some thought that this sickness may have altered his speech patterns somewhat, which may or may not be true. There is no record of how he was progressing in school; Carson-Newman cannot find any records and Dad did not leave any of his progress reports lying around just for this occasion. A more likely case for his departure from Carson Newman can be made from other family situations.

In 1923, Uncle George bought an adjacent parcel of land, about 108 acres, for approximately $1300. This not only increased the family holdings and opportunities but also its debt. It is likely that Dad was pressured to stay home and help in the family farm enterprises; whether or not, that is what he did.

By 1924, the Mincys, in addition to managing the farms they owned, engaged in the "threshing" business. This hardly compares with the mega harvesting businesses of the Midwest today, in which numbers of huge combines will start in Texas/Oklahoma and follow the grain ripening to

Canada. This "threshing" business had its day, however, as they owned the "thresher," a tractor, wagons, and all the implements necessary to take the "the Mincy" show on the road. The need was simple: with the invention of the McCormick reaper, farmers could grow much larger crops of wheat, oats, barley, etc. At the same time, this presented a larger volume of grain than could be "beaten out" by hand, as had been done for centuries. A thresher mechanically separated the grain from the straw, and could do so efficiently, in large volumes.

The thresher, a large, box-like implement, was pulled about by a tractor or mules but was operated by belts driven from the power take-off on a tractor. Crews of workers fed grain bundles into the thresher, bagged the grain, and piled the straw as it came out in a continuous flow. The "threshing crew" could be a dozen or so. The business itself was to "thresh" the grain on farms for payment in either cash or a share of the grain. Most farms, even of moderate size, simply could not justify a threshing machine, so farmers used the services of operators such as the Mincys. The threshing crew would work through a community wherever business was available, usually being on the road for a week, or more, at a time.

It was thus, on July 25, 1924, that the Mincy crew happened to be working farms in the Lawnville community and, in particular, the H.M. Hedgecock farm, on the Clinch River, a couple of miles from the Young's Chapel Cumberland Presbyterian Church and the Lawnville school. The usual protocol was for the host farm to provide meals for the entire crew, which could include parts of the host family. This, many times, presented a large congregation to be fed. In this case, the women present to do most of the kitchen work were Mrs. Alice Hedgecock, H.M.'s wife and three daughters still at home: Ada, Eva, and Ruby. We do not know what words were said, if any, but it seems some spark of recognition was ignited between Homer F. and Eva Estelle, as, that fall, they started to "date." With the evidence of Dad's rather reticent manner, the mores of the time, travel distances, and work requirements, the dating must have been a rather hit and miss affair; they continued this friendship until 1928, which was the year they became engaged. They were married in 1929.

Much happened following the time Dad and Mom first cast eyes upon each other; least was the fact he was 27, and she 23, at that first glance; both probably felt their biological clocks were racing away. Those happenings had nothing to do with ticking clocks but with the on-going pursuit of Dad's plans for the Ministry and the daily partnership in his family's farm enterprises.

Dad was ordained into the Ministry on April 17, 1926; the service was at Cave Creek Missionary Baptist Church. The council that was convened to complete an examination of him with regard to his Christian experience, call to the ministry, and views of Bible Doctrine included Ocsar Rainwater, Mrs. W.O. Harvey, J.W. Hardin, C.M. Dutton, and Charlie Helton. The simple certificate authorizing my Father to "Go forth...baptizing them in the Name of the Father..." is of wonderment to me today, and I am sure a source of pride and comfort to him, throughout his life. To follow through on a personal conviction and give voice and legs to a spiritual belief, in spite of all obstacles, is bravery shown by few and avoided by most of us. He never wavered in what he saw as his calling—the saving of lost souls. He never grew faint in that effort, sometimes to the consternation of others, who would have liked other interests to be first. More on that, later.

It is known that he preached casually at the New Midway Church (in his back yard), and I believe his family was somewhat perturbed that this church never called him to be pastor. He served in this period of time as Pastor of the Shady Grove Baptist Church in Knox County and, perhaps, other locations that we cannot confirm. Dad was a "Rev.," he preached, and pursued this calling.

The family farm seemed to be going well. The late twenties were prosperous times, prices were good, and no one imagined it would not always be so. Aunt Sophia had married Henry Littleton and moved away from home, but Granddad, Grandmother, Uncle George, and Aunt Olive were still there, along with Dad. Mom's father, H.M. Hedgecock died in 1928, but she was still living at home, with her sister Ada, her Mother, and brother, Frank. Dad and Mom may have dated others during this five-year period but nothing apparently serious. Homer (Jr.) remembers early on….maybe about 1935, a lady by the name of Emma Brogden showing up at the house one day, unannounced, and asking to "See Homer Franklin." (Homer, Jr.) Emma had apparently been a big thing to Dad; at least, he would mention her and Mom would good naturedly (?) bring her name up. Emma, when shown young Homer, "Kissed and slobbered all over him. Ugh, gross"!

Dad and Mom's relationship had one other certain snag, and that was religion, of all things. Dad was Baptist, of course, but Mom was Cumberland Presbyterian, which presented great social barriers to each of them. In truth, there is not great difference in basic beliefs between the two denominations, but one significant one was baptism, itself. Baptists believe in immersion, and the Cumberland Presbyterians believe in baptism by sprinkling. Each probably viewed the other as tainted goods, as they gave growing thoughts to marriage.

Meanwhile, in the mid-twenties, a strange agricultural phenomenon occurred: Roane County, with Kingston as the hub, became the self-proclaimed peach growing capitol of the world. While peaches as a casual fruit grown for canning or summer consumption had probably been around for some time, it suddenly took off as a cash crop and one with great commercial possibility (I believe this was somewhat driven by certain factors having to do with "Prohibition"). The area around Roane County…East Tennessee, for that matter, included many hills and slopes that were questionable for row crops but were quite satisfactory for peach trees. The climate seemed adequate for growing, and, in no time, this became "big time," both from a growing and marketing standpoint. High prices, potential for large volume growth, and, hence, profits, merged in these years; many farmers invested heavily in planning for peach orchards. The Mincys were not to be left behind.

Dad and Mom became engaged in 1928 and, although there appeared no notices in the social registers of the day, Mom always remembered it specifically, therefore, something occurred that marked the time. The wedding was to be in 1929.

I can only imagine, with this commitment, that Dad gave a lot of thought about what to do with a new bride and different direction; he was then what would be called an "itinerate" preacher and probably could not have visualized supporting a wife and family on such earnings. George, possibly in part for Dad, but more likely just being aggressive, sought to buy another farm. Such a possibility seemed to exist in property next door, owned by R.M. Calloway and A.W. Anthony and totaling some 522 acres. This addition would bring the Mincy holdings to over 800 acres. Why not make this investment? Prices were high, prosperity was everywhere, and the peach crops alone would pay for this property.

Dad would always say he (and Granddad) was not in favor of this purchase, but that George wanted to do it and just persuaded the others to go along. In any event, January 1, 1929, Dad and Uncle George entered an agreement to buy this property. Various transactions took place, with a mortgage and deed of trust ultimately being held by the Prudential Insurance Company of America, and one J.L. Britton, Trustee, of Greeneville, Tennessee. The final papers were dated April 26th and committed all the property owned by John Wesley, George, and Homer Mincy as collateral for $10,000, the approximate price of the 522 acres being purchased. Dad and Mom were married, April 29, 1929. How could they have foreseen that, economically, they had no chance?

The wedding was at my Mother's home, and was performed by Mom's brother, Ernest, a Cumberland Presbyterian minister. The "official" wedding party consisted of Aunt Ada and four nieces: Wayne and Roberta Hedgecock, (daughters of Uncle Ernest) and Helen and Edith Smith, (daughters of Mom's sister Verna (Hedgecock) Smith). I am sure some Mincy attended as well as others in Mother's family; there are just no pictures or write-up to confirm this. The newly-weds spent their wedding night at Dad's home, apparently along with Granddad, Grandmother, Uncle George and Aunt Olive. I cannot imagine a more stark, inhibiting way to start a life, but as proof that love conquers all, my brother Homer was born eight months and fourteen days later: tiny, premature, placed in swaddling clothes, and left in a drawer until he was big enough for the little baby bed.

Which of the many disasters that befell the Mincys had the greatest impact is arguable; undoubtedly, the events of October 24, 1929 probably led the list. The stock market crash and the ensuing economic disaster wiped out markets, prices, and made it tough for businesses, farmers, and most people to survive. Those owing a lot of money were twice burdened, as they were quickly denied an opportunity to earn enough to pay the required interest, let alone the principal.

Although the general economic situation was fatal, other blows were struck. In the summer of 1929, the peach crops were infested on two fronts: the Oriental peach moth and the brown rot fungus. Each was deadly and, as measurement, East Tennessee orchards had produced 1,120,000 bushels of peaches in 1928; the harvest in 1929 was barely 520,000, little of that first quality.

My cousin, Charles Norman, recalled a story of a neighbor relating that the only bill he never honored in his life was one during this time, involving peaches. The normal route to market was that a wholesaler would supply baskets to the farmers, who picked, graded, packed the peaches, and delivered them in bushel baskets to the railroad in Harriman (or wherever), for shipment to market. When sold, the price of the baskets and freight would be deducted and the balance forwarded to the grower.

One year, during the early thirties, the harvested crop of Charles' neighbor was sent in the usual manner and, finally, a $3.47 **bill** came for the net difference between the market price and the shipping and basket cost. Farmer (whoever) declared, "They can come and take everything I have; I am not going to pay that bill." He did not and apparently, they did not.

The point is that even healthy peaches, in large volumes, would not have been worth the price of baskets and freight. This went for most other farm products. Sure, costs were down also, but when cash was needed, sources were scarce.

The terms of our family's indebtedness were as follow: the balance of $10,000 was due in 10 years. Interest, at six percent, was due annually on the entire balance. By 1930, they were already in trouble. The peach crops were gone, tobacco allotments were being cut, prices were down, but, apparently, they scraped up the 1930 payment. In 1931, the interest could not be paid and, as security for that year's payment being *delayed,* the Mincys offered as further security (6) head of working mules, (10) head of beef cattle, (1) McCormick-Deering tractor, No. 4370, and (1) J.I. Case threshing machine, No.106092.

In addition, April 8, 1931, Dad and Uncle George borrowed $1200 under the Federal Crop Mortgage program for "seed, feed, and fertilizer," although it is more likely most of the loan was used for the 1931 interest payment as the "additional security" for that payment was released. No interest was paid in 1932, 1933, or 1934.

Those were tough times for millions of Americans; history, family lore, songs, and poetry of the era spell out the human tragedies that befell those caught up in the vise grip of deep depression and squeezed into life altering patterns of existence. Our stories are no more compelling, original, or enthralling than those of our neighbors and all neighbors from coast to coast in the early thirties; they are just ours, and describe how we lost everything that we had.

I was born February 9, 1934. That year, our property, that is, all the properties the Mincys owned or had title to, was sold on the steps of the Roane County Court House, Monday, December 3, at 1:00 P.M. I am sure no stone was unturned to avoid this. No one was willing to work harder than Dad or Uncle George, toward any objective put before them. There was never any chance, after the Plunge, in October 1929. I have a few of Dad's "time books" for the mid-thirties, and when he could find outside work, it seems the usual rate was 75 cents per day; if he could have worked, for others, five days a week, 52 weeks a year, he would have netted the grand total of $195 for the years work. This was hardly a dent in the $600 due in interest alone. I am sure they sold all they had and all they could scrape up, just to get by, ignoring the "debt." Dad preached when he could, I have notes of "chickens, calves, hogs," etc., being sold for a mere pittance, and I can imagine lots of praying and hand wringing. The life insurance policy was cashed in that year (1934); a wonder it was delayed that long. The farm(s) were sold and that was that.

I have no record, nor have found any to-date, to explain what remains a mystery. However, under whatever arrangement, we stayed put on the "farm" property for another five years. I can only imagine some agreement that offered us the chance to still make payment and redeem the property (it was bought back by Prudential for $7500). That was probably an everlasting hope, as time went by. These were not flush times for anybody, and the new owners probably preferred someone on the property, keeping it up, to it being left idle and vacant.

Very little farming continued during these last years. Most of our equipment and livestock had probably been foreclosed and it seems, other than gardens and such, the big time days were over. After the sale, Dad went into the business of selling "Watkins Products," I believe borrowing money from Uncle Walton Smith (Aunt Verna's husband) to get started. I doubt any was ever repaid. However promising that may or may not have seemed at the time, that road, too, was fraught with peril. We always said that Dad was no salesman, and that may or may not have been true. I am sure he applied himself to this work, put in long hours, and traveled, often away from home. His route, in fact, was mostly in McMinn County. The problem, in retrospect, seems to have been that most of his customers were in the same condition as he—no money. He sold on credit, could not collect, and, ultimately, failed at this.

Among the many efforts to "save the farm," none appears more pathetic or heart-wrenching than the episodes of "digging for buried treasure." It seems that, toward the end, Grandmother Mincy had a vivid and recurring dream that someone had been killed in the house where they lived. However, in the dream, the murderer, looking for supposedly hidden wealth, never found it. These dreams were so real and convincing that the family took it as a revelation of perhaps actual, hidden gold. Mom, though staunchly religious and most literate, bought into this idea and became convinced this was how they were going to "save the farm." Dig they did. They went through the back yard and garden, repeatedly, to no avail. Homer remembers joining in the fray, although he seems to remember no going under the house, which would be my first choice. Alas, in spite of all the digging, praying, peddling, plowing, and plodding, in late 1939, Mose Waller (Justice of the Peace), showed up at our front door and served us with an eviction notice. We had to get out, and get out quickly. It is sad to relate, but my grandparents, Uncle George, Aunt Olive, my parents, Homer, two-year-old Elizabeth Alice, and I were forced from that life with little but the shirts on our back.

What might have been different, if any of these life-changing events had not taken place; what if my family had remained farmers, and successful ones, at that? It is idle thought, just to contemplate; there may have been joys, but different ones than those since known. There may have been sadness and to an extent never imagined. Uncle George and Dad could have no more seen the depression coming than the many that jumped out of buildings or soon joined soup lines. Conservatism may have retained what they had but, as they say, rewards are always commensurate with the risks, and few get very far in life, always standing pat. Pestilence, disease, economic downturn of a magnitude never envisioned....one at a time could have been dealt with, perhaps. Occurring together, these events resulted in the "perfect storm" that sent my dad and all his family packing down different roads.

The next 10, or so, years were indeed different; years later, when I would drive my daughters (at still impressionable ages) by each house where the Mincy family had stopped and tell some of the sad tales attached to that particular real estate, I came to call this our "trail of tears." With due respect to those Cherokees, of whom the term originated, we, indeed, shed our share.

When Dad packed up what belonging were ours, in someone's borrowed truck, and loaded his family in his 1932 Plymouth, he headed with them to Riceville, in McMinn County, about 40 miles from where we were (perhaps then, as the crow flew). Why there? The best logic we can come up with is that was where his Watkins route was, primarily, and was all he had to hang onto, at the time.

He had made acquaintances during the five or so years he traveled into McMinn County and, when the end was clear, he probably learned of the first house we moved into and had made arrangements to do so. It came to be known as the "Brown Place," having been rented from a Mr. Harrison Brown. We do not remember much of him; it seems he was a principal in a feed-seed store, perhaps the Brown Supply Co., that I will touch on later. In any event, the house we moved into was a five-room, frame house, heated by fireplaces, drafty, shingle roof, and a step down from our previous home. More importantly, it was not ours.

Dad ca 1922
Carson-Newman College

Mother, Betty and Dad ca. 1950

Dad, with Betty ca. 1937

Left to right: Homer, Mom, Betty, Dad, me ca. 1938

Pam and Dad ca. 1960

Much could be written, hypothetically, of Dad's thoughts during this time. He had witnessed the loss of all that his family ever had; he had lost the security of his profession, which was farming, and a place to practice it. He was separated from his family, and his wife from hers; as it turned out, those 40 or so miles may as well have been an ocean, as the closeness that can exist only with proximity was forever gone. Further, he could have had no reason to believe his fortunes would improve significantly, soon. The Watkins business was a failing one, and its continuance would only deepen his problems. Truth is, none of us remembers him complaining, placing blame, or striking out at any of the forces that had reduced him to this state. He certainly never blamed the Republicans. He was lifetime of the school, "He always voted for Eisenhower, 'cause Lincoln won the War."

He simply plodded on. The Brown place was a small farm, although that was small comfort when we unloaded January 11, 1939. In the dead of winter, in a cold, windy house, what was required was to put things together, chop wood, and try to provide as well as possible. His business was still trying to sell that red liniment, push that vanilla extract, display the menthol-camphor ointment, suggest the petro-carbo salve, and most importantly, try to collect. Almost all those options fared poorly. He got Homer started in school, that being Riceville, a first through tenth grade, moderate-size school in the little town of Riceville, no surprise. Church attendance started equally soon, at the Riceville Baptist Church. Before long, he was Pastor at the Walnut Grove church, in the country, relatively near our home, and some normalcy returned. In truth, we were near neighbors who were wonderful people: the Kelseys, Guffeys, Brights, and others long forgotten.

When summer arrived, Dad worked at farming this place; he planted corn, had a tobacco crop, probably had a cow, and did his best to make a go of this. I doubt it would have been possible to make much of a living on this particular farm, as a renter, even in normal times. I can vaguely recall those activities, and I think the crops turned out okay. Into 1940, however, we moved again, and I just cannot relate the exact circumstances.

Dad must have been wallowing in a sea of debt, relative to the times and his situation. Technically, I am sure we still owed money on the Kingston foreclosure. The Watkins people had probably started pressuring for payment of bills owed. People charging rent usually want paid. I just suppose Mr. Brown asked us to leave, as kindly as possible, and we had to go somewhere else. I hope that Mr. Brown just had other uses for his property.

Rather than beat the point to death, addressing the debt issue this once will have to do. Dad or Mom would have given their life, rather than knowingly, with malice and forethought, cheat anyone out of a nickel. The idea of being dead beats was totally foreign to them, as it had been to their families for generations. Dad was in this situation, however, and was just ill equipped to deal with it, short term. It was not as if he could open a law firm, practice medicine or, with backers, start a new steel mill. He was trained to farm and called to preach; neither offered much support unless he farmed for himself or pastored a large church. At this particular time, debt could not be honored, and those times haunted Dad the rest of his life. He just was never, never, very vocal about it, as opposed to Mom, who sometimes seemed to take delight in dragging up this shame. They did the best they could, trying to survive.

Dad's next station was "Up on the Hill"; so proclaimed, because it was. Frankly, upon leaving the Browns, the issue was just a roof, as dead broke, his choices were rather limited. It would be difficult to ever explain the thin line between our absolute destitute circumstances and the pride and dignity with which Dad (and Mom) deported themselves, and, because of their character and basic integrity, the value of the friends they made and maintained. Such would be the case of this move.

Because of his Watkins routes, he probably knew most McMinn communities and seemed to have established friendships with many great families; they might not have bought petro-carbo, or might not have paid him if they had, but relationships had been established. Among those families were the Hutsells, an old line McMinn family with many branches, all with lineage to the early days of East Tennessee and McMinn County. A particular group, Frank, Floyd, and Horace Hutsell had adjoining farms, on the outer edge of the Mouse Creek Community and to the west of and between Athens and Riceville. These were solid and successful farmers who owned their land and weathered the depression by hard work and patience. On Frank's property, "up on the hill" above Floyd's home, and almost a mile from the nearest road, was a small house, if you will, shack if you won't, that Frank made available for Dad's use. I would have to believe it was for little but decency and charity that he let us in, as I doubt Dad had a dollar to pay up front for rent, if any was charged.

The time we were there had to have been the low point of Dad's life: the little four room house was pitiful, there was not even an out-house; the pretense of the Watkins business was drawing to a close; there was no money; and the issue of eating was even in doubt. We moved in during the winter of 1940. With no garden, not even "polk-salad" to pick, canned goods exhausted, and no money to go to the store, the task of putting something on the table three times a day must have been daunting. Homer recalls finding, in the attic crawl space, some type of discarded meat, wrapped in cloth, perhaps having been smoke "cured," but nevertheless, old; it was examined, thought to have been mutton, cooked, and devoured. Mom probably considered it a miracle, and who can say it was not.

Dad forged on; he worked all he could for the Hutsells, and they were generous and supportive people. He began to work on the nearby, huge, Layman farm. He was forever trying to collect Watkins debts. We struggled and somehow made it through the winter of 1940. Spring is always a period of renewal, and that probably included renewed hopes for Dad and his family. How could it get worse?

In the summer, at least, we had a garden and could eat off the land. Sunshine always makes things look less grim, and bare feet on a dusty road are a lot less tugging on a father's heart than bare feet on a cold floor. In the fall, I recall Dad taking me to school, at Riceville, for my first day; I do not recall much else of the day; I do recall his *being there*. These times remained a struggle; there was little money, a total lack of necessities, the house getting no better, and no help was in sight. In the winter of 1941, the block on our old car froze and burst, leaving Dad without owned transportation for another 20 years. In December, Uncle George came one night telling us Granddad had died; we had no telephone, and he (Uncle George) had someone bring him down from Lenoir City, just to get us the news. Then, barely two months later, the story repeated itself, only this time, it was Grandmother. He had been 84, she 74, and, just like that, the Mincy boys and girls were on their own. Dad was stoic about such things, but this had to have been a terrible loss, made no better by our dreary circumstances.

In spite of all this, our clothes stayed clean, we ate as well as we could, we were in school, and Dad probably never missed a Sunday being in church somewhere. When we moved "upon the hill," we almost immediately started attending the Union Chapel Methodist Church, a couple of miles from our house. The Hutsells, Laymans, and others of the community attended there, and Dad would probably have attended a Hindu Temple (not really!) rather than not be in church. We were actually nearer the New Hopewell Baptist Church, but, for whatever reasons, Dad just never warmed to that church.

What happened at Union Chapel is interesting; it has told me more of the character of the man, in a simple way, than pages of text I could create. Although this was a Methodist church, Dad (and Mom) pitched in and served as asked, faithfully, as long as they were there. Dad, from an overall standpoint, was rather staunch and dictatorial when it came to his beliefs and convictions. I am sure he would have debated Baptist doctrines with the Pope, never bending, given the chance and would have welcomed the chance. At Union Chapel, however, among his neighbors and friends, he slipped into a role of service and, to my memory, never uttered a peep that provoked denominational friction of any sort; that included delivering the message, on occasion.

What a small world, and lest we doubt, what trails we leave; if today, you access the "Union Chapel Methodist Church" on the Internet, to the background of **Amazing Grace**, Dad is shown as Sunday school superintendent, for 1941/42 and Mother, organist, for 1941/2/3; both are shown as teachers during this period. Dad did not always have a pulpit; he always found a place of service.

Dad had continued off and on to work for Gilford Layman and, in 1942, made "a trade" with Mr. Layman to move into a house on his farm and become an employee of the Layman enterprise. "Making a trade" was a term Dad seemed to use when a deal had been struck involving employment, work, or our residences. In this case, I believe it was an aggressive move Dad felt was for the better; it offered a chance of employment (as a hired farm hand), a house, stability, opportunity for gardens, and with it, more food, if nothing else.

Gilford Layman, and his father, Newton, purchased 212 acres from Elijah Montgomery Hutsell in 1918 and began what would become one of the premiere dairying operations in McMinn County. By the time we moved to this farm, it encompassed approximately 2800 acres and, at times, in addition to Mr. Layman and his family, four other families lived on the farms and worked for the Laymans. We called this home "down at Laymans"; it was below the "Up on the hill" house, about a quarter of a mile, as the crow would fly and was the lower, or most southern of the Layman houses. It offered rather few amenities that were improvements over our last place, but it was on a road, had spring water (and I believe an outhouse), Dad worked every day, and this seemed to provide some security.

This was a large dairy operation: hundreds of jersey cows to milk twice a day; barns to "muck" and clean; hay to raise, cut, store, and dispense; crops to raise, including corn, tobacco, oats…the list could go on. In the summer, Dad seemed to plow behind mules or horses most of the time; however, although he was good at it, this was on the low end of the totem pole. More senior or ranking employees drove the tractors, delivered the milk, or did preferred work. Dad never complained and did his work without a whimper. He still took us to the Union Chapel Church and, the first year, Homer and I attended Riceville School.

The second year, as school started, Homer staged a major rebellion over his desire to attend the Mouse Creek School, which was a two-room school about a two-mile walk from where we lived. I can understand Dad's view concerning the educational merits of a ten-grade facility versus a two room one; Homer's view was that he had met some friends who attended

Mouse Creek and wanted to do his eighth grade there. The battles raged around the table at night, as Homer had developed quite a talent for dissension and debate. In the end, Mouse Creek it was, and to Mouse Creek we went.

In spite of work, there was still no money; there was and is great commonality among mill-town, mining town, migrant worker, and hired, farm worker environments. The Laymans were not bad people; to the contrary they were fine citizens and gave us an upward opportunity. To people who have answered only to themselves for generations, working for "the boss" is difficult, and the economics of the situation dictated that the workers were all existing on the edge. These were still depression years, and the onset of World War II had not effected much change in rural McMinn County. So, at the end of the day, the till was usually empty.

I vaguely recall, and Mom would oft repeat, stories of Dad going to town, with not a penny in his pocket, just hoping (and she praying) someone who owed him money would pay him something. The scene that makes the story is the picture of Dad walking down the road from the Laymans, who had supplied the ride into town, with a box of groceries on his shoulder. Mom would always proclaim that many a prayer was answered in those days.

In 1943, Dad "made a trade" with Mr. Layman that involved our moving to another Layman farm about a mile beyond the Mouse Creek School and three miles west of Athens; we were responsible for the operation of this farm, which was a dairy farm and was separate from the other Layman properties. We were totally responsible for milking all the cows, although some of the harvesting or other operations were joint affairs with other Layman employees.

This "trade" yielded another four-room house, with bed bugs, holes in screens, fireplace heat, and an opportunity to work ourselves into the ground. One new feature was present; this was the first house we lived in with electricity. This provided us with one drop-cord bulb, in each room, providing a dim light by which we could read the Bible and fourth grade history. The deal Dad made was that we milked the cows and attended to all the barn functions, twice daily, seven days a week, 52 weeks a year for

$30.00 per month. We were provided the house, of course, and a garden space to grow all we could grow. Dad was paid an hourly wage for all the work (above cow stuff) he did on the farm, which was constant. This place on the trail came to be known as "up at Laymans."

When we moved to this location, Dad took us to the McMahan Calvary Baptist Church, which was a couple of miles from our house, on the Clearwater road; when distances are mentioned, this is what we had to walk, most of the time. The distance was never a factor in deciding to attend church, nor was the weather. If someone came along and offered a ride or picked us up, this was just an unexpected bonus. Attend church we did. Dad, as usual, served as requested: teacher, fill in preacher, song leader (not his strongest suit)—whatever opportunity presented itself.

This location almost worked us down. Dad was on the go all the time, as work of this sort was never completed. Mom, who was not the strongest physical person most of her life, became more prone to respiratory illnesses, and we always seemed short a person or two needed to "keep up." Homer and I often "ran barefoot through the frost" and milked all the cows before heading off to school. Try as you may, with no bathroom, hot showers, or multiple changes of clothes, a dairy farmer is going to be labeled a dairy farmer by anyone who catches a good whiff. Our friends at Mouse Creek whiffed us and let us know it.

We were operating a Grade A dairy farm, and that subjected us to regular inspection on an irregular basis; we never knew when inspectors were coming. Any little thing was graded: evidence of buckets not sterilized, barn cleanliness, milk temperatures, the list goes on. A negative report, of course, was on the Layman farm, not the Mincy household, so, bad marks meant bad mouthing by the Massa; deserved or not, it became tough to take.

By early 1944, the huge Oak Ridge atomic energy project was underway, although no one had a clue what its product was to be; it was known, however, that jobs were available. Uncle George had gone to work there and urged Dad to do so. Uncle George's further motive was to get us back closer together, although that never happened. In any event, Dad decided to leave the farm for all the imaginable reasons and found a job at Oak

Ridge; at the same time, we moved next door, into a residence we shared with Mrs. Bennett Guinn. She had a rather large home, a few acres, her twin sons were off serving in the Navy; her husband, Bennett worked at the TNT plant in Chattanooga, and was rarely home. He, in fact, probably never returned home, as Mrs. Guinn would listen to the "soaps" on the radio and liken them to "her situation."

Dad caught a bus to work on Sunday night or Monday morning and, for the most part, stayed in Oak Ridge during the week. He may have had some dormitory accommodations or just slept on a floor, at times. Memory has him working in construction, and I seem to remember his getting fired from the first job, over some misunderstanding as to how to hang fire extinguishers; in a day or so, he was working as a time keeper, which he did as long as he was there.

A couple of memories Dad provided from those days: first, he contracted pneumonia and almost died. As was so often the circumstance in rural areas, we had no phone, were not flush with cash for doctors, and it just was not our habit to call on them at the first sign of a cold. In this case, Dad got worse and worse and, finally, we had some neighbor call Dr. Ross Arrants, who made a house call in the middle of the night, diagnosed him, and gave him sulfa drugs, which probably saved his life...that, and Mom's never leaving his side during his crisis. I remember being genuinely terrified at the thought he might not make it. It was more than two weeks before he could get up and go and, when he did, his job had not been held for him. That was the end of Oak Ridge for Dad.

While he was there, I remember experiencing the first Christmas that seemed like the stories and the circumstances other people enjoyed. We had treats, candies, and several great presents for each of us. I remember a bow and arrow; I do not remember the others, but it was a slam bang success. We called this home, appropriately, the "Guinn Place."

A couple of developments happened toward the end of 1945; one, after brief stints working with a saw-mill crew and making concrete blocks, Dad went to work at the Brown Supply Co. in Athens (this was to become the McMinn Supply Co.). This was a feed, seed, and farm supply store, and Dad's role was clerk, delivery person, and general handy man. He would work there until his retirement, in 1962. They permitted him to drive a company truck home and doing so provided the Mincys their first regular transportation in over five years. Although it was a big truck, we made do and were thankful for it.

Dad still attended McMahan Calvary church; he may have filled in at various places, but had no regular church for quite some time (as pastor). In the course of events, he came to envision a Baptist church in our community, there being none between New Hopewell on the southwest and McMahan Calvary on the northeast. With cooperation and support from the Rev. Orlan Baker and a few interested neighbors, Dad started a series of cottage prayer meetings in the community, preparatory to the organization of a church and to plant the seeds for that interest. In time, the church was organized and Dad was called to be its pastor. He was justifiably proud of this step for the community and worked tirelessly in its behalf. The church was to be located along TN 30, about four miles west of Athens, and with many offered, Mom's suggestion that it be called Lakeview was adopted. Across the highway from the front of the church-to-be site, was the "Walter Craig Lake," although it had grown up, filled in, and, in truth, no water was ever visible from the church doors. Mom always was creative, with a great imagination.

From his days in Oak Ridge, Dad knew of a small church building that had been abandoned and was scheduled for removal; with some support from the new members, he almost single-handedly did the arranging and management of the movement of this building, in pieces, to the "Lakeview" site; presto, the people had a church building. With foundation, paint, and fixing up, it was a rather nice little church and was a source of considerable pride for Dad. I recall helping haul the first new pine pews from the Vincent Furniture Mfg. Co. to the church and shared the joy that first Sunday of their use (along with the lacquer odors).

This period was probably the happiest of Dad's ministerial career; he had a vision, doggedly pursued it, saw it come to fruition, and wanted only its success. He was not to cross into the Promised Land with it.

There are many issues with groups of people, be it church, clubs, schools, politics, or the military. No news here. Explaining those dynamics and, of more value, directing them, is the work for geniuses or very successful people. With differences of viewpoint, there usually seems to be villains or heroes; however, time tends to alter the hues that would color either. Thus it was with Dad and Lakeview.

As simply as it can be put, Dad was trained and believed, to the bottom of his soul, in a traditional type of worship service. That meant using the Baptist literature, contributing to the Cooperative Program, doing things in a traditional way, and, very importantly, using the Baptist Hymnal and singing traditional hymns.

Other factions in this community, as in many of that time, saw things in a different way: styles of "form and substance" battled, entertainment value counted more than tradition, and traditional music held little appeal, when compared with the faster, zippier, more modern church music available. The most widely used material was published by the Stamps-Baxter Publishing Company and usually was a small, paperbacked volume, with 100 pages or less, of currently copy written material. It followed that, to be able to understand and perform this music, a "singing school" was necessary to train the parishioners and, of course, to promote the material.

Then, there was style; Dad, admittedly, was no spellbinder, with his mild, low-key sermons. He was usually organized, made a point, but never shook the room. By comparison, there were others on the circuit of country churches, who had the shouting, gasping, and four word sentences down to a science and plied their trade. Such forces converged at little Lakeview in 1949, and their results were predictable.

Dad had a revival service during that summer and, with much pressure from some members, he asked the Rev. C.H. "Tuck" Dixon to conduct the services. Tuck was of the style described above, also related to some of the Lakeview members, hence, had a following. Dad was of the school that "outside" preachers, visiting or holding revivals, were to support and help build the church; he would have felt the same if Billy Graham had been the nightly speaker. Many, including "Tuck," were not above tooting their own horns, particularly if they were unemployed, church wise, at the time.

The church was also pressuring for a "singing school," and that would have led to the use of the Stamps-Baxter material. It has been lost on many congregations that little schooling is needed for *Amazing Grace* or *Rock of Ages*; it follows, however, that much leadership and practice is necessary to master *I've Found a Hiding Place* or *He Will Set Your Fields on Fire*. Some of the young people, probably prompted by their parents, were leaving notes around, to the effect that, "They would stay for preaching, if they had a preacher." A few were loyal to Dad, some openly against, and others quiet, but no help. Tuck had some of the members worked up in his behalf, after the revival, and the singing school crowd was loud. Dad, his discouragement mounting, resigned, and "Tuck" was called to become Lakeview's second pastor—a definite low point.

I have often wondered: if Dad could have somehow called upon himself to jazz up his sermons a little and given in on the singing schools and song material, might he not have wielded more influence and brought more to Christ? In modern terms, it was very simple: traditional versus contemporary. Remember those terms. They will be revisited. I currently attend a great church of Christ Followers and, on Sunday morning, when the band strikes up, the choruses are "power pointed" onto screens, most of them copy written last year, and the congregation joins in singing, the hair on the back of my neck stands up as I pass through the time warp between Lakeview, 1949, and today.

In reality, our family feelings aside, "Tuck" Dixon was not the Devil, and Dad was only a part-time Saint. He was willing to go down rather than give in to what he felt was wrong, and, in this instance, he felt the church's desired direction wrong. He moved on.

We left the Guinn place in 1946, when Dad made a trade with Earl Ensminger to move to his farm, which was about three fourths of a mile toward Athens. This offered a relatively nice house, one the Ensmingers had occupied for years and was surrounded by a nice farm. Earl had attended and was active at McMahan Calvary Church, and a mutual friendship had developed. I am sure, in Dad's mind, this would be an ideal situation; Homer and I, with Dad in his spare time, would farm this land

and make it shine. We probably were to pay rent and share in crop harvest(s). We called this home simply "Ensmingers."

It just never worked out. By then, I was twelve, Homer sixteen, and we were capable of any work. In reality, we just never applied ourselves to the task. Homer also left and worked out west the last two summers we were there. It is one of the few episodes causing me embarrassment when I recall the results. In defense, we had no animals or equipment to do a good garden, let alone raise tobacco, corn, hay, or other crops. Homer or I had to borrow from neighbors any mules we ever used, and I was old enough to realize that, however much the mule owners may have liked or respected Dad, borrowing gets old. Asking gets old too, plus, I remember walking along the highway for a couple of miles, each way, to borrow a mule, then returning it after using it during whatever was left of the day. Heavy work requiring a tractor always had to be contracted, begged, or otherwise obtained, and the completion was usually after the need. The system did not work. We probably did not work night and day to try to make it so, and our farm efforts were a disappointment to Mr. Ensminger and an embarrassment to us all.

I believe from the day we left Kingston that Dad always dreamed and believed he would one day own his own place, again. During the time we were at Ensmingers, an opportunity arose for Dad to acquire some property, and he pounced on it; in his mind, he visualized that it would all work out. It is only fair to say that Dad never seemed to aspire to great riches or required trappings of such, for his personal satisfaction. He did yearn for independence and the sense of accomplishment he had once known. His modest demands for himself, however, sometimes failed to take into account the rest of our little family unit.

On this occasion, having announced his plans, he took all of us one weekend to view our new home to be; I wish I could recall the exact location, but I know it was in a totally different community and pretty far off the beaten path. Again, with tools, equipment and time, the property was probably a good buy and could have been made to work. The house was simply unlivable. The area was nowhere Betty or I wanted to attend school and posed greater problems for Homer just to commute to town or wherever. In this case, we, including Mother, pounced on poor Dad like a broken dam and put an end to this particular dream. I believe he had to do some backpedaling to nix the deal, somewhat to his consternation. The dream never died, however.

Later, he talked with a Mr. Brock about some property located 3-400 yards out the highway toward Athens, on which Brock was going to place a house; this house was being torn down and transported in from elsewhere. This property was about seven acres, mostly hilly, covered with trees of all sorts, except an acre or two of tillable land on the back side, and came with a tobacco allotment. The house was, again, a small, four-room that was sparse, but livable. In this instance, Dad had his way, we consented, however reluctantly, and the deal was done. We left the Ensmingers, to Mr. Ensminger's delight and perhaps felt relief, ourselves. This was 1949, and we never really gave this place a name. To Dad, I believe it was just home, at last.

Dad worked continuously with the same employer until he retired. Shortly after he went to work for Brown Supply Co., a change of ownership took place and, with it, a name change. Fred Robinson and Earl Wilson, with other backers, took over in 1947 and, at the same time, changed the name of the firm to McMinn Supply Co. I believe the Knoxville Fertilizer Co. had an interest, as well as Fred's brother, Walter, who managed a sister company in Cleveland, Tennessee, the Bradley Supply Co. The firm gradually grew, as Fred and Earl were good managers, aggressive business people, and solid citizens with whom to work. They were generally respectful and accommodating to Dad, called him "Preacher" in a friendly manner, and treated him well.

Dad was sort of a utility person during his career with McMinn Supply; he just did everything in the store. He served as a clerk on the floor, he delivered products, he ran sales routes, he unloaded boxcars, he transferred goods from the warehouse to the floor, and he did anything asked. His manner at this work was similar to plowing or hoeing a garden: he was deliberate, and might appear slow, if you only glanced. He had a constant pace, however, and kept at it until, if you were working with him, he had run you into the ground. He was a short to medium height man, maybe

5'9" and, when trim, probably weighed 165 pounds. I never, in my prime, remember out-working him at anything: using a saw, axe, hoe, plow, hammer or carrying fertilizer into a barn. An image of him that will always remain is that of unloading 200 100 pound. bags of fertilizer (or feed) from the truck to a barn location; he carried a bag at a time on either his hip or across his shoulder and was just like a steady conveyor, until it was done. He was doing this into his sixties. I strap on my hernia belt, put on gloves, and stagger along trying to get a 40 pound. bag of salt into my water softener, wondering even yet, with every step, how he did it.

After the Lakeview experience, Dad attended the North Athens and later, the East Athens Baptist churches for a period. He then began pastorates at the Calvary Missionary, South Liberty, and Rogers Creek churches in McMinn and Meigs County until he was called to be pastor of the Valley View Baptist Church, in McMinn County; he was pastor of this church from 1953 until he died in 1967. This, I suppose, was the longest period of time he had been with one church in his life, and I believe it was finally a good fit between the man and the mission. Church members seemed to enjoy his leadership, and this full time responsibility, at last, fit his skills and purpose.

It would not be accurate to paint a picture of Dad as totally holy, giving and without flaw. He was all I have portrayed, with character above reproach. On a personal level, however, there were elements of his personality that, while perhaps commendable on one hand, caused some anguish on the other.

For whatever reason, Dad just never seemed interested in taking Mom to "see her folks." I know of no rift or disagreements; in fact, as documented elsewhere, Mom's family was, without doubt, one of the finest and most enjoyable to be around that I ever knew. It follows that they always had been, and were, to my knowledge, gracious and warm to him. There was, apparently from the start, something within him that just gave this a low priority; hence, it happened all too infrequently. When Dad and Mom were married, I believe leaving home after 28 years was an emotional and cultural shock for Mom that could easily have been tempered by this concession on Dad's part. At first, they lived only eight or nine miles from her home and had transportation. It is my understanding that, even then, she was practically cut off from this association. It was not that she was forbidden to leave; she did not drive, and he just did not take her.

As a defense, it could be pointed out that all his life, Dad worked five or six days a week and was always in church on Sunday; I do not remember debate about it, but he just chose and, in fact, may have sincerely believed it mandatory, that attending church came first. Later, we had no transportation, and living 40 miles from Mother's family, this gulf widened. He was an equal opportunity family avoider, as he did not make much effort to visit Uncle George and his other family members, either. This meant, of course, that Homer, Betty, and I had limited contact with our cousins, growing up, and that was a loss for all of us. This was not a source of continual strife; Mom just always felt this loss, and the issue was there. Church or family? Tough call, but Dad's choice was always pretty clear, with a price.

Each of us children perhaps has a different slant on the relationship between Mom and Dad. In general, we perhaps agree that during most of our lives, particularly early on, it was rather formal and perhaps strained, at times. Those days were so bad, financially, and living so hard, that any warmth and affection would have had to take a running leap to find a place to land. I remember no abuse, either way, few sharp words, and they supported each other in most of their endeavors. Mom was always there for Dad in his church work. It was not Dad's personality to be outgoing and affectionate, and some of us may have picked up a few of those genes, to our detriment. As a child, I vividly remember kindness, concern, pride, discipline, and all the traits of parental responsibility. I wish he had hugged Mom more and taken her to see her folks.

I must say, although I was gone from home for the last thirteen years of his life, my impression is that in the later years, they grew to be very comfortable with each other (if it had ever really been otherwise). I remember more warmth and affection seeming evident, and I believe they ended their lives happy and content for having shared that relationship.

How could I describe my Dad, then, to a stranger? A way to start would be to share his known **dislikes** and, if you were around him, these would have become evident in the normal course of his company: Democrats! Stamps-Baxter song books. Fords. John-Deere tractors. Shell gas. Loud, bragging people. Drunks (although he would sincerely work to influence a change in their lifestyle).

Likes? Chevrolets. McCormick-Deering tractors (or Farmalls). International trucks. Esso gas. Home cooking. Chicken gizzards. Smoking Camel cigarettes. Preparing sermons. Reminiscing about Carson-Newman College. His children.

Dad was a man who loved God sincerely and believed in the literal interpretation of God's Word, as recorded in the King James Version of the Bible, and as interpreted by Baptist scholars of his time. He was a victim of the tail end of the great depression and was forced to work hard, physically, all of his life because of that. He loved his family and did his best to be involved in it as much as he could. His work effort was beyond reproach, but he took a dim view of play. He never gave up on the task at hand, in spite of great odds.

He and Mom were very proud people; it defies logic to think that from the time the motor block burst (around 1940), until sometime in the late fifties, they were without motorized transportation (except, later, the company truck)

He (and Mom) was the model of plodding on, with his eye on the ultimate prize: heaven. They were both admirable people; we miss them still.

Eva Estelle Hedgecock Mincy

September 18, 1944

Son, always remember:

"A good name is rather to be chosen than great riches and a loving favor rather than silver or gold."

PROVERBS 22:1

"Mother"

With this Proverb, Mom christened the first page of my little, brown autograph book, early in the fall of my fifth grade at Mouse Creek School. And, on this Mother's Day, 2002, I begin an attempt to honor her memory with some of mine; more importantly, I will work to share a portrait of this lady with those who never had the pleasure of knowing or loving her. She was, indeed, a unique, an outstanding, and always serving individual; her story merits telling and remembering.

Mom (and sometimes I shall call her Mother; it was always back and forth) was just almost unreal. When she tucked us in on a cold night, in those early and difficult years, and added a blanket to our feet that she had warmed by the fireplace to fight the frigid shock of those sheets in an unheated bedroom, she was just being a loving mom. When she would skillfully lead, as a teacher, any group in her long history of church work, she became a biblical scholar who could rival any lay and most professional teachers of her day. When she repeatedly returned good for evil, in her immediate neighborhood of bootleggers, thieves, drunks, crazies, and other brands of troublemakers, she became missionary, witness, and miracle worker. When she would greet a Jehovah's Witness at the door, not let them in, but courteously listen, then give her testimony through the screen, she became an ambassador or mediator of sorts, acknowledging the other view point but holding steadfast to her own. Many who knew her outside the family would comment that she was the most outstanding, gifted, wise person they had ever known. How, then, can we best approach sharing the life story of this wise, gifted, and outstanding mother?

We perhaps could start by getting her "born and raised," before we canonize her.

Eva Estelle arrived December 9th, 1901, into the home of Henry Marion and Sarah Alice Roberts Hedgecock, the eighth of their 10 children. She never mentioned anything particularly memorable of her birth, or recalled her parents describing anything outstanding of her early days. Spaced between Ada Jean, born September 23, 1899, and John Virgil, born September 25, 1906, it perhaps is understandable that she and Ada, closest in age, would be closest in "spirit" as they moved through childhood. Now is as good a time as any to clarify her name; she was named Eva, to be pronounced "Evie," using a "short" E. This, of course, caused considerable confusion throughout her life; her family knew what to call her, but the rest of the world had difficulty. Her husband, my father, seemed to struggle to get the sound out and, in time, just called her "Mother." Her in-laws never even made an effort, to her considerable dismay, and, with time, the world as a whole not coming around, I believe she resigned herself to being "Eva." She forgave those not understanding. *You* keep this in mind, however, every step of the way: she was and is Eva, pronounced Evie (short E).

She was born in the "old house." Her father, Henry Marion, and his family lived in this structure, which was at the foot of a small hill, on which later was built another house, still standing in beautiful condition. The "old house" had three rooms; one, called the family room, had a large fireplace, large enough for the entire family to gather around, and included two beds. The parlor also had a fireplace and room for two beds. The third room ran the length of the house without a partition and served as kitchen, dining room, and, the far end, as another bedroom. While the dimensions are not known, it had to have been rather crowded by the time twelve family members called it home. Mom's memory and description, however, never included a negative and seemed always to emphasize order, manners, respect, duties, and a pecking order that covered work assignments, sleeping arrangements, and positions of responsibility.

The house had a couple of large maple trees in the front yard, flower beds on each side of the walk leading to the front porch, and a huge rose bush at the end of the porch. There was a cherry tree at one end of the house and an apple tree in the back; a cistern was on the opposite side of the house from the cherry tree and was the source of water unless, in dry weather, the water supply was exhausted. If that happened, water had to be carried from the spring in a valley below the house.

Among Mother's childhood memories were visits, with Ada, to (her) Grandmother Roberts' house, which were always pleasant and to be remembered. Ada would cook and Mom would help with small chores. After her grandmother died, Grandfather Roberts would visit and live for awhile with one of his daughters; before long, he always got restless and moved on to another one. During his stays at the Hedgecocks, Mother and Aunt Ada remembered doing small favors for him and his giving each of them a penny, when something special warranted it. This was always special to them and long remembered.

(Her) Grandmother Hedgecock died before Mom was born, but her grandfather married a lady, Almeda Scott Kreis, who became a wonderful grandmother to all the grandchildren; they loved her dearly. Their home was a great place to visit, especially at Christmas. All the grandchildren would receive a present; it would be small and seemingly insignificant but was always anticipated and treasured.

Mom remembered, and, would relate with pride, sitting around her grandparents and listening to them relate their Civil War experiences. She would always describe those memories, emphasizing their descriptions of "those dirty Rebels" with a twitch of her nose, as if she smelled something distasteful. I recall in later years commenting, "But Mom, that is us," to no avail. She was well aware that her great grandfather, Willis Hedgecock, had fought for the Union, also, but he died before she was born; she knew of his exploits, however.

Probably her most oft repeated story of the "old house" was the partial loss of a thumb. When she was very young, perhaps four or five, she caught her thumb in the fence gate in front of the house, cutting it off at the end. Her parents buried the severed portion in the garden, perhaps near the onion patch, as she always had an aversion to them. "Upset her stomach," she said. The end of her thumb was always a little misshapen; noticeable only if she called attention to it. She was never reluctant to recite the story of her loss.

The story of Mom's early days, family life, growing up, and the relationship with her siblings and parents is difficult to phrase in a manner understandable today. First, historically, families generally have trouble "getting along." They litigate, argue, fall out, steal and, in many sad instances simply split, and after a time, leave no trace of the original relationship. At best, loving families experience some of the negatives listed above.

Never, ever in my memory, or in that of my brother and sister, do we recall Mother uttering a negative word about her family; to the contrary, her words were always loving, kind, respectful, and seemed to paint a picture of absolute perfection, deserved or not. Further, I remember seven of Mother's brothers and sisters, and I recall the same of them—nothing negative. Mom, and I would believe all her siblings, viewed their parents with utmost respect and, while acknowledging their strict, authoritarian manner, felt blessed to be children of H.M. and Sarah, and were probably all model children. The most telling incident to make my point is to recall Mother relating, "The only time I ever disagreed with Papa….he had said something and I said, you know that is not right…he hauled off and almost knocked me down." She related this many times and, of importance, she was probably in her late teens or early twenties when this occurred. She always upheld her father as being "right." Such was this family's respect for parents and, as indicated, adoration of each other.

In any event, toward the end of 1908, this Hedgecock family moved into their "new" home on top of the small hill, above where the other house had been. A small garage actually was near the place of the old house, when I visited there during my early days; Uncle Frank kept his

Dodge there. Even though this was a larger house, no one ever had a room of their own, with the boys sharing a room and the girls doing likewise. Aunt Ruby seems to recall some of the boys actually sleeping down in the old house for awhile, as I guess twelve people, at best, over-taxed the new residence. Regardless, Mom remembered no complaints and their being a happy and contented family.

Mom would describe the family eating in the dining room, as there was not enough room in the kitchen for everyone. Her father insisted that the whole family, if they were present, be seated before the meal began.

This house had a parlor, also, with a nice fireplace over which a lovely mantel held a clock, pictures, and other nice items. There was a parlor organ and, later, a piano. For amusement, there was a phonograph (of the type depicted in the old "Voice of the Master" illustrations used by RCA) and nice chairs, but the children were only allowed in this room on special occasions when they had visitors. This was different, of course, when they were older. Two fireplaces and a heater, using wood that was in abundance nearby, heated the house. This house had no indoor plumbing or electricity, until many years later and was illuminated by kerosene lamps and lanterns. It was a regular chore to keep the lamp wicks trimmed and the globes cleaned. Old newspapers were the usual tools to shine the glass globes, which would become black, inside, from the soot.

Before the days of refrigeration, milk, butter, eggs, and other goods were kept in either a "dairy," (an outdoor cellar) or a box near the spring, to keep them cool.

Mother always indicated that, as the eighth of 10 children, she never really felt she had the responsibilities or burden of work that her older brothers and sisters had. She often said that she had no complaints. Her mother planned and cooked the meals for many years, until the girls grew older and took over this responsibility. Each of the five girls had to try their hand at ironing. With a family of this size, each person evolved into his or her "special" chores, and Mom always stated that hers was never cooking; it usually was washing dishes, setting the table, making beds, cleaning the house, but never cooking. She always lamented her lack of cooking skills and depreciated the abilities she actually had. We never complained about the many southern delicacies that graced our table; the early problem was not much available for her to practice with, as we grew up.

Mom remembered having the usual childhood diseases: whooping cough, red measles, mumps, and chicken pox, to name a few. Disease was always a presence: Uncle Burton, at the age of 27, died of tuberculosis in 1916; Uncle Hugh died from the same cause in 1926, when he was 38. It goes without saying that they suffered for years before succumbing. Uncle Virgil also contracted TB and moved to California in the late thirties, to improve his chances for survival. Mom's father died at the relatively young age of 59; so together with grandparents, aunts, and uncles, Mom knew her share of sickness, disease, and death.

I related in the story of Hedgecock families, the independent and self-sufficient nature of my grandparents. Grandfather Hedgecock farmed, ran a cannery, operated a store and supplied the sustenance for his large family with what he raised, grew, bartered for, or made by hand. Uncle Burton was a photographer; he, as well as Uncle Hugh, taught school; Uncle Ernest became a minister and school teacher, and in all these endeavors (until Uncle Ernest was married), efforts were for the common cause....survival. My Mother grew up doing her chores, feeling loved and loving in return, and felt secure and comfortable in this most admirable family unit.

Saturday nights were bath nights and that took a bit of managing on everyone's part. In the winter, the kitchen was the ideal spot where everyone took turns, as that area would still be warm from dinner, dishes, and such. In the summer, everyone used their own room; I can even recall when I would visit Grandma, the little table, "wash pan," and towels were a part of each bedroom. They, and I, made do. Mom always recalled her mother assuring that the clothes were clean, no buttons were missing, and no big fuss was raised as everyone got ready for church on Sunday morning. If anyone was sick, Grandmother Hedgecock was the one who stayed home from church, as otherwise, everyone went. Church, and the attendant religious faith of Mom's family, was a central part of their lives, and Sundays were dedicated to those activities. More on that later.

Mom always related that holidays were special; at Christmas, with no allowance and, usually, no money for presents, shopping and exchanging gifts were not part of the celebrations. She wished it could have been so. Rather, she always remembered that Christmas had a very special meaning. It seemed to bring glad tidings, good will, love, and cheer, with down to earth blessings such as special cakes, pies, candies, fruits, raisins, with oranges being one of the "way outs."

Easter was also a special time. Mom was taught early on the meaning of Easter and was probably grown before she learned of the custom whereby many folks got new clothes for Easter. In her family, it was usually May, and warmer weather, before they got their summer outfits. With her brothers and sisters, they would enjoy the quaint tradition of slipping around a few days before Easter, and, hopefully without their parent's knowledge, hide a large quantity of fresh eggs; these were brought in Easter Morning, and they would implore their Mother to cook them all. Some would get them fried, some scrambled, and some boiled; if there were any boiled eggs left, that meant egg hunting in the lovely grass yard that afternoon.

Fourth of July usually meant staying home. Occasionally, there would be a picnic and, across the river in the Sugar Grove community, picnics were also quite common. One year, when Mom was probably eleven, she recalled getting to go along with her older brothers and sisters to such an affair. This was quite thrilling, as it involved walking down to the Clinch River, riding a "skiff" across the river, then, climbing a steep hill that seemed like a small mountain, to reach the picnic site. She also remembered the huge (to her) American Flag that would be draped on the front porch each Fourth of July. It seemed to, somehow, fully express the true meaning of the day. One Fourth, when the older brothers and sisters seemed unable to reach any consensus as to an agreeable activity, someone got several buckets together, and they all went berry picking. She recalled it being successful, to the extent they harvested 35 gallons, that day.

Speaking of summers, Mom would relate the difficulty they had keeping cool during the hot months. The windows would be kept open, of course, in an attempt to capture any breeze that might have been passing through and, at night, they would try to create their own breeze with hand held fans that would even be taken to bed. She would tell of fanning until she would, "just drop off to sleep." Weather was always a consideration.

I think is goes without saying that weather patterns change: During my growing up and younger years, I just do not remember much severe weather or occurrences of any variety. Now, throughout Tennessee, it seems quite normal for the natives to be subjected to ice storms, tornadoes, floods, and even blizzards. Mother would describe anxious times caused by a tornado or cold so extreme that they would have to use axes to chop through the ice on the pond. Floods were common, as before the TVA, whose principle mission was flood control, the Clinch River would escape its banks and flood the bottom land, where most of the crop production took place. That was good news, bad news: This flooding over the years helped make this land rich and productive, but if it occurred in the summer, the crop went with it.

During my life, Mother always noted birthdays and other special occasions. As she was growing up, it was different, as she experienced no greeting cards, birthday cake, or gifts. She would relate that these dates were usually recognized, and she was made to feel very special on such days. At the top of the list of important dates, in fact, she would call it a "red letter" day, was the occasion each spring when she, her brothers, and sisters could take off their shoes and go barefoot. There was just something about the freedom and unique feeling of tender feet on the bare earth that always made one (me included) want to push the envelope and rush the occasion. Mom was made to participate in, and passed on to her children, the ritual of spending hours outside, picking up every piece of glass, nails, rocks, or anything that might be perceived as dangerous to a bare foot. This had to be done, and done subject to inspection, before those worn leathers could be removed. It must be said that this joy was a mixed blessing. After a winter of being contained inside, the bottoms of little feet become quite tender, and those first few days of "barefoot" are more hopping around than walking or running normally. This is particularly true on rocky roads or gravels. It takes time to toughen little feet to the point that shoes are not necessary. It must also be said that most dangers to feet lurked outside the confines of that house and yard. The serious nail holes, stubbed toes, stone bruises, cuts, and snake bites usually occurred out in the world at large; so, all that policing in the back yard usually offered only minimum security.

Mom's playmates were usually neighbors and cousins…often one and the same. The childhood recreation was seasonal. She reported that, "In Spring time, it was fun discovering the first Sweet Williams blooming. When the weather became warm, we loved to climb up in the hay loft and look out the side of the barn door over the pond, and watch the turtles sunning themselves on a stump, as well as the geese and ducks swimming along…" The Hedgecock farm was large enough, and the neighborhood between home and the Lawnville community familiar enough, that childhood for the Hedgecock children, including Mom, must have offered the ultimate in exploration, adventure, and fun.

The Lawnville School, next to the Young's Chapel Cumberland Presbyterian Church, was in a two-room building, which had been remodeled from a one-room structure the year Mom started to school. She remembered her room as fairly nice, with a stage across the end, a black board, desk(s) for two, and a shelf, for the water cooler. It was about two miles from the home place to school, and all the Hedgecocks walked this each day unless, by chance, a family member or neighbor happened along with a buggy or wagon and offered a ride. In those days, there were very few strangers. Everyone knew almost everyone else and accepting an offered ride, even if only part of the way, was a safe and welcomed relief—particularly after a day of classes, activities during two recesses, and that walk, in the morning.

Mom always seemed to describe her school days with confidence and joy. She loved the classes, seemed to do well, and would remark that the only help she ever remembered getting was from her older brother, Hugh, when she was in the eighth grade. Her favorite subjects were spelling, arithmetic, and English. At breaks, the children would play stickball, basketball (later), marbles, kick the can, and a variety of the made up games of the era. School, for Mom, helped fan her passion for learning but also was the base that denied her fulfillment of ambitions that she had.

When she had completed the eighth grade at Lawnville, she wanted to continue her education. It seems a combination of factors prohibited that from coming about. First, there seems general agreement that the next logical step would have been to attend a "Normal" school in Kingston; this type school was primarily for preparation to teach and, also, was a boarding school. She could not have commuted, as even though Kingston was only five or six miles away, daily transportation apparently was impossible. It would be a few years before a regular high school was available and bus or other transportation existed.

She always just said that, "Papa would not let me go on." Sometimes, there was an inference that cost might have been involved, but of note is the fact that some of her older brothers had continued. In fairness, none of her older sisters continued in school, either. Aunt Ruby, about eight years younger, was the only one of the girls to go to high school and, in fact, completed college.

The most likely answer appears to have been "the times" and the attitude toward women, then. The idea of a "girl" going off to board away from home at the age of fourteen was, probably, one that Mr. Hedgecock just could not bring himself to consider. All the words: improper, not right, out of place, lead to trouble, people would talk…probably came into play and probably did so with no malice toward Mom. He most likely thought her place, as he most likely thought with her older sisters, was in the home, and that was that. The boys, now, that was another matter.

But on to school Mom did go. She just went back to Lawnville and took the eighth grade over again. And again, then again. She went eleven years to the Lawnville School, in an effort to soak up all the knowledge she could. She recalled reading all the "good" books she could, at home and fed her thirst for knowledge in every way possible. During this time, on occasions, she would serve as substitute teacher for the lower grades and, in fact, harbored the thought that she would like to teach. Let her relate, in her droll way, what happened: "One day, when I was teaching in the lower grades, something funny happened. I thought we were moving along nicely, when, out of nowhere, a plane flew over the schoolhouse. Almost before I knew what was happening, I think the entire group of children was in the yard watching the plane, without my permission. At any rate, they got their science lesson for the day. That was when planes were scarce and, in this instance, something big was happening. I never became a school teacher; was that any wonder?"

She would, later in life, say that she got tired of taking the same material over and over, again; I think she also just lost hope of continuing beyond Lawnville and, in absence of that possibility, chose to get on with her life.

"Getting on with life" meant becoming immersed in whatever opportunities she could find at home and at church. It should, perhaps, be reiterated that the Hedgecocks lived on the river, and the "way out" entailed that two miles through the country to the little Lawnville community. Sure, there were neighbors, but even now, the area is not densely populated, along the road. So, most activities were at church or, in Mom's case, 4-H and "Home Demonstration Club" activities. She (and Aunt Ada) became very active in projects, won ribbons, went to the fairs, and seemed favorites of the Home Demonstration Agent, Glenn McClellan. She seemed to have stayed at the Hedgecock home more often than at other neighbors and always just marched straight to the kitchen to see what Grandmother was cooking. It also goes without saying that with the store, cannery, farm, large family, and illnesses, Mom had a full plate at home.

To say that she immersed herself in church work would perhaps imply she did so to a greater extent than other family or community members. A visit to the Lawnville Cemetery serves as a touching reminder that the Roberts and Hedgecocks were many; knowing this family is to know their faith and that little church was, and is yet today, a central focus in their lives. All the Hedgecocks were active, and Mom was no exception. I believe, however, her leadership abilities became evident, and she took increasing leadership roles at the Church and in the various organizational bodies of which Young's Chapel was a part. She regularly attended "Presbytery(s)," camps, sessions, and served as an Elder in her church (at a very young age). Betty, Homer, and I concur in our memory that she had wanted to become a missionary; her inability to continue in school probably thwarted her pursuing this through the usual channels. It was always evident that those years, from finishing her "schoolin'" at Lawnville until her marriage, forged her gifts of scholarship, willingness to serve, leadership ability, and conviction of faith. She never was able to continue in school; she never stopped learning.

We can only imagine her range of friendships during this period. She was part of a large family; it extended through countless cousins near and far, and she must have gained many new friends through her varied activities. Later, in addition to her family members, she seemed to devote the most conversation in memory of special friends Annie Kidwell and her cousin, Ola Roberts. Verna Briggs seemed an influential leader and coworker in many church activities. Mom's dating activities were more obscure.

Memories of her mentioning serious relationships with young men are few; when Mom was in her teens, many men her age, and older, were "off to war," with the United States. joining in the last part of World War I. Pictures of her as a young person make her appear attractive, at least to me, although she may have suffered from the fact she was surrounded by Hedgecock sisters equally attractive, or more so. Maybe the women to men ratio in her community were not to her favor. Perhaps living at home, a home somewhat dominated by a demonstrably stern father, had a dampening influence. There is just not any evidence that she dated a lot.

She would mention a friendship, or at least an acquaintance of note, with Miser Richmond, who later became Dean at Tennessee Tech. She and millions of other young American women idolized and dreamed about Charles Lindbergh. She was probably as normal and aspiring as anyone her age was, in similar circumstances.

Recently, Aunt Ruby recalled instances when she, and her brother, Virgil, would be playing and happened upon Mom and Aunt Ada talking. Invariably, all conversation would stop, with either Ada or Eva admonishing them to, "Just go along and play," insinuating that the conversation was perhaps too mature for their little ears to hear. I am quite sure those interrupted conversations were not about the weather, war, or church work. Aunt Ada never married and Mom did late; in Aunt Ada's (as well as Uncle Frank's) case, caring for their mother was perhaps an influence. For both, I think there were suitors, but the circumstance was never right.

If I could visualize Mom, as I believe she was then, in light of today's terms and situations, I can imagine that she would have intimidated most of the farm boy beaus of the day. She was rather tall, attractive, serious, studious, and active on a lot of fronts. She was interested in reading, loved memorizing poems, could remember sermons almost verbatim, (she could, in fact, recall sermons 50 years later) and had taken leadership roles in many activities at an early age, relative to her peers. She was from an outstanding family in the community and was on all fronts, quite a catch. The right party had just not crossed her path. Whether or not it was an influence, she had to endure much sickness in her home, with her two brothers and father and, in fact, questioned her own health, as she did to a degree throughout her life.

That someone did cross her path in the summer of 1924: Homer Franklin Mincy. I have related in the chapter of Dad's life about his family's threshing business, how they were working in the Lawnville Community, and how at this time they were working the Hedgecock farm. The nature of our rather reserved parents, conversation-wise, and the fact we were not inquisitive about important to-be things, has resulted in the details of this courtship and period of time being left unknown. Obviously, they met then and remembered the meeting; they both always acknowledged that fact. Mom stated that they "started dating" the following autumn and became engaged Christmas, 1928. They were married, of course, April 27, 1929.

On paper, this was a good match. Dad appeared to be a prosperous farmer, was a serious person, was soon to be ordained as a Baptist minister, and, I can imagine, a pleasant person to be around. He drove a car, seemed to collect many pictures of girl friends, with their hats or bonnets usually displayed on the radiator of his car. It would seem he got around. We will just never know if "dating" was once a week, month, quarter, or year. It apparently did occur. There are no surviving letters or mementos of the period to account for this relatively long courtship; I could imagine, as I did in describing Dad during this period, that he was working toward some reasonably sound economic basis for life with a wife and moving forward with his ministry plans. Whatever, date they did, and wait they did.

The wait ended on that April date in 1929, with their marriage in the front yard of her home. It should be said that the settings was probably beautiful then and, in the same spot, would be today. The stately, white, framed home sat on top of a hill, with a view overlooking the immediate area and across a small valley, to an opposite hill, to the west.

There were thick forest to the back and east side of the house, and young maple trees shaded the front yard, down to the road. The leaves would have been out, the grass green, and flowers would have surrounded the house: hollyhocks, sweet Williams, roses, lilacs, and many others. In her white dress, hose, and shoes, Mom was a beautiful bride, carrying a lovely flower arrangement. This was most likely a family affair, with the Hedgecock's and a small contingent of Mincys rounding out the party. Her older brother, Ernest, a Cumberland Presbyterian minister, performed the ceremony. I can envision Grandmother Hedgecock supervising the serving of a spread on the dining room table, fit for (southern) kings. Good-byes, last hugs, hand shakes by the men, and Eva Estelle probably got in Dad's Star automobile for the seven mile trip to his home on the Kingston Road, now U.S. 70. There was a small catch: that was also the home of Uncle George, Aunt Olive, Grandmother, and Grandfather. I have often wondered if Mother foresaw what she was getting into; I know I never heard her utter anything close to the proverbial, "If I had known then...."

To properly set the stage and fill in the blanks of the next stage of Mom's life is difficult; I (or anyone) can only look at the circumstances Mom and Dad faced, as they started their life together, through my eyes and experiences. These views are probably a far cry from the way they looked at it and experienced it. Within a few years, and for the balance of our parent's lives, my brother, sister, and I were witnesses to all our family circumstances; yet, each of us has a different slant on some things. In the final analysis, sometimes, what we saw and what we thought did not, and could not, reflect what they thought, particularly about each other. In many instances, they just did not talk about things; at least not openly; certainly, not things about each other.

Having said that, there are some basic facts that have always been evident: I have tried to describe the home life Mom experienced for 26 years. It was always congenial, loving, supportive, positive, and fostered an atmosphere that nurtured learning, self-development, and independence. On the other hand, Dad's home, insofar as I know or can imagine, would have been almost the opposite: insular, crude, suspicious, self-centered and intellectually limited. I am not being contradictory regarding the overall descriptions I have previously given my grandparents, aunts and uncle; they were God-fearing, loyal, supportive of each other, and, I believe, proud of my father, the baby of the family. Their lack of social graces would extend, however, to being rude at times and somewhat overbearing with respect to social contacts. Dad had experienced the outside world at Carson-Newman, was exposed to a little more education, was by nature quieter, and stood a little outside the rest of his immediate family. But it was *his* family, and into it Mom moved on her wedding night.

I never *knew* my grandparents, although I vaguely remember them; by the time of Mom's marriage, Uncle George and Aunt Olive were the driving force of this household and the prime ones with whom Mom had to reckon. I believe, and can imagine, that Mom, from "way over" in the Lawnville community and a non-Baptist at that, may as well have been from another country; while I believe they were proud of Dad finding a wife and potentially fathering little Mincys and, basically, felt "Christian love" for Mom, they were just intellectually incapable of supplanting Mom's own brothers and sisters. I doubt they made much effort to or would have imagined the need.

Into this new life, Mom was plunged, spending her first night and first month with the Mincys. At the end of this time, she and Dad moved almost next door (around the curve on "Kingston Pike") into the little five-room house that was part of the farm the Mincys had bought, just a few months before. Their possessions would have been a collection of pieces from both sides of the family: quilts, beds, dishes, stoves, tables, an organ, and their personal Bibles. I doubt that first night in their new home, there was a piece of new furniture. With all this, I believe Mom truly loved Dad, and I have no evidence that feeling ever changed.

Mom's new home presented many immediate challenges. First, this house, its sparse furnishings and minimal equipment was a far cry from her "home place." Even though her parents and family were not wealthy, compared to many, they were comfortable, and their home was a comfortable one, in every aspect. Mom suddenly was the cook, planner, wife, social chairperson, and had to provide, with the resources she had available. The Mincy women (Aunt Olive, Grandmother, and on occasion, Aunt Sophia), I am quite sure, meant no harm but, rather than be totally supportive, probably made sure Mother knew how much better they were at cooking or anything else they could dream up to make themselves feel important.

To add to the equation, within a couple of months, Mom was "great with child," an event I doubt she welcomed so quickly. So, in addition to adjusting to a new home, with its shortcomings, and a new family that could be trying at times, she faced the prospect of motherhood within a short time. I do not remember her complaining, even of morning sickness, but rather, think she looked upon it as a new challenge and adventure. A singular event occurred, however, that I believe influenced some things that followed and not in a positive way. Mom decided she would learn to drive.

On the surface, this would seem no great thing. Cars were not that common, as Mom grew up, and it was probably around 1918 when her father bought the first car the family had owned. Again, even though all the "boys" learned to drive, I do not recall stories about any of the "girls" learning to drive at that time. Women drove, of course, but that just did not seem common in the Hedgecock household. I can imagine, however, this being mutually agreed between Mom and Dad, and I can further imagine Dad being pleased to teach her. A couple of mannerisms that were trademarks of both Mom and Dad are important elements of this story:

I never heard my Father utter a profanity, blasphemy, or sworn word in my life. He just did not, even in the most trying of circumstances. He was, of course, "tried" many times in his life, and he did have one common response to some occasions. He would utter a resounding "shhhht," the intensity and duration signaling the measure of his displeasure. He could be, at times, also impatient with those not possessing his plowing, hoeing, and milking skills or, we might imagine, driving.

Mom told a thousand times of the occasion of her initial driving lesson. I believe it occurred in the Chevrolet "coupe" Dad had just obtained and, as her story would have it, driving down some dirt road, she inadvertently ran through a "mud puddle," splashing the probably clean and shined Chevy. Dad, she reported, let out a noticeable "shhht," and inquired as to, "Why she had to do that"? Mom's response was to pull over, end that lesson, and vow to never learn to drive. She showed him!

This was always Mom's story, and Dad never disputed it. With its many tellings, I do not recall Mom expressing anything other than vindication for her position nor do I recall her second-guessing her decision to end those lessons. I know she never again attempted to learn to drive.

The result was, however, that she became trapped into dependency upon Dad to take her anywhere she wished to go and, for most of her life, he did not wish to go when and where she wished.

I just cannot imagine Mom believing that becoming Dad's wife would separate her from her family and church. If she could have envisioned that possibility, I wonder what her choice would have been. Separation came, however, almost at the outset, and was surely set into stone, when we moved to McMinn County, some 40 miles further from her home. She had made that frivolous choice to give up on the driving lessons, but at the price of an increasing distance between her new home, the Mincys, Dad's church activities, and her "home place," family, and friends.

Driving aside, she settled into home life, which included cooking three meals a day on the wood stove, washing all clothes on a scrub board set up in a galvanized tub, and heating the water, weather permitting, in a large cast iron pot, outside. Starch would be added by hand into the hot water, along with a little "bluing," to add sparkle to Dad's white shirts. An outside clothes-line and Mother Nature were the drier, and a prediction of her tendencies greatly influenced which day would be wash day. The heavy, cast "irons," heated on top of the kitchen stove, were rotated in use, during the course of an ironing session; washing and ironing could rarely be completed in one day. She canned all the goods available in the summer for food in the winter (I recall, when I was three or four years old, going with Mother up the road to a neighbor's house and watching them work all day, chopping cabbage for "kraut", in a cooperative effort). She helped prepare pork hams and shoulders after the "hogs were killed," just to mention a few of the daily highlights in the life of Mrs. Homer F. I am quite sure she had to do all this up until the day Homer F. Jr. was born, January 12, 1930.

Mom's lament was always that the "Mincys (next door) just took over Homer Franklin." I believe this view must be tempered by acknowledging that little Homer, being breast fed, was at least cuddled several times a day, for some time. Further, as a practical matter, I cannot envision my grandparents, aunt, or uncle changing many diapers or washing any of them. It is a fact that Uncle George and Aunt Olive, for the rest of their lives, loved and admired Homer, and I think, in some ways, saw him almost as their own. Neither ever had children, and Homer was as close to that as they would ever know. They were always loving and supportive of Betty and me (very much so), but Homer was the first, was "Homer Franklin Jr.," and was special. That said, I think it likely that as Homer started to grow, the Mincys just came to be more possessive, bossy, perhaps interfering, and certainly opinionated regarding his "raising." It would have been their nature to share freely with all those traits.

Homer remembers Mother commenting early on that the "Mincys acted as if they had more than they did," and I am sure, regardless of any act, that it soon became evident the family was in trouble. The year Homer was born, with the Great Depression getting a full head of steam, they were unable to pay their bills, and, in 1934, the year I was born, the farms were all sold at auction on the steps of the Roane County Courthouse. This meant that, in addition to washing, ironing, cooking, and attending to children's needs. and religious activities every weekend, Mom had to contend with the possible effect financial failure might have on her family. I cannot imagine that she had any background, training, or preparation for this situation. She most likely, along with her sisters, had grown up in a home where the women did women's work, and the men took care of men's work. That would have included taking care of the financial aspects of running their family's affairs. How, then, could she have sat down at the kitchen table and entered into a practical discussion with Dad regarding what they should do or not do in their new-found circumstances? Dad and his family likely had few ideas themselves other than whatever flowed from the hand-to-mouth, day to day struggle.

It is as good a time as any, to relate now the practical side of growing up under these circumstances. I have already told of, from Dad's perspective, our trip down the "trail of tears" and often, tongue not so firmly in cheek, have added my personal flavor to the tale. It seemed we were always poor, had it tough, and struggled to get by. Homer reminds me, correctly so, that from our rock bottom days until Dad went to work at Oak Ridge was only about five years. Yes, those were rough times. However, he (more so than little me) states that the Kingston years for him seemed normal, and he recalls suffering no deprivation. After Dad left the farm and worked first at Oak Ridge, then, soon, for the McMinn Supply Co., he had a regular income, albeit a rather modest one. So, taken as an entire life, we have been blessed, and those few years after we "lost it all" were a drop in the bucket, to the sum of it all.

To Mom, however, who must be credited most of all for holding family life together as normally as possible, each new indignity must have been a bitter and disappointing pill to swallow. She almost immediately found herself unable to pay bills, buy accustomed and needed family supplies, or know what the future held. She was apart from her large and close family. To support Dad in his church efforts, she suddenly was thrust into the "Baptist" arena and was faced with the dilemma of either fighting them or joining them; she did neither but, rather, chose to just enter into the work, doing all that was asked and more. However, she refused to join the Baptist and held out on that issue until many years later.

Through the thirties, in spite of it all, Mom settled into the routine of homemaker, wife, mother, neighbor; I came along in 1934, followed by Elizabeth Alice (Betty) in 1937. There was never any "household help," and each child just added that much to the burden of managing it all. If I have made my grandparents, aunt, and uncle out to be ogres of the worst sort, shame on me. They were far from it. Grandmother was warm and friendly to Mom and all of us. Uncle George was always outgoing and gracious and their home, as long as we were in Kingston, was a place to go and a place of close relatives, almost next door. They collectively were just sort of rough around the edges, Grandma and Granddad were getting pretty feeble, and Aunt Olive and Sophia were just prone to be rather short and critical, at times.

As the decade drew to a close, we were finally evicted from our first home, and Mom faced the facts of separation from her family, a step down into poorer housing, and our being broke and in debt.

In early January, 1939, Mom, Dad, and the three of us made the first of what would be several moves into different homes. This one, as mentioned before, was to McMinn County, Riceville community, and to a place we always called the "Brown Place." Again, the only reasons Homer and I can conclude (for this location) is that McMinn County was the prime focus of Dad's "Watkins business," and during his visits to this area, he had probably become aware of this particular location being available. Betty and I plead ignorance, as she was two and I was five at the time of the move.

I could go into great detail about all the trivia of this new home and repeat it for each location we were to endure for the next five or so years, but I described these houses through Dad's eyes and, rest assured, they assumed no softer image through Mom's. What is significant was the impact this move probably had on Mom. In Kingston, she did not get to visit her Mom and other siblings as often as she wished but, at worst, she was six or seven miles from them, did get back to her family church on occasion, and the proximity was real, if not always apparent.

The move to Riceville severed that proximity, as we were 40 or so miles from her "home," had no telephone, and even irregular visits were, for the most part, a thing of the past. Cut off from her lifelong support group, to the extent she had one, and facing a rather dreary future, she was left no choice but to dig in and make the most of it. It is at this point that I do begin to remember our home, the circumstances, and Mom's attitude and reactions, and also began a lifelong respect and appreciation for those traits that made her the "special Mom" that she was.

It cannot be overstated, in light of today's opportunities and conveniences, how demanding, tiring, and challenging mere survival was for us and, of course, for the millions who were in similar circumstances, or worse.

Mom always had a droll, understated sense of humor. In those days, and in those places, life was fairly simple, the world was "out there"; what was worth discussing was recent and nearby "happenings." Humor was observed, imagined, and expressed in whatever manner fitted the personality involved. So it was with her. Actually, all Mom's family, her brothers and sisters, and Grandmother Hedgecock to the extent I remember, shared similar inflections of speech, speech patterns, and style of conversation. Generally, they spoke softly in a quiet, reserved, conspiratorial style, seeming to convey they were not sure they wanted to be overheard or that almost any telling was told in confidence. The laughs were more chuckles, they were good listeners, they were always positive and friendly, and words were not wasted. Anything I credit to Mom, henceforth, must be remembered with those descriptions and caveats in mind.

An event at the Brown Place illustrates the point. One weekend, Uncle George and Aunt Olive came to visit us; Aunt Sophia may have been along. I just do not remember her. On Sunday, we "men" all went to church at the Riceville Baptist Church, and the "women" stayed home to have dinner (lunch) ready for us when we got back. Upon our return, as we approached the house, it became apparent some disaster had struck, as a large crowd of neighbors was gathered in the yard, milling around.

Our house had caught fire; either sparks hitting the old, wooden shingle roof, or an exposed spot between the "flue" and the roof had ignited the roof, which had quickly started to burn. The only water supply was our cistern, and the nearest neighbors were several hundred yards away, down the road in either direction. There was nothing Mom and her guests could have done, and I have no memory of neighbors noticing the problem in time; my memory has always been, handed down by Mom, that as the blaze picked up steam, it started to rain, and rained in sufficient strength to quickly extinguish the blaze. A hole was burned in the roof, and rain was coming into the kitchen, but the house was saved. To Mom, this always illustrated to her the power and presence of God in times of need. This part, however, was not the part she always took the most delight in telling:

Aunt Olive, a large, heavy, slow moving woman, was at work preparing "deviled eggs" for lunch, and when the commotion started, she had her apron full of eggs in progress. Reportedly, she dashed out of the house, took in the tragedy about to befall them all, and with a resounding, "Whooo, Whoop, Whoooo......!!!!, ran aimlessly around the front yard, waving her apron up and down, scattering boiled eggs in every direction. Such was the aftermath we men took in, as we pulled in from church.

Homer recalls moving around, unobtrusively, picking up all the eggs he could recover, washing them off and recycling them for dinner. Mom, for years, took great delight recalling her sister-in-law's fearful flight; it was sort of score one for Mom versus the Mincys.

A "still-frame" of memory that has always lingered from the Brown place, and one I have always used as a "phrase of poverty," was during a large snow, either that winter or in 1940-41; Mom gathered up a pail of snow and made us "snow ice cream." The pitiful irony is that as we partook of this rarity of nature's delicacies, we all hovered around the fireplace, trying to keep/get warm. That was the only heat in the house, and I remember it as drafty and cold at best; freezing at worst. "Shivering around the fireplace, eating snow ice cream" has been my oft used whine of childhood days. The underlying truth is that Mom always used what she had, or could conjure up to relieve the tedium of day-to-day existence.

We moved almost yearly for the next five years; the scene, circumstances or challenges for Mom varied little-not much to cook, not enough to wear, not many conveniences to help make it bearable. I have told about our houses, household life and hardships; it just is more joy to remember the person than the places, and I am just going to ramble around and talk about Mom, the person.

This fine lady did have a temper, and would let her displeasure be known; needless to say, she often admonished us that to "spare the rod was to spoil the child," and I think she did not leave this world with her conscience bothering her in that respect. As a benevolent but responsible shepherd, she tried to keep us moving in the right direction....by whatever means it took.

She was not always benign to what she took as slights by others, either. I recall one Sunday morning at Union Chapel, the regular teacher of my group of (perhaps six year old) children, Mrs. Floyd Hutsell, was late arriving. Mom had taken us on and was moving along very well, with perhaps two-thirds of the time for Sunday school having passed, when Mrs. Hutsell arrived. Walking non-stop down the center isle of the little church (we were being instructed in the back left corner) she called to us, "Come along, little 'uns."

I think we all took off, leaving Mom stranded and ignored; she said at home that day, and many days thereafter, that she was "spittin' mad" and inclined to "tell her (Mrs. Hutsell) off, right there."

Mom could sense sin. She could surmise it about to happen, she knew if it had happened, and she would warn you about the temptations of it, even if one had not thought about it, before it happened. Homer or I could never smoke anything: "rabbit tobacco," the real weed, newspaper, or anything combustible that would arouse our curiosity, without her getting a whiff, figuratively. I can recall playing around down in the field on the Layman's place with a neighbor, Lucille Green. We had not progressed to the birds and the bees but more likely were creeping toward butterflies and beetles, when Mom would come charging from hundreds of yards away, admonishing Lucille to "get on home," and me to get on about my business, as if I had business when I was eight. Lucille, Betty and I could be playing down at the spring house, out of sight and a couple of hundred yards away and, if too much time had passed, here would come Mom to send us on our separate ways; she would just make sure we did not have time to even *think* of trouble.

Another of Mom's memorable, explosive moments involved Lucille. She lived down the road with her father and brother, R.C. Her mother was dead and it was a sad family, as however bad we had it, they perhaps had it worse. Mr. Green worked for the W.P.A., and times were tough for them, too. Mom was always trying to get Lucille and R.C. to go to church.

Mom's wedding; (at Grandmother Alice's), 1929

Left to right: Uncle Ernest, Dad, Mom, Helen Smith, Edith Smith, Aunt Ada; standing, front: Wayne Hedgecock

Mom, Dad, Betty
The house, on US Route 70, where I was born

Eva Estelle Hedgecock Mincy 173

Eva Estelle Hedgecock Mincy

Virgil and Eva
1982, at Betty and Ed's

Left to right: Aunt Ada,
Mom, Betty, Karen,
Angela, Ed Axley,
Uncle Frank

One week, Mom got Lucille to promise she would go to church, if she (Mom) would "do up" Lucille's dress. She did. I can still see Mom washing and ironing (with those old cast iron, kitchen stove heated implements) that little, white dress, trimmed in yellow, with a sash that pulled around and tied in the back. Lucille had wanted it starched, "stiff as a board." She picked up the dress on Friday and solemnly promised she would go with us to church, Sunday.

Alas, on Saturday afternoon, Lucille (with some other people) skipped by the front of our house, up the dirt road, on the way to her cousin Imogene Burke's house, to go into town for fun and excitement. You guessed it; she was all spiffed up in her newly starched and ironed pinafore. Mom left no doubt that she would have "pulled her hair out, if she could have caught her."

Every year that passed found each of us children a year older; the grades flew by, teachers changed, and the expectations of behavior and deportment were continually raised. On the one hand, we went through times when Mom and Dad could only be described as poor tenant farmers. On the other, our parents' expectations were that we learn, behave and contribute. The grade cards were carefully scrutinized and usually signed by Mom. She was not a troublemaker, but an interested participant, with the teacher, in our progress. At home, she read to us, with the "bible story book" being the most common source. At church, we were persuaded (i.e., forced) to be involved.

I remember, starting down at Union Chapel, with Mom playing the pump organ and Dad perhaps coaching from the side, Homer, Betty and I getting up and singing little "choruses": *"One door and only one, and yet the sides are two; I'm on the inside, on which side are you?"* and others. I still shudder from the memory of, at Lakeview, getting up and trying to sing *America the Beautiful*. It is in a key I could not do then or now, but this did not seem to have been worked out beforehand: *"America, America, God, shed your Grace on thee........."* The only comparison is the little guy from "Our Gang," who would sing in his squeaky, cracking voice. A little later, with my crude guitar accompaniment, Homer, Herbert Marshall and I did a Carl Story version of *"Rocking on the Ocean Waves"*; I am still unsure how that slipped by Mom and Dad's censorship, considering their view of non-traditional music.

All this is to simply say that Mom (as well as Dad) did everything in her power to help us rise above the plight we may have been in at that time; she knew the worth of the mind and the spirit, and, I think, felt that though she might not, we stood a chance of escaping that pervasive, vice-grip of poverty. We were poor; we just did not have to think poor.

Suffice to say that, from "up on the hill" through "up at Layman's," Mom's life, activities, duties, and circumstances changed little. She worked hard, had to "make do" with little in the way of creature comforts, tried to direct the growth and development of three children, and continued to show by word and example her faith and belief in God and his teachings. "Up on the Hill" was rock bottom, but duty on the Layman farms was only marginally better. We had a little more security, but not the means to cope with any disaster or be more than dirt poor tenant farmers.

It must be clearly understood that the Laymans were fine people and benevolent employers. The subtlety at work was that Mom (and Dad) had been independent all their lives, as had their parents, and becoming little more than servants took some adjustments. I think Dad was more stoic about his circumstances than Mom was hers. She was quicker to notice a perceived slight or imagined insult and just "chaffed at the bit" at times. Being increasingly worn down by the totality of the work load took its toll.

By the time we were given responsibility for the "Up at Layman's farm," that toll had become almost too much to bear. The work was never done: cows had to be milked twice daily, seven days a week, 52 weeks each year. If any of us, i.e., Mom, Dad, Homer, or I missed a turn, something was left undone. If something was left undone, the "milk" inspector might show up, report negatively on the Layman farm, and Mrs. Clio Layman would usually make a visit and give us a performance review (rightly so). Mom's health seemed to suffer increasingly; she always seemed prone to respiratory problems, part real and some, perhaps, imagined. I say imagined, in the sense that she had watched two brothers die of tuberculosis, another suffer years from it, and had been told she "had a spot on her lungs" somewhere in her young life.

She would do simple "breathing exercises" and try to address her health fears, but much was likely caused by stress, overwork and exposure. I just remember her often being not well. I never remember a lack of her presence, support, love, or concern; more frequently, it just seemed she was sick, which would certainly cause us concern. On the health note, an interesting sidebar: Mom always took "patent medicines." You name them: Retonga, Scalfs Indian River Tonic, G.M.D., and Hadacol, among others. The claims always tackled whatever Mom believed afflicted her, and I suppose none ever did her harm. These names, however, not only on the airwaves and newspapers, but in our home, became household words. To children, the business logistics of where these various bottles "came from" was of no interest; they were just, mysteriously, from "out in the world" somewhere.

It was with a jolt that, in 1992 after moving to the South Bend area, I noticed, on the side of an old restaurant in Mishawaka, a mural covering the entire building: "Doc Pierce's Golden Medical Discovery. (GMD) For the blood, lungs and liver." As it happened, old Doc Pierce had apparently conjured up this concoction and distributed it straight to Mom, down in Tennessee, (along with the rest of the world) during those years long ago. Further, researching family matters in the last few years, I came across a "newsletter" dated several years ago, that described early community activities in the Dogwood Shores community, near Dad's birthplace and only a few miles from mine. It reads: "In the early 1930s, a man by the name of Scalf camped in a tent in the spring and fall to gather herbs for his Scalf's Indian River tonic. He also hunted squirrels. He came to the Brabson Bend for four or five years." Truly, these "Wizards" have been found hiding behind their curtains of mystery.

Church was a constant, usually interrupted only by weather or some other reasonable circumstance; going to church then always meant walking, and long distances, at that. When we lived "up on the hill" and "down at Layman's" we attended Union Chapel, and Mom pitched in wherever needed-playing the organ, teaching, singing, and working. After we moved to the upper Layman farm, we began attending McMahan Calvary Baptist, which was a long walk. Again, Mom, as well as Dad, worked as needed. Going to church meant more than her desire to worship: washing, ironing, mending what clothes we had, in order that we were clean and respectable, enduring that long walk, and having dinner for us, when we returned. If she did not make it now and then, small wonder. Keep in mind, during these times of her serving in the Methodist and Baptist churches, she was still a card carrying Cumberland Presbyterian and proud of it. Mom was with Dad, supporting him each step of the way, during the Lakeview experience. I do not recall any hint of rejecting her services, although both denominations may have officially frowned upon those of different denominations serving in certain capacities.

The move to live with Mrs. Bennett Gwinn, sometime in 1944, was perhaps a Godsend; we were getting nowhere as tenant farmers, and Mom was just worked down. Mrs. Gwinn lived across the field from the Layman place, and we had become acquainted with her, as neighbors. She lived in a much larger two-story frame house that was quite nice, sitting on eight to 10 acres of land—plenty of space for a large garden, and to graze a cow. I think we also raised a hog or two while we were there.

Dad, having decided to leave the farm and having obtained a job at the huge "Oak Ridge" project, arranged for us to move in with Mrs. Gwinn and share her home. Bennett was rarely there, as he worked in Chattanooga at the Dupont powder plant, and their twin sons, Reed and Creed, were away, serving in the Navy. It sort of worked out that we moved into one side of the house and Mrs. Gwinn (Mae) took the other. This was the nicest place I had ever lived and provided a breather for us all.

The only problem was Dad's being away most of the time, in the beginning. This meant Mom had to do something she had never done before—shopping in Athens for groceries or whatever was needed. Remember, we had no car and even if we had, Mother could not drive. We all remember Mother starting on that three plus mile walk into Athens, during this period, and sometimes walking all the way; other times someone would pick her up....occasionally, strangers.

The most common return transportation would be a taxi; or Mr. Land, with whom we did most of our grocery shopping, would bring Mother home with her little box of groceries. As a lifelong logistics professional, I often pondered how this was profitable for Mr. Land; I usually concluded he was just a nice man helping a nice woman. Those were, indeed, different times.

Mom, during this period, had time to "visit" with Mrs. Gwinn when she (Mrs. Gwinn) was home. She was permitted to borrow Mrs. Gwinn's radio and gained a slight addiction to "Stella Dallas," "Our Gal Sunday," and "Helen Trent," the soaps of that day. The biggest negative came during Dad's bout with pneumonia…..one that was nearly fatal. Dr. Arrants intervention with sulfa drugs and Mom never leaving his side were what pulled him through but, during this time, I think we all grew up a little.

I recall it was spring and, before Dad had strength to work, it was time to plant a garden. We got someone to "plow up" the garden patch and, with nothing but a little "push plow" and our hoes, Mom directed and Betty and I planted the basic stuff. I remember her being warm with her praise, calling me her "little man." I have a picture or two of that scene: Mom, Betty and I standing in the garden space, I with a straw hat for effect, commemorating that spring planting.

You will recall the circumstances of our moving to the Ensminger place; I am sure Dad thought this would work out well for all concerned, but it just did not. From Mom's perspective, she now had to deal with teen-age boys who were not always her "little men."

I will ever remember her imploring/scolding/pleading/ordering us to get out and address any of the many things needing doing, with such admonishments as, "idle hands are the Devil's workshop" or "a little sleep, a little slumber, a little folding of the hands to sleep." I never quite got that one. Homer will admit that during this period, he was not the most cooperative pilgrim and was off to Texas to work the last two summers we lived there.

I think it was after the move "up on the hill II" that Mom regained some of her natural spunk and enthusiasm. The house itself was not much, certainly not as adequate as the Gwinn and Ensminger place. But it was hers! She could work on it, paint it, paper it, panel it, or not; it was her call. I think, even in these humble trappings, she began to regain a sense of independence and dignity that had been forced beneath the surface for almost fifteen years (Since our property in Roane County had been lost). She was home at last, and she never left it until the day she died, 30-plus years later.

It was there she saw her children complete school, launch careers, get married, have children, and thus, give her grandchildren. It was there she said good bye to her husband of 38 years. It was there, I think, she just, finally, felt at home.

Funny thing: When Dad died suddenly in 1967, Homer and I rushed in for the couple of days we grudgingly could spare and were sure we had to make some life changing decisions for Mom, given her inability to drive and the apparent, to us, problems of maintaining this "home place." She sent us packing. Sure, Betty and Ed became caregivers in many important ways, but she survived, happily, for sixteen more years, quite independent, content, and at peace.

As an adult, it was from this base that I remember more events of significance that occurred during the teenage and college years, and it was there that I conversed with Mom for the 27 years from the time I left home for good, until she was taken from us. There is where the adult memories originated.

Where do we go from here? We talked about her cooking and her insecurities about it; however, she almost always had something special when I would return home from school. It would seem to violate every rule of dinner etiquette, but it seemed she always allowed me a sample of the banana pudding, blackberry custard pie, cobblers of all kinds, cookies...whatever the dessert of the day was...before I hit the chores of the afternoon. Mom's cooking was just fine.

Berry picking: Mom had picked blackberries all her life; it was a source of fresh fruit in the brief season, but more important, sources of jam, jelly, and canned berries for the winter. That was the given. I have picked blackberries and hated every minute of it. Occurring in hot June or July weather, the conditions were always extreme. They (blackberries) grow wild in patches of dense vines and are punctuated by razor sharp thorns that are a part of each vine. Any place that has blackberries has chiggers, ticks, snakes, and wasp or hornet nests. "June bugs" are always at their most active at this time and are all over the place. At any moment, and usually every two or three, one will buzz out in your face with a noise like an angry rattle snake. (There were no rattle snakes in our part of the woods, but you get the point.) Given the choice between starving and picking berries, starving loses only by a nose. Mom declared to her dying day that she loved it.

To see her prepare was something else. She, throughout her life, protected her skin from the sun; that skin, surprise, surprise, was baby smooth in her eighties. This protection started with the widest brimmed straw hat she could find or, in absence of that, a large bonnet. Then, she proceeded to dress herself in an assortment of garments: dresses, aprons, overalls, sweaters….layer after layer, until I believe she felt a coating of armor against every evil lurking to thwart the task. Her gloves were usually a pair of old socks or worn men's cotton work gloves; the backs and palms of the hands were protected but the fingers were free for picking. She would do justice to the most extreme street lady you can imagine and thought nothing of your appraisal of her appearance. "I love to pick berries." End of story.

This home, sitting atop a hill above TN Route 30 west of Athens, was in the middle of an assortment of neighbors. The Edgemons and Hutsells below us were prosperous and nice people, but, in general, the others surrounding us were an assortment of bootleggers, ner-do-wells, and belligerents or at best, people just struggling to get by as we had been (and still were). Mom ministered to, returned evil with good, ignored, extolled her faith and, I think in time, just came to be respected as being above it all. In a rough neighborhood, I do not recall her ever being robbed, vandalized, abused, or taken advantage of, even when she lived alone. Children my age when we were there, who grew up with parents who, at times, might have harassed us over something, have approached Homer, Betty or me to give testimony to their respect and memory of Mom; this has happened over and over.

I was married five years after we moved there and being gone, my relationship and communications with Mom came through increasingly fewer visits and more letters and phone calls. The pattern was always the same:

"Have you found a church home, yet?" From North Carolina, Memphis, Chattanooga, Columbus, Ohio, and New Jersey: "No Mom, but we have visited a place or two." From NC, later: "Yes, Mom." From Texas and Pittsburgh: "I'm looking." I wish I could tell her now: "Sure have."

Of course she always asked about the children: "How are the little darlings?" She would ask by name and want details of their lives. She would seem to lament that she could not see them and seemed so interested in doing so. For some reason, she would rarely visit us. Time seemed to have reversed whatever psychology governed her spirit, as one (the only) time she and Dad visited us in North Carolina (probably about '64–'65), Dad, in an aside, said to me: "You know, I would like to come more often, but your mother just won't come." Guess in some way she was paying him back for all those years she had to stay home from her family.

I must relate her first (and only) plane ride, which coincided with the birth of Debra, my third born. Mom had agreed to come up to New Jersey to help us with this situation, with the visit to be rather loose, depending on the actual delivery date (which was October 11, 1961). This must have been some experience! First, the ride itself, from Knoxville to Newark, New Jersey, with a stop in Washington, DC, was on a DC4 (I think), a four engine propeller craft that was loud, shaky, and flew at an altitude causing it to just bore into any bad or rough weather. Turbulence and popping ears were a given.

She hopped right on and as would be her wont, kept a little diary of her trip. Most of it survived: A little note pad in her handwriting details her experiences and, better than any words I could ever put together, tells us of her. It is so Mom: poetic, mystic, serene, humorous, and woven through the fabric of it all is her obvious faith in and love of God.

"…(to New Jersey) I get glimpses of the mountains…we're nearing the end of our flight; just brief glimpses of earth. Houses look like tiny blocks shinning in the sun. The green fields look refreshing. Mountains, valleys, streams…breathtaking. Still a tint of yellow leaves left makes the mountains peaks look like giant bunches of yellow mums. Going over Smokies…believe I saw a ghost town. The beautiful valley, farm lands, cities, small villages look like one beautiful jig saw puzzle. The plane is rock-

ing...don't just know what. Guess we are getting ready to land; an old guy snapped a picture of a lovely stewardess....don't they ever give up? Heh heh." Missing pages

"Left Newark 8:45; stewardess took tickets. Plane now going around runway, warming up. Flew over large city. Up above the clouds and a bit frightening. The sun is so bright.looks as if one could walk on the clouds. Don't care to try it just yet. Now I can see city below; fog is lifting. Yawning acres of beautiful green fields. Closed off again, but okay. God's sun is shining; a sight indescribable; makes one feel very near the creator. The stewardess asked, "Mrs. Mincy, do you want milk, tea or coffee with cakes? (Note: Mom's disdain for coffee approached that of "sin") Of course I took tea." After quite a while above the clouds, I can see a river and city; now it looks like a 20 foot snow banked in high peaks; but for the temperature, which is uncomfortably warm, it is easy to imagine you were at the North Pole, but, I have not seen a single dog sled. I wonder why we should ever even entertain a single little doubt that a creator made such a wonderful world just by speaking and then made man in His own image and gave his Son to redeem us from our sin; I can safely rest in the shelter of his love because I am persuaded that neither death, nor life, heights nor depths, angels nor principalities; things present nor things to come can separate us from the love of God, which is in Christ. Although we are high above a lot of things, I am sure our human natures are still with us. The couple across the aisle are getting their enjoys, smoking...I am almost suffocated. Recon I'll just have to grin and endure.

We're riding above the clouds. I hope the clouds will lift before landing; it must be pretty soon. Okay, now I can see a city below; have been flying an hour above the clouds. It is now 9:55; landed in Washington. Thanks to the good Lord above. The clouds are beautiful but I sortie like good old terra firma. There were just three: Two men and I left on the plane.

Washington is really something from the air. Could see the Capital, Washington Monument, Lincoln Memorial, and the Potomac River. The engines are warming; will soon be in the air on the last leg to home sweet home.......from here, can see a large boat or barge on the Potomac. Now taking off. Stewardess said we would be in Knoxville in two hours, 10 minutes. See the Washington monument again; now we have left the ground again. Right over the Potomac…higher, higher; the sun is shinning brightly over water; almost blinding. Seems we will soon be shut off from earth by clouds. The leaves are breathtakingly beautiful. Painted by the Master Artist. Now we are riding on snowy wings of clouds, again. No wonder Jesus said he would come in clouds of Glory, because on the top side of them, they really are majestic. If I could just find the right words to explain, at one place it looks like a canyon; just heaps and heaps of clouds. Now the clouds are in heaps; looks like huge piles of snow the day after. Now there is an opening; see earth again.

This is my last page; looks like I'll have to turn my attention to something else; as much as I hate to put forth the effort, I think I will have to remove my coat; so hot. Lunch again. I haven't begun to get………"

And, on the back cover: *"They that wait upon the Lord shall renew their strength; they shall mount up with wings as eagles; they shall run and not be weary; they shall walk and not faint. Isa."*

Just Mom, talking like Mom talked.

A couple of insights surfaced on that trip. First, Mom expressed her disinterest in television, early on. I am not sure if she had a set at that time, but she rather contemptuously let us know she thought it a great waste of time. It became apparent early on, however, that her curiosity soon grew.

During the day of October 11, 1961, June was probably beginning to feel labor pains; she was scheduled to see our family doctor, Dr. Trachtenberg, who told her "no, nothing was happening, so go on about your business." That business actually included a shopping trip to what passed as our nearest mall, where we bought a bike for Pam. Through dinner, June's discomfort increased, but the doctor had spoken, so Mom, Pam, Tina, and I went about our business and practically ignored June. Late evening, I finally observed that poor June was almost out of it in her corner of the living room and quickly discerned in my non-trained way that her labor pains were not minutes apart, but almost constant.

Suddenly, in a panic, I sprang into action, called the doctor's office, and set about the rushed trip to the hospital. Mother, of course, was to be in charge during this phase of the program. You guessed it: she was so engrossed in the action of the evening on that little tube that I could not get her attention to give her a final briefing. So much for her TV story.

The other truth that came to light dealt with her claim that she could not sleep: "Just didn't sleep a wink last night," she would say. Not long after the rushed trip to Middlesex County Hospital, where I am sure Debra was delivered by a nurse on duty, we were home and the universal routine with newborns set in: frequent feeding, crying, walking the floor, and, truly, some of us not being able to sleep a wink. Mom? I don't believe the "crack of dawn" could have jarred her loose from blowing those Zs and, after a night or two, we just gave up hoping she would hop up and take her turn. She needed her rest, after all that TV watching.

After Dad died, I think she sort of settled into a routine of study, worship, service and family interests. When Dad was called to pastor the Valley View Baptist church in the fifties, Mom finally decided to join the Baptists. It would seem neat if she had done so in his church and let him baptize her, but she actually joined the East Athens Baptist, where Betty and Ed attended, and was baptized there. I think her point of view was to simply make it a surprise, and more importantly, make this final step toward truly joining him in a supporting role, as they worked together in this little church. I believe she felt limited, either in her imagination or her perception of Baptist doctrine, still belonging to another denomination; she did want to serve. In her heart, she was still a Cumberland Presbyterian and proud of it; she was most sure that the "water" did not change anything.

During her last few years, she would go to her "home place" and stay with Aunt Ada for the winter. They would hunker down and just soak up the love and fellowship of each other, nieces, nephews, cousins and, of course, Aunt Ruby. Uncle Frank had died and Aunt Ada was alone; I guess it could be said she had returned to her Promised Land, after wandering 40 years in the wilderness.

Without Dad and with her transportation always provided by Betty and Ed, she attended East Athens Baptist Church with them, where she worked constantly. She, for many years, taught a ladies' Sunday school class. In fact, August 7, 1983, Mom had taught her class and, as she would do on occasion, risen from her pew down front and offered a few words of testimony following the invitation at the close of the service. She was always engaged in conversation and usually among the last to leave any gathering. That morning, Ed was at the rear doors of the sanctuary and, hearing a noise, turned and saw that Mom had collapsed. She died, suddenly, at that spot, doing what she always enjoyed most: worshiping and enjoying the fellowship of fellow travelers. Perhaps, as had been Enoch, she was just "taken."

There are a few thoughts from her that must be preserved: Mom answered a rather lengthy questionnaire many years ago, as part of a project Karen (Axley) had undertaken in college. One specific question was: "What do you remember of their (her children's) baby days and childhood." From Mom: ".....as for their baby days, that indeed would make a book. We will not go into that. I will say it was a great responsibility as well as privilege, and am happy to say very fulfilling and rewarding. What greater privilege could any Christian woman ask than the opportunity to be co-laborers with God in helping to rear and train children for eternity?"

What did she consider her most important achievements? "I can truthfully say, if I have accomplished anything for Jesus and in his name and for his sake, that would be the most important achievement of my life."

A poem she dearly loved: (and may have written)

Heralds of Spring

*When farmers turn the furrows deep and cattle graze on yonder hill, Turtle doves build homes in cedar trees; we **rest assured** that spring is near.*

*When March's siren sounds through trees and lilac fragrance is in the air, When come butterflies, wasps and honeybees, we **then believe** that spring is here.*

Then shouts are heard from hill and vale of happy youngsters, who've been set free,
From walls and books and teachers severe; it's then **we know** *that spring is here.*

Then, this final note: I knew Mom taught that class at East Athens Baptist and was vaguely aware of being told that, after her death, the class had been named for her. It may have been in the back of my mind, but I attached little significance to it, as I did not equate that honor to anything material or lasting.

A couple of years ago, I visited East Athens with Betty and Ed and, waiting for them, found myself alone in the assembly area of the adult education wing, with small class rooms all around me; I looked up, and beside me was a door leading into a room, clearly marked: "Eva Mincy Class." It was a shocking and moving moment; yes, her memory has permanence.

My next visit, Betty arranged for me to speak briefly to this class; many remembered Mom, and they seemed pleased to share my remarks. I told them a few things about her, with my emotions surfacing along the way.

I closed by telling them one thing I was sure they did not know and asked that they always remember it: **"Her name was Eva, pronounced Evie, with a short E."**

Early Days, School and the Learning Years

Samuel Langhorn Clemens, 1835-1910, grew up in the little Mississippi River town of Hannibal, Missouri. He became wealthy and famous; he traveled the world and, arguably, was America's greatest author. His reigning masterpiece(s) were works recalling his life as a "young boy," growing up in a small town, and tasting life's new experiences.

A nagging question comes to mind as to how Mark Twain's "childhood" days were different than yours and mine or, for that matter, those of Franklin Roosevelt (or Teddy), Bing Crosby, Abraham Lincoln, Joe Dimaggio, Susan B. Anthony, Marie Curie, or Billy Graham. What is childhood? If we suppose most of us remembered little until we were five or six and, by the time we were 14 or so, certainly did not call ourselves children, we are left with only about eight years before we tried to act like, or bluff ourselves into believing, we were adults. What did all of us do in those eight "childhood years"? Did Samuel Langhorn, all those above, or you and I do much that was really different? Did we not all walk, talk, eat, and sleep? Were we not happy, sad, afraid, and brave? Might we not have dreamed, schemed, fought, and sought? Overall, would it be fair to say that we tested the limits of our imaginations and environments, then went beyond them to the extent we could and get away with it….or survive? In the final analysis, might not the grandeur of the tale be the result, not of the tale itself, but the telling of it?

I want to tell of my early days and learning experiences from babyhood until manhood. I have considered this carefully, in light of the thoughtful evaluation I have just shared with you and understand that I probably should not arrange a book signing tour, just yet. I also believe this can be handled in a fair size chapter. I just do not concede that, at times, my heart beat less fast, my shame was less degrading, or my idle time less enjoyable than young Huck Finn's, or my croup any less a problem than Teddy Roosevelt's asthma.

You already know that the year I was born was the year we lost our earthly possessions. What a treat for my parents that February morn: a difficult delivery, a cold winter day, another mouth to feed, and another day to mark off the calendar on the road to financial ruin. The records indicate that at 6:26 A.M., Friday, February 9, 1934, I was white, legitimate, and the son of a farmer and a housewife.

I guess things were bad all over: Mussolini had ordered all schoolteachers to wear uniforms; his next suggestion to the Pope was probably how cute it would be if Catholic school children wore them, also. Bonnie and Clyde, Pretty Boy Floyd, and Dillinger were all killed. A loaf of bread cost eight cents, and the Dow Jones Average was 98. Life expectancy was 59.7 years, but it was only Friday and, by the first of the week, my chances had probably improved.

Mother always told me I was a difficult delivery, and, throughout my life, when I have tried to find headwear for my size 7 7/8 head, I have understood why. In some way, the difficult delivery seemed to endear me to her. She was a sweet, caring, giving, loving, and special mom. I have related her attributes before but, all other disasters aside, my entry into life's sorrows was shielded by the loving arms of caring parents.

I do not recall the birth, did not read at 18 months, and Mensa did not come calling, led by celestial guidance. I was told my grandparents, aunt, and uncle, who lived almost next door, did not "take me over" as reportedly they had Homer. This perhaps overstates it a little, but Mom always resented the fact that her in-laws were so intrusive into the early care and management of her first-born. If I were denied their initial oversight and affection, it was perhaps more my lack of infantile charm than my Mother's aggressive stance. In any event, I felt a special bond with her; it could be that she saw me as "her own" for the first time.

My experiences during the Kingston days are more images, vignettes, and scattered memories than specific recollections of continued occurrences. For instance, I cannot recall being aware of the terrible financial burden that my parents were bearing during this period. I vaguely remember the "peach sheds" and the fact that we grew peaches. I remember images of attending church at New Midway but not of Dad preaching. I have memories of my grandparents, but I am not sure whether they come from pictures or personal contact; I do not recall a conversation with them, although they lived almost next door.

I do remember having the croup several times. Although these bouts were very real, they went away by the time I was five or six. Having been a parent many times over, I can just imagine the angst my parents endured during those occurrences as, in truth, they probably had no clue of what to do that would have been effective. I was subjected to homemade "tents," under which I was made to breathe melted Watkins "menthol-camphor ointment"; I was given liberal doses of almost 100 proof Watkins red liniment in water. I was given a spoonful of kerosene, at times, to cause me to throw up. My chest was greased with the menthol-camphor, over which hot clothes would be applied. All this time, of course, I could not breathe. I know of no logical reason any of this would work, but my parents tried feverously, each time, to bring me relief. These treatments were awful, as you might imagine; in a speech designed to be humorous a while back, I commented that I finally figured out if I did not have the croup, I did not get the "treatments"; so, I just quit having the croup.

I very well recall a few instances of sticking nails in a bare foot; not a little nick, but straight in, full bore. Seems this usually occurred when I would walk bare foot, of course, around the old peach packing shed, with its wealth of boards, timbers, and exposed nails. Tetanus may have been known, but treatment for exposure was not, by our family, who felt liberal applications of turpentine would heal all ills. I have been blessed by the presence of that guardian angel over and over, beginning even then.

I remember hobos, tramps, or just poor souls moving on, stopping by the house asking for a handout or a meal. We lived, remember, on what is now U.S. 70; then, this was one of the few east-west roads. Mom would never give handouts (we had no "outs") but would try to find a chore for the person at our door to do in return for a meal. Some would not work for food, but I do remember a few who would. I can still see some hungry pilgrim cleaning and scraping the rock steps from our front porch down to the highway, then, sitting on the porch eating his food. Mom probably was giving him a sermon, as he tried to digest the cornbread, vegetables, and beans. It is rather telling that we were losing it all, yet, still held out a hand to those who were also in need.

The rock quarry around the bend was a constant factor in our lives. This quarry, operated by the county, was going all the time of my memory. I can find no record of its creation in any of the property actions of the period, although there were transactions for road and power line right-of-ways. It would seem to have been carved out of our properties; whatever the route, it was there. Operated by county prisoners who were guarded by armed personnel, the threat factors were twofold: constant blasting and runaway prisoners. A good blast would send some rocks our way, and I guess there had been escapes, with guns firing and dogs barking, to remind us of that threat. Seeming so big then, today, covered with kudzu vine, one has to look to find where it was.

All the problems, stress, and upheaval that we endured were not really key to my memories of those times; I had the luxury of a caring family and was protected from outside pressures. It was after we moved to Riceville, and later, that I was even aware that we just did not have what many others did.

I do remember much more about the Riceville home, named the "Brown Place" after the owner, although we were there only a year or so. To begin, I was almost five when we made this move, in January, 1939; in fact, the Kelsey boys next door, being older, would tease me by asking how old I was. My answer, "I am size" would amuse them, and they asked often until I learned to pronounce my "Fs" and grew a few front teeth. Dad taught me how to "hand" tobacco there, and I was quite proud of my graduation to helper, of sorts, around the farm. Most of the time, particularly during that summer, I did little but hang around, while the plowing and hoeing were done. I probably helped pick blackberries, but I doubt with much skill.

Mom, while outside working in the fields or garden, was always finding arrowheads and Civil War artifacts. At one time, we had quite a collection of "minnie balls" and other relics, as this was probably the scene of an encampment during the War of Northern Aggression. What I could never comprehend, then, was what a "Silver War" was or what it was about. No one seemed able to explain it to me in a way I could understand.

There was the time of the Christmas program at the Riceville School auditorium, when Dad had gotten a new "little red wagon" for Homer and me. I believe this was, actually, a Riceville Baptist Church affair, being held at the school, but, in any event, my family and I were there. An elaborate plan had been hatched for Santa to deliver this at a climatic moment near the end of the program, but, for some reason, Santa forgot and had to be reminded. Finally, with a hearty "ho, ho, ho," Santa rolled the wagon down the aisle to me and, upon delivery, I promptly took the wagon tongue and rammed the wagon into Santa's shins, nearly breaking his leg. I must not have been all that warmed by the jolly old elf, at that time. Mr. Roscoe Parkinson, forgive me, for I knew not what I was doing.

It has long been told that I created a Kodak moment during the time Dad was pastor of the Walnut Grove Church. We were invited to Sunday dinner (lunch) one time at the home of Mr. Scolar Womac and his family, and I am sure I had been admonished to behave. Manners were always stressed by Mom, as Dad was more likely to take corrective action after a wayward deed, than to try to prepare you to avoid it. On this occasion, after the fried chicken, vegetables, slaw, and cornbread, during a lull in the conversation, I proclaimed, "Give me some pie, or I will die"! Such was my parent's remorse over my exuberance that this incident was recalled repeatedly, as evidence of my misspent youth. It was willed to my brother and sister, for use as appropriate, and the reminder has never gathered rust. I was never praised or encouraged regarding my early literary tendencies.

A memory Homer and I share from the "Brown Place" is playing in the dirt under the front porch. The house sat on a gentle downward slope, and the ground under the front porch was lower, of course, than the back of the house. There was room for children to almost stand or, at least, sit. We had few, if any, real toys and had to use our imaginations and whatever was handy to create our fun. In this spirit, Homer led in the creation of little roads, scraped out of the dust and dirt, with fences and telephone lines fashioned from toothpicks or match stems and string. For vehicles, we would get our hands on a "clevis" or two (a U shaped iron device for hooking a plow to the singletree and, hence, the horse), and slide these up and down our dirt roads. This action, of course, was accompanied by lusty "hudden, huddens" (or whatever car sound we could originate). It may be jealousy, but I am a little sorry for children today, who have to use no imagination to create their fun. Games invented often provide the most satisfaction.

When we moved to the Frank Hutsell property, a.k.a. "Up on the Hill," I had matured by a few months and was more aware of our problems and the inconveniences they caused. The lack of heat, non-existent bathroom facilities, food issues, money, and work, or lack thereof, were either endured or observed. Those were tough, sad times. Looking back, though, I believe Homer, Betty, and I have laughed more than we have cried as we recall those times; in any event, we survived them.

One of the disappointments of that period had to do with Homer and the radio. We had no radio, of course, and electricity was not yet available, even to wealthy farm families. TVA was just beginning to build those great dams and distribute electric power to rural families. Ever industrious, Homer had tackled the project of selling some product, with the commission to be a small radio. This was a quite popular method of distributing various products in those days: seeds, candy, Cloverine salve, you name it. When the box (or boxes) of the product had been sold, the money was sent in, and the prize was sent out. It usually was of very nominal value, and the selling of the product was no easy task, because no one had much money....even at a nickel a clip, to help a young vending urchin.

In this instance, whatever the product, Homer went to work, knowing in advance that the payoff would be that radio. In the pictures, it appeared to be of parlor cabinet size and we were assured we could receive WSM, WCKY, XERF, WNOX, and all the known stations of the day. The Lone Ranger, Tom Mix, boxing matches, country music, the radio soaps....all would be within our reach. We would move into the modern age, all due to young Homer's early on abilities in the art of door-to-door. Alas, the work done and the prize received, our hopes were dashed-dashed-dashed. The radio was slightly smaller than cabinet size; an accurate measurement was probably in the neighborhood of three inches by three inches. It was perhaps a crystal set, with a little single earphone; whether it was designed to work at all, only God knows, as we did and do not. We strung up an aerial to an outdoor clothesline and turned it on...., listening intently for any sound. None came. Not the Lone Ranger, not music, not boxing, not even static. Whether it was our lack of expertise as radio operators or that we were flim-flamed again, the radio never worked. I guarantee you, though; Marconi never listened more intently for a sound....any sound, than did the Mincys with that little "salve" radio.

Down below our house, on the road in from the "main road," lived Floyd Hutsell and his fine family. There were three daughters, Frances, Helen, and Evelyn. The daughters were older, with Frances and Helen already gone from home and working in Athens. We had to pass their house on the way in or out to civilization, even to get our mail. In the summer, this trip to pick up the mail or meet the "rolling store" was a pleasant journey. Walking along or loping on a stick horse, trying to stir up dust as imagined from western cattle drive stories, barefoot and not worried about the Dow-Jones, these were fun moments. In the summer, Evelyn would often be on the front porch to greet us as we (or I) walked by. It was at this juncture in my life that I discovered, as did Adam and Eve in the Garden, that I was "naked," literally. I walked out, one day, noting Evelyn on the porch and observed on the way back, to my horror, that the entire seat was out of my overalls, exposing my small but developing butt to the world at large. Knowing I had to pass Evelyn on that porch and thinking it impractical to wait for dark, the only solution I could find was a rusty nail along the road, which I promptly stuck through the material in my overalls, fashioning a closure of sorts. She must have thought me somewhat weird and forward as I walked, sort of crabbing sideways, facing her all the time, until well passed line of sight. Ernest Tubb stole my life experience and wrote a hit song, "Driving Nails in my Coffin, Over You," without so much as a royalty check or thank you.

The experiences that really mattered—my grandparents dying, our car broke for the last time, food in question, and all the hardships—were primarily issues that my parents handled. These were of less importance to a child as, whatever happened, they had the answer. That they did not always was a lesser concern, as today was what counted. They would fix tomorrow.

Now is a good time to describe our home setting. It did not vary much, from house to house, as most were small, four rooms give or take a little space, and we certainly never added any furniture along the "trail." Starting with the living room, there was a fireplace, our only source of heat until we moved to the Guinn Place. In the winter, Dad always started a fire in the kitchen stove early each morning and, sometimes, in the fireplace also, depending on how cold and what day of the week it was. In the living room, which we usually referred to as the "front room," was the pump organ, the old rocking chair with one arm broken, a dark table, a small bookcase, and sometimes the bed, in which Mom and Dad slept. In some instances, a mantel over the fireplace held the old clock that was our only timepiece, matches, and whatever else needing to be there. The organ was called a "church" organ, distinguished from a "parlor" organ only by its lack of fancy woodwork and trim. The bed was a small double of some dark wood and obviously hand crafted.

In the "dining" room was a "claw foot" dining table with four to six chairs, a china cupboard of sorts holding what "nice" dishes existed, and various "tea" glasses and odd pieces of crystal. In some of those houses, the dining room was where Betty slept on her cot.

The kitchens varied little: a wood stove, with warming cupboards above the eyes, and an attached water heater on the side (It only warmed water poured into it). All cooking and, usually, iron heating took place on this stove. Cutting wood of proper size and having a means of starting the fires efficiently, were constants. The stove served to warm that side of the house, and its oven baked the biscuits, cornbread, jam cakes and sugar cookies that gave rise to memories ever present.

The fourth and (usually) final room was a bedroom, always housing Homer and me and, in some houses, Dad and Mom as well. Our bed was an old iron affair; it, as well as Mom and Dad's, had a straw tick with a feather mattress. Crude as it was, I will have to say it could be comfortable. The forerunner of waterbeds, when the straw tick was recently filled and the mattress fluffed up, it was somewhat unstable, but certainly cozy. There were always bed bugs. There was an old dresser and another piece of furniture we called a "bureau," which was a chest of drawers with the size inverted—the deepest drawer on top, the most shallow on the bottom. This gave it an inverted pyramid look. This contraption housed mostly junk, odds and ends, the mysterious "sex" book we would peek into when we dared, and various memorabilia collected along the way.

Those little structures were shelters from the storms of life as it existed then; always clean and often ringing with hymns from a Broadman Hymnal (Baptist), as Mom pumped and played the organ, singing alto, as Dad led in his usual, off key manner. Whoever else joined in was usually the one(s) who caved in to our parent's pleadings first.

In 1940, I started to school at Riceville, the school Homer was attending. I remember Dad going with me that first day, making sure I got where I was supposed to go and just being there with me, my little hand in his big one. This experience was just as intimidating to me as any of the stories make it out to be. Riceville was a one through 10 school and very large in my eyes. Dad started me, however, and Homer was there, so I do not remember ever feeling fright or concern, after those first few days. Mrs. Ella Grubb was my first-grade teacher.

There are three highlights from this introduction to the world of academia, beginning with my first "whipping." Corporal punishment was allowed, even encouraged, then, and I knew going in that one at school meant one at home, also. Even this did not always deter me from the paths of sinfulness, although most of my transgressions were not premeditated; rather, they just seem to happen. This one was caused by such a minor infraction that I really felt I should have been sent to the corner, or such. Students were sent to the rest rooms in groups of three-four at a time, and one day, returning with my group, I must have been feeling my first-grade oats, as I led my squad in an exhibition of "rooster-crowing" as we came back down the hall. Since the entire wing of the school was witness to the offense, I was convicted before I could think of an excuse and was sent to my seat with it having been thoroughly pre-warmed.

Another happening prompted a life-long memory: Mrs. Anna Puett, the second grade teacher, also taught "music" and would come into our room each week for "music" lessons. These usually consisted of songs, little dances, and whatever else she could conjure up to spark our interest in the arts. One particular day, she was leading us in folk dances and asked me to be her demonstration partner. When the class was over, she commented to me, "What a good little dancer you are." Bear in mind, in our house, dancing was connected to drinking, which was connected to smoking, which was connected to sex, all which pointed one toward the road to perdition.

Well! To home I go, proudly proclaiming to Mom that Mrs. Puett said, "I was the best little dancer in the class." Mother, the rest of her life, would recall this tale, adding mournfully, "That just almost broke my heart."

Finally, Mary Ellen Kimbrough, a fellow student, to this day declares that she and I took apart a family heirloom broach watch she was wearing, just to "see what it looked like inside." I really cannot confess, although I vaguely remember some conversation between our parents.

My academic results were Es and Ss (E=Excellent, S=Satisfactory) and no bad marks, notwithstanding the pitiful, little, snaggle-toothed soul that I was.

Mrs. Puett's second grade was certainly memorable for several reasons. World War II started, and it became common to see large convoys of trucks, tank-carrying vehicles, and personnel carriers moving down US 11, which ran by the school. Large numbers of planes were also to be seen overhead, moving from one assignment to another. I remember seeing Mrs. Puett, at recess, on the bank beside the school, sitting with her head down on her knees sobbing; I suppose it was for her husband, Fred, who had "gone off to war." She was a fun teacher; however, I got caught up in an event that brought on her terrible swift sword of justice. Being seated alphabetically, I sat behind Mary Ellen (Kimbrough), upon whom my affections were truly lavished. To no avail, however, as she, being the epitome of sunshine and all things desired, had the same effect on all the guys, so she just played us one against the other. And at all of seven years old.

Anyway, this day, during class, she turned around and painted a "Zorro" mustache on my little slick face, and I, entranced at the attention, sat and let it happen. I do not know where Mrs. Puett was during all this foreplay; however, she appeared soon enough after the deed was done and dragged me by my arm to the front of the room. After exhibiting me to the class as the mindless moron that I was, she took my arm, covered in a modest, blue, work shirt and proceeded to try and scrub off my temporary mustache. It would not come off, but my skin almost did; that was not enough. She then gave me a sound whipping and sent me to my seat to be greeted by sweet Mary Ellen, who was laughing her little butt off. What a lesson I should have learned. Oh well, mostly Es plus "Very commendable, very satisfactory and very good." Seems redundant, but I did not print or design the report cards.

Some important facts need to be pointed out regarding the logistics of getting to school. When we (Homer and I) attended Riceville, we rode the school bus; however, we had to walk about two miles, from both "up on the hill" and "down at Laymans," to catch it. There were a few times when we just missed it. It was 6.3 miles to Riceville School from the "Up" place and 6.4 from the "Down" place. Never did we turn around and go back home, when we missed that bus, as Homer just led my tired little legs all the way there. It would be late morning before we could make it, but make it we did. This is but one example of the tenacity and drive that Homer has always shown when focused on a particular goal. I doubt we would have been strongly rebuked had we just tucked tail and gone back home. I also doubt that ever entered his mind, however, as we were supposed to be in school, so he just dragged his little brother along and off to school we trod.

During the summer, after my second grade and Homer's seventh, he decided he wanted to go to the Mouse Creek School to finish the eighth grade. Mouse Creek was a two-room school, also about two miles from our house, and seemed to our parents to be less an opportunity for scholarly achievement than was Riceville. Quite heated discussions ensued, and I can recall vividly the arguments between Homer and Dad. Homer, even in the eighth grade, could out-debate Dad or at least out last him, as he did in this instance. That fall, to Mouse Creek we went.

The classrooms at Mouse Creek were typical of those times: full desks, with space under the top for books and supplies, a hole top-right for an ink bottle, and the little groove up top for a pencil. The stove sat right-rear corner in the big room and left-rear corner in the little room, sharing a common chimney. A partition separated the classroom from an area in the back of the room, where the coats and lunches would be stored. A large blackboard graced the front of the room; a coveted chore was "dusting the erasers" and cleaning the blackboard, as it included going outside to beat the erasers clean, getting one out of class for a short break. There was a large, folding partition between the big room and the little room that would be opened for pie suppers, occasional hillbilly shows, or other large assemblies. The large, heavy, wooden sections were on tracks, but time had diminished their ability to slide, so it was quite an affair to open the partition; the bigger boys, with crow-bars and hammers, had to work an hour or so to force it open. The excitement of watching this happen usually exceeded whatever was to follow.

The drinking fountains were outdoors, with water drawn from a well with a manual pump operated by a long pump handle. The water was pumped into a pipe, over a "trough," with six to eight holes through which the water would rise. One person had to pump for others to drink. Two tricks passed down through the years were pumping with rapid strokes, followed by a full one or two, causing the water to "geyser" up into the drinkers face; and, creating just the correct water pressure to cause little resistance and with a swift down stroke, breaking the pump handle. No water, no school, until the county could send someone to "fix it." The welds on the pump handle were testimony to devious scheming by the little Mouse Creekers of those days. Two large outhouses, one for boys and one for girls, on opposite sides of the playground, served their intended purposes.

I went two years in elementary school to Riceville and one year to the Forest Hill School, in the Athens City system. However, I have always referred to and been associated with Mouse Creek in any reference to my elementary years. Those years and experiences just dominate my memories and everybody else's memory of me. In high school, I always felt, particularly at first, somewhat snubbed by the "city kids" and embarrassed about my background, because of what and where it was. It took me more than 20 years and being PTA President for life, to appreciate the Mouse Creek School and the real advantage and opportunity it afforded me.

First, in each of the two rooms were four classes, with probably no more than 25 students in each room. Every day, each student was subjected to (overhearing) four doses of reading, 'riting, and 'rithmatic. I have come to believe that on the subject of small classes, individual attention, and emphasis on the basics, we were ahead of our time. Further, I was fortunate to have the same teacher for four of my eight years of elementary education; fortunate because Mrs. Effie Bigham (Principal,1936-1947) brought quality instruction, discipline, and interest into her classroom each day, five days a week, for the entire school term.

A sweet lady, Mrs. James Tate, taught my third grade. I received a whipping for cussin' on the playground, (I also remember going home that night and crawling under the house; I knew another whipping was coming. Long after dark, Homer crawled in and negotiated me out) otherwise, all Es, except a U for drawing (???) I was also very commendable, satisfactory and good.

During the third grade, I had an all-out fight with Bobby Torbett on the way home, over what, I do not know. The boys could be very cliquish, with different groups siding with each other at different times. For some reason, Bobby, who was about my age, got on me, and encouraged by a "mob" of others, we squared off no further than three hundred yards from school; I believe it was in front of Tom Bohannon's house. Homer was there and helped to make sure it was a fair fight, although they may have been on his case, too. In any event, we went at it, wore ourselves out, with me bloodying his mouth and he banging my head pretty good. Finally, satisfying the lust of our audience, we sniveled and sniffed on home; funny thing, though, how friendly he was next day. ("*Sometimes you have to fight, to be a man.*" Kenny Rogers)

A funny thing happened with my fourth grade, which normally would have been taught by Mrs. Tate. Due to class balance that year, Mrs. Bigham taught the fourth through the eighth grades; therefore, I was moved into the "Big Room." During my entire experience with Mrs. Bigham, she always thought I was very commendable, satisfactory and good, but further, thought I whispered too much and talked too much. Alas, the story of my life

Mrs. Bigham was the wife of Ernest "Pooch" Bigham, a career policeman on the Athens force, and was a tall, imposing woman, to say the least. Standing probably six, six-two, she possessed a paddle that was likely two-plus feet long, and she used it not sparingly. Mouse Creek School was in the country and, while it's students were not delinquent in a now inner-city sense, some were aggressive and strong willed, subject to mischief at any time. She ruled her school, tolerated no disorder, and conducted our classes without interruption. Occasionally, she had to deal with parents over her dealing with their little darlings, but, usually, did so successfully, with no vendettas originating from the Shells, Womacs, Torbetts, Rockholts, Norwoods, or other families in the neighborhood.

We had pie suppers, played basketball and softball, and were shown movies (the first I ever saw); Mrs. Bigham fostered a strong P.T.A. and encouraged strong inter-action with parents. We were introduced to the 4-H Club, which came to mean so much to me later. The school served as the center of the community, the nearest church being almost two miles away. Being very commendable, satisfactory and good, I was rarely in trouble with Mrs. Bigham; I often served as janitor for a month at a time, as did many others. We were usually rewarded with a book; I remember *Dick Donnely and the Paratroopers* and Zane Grey's *Spirit of the Border*.

There were many elements at work, early on, at Mouse Creek. First, these were the **war** years and, for some reason, word often got around that the "Mincys were German." Once accused, there was no good answer, as, truth to tell, we did not know what we were, in a classic sense. We had been told we were "Black Dutch," however, since we did not know what that meant, it was of no use as a defense. It was difficult to get that swastika off your back. One could be among the best athletes on the playground, but there was room for only one best. One could lead his army of fourth graders into battle, as it attacked the other army encamped inside the outhouse, and fight furiously in hand to hand combat, losing blood in the process. It helped if one were the most obnoxious troublemaker for Mrs. Bigham. We were none of those, although I threw many a rock or corncob at that outhouse, as we swept to vanquish the Huns barricaded inside. Homer and I were thankful we showed no Oriental lineage, or we would have been stoned. Then, there was the issue of religion: my father being a minister, I was in a lose-lose position. I would be asked, "Are you a Christian?" and any way I answered, I was in trouble. If I said yes, then I was asked why I had done so-and-so, and if I said no, the questioner would want to know why not.

Because I behaved, made good grades, and caused no trouble, of course Mrs. Bigham gave me none. I was labeled a "teacher's pet," from time to time, and in one instance it really backfired. Hanging out with the boys one day after school, I slipped and referred to Mrs. Bigham as that "Slim-seven-footer." It was no more than a day or so until Bobby Torbett, while being whipped for something, blurted out "You would not pet Virgil so much if you knew what he called you." I was called to the front of the room and, to my shame, made to confess my blasphemy. Mortified as I was, and notwithstanding the look of hurt she showed, I think Mrs. Bigham was more amused than angry.

A memory that lingers to this day was the "Jimmy Hutsell" escapade. Jimmy was a year younger than I, but we would play together from time to time. He lived about a mile from the school by road, closer as the crow would fly. Their farm was next to the Jolley's and Patterson's, and actually close to the southeast corner of the school property. His father, Ralph, was brother to Dick and Bill Hutsell, who were our neighbors "Up at Laymans."

One day Jimmy and I were playing quite a distance from the school building, in a large open part of the playground, when an older girl rode toward us on a bicycle. Whether Jimmy just fell and the bicycle struck him or whether the bicycle struck him first, if at all, Jimmy hit the ground injured, as it turned out, with a broken leg. She immediately claimed I had pushed Jimmy into the bike and carried this claim home with her. Her parents were respected, established people in our community and the value of their word against that of a German, Christian, teacher's pet would seem overwhelming. I recall Jimmy's Dad and either Bill or Dick, visiting our home to "see about this," however, this being before the day of a lawyer on every corner, it blew over. Jimmy, to his credit, did not remember anything other than simply falling and breaking his leg, which was what I always thought. Now, for the rest of the story.

Major, Virgil and Homer

Virgil with wheels
An obvious early interest in logistics

Virgil, Betty with cat, Homer
The "Brown Place"

Early Days, School and the Learning Years

Left to right: Homer, Betty, Virgil ca. 1944
"Up at Laymans"

The Little Angel with adoring big brother

Jimmy was laid up at home for a couple of weeks and, while there, started fooling around with a guitar his mother had. He apparently could sing, as he did not learn that in just two weeks. I will never forget, however, the scene when he returned to school, with his leg in a big cast; he propped it up on a chair in front of him, held that big, white, arched-top guitar and sang, "*There's a star spangled banner waving somewhere,*" in his perfect, young tenor voice, just wowing us. That guitar was the most beautiful instrument I had ever seen and helped spark the lasting love I have for guitar music.

Jimmy continued to work on his talents and, in a year or so, was appearing on our new, local radio station, W.L.A.R. ("Watch Little Athens Rise"). He was head and shoulders above the rest as, in those days, everyone who chose to walk into the station could get on in some format or another. In a short while, he had programs of his own and did some announcing...long before he completed high school. He appeared often on the Knoxville stations and made it to the Grand Old Opry. Broadcasting became his interest and life-long profession.

I often wondered: if I had to shoulder the blame for Jimmy's broken leg, should I not share the success of his musical and broadcast career? Jimmy, rightly so, never gave me credit for either.

Before the start of my seventh grade, word got around that Mrs. Bigham was not returning; she was moving into the Athens City System, and our teacher for the "big room" was to be Mrs. Clifford Duckworth. This was good news, as she was usually well liked, so the rumors went, and also a great basketball coach. School started well, but within the first month, Mrs. Duckworth left Mouse Creek to become principal at the larger and hated Idlewild, our archenemy across the ridge to the west. For a short while, we had substitutes: Mrs. Deason, Mrs. Lovingood and perhaps others. Finally, we had no teacher, and the big room just closed for the year. A couple of my classmates lost that year of school and were a year behind the following year.

With much persistence, Dad was able to get me admitted to the Athens Schools and, about the third month, I started attending Forest Hill. Guess who my teacher was: Mrs. Ernest (Pooch) Effie (Slim-Seven-Footer) Bigham. I was a little behind, but still got through. No longer deemed commendable and very good, I was just satisfactory in all respects. I think Mrs. Bigham was a little tougher on me than the others, as she let it be known that I, "had been her student before" and expected me to perform above the rest. Trouble was, many of the rest were bright, affluent, well-behaved young men and women, and the competition was tough.

That year was probably my most enjoyable in grade school: I was a fresh face to the rest of the class, and I actually believe the girls got together to decide who "got me." In short order, I do know I had a steady, with no idea how I had been so lucky. As Jerry Clower always said in one of his stories about football, "I just thought I was good!" As important, I quickly made friends with many of the guys....friendships that lasted through high school. I have been gone from Athens for 52 years, but meeting some of the Forest Hill (and high school) crowd always brings back those memories, and some of the tales.

An incident that always stands out from that part-year had to do with "autograph book signing." Even at Mouse Creek, near the end of the school term, students would bring in their "autograph books" to be signed or noted by fellow students. Sometimes, it would be a new one; other times, just the same book from the previous year. This was sort of a warm-up for high school "yearbooks." We did this at Forest Hill, also.

In the spring, out came the books; I still had my little brown one, with the first entry being that entered by my mother in 1944. At Forest Hill, her challenging words were soon joined by such prose as: "When you are married and live down South; don't forget me and my big mouth." **Jimmy Dodson** Or, "Virgil, never kiss by the garden gate; love is blind but the neighbors ain't." **Regina Lawson** You, perhaps, get the picture. In the front seat of my row sat the cutest of the cute of the seventh graders, Sybil Wyner. Her book finally found its way to me and, with my early budding writer's skill, I penned something profound, like, "Sybil, always be good, and don't go hanging around the boys too much" or something close. A few minutes had passed when, suddenly, Sybil arose from her seat, stomped back to my desk and flung down a folded piece of paper. With a smooth pirouetting move, she marched back to her seat with those cute braids tossing in her wake. Thinking whatever was on that piece of paper could only be some new words of praise, I admired her greatly and, through the eyes of memory, do yet.

Well! I opened the little piece of paper and I believe this is exactly what was written: "I will have you know I do not hang out with the boys; I am a Jew!" I was crushed, baffled and without a clue. Crushed that my simple little message of nonsense had been rejected, baffled that I had somehow offended and without a clue what "being a Jew" had to do with our seventh grade friendship. I knew of Moses and the prophets, but was ignorant of ethnicity and could not comprehend any differences between us thirteen year olds, other than pretty, ugly; nice, less nice; dressed neat, ragged, or she likes me, she likes me not. I am still saddened that I had to find out there was a little more to it than that.

Girls, escapades, Mrs. Bigham, city people, all paled in comparison to my brush with fame that year. I was a nightly listener to all the adventure soaps: my favorite was Tom Mix and his Ralston Straight Shooters. (Ralston-Purina was the sponsor, hawking their cereals and such.) Those shows were always peddling stuff, running contest, or pretending give-a-ways, achievable only if accompanied by many box tops from the promotion of the moment.

This particular time, Tom was running a contest to name his new pony, the offspring of his famed horse, Tony. The prizes were varied and worthy of interest, so I entered. My creative juices being totally absorbed by Mrs. Bigham's expectations, my dear mom came up with a name for me to enter: Ruff-N-Tuff. Having never hit the lotto in that day, I thought little of it after the mailing. Time passed and coming home one afternoon, Mom, with emphasis, made sure I completed all the chores by radio time. I was listening with disinterest when, at the proper moment, the network switched to the local station to announce any winners. My little heart stood still, as W.L.A.R. proudly announced a winner in one VIRGIL MINCY, with his prize being a pair of Red Rascal roller skates. I was a greater celebrity next day at school than President Truman would have been, had he dropped by. Alas, those skates were not much use on our wooden front porch or the steep dirt driveway. Guess they rusted into extinction, along with other Tom Mix paraphernalia I had collected.

I swear this to be true: Fifty-five years later, I was introduced to Bill Paisley, whom I vaguely remembered, but had never known personally. He had been a student at Long's Chapel, the small school where Homer first taught. I may have visited it, a time or two, but that would have been several years after Mom named that pony. This man, upon our introduction, related hearing that winning announcement all those years ago and actually remembered the pony's name. I have uncovered no collusion or fraud, so you go figure.

The next year, Mouse Creek had a teacher for the eighth grade and I had to leave Shangri-La and return to earth. The Rev. George E. Erwin, a Methodist minister and teacher, was to serve as usher into the next phase of my life, and he did so in a rather uneventful manner. He was a stern, plodding, humorless man; however, he applied himself to the reading, 'riting and such, and the year went by. His most lasting impression was his handwriting; he was very skilled in the cursive style and would often entertain us putting fancy script on the blackboard. (It was then, indeed, black.) He always kept our attention when he was showing off. I received Es in every subject each month, except one S in English. I never understood why he gave me that one S in an otherwise perfect year. (Perhaps the good Reverend was prophetic?) After eight months, Junior Petit, Anna Ruth Torbett, Paul Rockholt, and I were passed on to the ninth grade and the next learning experience.

Volumes are written, far more eloquently than this, chronicling that time in history and that period in lives. Almost as much time has passed since I began school, as had from Custer's Last Stand, until I started. I know when the past seems quaint and uninteresting, as I can remember when it did and was. That said, my early days in school were between "then" (the quaint and uninteresting) and "now" and certainly were different than now.

I never knew a black child or young (black) person. I bought the first radio our family had, when I was in the seventh grade. We recited the pledge of allegiance AND the Lord's Prayer; however, I never felt that practice or the lack thereof significant as I learned the value of democracy in school and in life and the circumstance of the model Jesus suggested at home and in church.

We sang Stephen Foster songs such as *Old Black Joe, Uncle Ned,* and others that are politically incorrect now. We sang them with enthusiasm and respect, because this was music appreciation we were learning, not history. To the extent our history may have been distorted, our lessons in the value of life and the dignity of man were not shortchanged by Messrs. Puett, Bigham, Tate, Erwin, Foster, et.al. Those hearing these lessons and getting a different one at home perhaps have been guilty in life of some dreadful things. That has been sadly true, in equal measure, of young people growing up in Tennessee, Mississippi, AND, in New Jersey, Indiana, or Watts. Great classroom experience has a difficult time overcoming a poor home environment, just as love and direction at home can often balance mediocre classroom exposure. I was curious, yet respectful and open, when I met, as an adult, the first African-American I knew. I knew the value of work, by the time I had my first job. I voted my first chance. There were classroom experiences I was probably not afforded at Mouse Creek, but those we had were dead-on. Thank you, family and friends, for kicking me out into life better prepared than most.

In the fall of 1948, McMinn County High School opened its doors to me and all the others of the huddled mass that made up the Class of 1952. It was not quite the experience of Dad holding my hand and leading me into Riceville eight years before but perhaps got the juices flowing a little faster than would Tennessee Wesleyan, when I entered college four years later. I had left the safety of my little cocoon at Mouse Creek and my three classmates, to become one of 161 entering freshmen; I knew very few. I had no identity, not many close friends, and the in-crowd seemed to be those who did, or those entering from the three large Athens City Schools. My seventh-grade acquaintances from Forest Hill were not unfriendly, but decidedly cool; a year had passed and they had gone on with their little lives quite well without me, formed new alliances, shared new experiences, and that year was exclusive to them. It did not include me.

McMinn, in Athens of course, was but one of several high schools in McMinn County. There was Etowah, in Etowah, Englewood High School was in Englewood, Calhoun in Calhoun, and other junior high programs were scattered around. McMinn was the largest school, or so it seemed, as we usually beat Etowah in football, did not play the others, and that seemed to be the determinant of size to ignorant little freshmen. By contrast, we struggled to hold our own with Bradley (in Bradley County) and usually got drubbed by Oak Ridge in Anderson County; therefore, we assumed these schools were much larger than ours. As a point in fact, I never laid eyes on Englewood High School, about five miles from downtown Athens, nor Etowah, which was nine miles away over that curvy, treacherous highway leading there. Such was our understanding of how we ranked in the pecking order of surrounding schools.

There were some positives that helped create order and routine in those first high school days; I caught a bus in front of our house (the Ensminger Place) and it returned me there at the same time each day. It was predetermined that I would take English I, general science, civics, Algebra I, and health education; all I had to do was find the classroom and the teacher would outline the rest. In some classes, we were seated alphabetically; in others, we randomly chose our seat, which by habit, became the same place. This force-fed us new friends, speaking acquaintances, or antagonists. Lunch was available in the cafeteria, for the sum of one dollar for the week. Lunch protocol needs to be discussed, at this point.

When Homer, then I, started to school at Riceville, we could not afford to eat in the cafeteria, because it cost 10 cents per day. I remember one time when Grandmother Mincy gave Mom a dollar, with the admonishment that, "Homer Franklin was to use this to eat in the cafeteria for two weeks." Or, it may have been, to buy 10 loaves of "store bought" or "light" bread, for proper sandwiches. The issue was that lunch, for us, was usually ham or sausage on biscuits or potted meat on crackers. There was no money to buy those common lunch items that came from a store, so Mom had to "make do." I remember one occasion Mom, with nothing else available, baked sugar cookies, some with icing, some plain, and sent along a supply of those for lunch. While my grandchildren clog their arteries with ham and sausage biscuits from Hardees or Biscuitville, they, taught by my children, (their parents) roll in the floor with laughter as I try to poormouth my past with sugar cookie and ham biscuit tales. There were issues, though; children who could afford it brought "light bread" and peanut butter or bologna sandwiches to school, usually accompanied by cookies and/or fruit. This lunch would usually be packed in a new, crisp, paper bag. Actually, a proper lunch box was considered rather square, and a thermos in that box was definitely over the line. A good lunch wrapped in a newspaper was a step in the other direction, and ham biscuits, with grease leaking through the newspaper stamped one with a sign: "he's poor." There were other indicators: a "mackinaw" coat, covered with cow hairs and smelling of barns, indicating one had to wear his "work" coat to school; one's teeth never brushed; hair gaps indicating "home hair cuts," and the same outfit worn each day of the week. Check any two of these and your family was seeing hard times.

By Forest Hill, I could eat in the school cafeteria and usually did, except for an occasional foraging run to Kenneth Minge's folk's store behind the school for a junk fix. This brings us home to freshmen days and the routine at McMinn.

One would think, as I had struggled up from poverty, marking off those checks that would identify me, I would take advantage of all perks possible. Dad gave me one dollar each Monday, for a meal ticket to the cafeteria that week. Did I get in line for the meatloaf, mashed potatoes and gravy, salmon patties, peas in sauce with pearl onions, etc., etc.? Not when greater perks were possible! For a while, along with some other little geniuses, I would go down to the Farmer's Supply, a combination grocery and general farm merchandise store, owned and run by Mr. McKenzie, and feast on a Moon Pie, a "big orange," and a cup of Mayfield ice cream. Total fare: 25 cents. I would, as all you math majors have already discerned, eat four days and starve one, just for the freedom of choice to partake at the table offering this creative cuisine. Occasionally, I would take in a movie and not eat two days. There are those who might suggest that I was not quite ready for prime time, not the sharpest knife in the drawer, or a few ears short of a dozen. That is why we were called freshmen.

Principal J. Will Foster governed McMinn County High School. He was there five years before I arrived and served long after I left. He and Mrs. Bigham were adopted twins (just kidding), as each believed in ruling with a stern hand, applying discipline as needed, even if it meant shooting first and asking questions later. Mr. Foster, in appearance, was a blend of John L. Lewis and George Wallace, though a little taller than either. As an adult, I vouch for his humor, outside interests, family concerns, and outstanding character; as a freshman, I never wanted his shadow to cross my path or for him to have any reason to know my name. Problem was, students were required to go by his office and get a "tardy" slip for admission to class if they missed the bell for first period. Bus late…go by, sick…go by, goofing off…go by; sooner or later, he knew me along with everyone else. With Homer having passed through before me, he had an additional reason to acknowledge my presence; he even called me "Homer" on occasions. I never had a discipline problem with Mr. Foster and, if I had been there 50 years, I doubt I would have. He was definitely a nuclear deterrent, before that term was imagined.

From high school on, I was never an "outstanding student." Some of the reasons are not very pleasant to contemplate, and when I look at old pictures of the National Honor Society and consider its members, I feel embarrassed not to be among them. Some were just sharper than I was; in several classes, for example, I would be ranked number two, but rarely number one, if Joyce Lovern was in that class. She was just that good. I do not know if it was superior intelligence on her part or that she applied herself all the time. Either way, she always took me. Others were more consistent, and even though they might have ranked only in the top 10 in English or history, they would rank as high in Latin and chemistry.

I, on the other hand, generally did well in social studies, but faltered in the technical or scientific areas. I have no specific reason, other than I did not dig in and apply myself when confronted with difficulty. In Algebra I, I breezed through and just ate it up. Mrs. Peggy Long was a "favorite" teacher, and I choose to believe her presentation made the subject understandable and her style made her class, therefore the material, enjoyable. What followed still puzzles me.

In my sophomore year, Mr. L.J. Harrod, a local grocer and part-time teacher, was my Algebra II instructor. I just never seemed to understand it and, although it is a lame excuse, I always thought I would have comprehended the material if Mrs. Long had been the teacher. I must confess that Joyce Lovern and all the other Honor Society members-to-be seemed to breeze through, so I rather sadly concluded the problem was I, and not Mr. Harrod. This trouble followed me into geometry, chemistry and a few math-based college courses. If I had kept the books open and stayed with it, would I have ever understood it? I believe so, but I did not. In my sophomore year, I was starting to make some headlines in 4-H activities, and I remember Mr. Harrod confronting me one day asking, "Since you are having so much success in outside activities, why won't you apply yourself to succeed in this class?" I had no answer. I never failed a class, and my lowest performance was 16th out of 21, in Mr. Harrods second semester Algebra II class. I do not know how I ranked in my class at graduation. Mathematically, in all my classes, I averaged ranking 6.90 in an average class size of 27. The 6.89 who did better in my classes, plus all those top students in classes I was not in, strong armed me, rightfully so, out of scholastic honors. A **good** student applies him/her self all the time, up to the limits of his/her capabilities; I was capable and excelled in some areas, but lacked what it took to be consistent. I **earned** that 6.90 ranking; both the grades raising it that high and those pulling it down that low.

The most lasting memory I retain from four years of class work is of an occurrence in Mrs. Judson Daughtery's sophomore biology class. We were assigned a project to assemble a "scrapbook" of something relative to the class material, i.e. leaves, plants, etc., and make an oral presentation to the class. On judgment day, we were making our little speeches and it came the turn of Bill Casteel, a North Athens athlete, who was quite good at basketball and baseball. He faced the class and began: "Biology is about plants; trees are plants, baseball bats are made from trees, baseball is played with bats, the New York Yankees, an outstanding team, plays baseball, and Mickey Mantle is one of their star players. My project is about Mickey Mantle, and I will tell you about him." And, he did. Mrs. Daughtery just gave him a look, shook her head, sat back, and enjoyed the moment with the rest of us.

Bill enjoyed an outstanding career as sports reporter, editor, columnist, and writer; who's to say what is important in the learning process?

Oh yeah, I forgot to mention one other lesson for life that I retain from Old McMinn High: how to make up a bed. Lucile Anderson, everyone's favorite, was our junior year English teacher; she made literature interesting, and no one ever sat through her class and went into life without associating Ms. Anderson, throughout that life, with "Macbeth and the Witches." All of us budding scholars from Mouse Creek, Riceville, North Athens, Forest Hill, etc., would suck up to Teach by inserting every Shakespeare icon we could into our papers, workbooks, or tests to try to cover our ineptness in the subject matter by implied interest. She usually would note our feeble efforts with pithy, witty little responses. About the beds:

Lucile had been/was a nurse, and would occasionally tell us about those experiences; one included how to prepare a bed. I know she demonstrated how to miter the corners with a sheet and, although I may have not memorized Beowulf, I took to the tucking and it stuck. I perhaps would have picked up on that elsewhere but, in fact, I got it there. And who would decry a public education?

And then, there were the sports. I played none and wish I had. First, there was the inspiration of Homer who, with all his 145 pounds, had gone out for football, stayed with it all four years, rising to be captain of the B team his senior year. Coach Baker, in appreciation for his efforts, awarded him a "Letter," perhaps the only time he ever did so to a non-varsity player. Sometime during my late freshman or early sophomore year, Coach put my name with my not too athletic looking body, and asked me why I was not out for football; I mumbled something and for my effort, got to hear the Homer story.... as it happened, just as I have told you. He laid a pretty good shame act on me.

I was asked the question and heard the Homer story about every four or five months, on a regular basis. By my junior year, I was actually pretty good at gym class tag football, which would include the football players, out of season. One day, a boy named Marvin (Mop) Melton (the son of Henry Melton, my mother-in-law to be, Bess's fifth husband) and I were just lighting it up with his passing and my receiving. Mop did not play football either, but could pass a spiral, left handed, with the best. With some skill, I could go up into a crowd and come down with the ball and, this day, he and I had the other team shaking their heads. We were unstoppable, and I was the Jerry Rice of third period Phys Ed. At a break, Coach ambled over and said, "What is the matter Mincy; are you a sissy"? Then, on cue, he brought out the Homer story and refreshed my memory.

Our football team did not win a game my senior year; I know I could have played, and helped but, by then, it was too late.

The reasons I did not play, that I have dragged out to excuse myself all these years, are many: first, when I was a freshman, the team was quite good and just looking at and being around guys like Paul Murphy, Hal Crittendon and a few others positively made me sure I did not want to go near a football field. Paul was the kind of guy who looked like he would not only knock me down, but also walk up my back, ventilating me for life with permanent cleat marks. There was the transportation issue: Dad and Mom discouraged football (they had also, with Homer) and were of no help with the prospect of not having a ride home after practice. Others, living in the country, overcame this; I could not imagine how I might. I had no close friend to hold my hand, as I dug some used shoulder pads out of the pile, and show me how to put them on. I am sure I conjured up others.

I did, along with some other sissies, get selected to be in the "junior play," my introduction to the theater. We put on *The Campbells are Coming*, fresh from its run on Broadway. (Broadway is the main street in Lenoir City, Tennessee) Casting was held down at McKenzie's grocery at lunchtime, and I was selected to play the role of Dickie Boy, the family idiot. I was spotted, sitting on empty Coke cases, gulping a Moon Pie and big orange; I definitely recall someone whispering, "He's a natural."

During the night of February 16, 1951, a large section of our high school was destroyed in a fire; if the cause was determined, I have forgotten it. In what I still believe to be an effort above and beyond, we were back in class within a week. The Athens Armory, which was a block from the school, was partitioned into classrooms, and business went on as usual. Although this gets ahead of the story, I always felt this event and the split classrooms had a negative affect on our class; we had some morale/behavior problems our senior year, and our class (in my opinion) just never was as focused as other senior classes I observed.

Near the end of my junior year, the faculty and principal selected me, along with the class president, Jimmy Dodson and Coach Baker's son, Kenzil, to attend "Volunteer Boy's State," which was quite an honor. First, I had at least done something right, in the eyes of all the teachers, and this was the finest, most enjoyable all-boys event I ever attended. Sponsored by the American Legion, it was a one-week event held at Castle Heights Military Academy, in Lebanon, Tennessee. The premise was to divide everyone into governmental units and involve them in running that unit all week. We organized cities, counties, and the state, with elections, campaigning, and speeches...just like big folks. Over two thirds of the boys were the top (junior class) high school athletes in the state, and the organized sports were something else. I played (fast pitch) softball and got a big (private) laugh when some of the other guys, watching me play, were complimentary, asking me what else I played and where I was going to college. If everyone ASSUMES you are a big time jock, you can almost fake it for a week. Take that, Coach Baker! My team reached the finals for the Boys State championship. In the middle innings of that game, I had the only hit and had managed to score the only run, when we noticed some whispering on the side. Turned out, one of our guys had signed up for football, never played, but joined our softball team and, upon being discovered, was, along with our team, disqualified on the spot. They were that strict all week. I was a four and one-half inning star.

The yearbook staff picked Jean Riddle and me to be on the staff our junior year, which meant we would be the editor and business manager our senior year. We, along with a lot of help, got it done. Of course, we will have to live with the shame of spelling Bill Casteel's name incorrectly, horror of horrors. Juvenile writers messing with a real writer to-be are certainly tugging on Superman's cape. As editor, I must accept the responsibility but, hey, even Bill did not catch it at the time (??); the statute of limitations has expired, and we were minors.

In my senior year, I took D.O. (Diversified Occupations) and worked four hours each day, being in class only a half day. While I missed some of the at-school stuff, this was offset by getting started on my life's profession, transportation. I also beat out Joyce Lovern, first semester, by ranking first in this class. She must have tied me the last semester, as I ranked only 1.5, whatever that meant.

I have always felt that after those early freshman days, my 4-H successes outside of school caused me to get noticed. When called upon, I tried to succeed at whatever I was asked to do. Success breeds success, and my senior class voted Jean Riddle and me "Most Likely to Succeed" and "Most Dependable." Another senior girl, June Canupp, and I were voted "Most Versatile." This leads me to the other major regret, in addition to football, that I carried from high school. I wish I could have dated more.

When I was a freshman, I do not remember much hot action between non-driving little pimple heads, but that did not mean hearts were not set a-flutter. I remember having a crush on Laura Walker, brought on primarily by our cutting up in Mrs. Long's Algebra class, and her seeming very friendly and open. The problem was Laura being undoubtedly the wealthiest girl in Athens and in the running for lead in East Tennessee. What was I to do? Even my pea brain understood that I could not say, "Laura, I am having my dad drop me by your mansion tonight in the feed truck; he will take us to the movie, wait on us and return us to your home where I will suck face with you on the front porch until your grandfather, Tom Sherman, sends one of his bodyguards and the dogs to take proper care of me." That was not meant to be.

I recall cutting up with June Canupp in Mrs. Drumwright's sophomore English class, primarily, because she could match my sarcasm and clever back and forth. Come 3:30, however, it was bus time, back home, and chores to do. I did not even have a telephone. This was the same June Canupp who visited me in the fall of our junior year, as I lay in a hospital bed getting over an appendectomy; as class secretary, she delivered to me the best wishes of the class. My first official date occurred during my junior year and came about in soap opera fashion, with a lot of notes, looks, third party intervention, she-said, he-said kind of stuff, which did not help either of us.

I do recall, with mixed emotions, attending a party for the cast of our junior play; I believe it was at Dorothy Trotter's home and was chaperoned, of course, by our director and Home Economics teacher, Ann Crox. As the evening wore on, we drifted into playing a combination of spin the bottle and post office. An alignment of the sun, moon, most planets, and unequal weighting of that empty coke bottle must have occurred, as it spun at a climatic moment toward me and Sybil Wyner; yes, **that** Sybil, who was now actress, majorette, and all around neat classmate. I have forgotten whether it was as prize or punishment that we were dispatched to a small, dark closet, without any instructions as to what should happen; I think I knew, but all bluster and sarcasm aside, I was inexperienced, lacked self confidence and was hardly prepared for close-quarter lights out. Sybil was sweet, and I hope she has forgiven me for probably not getting the stamp licked; she did, however, postmark my heart, and it never quite wore off.

My senior year, with no wheels, mobility was somewhat limited. "Going out" usually had to be shared with someone who had a car. I had many friends, and there was much kidding around in the many activities we shared. My most serious heartbreak had been with Doris deSha, a 4-H connection from Hamilton County, and nothing had happened at home rivaling that. In the fall, as the weather grew colder, after each football game it was common to pair up with somebody and join whoever had a car; the ride to wherever was important, but just getting warm was equally so. For some divinely inspired reason, I started pairing up with Leatrice Mason, an attractive girl I was conspiring with to help through Mr. Benton's history class. Leah was engaged to a guy who had already finished college and was working for the TVA, in Knoxville. Jim wasn't around on Friday nights, however, and, from shivering in the back seat of Jessie Guinn or Jackie Hill's car to the natural inclination to experiment with some heavy smooching, this got prolonged through the rest of the football season and into the first of the next semester. We had fun.

One day, in January, 1952, Leah said that, "I am going to have to stop fooling around with you, because my best friend is going to kill me, if I don't; she wants you, herself." Well, I knew all along Leah was spoken for and my male ego, being the monster it is, said, "This is a good thing." And it was.

The point of my regret for not dating more is that I did not have enough girl "friends," or become comfortable being around girls, without being influenced by going steady, jealousy, marriage, limited activities, or other things teen-age kids need time to grow into. I never wished the ***result*** to be different; I have wished that I could have been prepared to deal with it in a more mature way.

All too soon, those "happy days" were behind me and I was, again, ushered into the next phase of becoming big people. Leah's best friend turned out to be Ms. Most Versatile, June Canupp; the last semester, we became an item, enjoyed our senior trip to Washington, DC, worked on the yearbook, went to the basketball games where she played, and graduated. At year end, we passed our yearbooks around, where everyone wrote, "Take care of June," "Hope you and Virgil have a happy life," "Be sweet to Virgil; he's the best," "You two make a great couple, and deserve the best," and other such inspired prose as eighteen year olds are wont to offer. She went to work for Pat and Trim Love at the Farmers Bank, and I continued my career at the Athens Coal & Transfer Company. Overall, high school had been an enjoyable growing and learning experience. I remember, and consider outstanding, teachers that include Peggy Long, Bob Benton, Lynn Bevins and Mrs. Lucile Anderson. The rest include many who were average and some less so; all were doing their jobs, and none harmed me in any way. There was a male teacher, perhaps two, who should have been in jail for their actions toward young high school girls under their care, who were entitled to respect and protection; they callously violated that trust.

I do not recall a planned approach or definite thoughts concerning college. Just as had been Homer's plight, our parents did not have the money to send me and, although I am sure they hoped I would go, in absence of the means to make it possible, the leadership and urging that I go was sort of weak. Further, with no disrespect intended, I believe they thought a "good job," a wife, and regular church attendance were worthy ambitions, as well. In any event, the only role model or person I knew who had actually shown a possible path was Homer, who had gone to Tennessee Wesleyan College, a Methodist Junior College in our home town. Living at home took care of the room and board, leaving only the funds for tuition and books to somehow find. He had managed to do so, although that was never easy.

There were many days when I imagined continuing my career in the local freight business. I shudder to think how excited I got when Sam Queen's (a co-worker) son, Bill, recently returned from the service, outlined a plan for us to buy a truck and hit the road. His plan turned out to be about as dependable as he was and, sad to report, he was dead from a horrible automobile accident within a year. I had been interested, however.

I did realize the value of college; it just seemed, overall, to be a goal and project somewhat beyond my reach. With several of my classmates planning to enter college, and many enrolling at Wesleyan, I think I gradually came to the conclusion during the summer of 1952: "Why not." I was working, and the idea of "working my way through" did not seem that foreign, as I had actually worked all my senior year in high school, indulging myself in clothes and such that I had not been able to afford before. By enrolling at Wesleyan, I also had the benefit of moral support from friends and classmates, and I did not have to leave June. Sounded like a plan.

At the start of school, I changed jobs, but the hours and pay were about the same. To describe the college experience for me is to suggest that it differed little from high school; I lived at home, I went to class, I worked, I studied (too little), I saw my girlfriend, and the next day, did it all over again. Much could be written about the "college experience," but it has been and must be written by others. I missed it. I was spending my time growing up outside the ivy-covered walls, and my experience probably relates more closely to those today, who make it through in "night school."

Money was always an issue. Quaint as it may seem today, the tuition at Tennessee Wesleyan was $75 per quarter, plus the cost of books, fees and whatever other incidentals may have been needed. In spite of living at home and working, coming up with this much cash on the barrelhead was difficult. I must acknowledge that June, during my two years at Wesleyan and before we were married, pitched in a time or two. During my second quarter, I searched the college catalogue with a microscope, trying to see if there was any aid or scholarship I could pursue. I noticed an entry: "scholarships for children of ministers." My now bean-sized brain naturally assumed that, since I was a Baptist, this Methodist Institution would laugh me out of the sanctuary where the money was handed out; however, desperation occasionally makes heroes of us all. I sucked it up and called upon the President, Dr. LeRoy A. Martin, and pled my case. I vividly recall him drolly smiling, then responding that, "Yes, he thought they could accommodate a Baptist." Even though this was like hitting a modest lotto today, I went for broke, and asked him if he could find it in his heart to make it retroactive to the first quarter; he did, and I left his office a grateful and happy man. That $25.00 per quarter made all the difference in the world.

Tennessee Wesleyan College, affiliated with the Holston Conference of the United Methodist Church, was contained in a neat, small campus, north of downtown Athens, Tennessee. During its storied history, it has struggled for survival, its troubles almost always rooted in the maintenance of an enrollment sufficient for that survival. It has survived, and, now a four-year institution, seems modestly successful. In 1952, it was in the struggling mode, although that was not obvious and of concern to the students there.

Living off-campus, attending Wesleyan, as mentioned before, seemed an extension of high school. The most noticeable difference was the make-up of my classmates; being a Junior College, we were closer in age, except for the Korean War Veterans returning to school; there was more diversity, with students from North, South, Middle East, and Latin American countries and, in general, we saw ourselves as more adult. The campus students were, indeed, on their own, and no one got them out of bed to attend class, if they chose not to. The professors and instructors were dealing with specific professional matter, as well as the humanities, resulting in a somewhat more mature atmosphere in most classes.

I did not start off particularly well. During the first quarter, I won my trip to the National 4-H Congress in Chicago and was out of class for about 10 days. In addition to the simple fact I got behind, a couple of the instructors were not at all sympathetic with my choice of time; this caused my immediate task to be not only catching up with class material, but also re-building the bridge with an instructor or two. Of particular note was my experience with Professor Kenneth D. Higgins, a local, Athens attorney who was moonlighting as an economics instructor at the time. He was very perturbed that I would cut his class for more than a week and was totally uninterested in my reasons. I struggled that quarter, with no help from him, and he rewarded me with a well-deserved D. We kissed and made up next quarter and I earned an A, perhaps restoring both our faiths in me. A side note: Professor Higgins served the City of Athens in many legal capacities during a long and productive career and was equally supportive of Tennessee Wesleyan, during that time. I underestimated him, and I hope he did me, during those testy days back in 1952.

The only other difficult time I had was in English composition; I seemed not to "get" Ms. Hampton, but I thought a few athletes in class did. My feeling that she was condescending and preferential to one or two gave me an excuse to cop an attitude, and she rewarded me with another well-deserved D. Otherwise, I was B's and A's with a C here and there, for good measure. I transferred a 2.90 average from Wesleyan; mathematically, it takes a long time to average B with a D or two lurking around to drag it down.

I pledged a fraternity my freshman year: Phi Sigma Nu. I endured an initiation from the old school of hazing, then drifted out of active participation before year-end. My only memory is of just not being very interested in what we seemed to be doing. I do remember with some glee, however, something that occurred during that initiation. After we had been humiliated in about every manner imaginable, we were taken in small groups and dumped out in the country, presumably lost; we were left to find our way home, in the middle of the night. Turned out, my group was stranded on a dirt road, which I immediately recognized as being below the Union Chapel Methodist Church and along the path where Homer had death-marched me to the Riceville School, twelve years before. We gleefully started home, thankful that I was along, and I believe we actually caught a ride before long. Our group turned out to be no fun at all, when we returned in record time.

With some urging from old friends and new acquaintances, I ran for president of the Student Council. With Pete Wilson, our football quarterback and an Athens native as my campaign manager, I mounted an all-out campaign to capture the office. My card read: "Your vote is your decision. Your decision to work with Mincy gives him the opportunity to work for you. He wants to do it." I gave a spellbinder of a speech at a gathering of the entire student body; gave it my best shot. Dallas Anderson, a great guy living on campus, narrowly beat me out and made a very good president. The Campus Party was just too much for the Living-at-Home Party, although my platform of God, Mother and Country should have been compelling.

Several factors converged my senior (second) year that ultimately headed me in the next direction. I do not remember envisioning life beyond Wesleyan; I was a business student, taking all the business courses available. I took every accounting course and, after a couple I later took at the University of Tennessee, I always viewed myself as having a minor in accounting. Years later, when I took over the family budgeting, I set up a double-entry book keeping system that worked, but took about a half-hour just to write a check. That zealous approach was tempered with time but, to this day, my budget is some "T" accounts on a single piece of paper. Once an almost accountant, always an almost accountant. Anyway, I perhaps envisioned an "office job" after graduation.

June and I were married November 25, 1953 and, instead of going home, then to June's, I just went directly there after school/work. My serious thoughts, however, were directed toward what I could do, the quickest, to realize my little share of the American Dream. I had received a student deferment from the Selective Service System, which exempted me from the draft only as long as I was in school. A huge industrial development was underway near Athens, being built by the Bowater Southern Paper Corporation; many of my buddies and I were there the first day possible, filling out applications for employment. The owner of the Williamson Hosiery Mills, John Williamson (where I worked), often touted his friendship with Sen. Estes Kefauver, indicating he could arrange to get me an appointment to the U.S. Naval Academy, if I were interested. I have been forever curious about that possibility but, even then, I doubted my qualifications, was discouraged regarding a career in the military, and could not have been married and attended. All these issues were floating around during the spring quarter of 1954 when, one day on the bulletin board in one of the accounting classes, I noticed a flyer announcing the availability of scholarships to "study transportation" at the University of Tennessee. All my outside work, thus far, had been transportation related, and I thought, "Study Transportation?" "They would give me money to do this"? With nothing to lose, I sent in an application. I asked some friends who were attending Tennessee and was assured that I "could make it," although the thought of the big state university was somewhat daunting.

June and I concluded that we would go to Knoxville and I would enter the university, if I was awarded as much as $300 in scholarship assistance; less, we would not go. As we waited, during the summer after graduation, I received a call from Bowater, to come down for an interview. I do not remember ever doing so, as it must have been about the same time that I got the letter from the University of Tennessee;....$150.00.

It is laughable what can ride on such trivial happenings or circumstances; to us at the time, the money difference between our go, no go, decision was palpable to the extreme. In the end, however, we decided to go and, in the fall of 1954, off to Knoxville we went for two more years of school. A small, upstairs, furnished apartment at 1006 Churchwell, in Fountain City, which is on the Northwest side of Knoxville, was our dormitory for that first year.

As apprehensive as I was about leaving my hometown permanently and perhaps humiliating myself in class at the "Big Show," it turned out to be just more class, work, home, study, and class all over, again. There developed so much pressure and eagerness to get out and get started in grown-up stuff, as we observed other married couples doing, that it was unthinkable not to carry a full academic load or pass every class. I was a father my senior year in school, and I can just imagine (no, I really cannot) the scene of my coming home and stating, "You know, I just do not believe I can handle eighteen hours this quarter; think I will enroll for only twelve. Of course, that puts us into another year here." Or, "Guess what; I flunked statistics. Got to take it over." I was proud of my 3.11 at UT, considering I worked full time, tried to be a good husband and father, went to church, and caught an occasional football game.

I majored in "Transportation," of course, and received another scholarship my senior year. Tennessee's approach in the College of Business Administration was different from most Liberal Arts schools, in that the student was smothered with profession specific courses, rather than a broad sweep of generalities and humanities. I took fifteen three-hour courses directly relating to the Transportation industry and most of the balance was general business courses. Fortunately, every course I had taken at Tennessee Wesleyan was accepted at UT, and I did not have to "make-up" any "required" courses. I was able to follow the progression of core courses; by my last quarter, I actually was able to loaf through with a slightly reduced load.

Again, living off-campus sort of removed me from feeling a part of the university. That was not the university's fault; it was just that other than class, I did not connect with much going on elsewhere. All too soon, it was over, and the paradox of achieving my dream was having to leave what I had appreciated all too little while experiencing it. My Uncle George bought me a class ring, and with cap affixed and gown flowing impressively, Monday, June 4, 1956, I marched across the stage in Alumni Memorial Auditorium with 2,479 others and received my diploma. There were 288 from the College of Business Administration. I recall celebrating a little with our good friends, Dave and Audry Kirk, then, it was off to pack up, say good-byes, and report to work the following Monday.

I often say that college, or all school for that matter, teaches us to learn, more than to do. Perhaps that is truer in general education and professions, such as business, than it would be in the technical, legal or medical professions. I know that few of all those accounting and transportation courses were worth a hill of beans in the daily tasks I came to face. I generally felt I was prepared to face them, however. Upon graduation, I am sure that I, like most of my classmates, felt overly cocky, 10 feet tall, and bullet proof, when put to the test. Time soon tempered that. And we, my classmates and I, did not get there alone.

From Mrs. Grubb to Professor William Way, the road was paved with the efforts and dedication of teachers, workers, parents, friends, family, and strangers, who, in our system of doing things, make it all happen. Chance, ability, ambition, work, circumstances, need, support….all came together for me. Those factors made possible the delivery of that little scroll, which conferred to me, Leonard Virgil Mincy, a Bachelor of Science in Business Administration. And that's no BS!

4-H Days

It is fair to say that my Four-H Club activities and experiences, more than any other single happening, helped make possible later successes. We can never relive the past nor second guess ourselves with much practicality; however, I know how those experiences made me feel about myself. I cannot prove that, without them, many other opportunities that followed would have turned out as they did. A little background may be helpful regarding what Four-H is and from whence it cometh.

In 1862, the Morrill Act was passed, giving the states federal lands to establish colleges offering programs in agriculture, engineering, and home economics, as well as in the traditional academic subjects. The University of Tennessee, founded in 1794, was one such college.

The Smith-Lever Act in 1914 established the Cooperative Extension Service to support informal adult education and development. This constitutes one of the largest adult education programs in the world and consists of three levels of organization—federal, state, and county. Its overall objective is to plan, execute, and evaluate learning experiences that will help people acquire the understanding and skills essential for solving farm, home, and community problems. This objective was and is met through educational programs that make use of research funding emanating primarily from the U.S. Dept. of Agriculture and the state land-grant colleges and universities. The Extension Service also sponsors Four-H Clubs for youth throughout the country.

Four-H clubs or "4-H Clubs" are organizations for boys and girls from nine through 19 years of age. This organization is part of an educational program designed to improve techniques of agriculture and home economics, promote high ideals of civic responsibility, provide training for community leadership, and foster international understanding. Founded about 1905 to enable rural youth to "learn by doing," the American 4-H program is run by the Cooperative Extension Service of the U.S. Dept. of Agriculture, with the aid of state land-grant colleges and universities. Extension Service workers and volunteer leaders guide local groups. Each group elects its officers and plans its activities and programs. The club motto is "To make the best better;" its pledge, "My Head to clearer thinking, my Heart to greater loyalty, my Hands to larger service, and my Health to better living, for my club, my community, and my country."

The 4-H movement has grown to include cross-cultural exchange and training programs with similar groups in over 85 countries. A national 4-H Club congress is held annually in Chicago at the same time as the International Livestock Show; club members display their achievements in such fields as breeding and raising poultry and cattle, cultivating vegetables and fruits, canning and preserving foods, handicrafts and needlework. In response to the steady decline in the United States agriculture population since World War II, 4-H has expanded its program to include groups for youngsters living in the nation's cities and suburbs. There are more than 5.5 million members in the United States. Indeed, I was once among the numbers.

It would be a disservice to parents, family members, teachers, and a safe community environment to moan that, in grade school, I was drifting aimlessly toward a life of sharecropping or minimum wage work in the stove foundry. It is true, however, that I was not afforded the opportunity of Boy Scouts, summer camps, travel, competition, and those things that *can* build self-confidence and success.

Then, this happened: from 1948 (8th grade) through 1952 (high school), I served three terms as president of the (4-H) county council, won the first public speaking contest in the county, won the county Jr. Leadership contest three times, and was State winner in the Jr. Leadership project. That qualified me to attend the National 4-H Club Congress in Chicago. I was the first winner of the Vol-State award, the highest award offered (at least then) to a county 4-H member. I was a member of the county dairy (cattle) judging team for three years; our team placed fourth in the state in 1950. I was also a member of the county livestock judging team that won the state championship in 1951, qualifying us to compete in the nationals, held in conjunction with the International Livestock Exposition (and the national 4-H club congress) in Chicago. More on that later.

I was selected to attend the Tennessee 4-H Club Congress in Nashville twice and the 4-H "Roundup," held annually in Knoxville at the University of Tennessee, three times.

I presided at countless meetings, rallies, elections, and other activities. I served as Jr. Leader of my local club. I completed projects, met important people, was in the presence of famous people, and traveled to see parts of a world quite different from the Mouse Creek community. Who could argue that these experiences had no lasting benefit?

How did it happen? It would make good fiction to describe a yearning to be part of something, a longing to get away, or a burning desire to succeed. None of this would be true. It perhaps was destined to happen but, most certainly, it started by the purest of chance; I was in the right place at the right time.

I have vague memories of 4-H club activities at Mouse Creek School when I was in the sixth or seventh grade....perhaps earlier. I do believe these were rather irregular, as the Extension Service personnel responsible for these activities were the County Agent and the Home Demonstration Agent. These people had names: L. M. Amburgey and Ms. Mrytle Webb. Their primary focus being on the adult issues of agriculture and home management, I do not remember regular "meetings" or much discipline with respect to projects.

I have memory of only *one specific meeting* of the 4-H club at Mouse Creek; it involved Mr. Amburgey giving a demonstration of how butterfat is extracted from milk. He had with him a small spinning device that, combined with the use of some type acid, would cause a visible separation (in the small containers that were part of the machine....not on the floor of the room). I remember him having those watching feel the containers, as they became quite "warm" in the experiment. Naturally, we supported Mr. Amburgey with sincere "oooohs" and "ahhhhhhs." Interestingly, during the summer of 2001 while visiting the Mayfield Dairy in Athens to test some of their widely acclaimed ice cream, I noticed in Mayfield's "museum" a model of the very device L.M. wowed us with, long, long, ago.

About 1946-47, I decided to pursue a project; I was going to raise a hog. Actually, this was not much of a departure from our normal rural life. Dad, along with church, garden, voting Republican, worship, and rather limited views of youthful pleasures, firmly believed in raising hogs. We always had one. I never remember an economic analysis as to whether or not we came out ahead raising, butchering, canning, and preserving pork, versus just buying what we needed or doing without. He believed in it so we always did it.

This was different, however, because it was *my* project. I was going to buy a baby pig (Porky, if you will), feed it, keep expenses, take it to market at the appropriate time, and start my fortune in sowbelly futures. I also believed I had a chance to enter all-grown-up Porky in the hog show and reap rewards that would make me further rich and famous.

Table scraps alone rarely sustain a growing, always hungry little porker, unless, of course, those scraps come from the tables of a 100-seat restaurant, which we did not have. Even if one has room for little bacon bits to roam, graze, root, and do what pigs do, feed from some external source is needed. My little Porky had only a small lot and insufficient scraps, so purchasing feed was necessary.

Come roundup time, my "project" was hauled off to Chattanooga to the hog show and sale, and I went along expecting to see it judged. I really, really thought I had a chance.

What I did not know, and perhaps should have, was that those worthy of competition were sort of pre-ordained through registered bloodlines and previous competition. When I finally located poor Porky in the company of many other lower caste porkers in the holding pens, I noticed a few dudes brushing, polishing, "finishing" and otherwise preparing their prize hams for the competition. What was at stake, of course, was the sale price; prize winners were bought for boar or sow duty, and the rest of the lot would soon find a home at Oscar Meyer.

I did win some small notoriety; I attended the "show" where the grand champion was decided and was on the front rail, leaning over dejectedly, looking on. After the final competition, the winner and his finely coifed, Poland-China, high bred, and quite handsome hog were having their pictures made. As I was only a couple of feet away looking on, I became the background of pictures making the Chattanooga papers the next day. The word was, "Well Virgil, you did not win, but you got your picture in the paper."

When the books were closed and audited, my project cost me $16.47. So much for the pork industry.

Thus, on a spring day in 1948, I was at the Athens Armory attending what I remember as an "officers and leaders" meeting. Included were the officers of the individual clubs in McMinn County. I must have been an officer in the Mouse Creek Club to receive a ticket for the day, which probably included some rah-rah, hot dogs, pop, and a chance to mingle. Mrytle Webb oversaw the activities.

This is a good time to pay tribute to Ms. Webb, who spent a lifetime in McMinn County, helping to teach rural homemakers how to improve their homemaking and craft skills. To recall, the rural south in early years of the 20th century included many poor, undereducated, and unskilled people. Even though young ladies traditionally learned to cook, sew, and care for their (anticipated) children, assuming that homemaking would be their career, the purpose of the Cooperative Extension Service was to teach new, improved, and more efficient ways to do this. Home Demonstration Clubs were established in communities, with the Home Demonstration Agent being the organizer, leader, and program focus of most meetings. Such had been and was Ms. Webb's life. In between, she and the County Agent squeezed in 4-H Club activities.

On this Saturday in 1948, near the end of the planned program, I remember our having lunch, which was mostly a stand up affair. As we stood around, I can still see Ms. Webb coming over and announcing that we were going to elect officers for the "County Council." We had gotten by for 1948 years without one, but I guess in the post war prosperity, it was deemed we needed one. Anyway, she came up to me and said, "Virgil, you are one of the biggest boys here; you can be president." In turn, she selected Emma Lou McKinney, Blan Parks, Marion Moss, and Franklin

Roderick to round out my staff. I was not the biggest (Roderick was taller and, later, a basketball star), brightest, or best qualified to do this, or much else. Just like that, however, I was in and all the rest followed. Had it not happened this way and at this time, most of what happened next would never have occurred.

For a year, I do not remember any other event; I was not aware of any changes within the county agent's office, nor do I remember any 4-H activities of significance taking place. I certainly had not initiated any sweeping changes to the Department of Agriculture.

One day, in the spring of 1949, I was called into the principal's office at McMinn High, where I was a totally obscure freshman, and introduced to Russell Humbred and Nellie Robinson. They were, they said, the Assistant County Agent and Demonstration Agent, respectively, and were responsible for 4-H activities. Russell was short, and possessed an average build, fair complexion, light hair, a raspy voice, an infectious smile, and an attitude that exuded confidence. Nellie was, on the other hand, quiet, had dark hair, and was somewhat plump, with a perpetual smile. They told me they had big plans for the 4-H clubs of McMinn County and, since I was president of the County Council, they were paying me a visit to solicit my advice and support for what was coming. Further, I was told that, in a matter of days, there would be a "rally;" all the clubs in the county would meet in Athens, parade around the square, then take part in various activities. The Governor of the Sovereign State of Tennessee, the Hon. Gordon Browning, would be present and speak. I was to preside, serve as master of ceremony, and introduce Governor Browning.

To my knowledge, no one had ever (with good intent) called me out of school, made a special trip to do it, and signed me on as an important part of any project. Had I not been "selected" to be president of the "Council," I would have never received that visit. In addition, Russell made this sound like fun, not to mention the added excitement he created talking about camp, judging teams, roundup, and all the things we were going to do. Although our shared experiences were short lived, he became one of the influential adults in my early life.

On Friday, April 20, 1949, march we did! Fifteen hundred 4-Hers, representing every club, stretched out from one end of Athens to the other. If we had trumpets to blow and could have held out for seven times around, I believe we could have brought down the old courthouse.

The crowd was divided into two groups: one to the Athens Theater and the other to the Strand Theater. At the Strand, movies and ice cream (courtesy of Mayfield "Creamery") was the order of business, while at the Athens, we put on our show of me, the Governor, a few other dignitaries, pledges, anthems, prayers, and minor speeches. The "show" then switched theaters.

Gordon Browning was a tall, stout man, whose trademark was his rendition of the "Tennessee Waltz." He could certainly carry a tune but, after a bar or two, everyone prayed for him to carry it in another direction. That day, he spared us and to this day, I cringe when I remember my pathetic performance. For instance, I distinctly recall quieting the crowd (remember, a packed theater) and thanking them with, "I really appreciate yaw'll com'in out to see *me* today." After a few titters ran through the audience, I tore into the program. *I was in charge*!

Thinking back, all embarrassment aside, no one told me that *I could not pull it off*. That is the benefit of opportunities like this and the positive results that can follow. You never know what you can do, unless given a chance and you try.

From that point on, it seemed my divine right to go to 4-H camp, to Roundup, to enter speaking contests, to be part of the judging teams, or to tackle projects. It was not then, nor now, my nature to be aggressive or to volunteer for much of anything. There is a thin line, however, between that state of mind and being willing to try anything, if encouraged, led, and supported in the effort. Russell would just say, "By golly, we're going to do this, or do that," and we jumped at the chance. Given the opportunity, I endured the work and ate up the successes that came with it.

There were so many positive experiences that to detail them all would only amuse me, even if I could reconstruct them. By far, the most lasting memory is of the friends made during those shared times. I find myself wishing I could have bottled those feelings, popping the cork from time to time to fill the void time creates as it passes us by.

I want to share with you descriptions of some of the key players in those little dramas.

From a 4-H standpoint, the important unit was our county (McMinn), which was part of a district made up of several other counties. I certainly do not remember them all, but the key ones were Bradley County (Cleveland), Hamilton County (Chattanooga), McMinn of course, and at least Marion, Polk, Franklin, and Grundy. County activities pitted us against each other, sometimes, but more often against the other counties within our district. Our district, on the other hand, often faced other districts or would be involved in coalitions with other districts in such things as state elections, campaigns or the like.

County friends were more like brothers and sisters; you would date a girl from another county before your own, although that did happen. You teamed with these "brothers and sisters" against other groups in the competitive stuff; yet, come night and recreation time, these geographical differences were put aside, the music started, the square dance caller went to work, and boys and girls tried their best to be boys and girls.

The closest knit group to me, during most of this three-four year period, included those who became members of our livestock judging team: John Henry Gilbert, Kenneth Grubb, and Lane Parkinson. Ultimately, we were just together more, shared more, endured (including each other) more, and succeeded more. Others: Franklin Roderick, John L. Baker, Clyde Anderson, Earnest Bacon, J.C. Cates…. to name just a few, were soul mates at various times.

And oh, those girls: within our county, Emma Lou McKinney, Emma Lee Brown, Blan Parks, Carolyn Fillers, and Regina Womac were sisters, true, but more. I just wish I could recall all those scattered throughout the state; however, June Hill from Bradley County, the Boyd sisters, Ann and Carol, Martha Byles, Patsy Crites and Doris deSha…. all from Hamilton County…will never be forgotten.

John Henry Gilbert was absolutely the most charismatic, crazy, gifted (in some ways) person I ever met. In the context of those times and experiences, he was a virtual magnet; boys vied to be part of his inner circle, and girls seemed to line up for his favors. He could be quite generous.

First, in a classic Grecian sort of way, he was handsome, with broad shoulders, narrow waist, blond wavy hair, and features similar to the Adonis statutes. While those attributes never hurt him, it was all the other stuff that could make him captivating.

He could sing, although not in a formal, trained way. In fact, in a disciplined, structured, musical setting, he sort of froze up and became bland and ordinary. He had a repertoire of songs he could pull out (God only knows where he got them), deliver them acappella with total non-chalance, and leave his peers howling and screaming for more. He did things like "You made toothpicks of the timbers of my heart," and "Cigarettes, Whiskey, and Wild, Wild Women," to name a few. You had to be there.

He had strange abilities. For instance, he could say many words beginning in "S" and sort of whistle through his front teeth at the same time. A favorite greeting was, "Whatya say, Sam,"…whistling on "say" and "Sam." He could absolutely throw his right knee out of joint at will. He would walk with a deformed leg-dragging style that looked pitiful. Imagine the mayhem he caused by walking into a slow moving car on the street and going into his routine. I had and have no idea how he physically did it, but he could.

He would preach. Lord, forgive us, but get a group together and with a little encouragement, he would cut loose a spell-binder replete with all the gasps, arm waving, and fundamentalist trappings.

He was also tough. He lettered in football at McMinn as a freshman, a feat not often accomplished. I remember a few years later at Tennessee Wesleyan College, we had gym together; one of the little torture things Coach Hudson would do was have us play "horse." The game was simple: get a partner, decide who was up and who was down (the rider just straddled the "horse's" back, upright), and turn the entire class loose on the gymnasium floor. The last team standing won (Coach always gave the winners a dollar). It was like stand up wrestling, two-man style….. anything went. John Henry and I teamed up and always won. I had good legs, he was strong up top, and we did not give up. We just would not go down.

I could go on. John Henry and Lane were a grade behind me, although I believe John Henry was my age. Kenneth Grubb was a grade ahead. When we practiced or traveled, we played off John Henry a lot, but together, we had a lot of fun.

To highlight some happenings of those days, I am going to divide the experiences into two groups: the fun things and the work things. This gets rather arbitrary, as most of the work things were fun, and most of the fun things were designed for useful purposes. Nevertheless, activities that tended to be "awards" include (in my grading system) state 4-H Congress, Roundup and camp. That leaves as work: projects, team activities and all the training that went into our being successful.

The first time I traveled more than 60 miles from home was in 1948, when I was selected to go to the 4-H Congress in Nashville. We were given white pullover sweaters with a green "Tennessee" state outline on the chest, with four H's highlighted in a cloverleaf in the center of the "state." This was the official uniform at the state Congress, as well as for those attending the National Congress. No other state had anything as distinctive; we were always a sharp looking group.

I was in the eighth grade, in the big city for the first time, and quite in awe of the experience. I stayed at the old Hermitage Hotel and, as all our activities were in one of the hotels around Capital Square, in the War Memorial Auditorium, or even in the State Capital, it was all heady stuff. There were outstanding speakers, meals above my normal fare, and sight seeing to behold. We visited the Hermitage (Andrew Jackson's home), the Parthenon, Fort Donalson, the Capital, of course, and other sites of local fame. There was politicking to do, as officers of the state group were elected each year. At Congress, we elected a Governor, (although at Roundup, the "chief officer" elected was "President"). As a lowly fourteen year old novice, I had no grass roots support, nor was I a behind the scene mover and shaker that year. However, my memories of the process include the young man elected Governor, Murray Miles, who was not only impressive then, but throughout a long career of public service as a state legislator and executive. Even then, Nashville sights notwithstanding, the most memorable benefit was association with outstanding young men and women.

There was always entertainment of one kind or another. This was Nashville, home of the Grand Old Opry. The National Life and Accident Insurance Company was an active participant in our events as well as sponsor of Opry segments. This company also owned powerful radio station WSM, clear channel 650 on your radio dial. It was a natural, then, that one night, the entire Congress, some 250-300 strong, was packed into a rather small "studio," seated on the floor in a tight semi-circle, and entertained by Opry stars. In a little book somewhere, I still have autographs of Odie and Jodie, Zeke Turner, and Milton Estes (and his Musical Millers) among others.

Emotionally, though, what could only be compared to a similar age group today being given a free concert by the Back Street Boys, Brittany Spears or U-2, was our reaction to a performance by Eddie Arnold. He was then the Garth Brooks of country music and, although that might be a rather limited genre, it was enough for us. The setting lent to the occasion, as the front rows, sitting cross-legged on the floor, were literally at his feet. With his band, the Tennessee Plowboys, including "Little Roy Wiggins" on steel guitar and the Willis Brothers, he went through his hit list of the day. There was one highlight for the group and a lifetime one for me. During the course of his stint, he said, "I'm sure happy to be here with you tonight; you know, ah was once a Fo H club membah myself." I am sure if there could have been a measuring device, almost 300 teenagers would have registered an emotional climax that very moment.

Mine came when he sang his latest hit, "Anytime." Okay, so that is just one among scores of hit tunes from his 40 years of entertaining. Until that night, however, I had never seen a band or performer of that caliber in person, let alone up close and personal. The music just immersed my brain.

The next morning we left Nashville by bus on a dreary, rainy, day on our journey back to Athens. I simply could not get the sounds and words of that song out of my mind. It reverberated over and over: the lines, that band, his voice. To this day, I can download that memory and almost play the emotion of that night over again.

The McMinn 4-H County Council

Left to right: Emma Lou McKinney, Blan Parks Virgil Mincy, Marion Moss, Franklin Roderick   1948

Arkansas Shirley and Tennessee Virgil

About as big time as it gets: National 4-H Club Congress, Chicago

Spring Rally 1948

Gov. Gordon Browning; speaking after a rousing introduction by Virgil, seated.

National 4-H Club Congress Tennessee delegation, 1952; I am third row, fifth from right; John Henry is (standing) to my right, John L. Baker is behind and to John Henry's right.

Standing Stone State Park, lying in the North Central Cumberland Mountain hills of Tennessee, was home to 4-H campers from our District. Located northwest of the little town of Livingston, south of the Kentucky border and southeast of Dale Hollow Lake, it was isolated enough to present a legitimate claim to "roughing it."

Now, it has been expanded, hosts a championship golf course, and is part of continuous efforts to improve the park system within the state. In 1949, the picture was quite different. By today's standards, it *was* rustic: isolated, single structure for meals and meeting, cabins housing from eight to 10 people, and common shower-bath accommodations. A lake had a concrete (actually, rock wall) section off one side that served as a large "pool." From the main hall leaving the front, the gravel road split, forming a "Y." The left road went up and around the side of a hill to the boy's cabins, the right to the girl's.

Sound somewhat crude? It was heaven!

Getting to Standing Stone was another matter. Visualize that in East Tennessee, the Appalachian Mountain chain lies northeast to southwest, with its peak being Mt. Mitchell, just within North Carolina. From that point west, the ridges diminish until toward mid-state they pick up the eastern ridges of the Cumberland Plateau. The state, from east to mid-state, is a series of northeast-southwest ridges and valleys. Examine a map and immediately obvious (certainly in 1949) is the fact primary roads run parallel, in the direction of the valleys between corresponding ridges.

No main roads ran from the southeast (Athens) to the northwest (Livingston), therefore, travel in 1949 was rather torturous. There were paved roads, of course, but just no direct route. We had to "gerrymander" our way in the general direction, which made the trip a long, tiring, impatient ride. The non air-conditioned school buses in late June-early July did nothing to lull us into comfortable sleep. *It just did not matter*! Padded with our blankets and earthly possessions, fueled with energy, mischief, and anticipation, we could not have cared less. Let the games begin!

Camp was generally a Monday to Saturday deal, with Monday spent arriving, settling in and getting organized by dinner; Saturday was pack up and go. The days were structured and full: by lights out, everyone was ready for lights out unless John Henry felt called upon to preach. The program did not vary much: breakfast, flag-raising (with salutes, pledges, prayer), clean up cabins, morning lectures, field-trips, crafts, lunch, brief rest, recreation, clean up, dinner, fun and games, vespers or such, and lights out.

The business of camp included lectures or demonstrations on dairying, poultry, electricity, fashion, crafts, wildlife, among others. These "ran" every day, and we had to plan our time to attend most of these before the week was over.

We could choose from many activities; softball was my main thing. There were other organized competitive games, but softball was the loudest, took up the most space, and required the most people. It was "county" competition, with the teams made up of your best: agents, leaders, members....anybody,.... against their best. If you had a "fast pitch" pitcher, all the better. Forget that bit about letting everyone participate; if you could field nine studs, well, suit them up!

We had a good team that year; Russell was quite an athlete and, with Kenneth, Collins, Hanks, Clyde Anderson and others, we just went through the other poor counties like Sherman through Georgia. I was not the star I would later become, but got to play outfield. I contributed and did my best to remain inconspicuous by not messing up.

Swimming usually came after softball and, actually, we had swimming competition, too. Most of the people were like me; we could swim but had no serious "lap-training." When it came to competition, if the event was four or five laps, we just did our best not to drown before it was over.

The main event, hands down, was evening fun and games. There were talent skits, square dancing, hanging out, checking out, pairing up, breaking up, and good times had by all.

It's time to introduce another memorable person from those days, Fred Colby. Fred was part of the Agriculture Extension service and worked out of the University of Tennessee. I do not recall his exact title; he always was the recreational leader, not only at camps, but Congress and Roundup, as well. I think his duties and skills were broader, however, as he also led us on forestry and wildlife field trips, did crafts, and was quite a generalist.

The best analogy I could draw to him would be that he resembled a middle-aged Walter Mathau, with a more cheerful demeanor.

I remember those evening activities best. He had the music, set up the sound system, announced the type dance, instructed, encouraged participation, and would wow us with his "buck dancing" exhibitions. Of course this was "dancing," but those voices of conscience that nagged about eternal damnation had to compete with the fact it sure felt good, to be so bad.

The memorable event of this camp, however, was not to be framed in the pool, on the field, or over that slick, meal-covered, dance floor in the main hall. I eternally wish it could have been.

About mid-week, there was news that one of our campers, Tommy Spurlin, was not feeling well. He was not in my cabin and was a year or so younger, therefore, I was not as close to him as to others. I did know him, though. He was full of life, very active, and was developing into an outstanding 4-Club member. From a fine farm family and great community, he definitely was a rising star.

By Thursday, he was no better, seemed to have a fever, and I believe had been taken to the nearest doctor for a check-up. I guess the advice was wait and see, as apparently we did. Friday morning, Tommy seeming worse if anything, the leaders decided to take him home. The logistics were: Nellie Robinson would drive back (she had brought her car) and someone would volunteer to ride along. I cannot say if I was asked, volunteered, was in a bad romance and wanted to escape, or what; however, I did go.

What I do remember is that long ride of probably five to six hours. We were in Nellie's new, four-door, Studebaker, and I remember what a smooth, gliding ride it offered, particularly, when she put the pedal to the metal. I wish I could forget this, but, by then, Tommy was already in a semi-coma.

When we finally arrived in Athens, Nellie went directly to the hospital....Foree's, I think, although that is just a guess. We left Tommy there, I went home, and camp was over for me one day early. While I appreciated the nice ride home versus the old yellow bus, I wished it could have been the other way round. It got worse.

Tommy was soon diagnosed with polio. Remember, in 1949, polio was still rampant, there was no cure, nor was prevention possible. Everyone was shaken upon hearing about Tommy, me included. I was doubly shaken, knowing that I had maximum exposure to a very contagious disease. In all seriousness, I am sure I pledged to never square dance again, to not even think about it, if I could be spared.

I was, but Tommy was not. He lived, but was totally paralyzed. Shortly after our return, he was rushed to Warm Springs, Georgia, for treatment, with police escort all the way. Reports were that had he not done so, and in such a timely manner, he might not have made it. Warm Springs, you may recall, was where President Roosevelt spent quite a bit of time.

Tommy lived to make a lasting contribution to many, many others. With a lot of special assistance, he completed high school and attended Auburn University. (He probably graduated....I am just not sure.) A close friend and outstanding 4-H member, John L. Baker (I mentioned him before), went to Auburn with Tommy, with help from Tommy's parents, and served as friend and companion while they both attended school. Tommy's star burned out all too soon, and his life ended prematurely, but he inspired many people with his smile, his courage, and his never-give-up attitude.

A final footnote: how could I have known that 50 plus years later, I would drive daily through what is known as the "Studebaker Corridor" in South Bend, Indiana, on my way to work. The factories shut their doors for the last time about 1965, and the city has been slow to do much other than watch the deterioration of those old buildings where Nellie's four-door prize rolled down the line long ago. I thought of Tommy almost every trip; I often wondered: if we had dashed to Athens earlier, would it have made a difference? Probably not, but who knows? In life, many things are not fair, some things you cannot foresee, and others are just never known.

Camp Standing Stone in 1950 offered more of the same, with heightened anticipation that came with an additional year of what we believed to be maturity. Another year of activities had passed, and Russell had us off running on several fronts. We were practicing for judging team competition, working on projects for state competition, remembering another successful spring "rally," and completing our individual projects. Nellie Robinson had gotten married and was replaced by Grace Stowe (a doll). Russell was just everywhere; encouraging, leading, coaching, planning, and causing us to increase our affection and respect for him. He, of course, had graduated from the University of Tennessee, with a major in agriculture, and seemed to have access to all the professors, specialists, and facilities to aid in our practices or development. He charmed us with his "poor boy" tales about sleeping in the barns and cleaning the stalls, as he worked his way through school.

Our dairy cattle judging team placed fourth in the state. We were beginning to work on livestock judging and were about ready to take on all comers.

I had a couple of interesting projects that year: tobacco and yard improvement. A neighbor who lived at the foot of the hill from our house asked me to help him with his tobacco crop, and we worked out a deal whereby I would manage about half of his total crop (one specific "patch") and assist him with the rest. Nat Edgemon seemed old then but was probably in his fifties.

His farm, which faced TN 30, was a hilly affair, but was large enough to have afforded him a living for a long time. He had a nice home, barns, equipment, and all I needed to do the work. We were to split the anticipated profits from my patch.

I will not digress to explain tobacco farming, except to reaffirm it as the most reviling habit at end use and the nastiest, most loathsome work on the front end. Getting the patch ready, "setting it out," applying arsenic, "suckering" it, de-worming it, topping it, cultivating it, cutting it, hanging it in a barn, grading it, "handing" it and, finally, taking it to a "barn" for auction sale is truly a work of the devil.

My crop went well in every respect. The result, though, proved somewhat disappointing due to circumstances beyond my control. In early November, as I started "grading and handing it off," I had an appendectomy, putting me out of commission for a couple of weeks. Nat got impatient and insisted that I hire some help to get back on schedule, so I enlisted the services of a buddy, Cliston Riggs, and the Standridge boys, and together, we soon knocked it out.

We had a good crop and received a fair sale price, however, after I paid my migrant workers and the hospital bill (yes, that was the case because we had no insurance and my parents did not have the cash), I was left with just a few bucks for a summer's work.

The yard improvement project was another matter. Our house had been split up and moved from another location. It had been placed on a wooded lot that was part of about seven acres of mostly trees, rocks and brush. The yard was no different than all the other rough stuff that surrounded us. I set out to "improve it," as "Yard Improvement" was a recognized activity, therefore, an official "project."

The task was simple: lay out some perimeters, dig up the stumps and rocks, smooth it out, plant some grass seed, and start mowing it. If I have described tobacco as nasty, this yard work was nasty in another dimension. With no power equipment and relying on an axe, a "mattock," a shovel, and lots of sweat, it became a pioneering enterprise, to say the least. At 16, Honest Abe I was not.

Truth must be told. Homer was home that summer and joined in the project. Fairer yet is to admit that he led the project, and total truth in advertising calls for admission that he did the lion's share of hard work. This, to say the least, caused some friction, as he seemed to lack understanding of my planning, organizing, camping, traveling, and having to practice other skills while he swung the axe. At times this lack of understanding spilled over onto the yard itself, and I still have an image of our rolling on the yard in mortal combat, Mother beating us with a broom trying to restore order, as Johnny and Cordie Fritts passed by, calling out, "Morning, Mrs. Mincy."

She would claim, "You have no decency," and at times, I doubt we did.

Camp 1950 was another highlight reel. The routines were the same and I shall not belabor those points again, except to say our softball team was even better. Clyde Anderson was a good "fast pitch" pitcher, and that year I was his catcher. I had caught some in grade school and seemed to have a knack for it. By camp time, modesty prohibits undue bragging, but let's just say I was quite good. Without mask, pads or protection, I just squatted and gave Clyde a target, encouraging him to let it rip. I also could hit and still have some pictures someone took that include a shot of me in full, graceful swing. One particular shot supports my claim that the ball surely was still rising when it sailed over the capital, in Nashville, 137 miles away.

The only other softball issue to report was the field: it was small, irregular in size, with limitations. Almost by agreement, we tried not to foul to the right, as we had to go into a ravine to retrieve the ball. A home run to left field might include a sprint up the gravel road toward the girl's cabins, before the ball was fielded.

We still kicked butt!

That camp will be remembered, though, for the girls, young love and global news. The girls first.

The difference between 15 and 16 years of age is substantial, particularly when that year has been spent in thought, practice, scouting, and planning. We had been there before, knew most of the people, grown to like some of them, and now were ready to get on with it. For the sake of understanding, however, a definition, if you please:

Dating *adv,* dat-ing. 1). To date 2). An occurrence whereby two members of the opposite sex are together at least five minutes, say at least five words during that time, and have pre-arranged to do so, with neither side failing to complete all requirements.

Dating has some subtle differences from "going together," as going together can lack some of the requirements of dating. For example, it sometimes is assumed a couple is going together, when, in fact, they may not (be). Also, a couple may say they are going together, may allow others to think they are going together but, when together, may not fulfill the actual requirements of dating: i.e. saying five words, together five minutes, or have pre-arranged to do it. This definition, of course, is circa 1950; I do not want to entertain the definition of that term today or what it might entail. Period!

By Monday night of camp 1950, most of us 16 and older were checking out, being checked out and making plans. By the end of fun and games, couples had been established and many girls were walked up the hill to their cabins. I was no exception.

Intending no disrespect, I do not remember how it occurred, but right off, I was "dating" a blonde girl from McMinn County. She was nice, friendly, reasonably attractive, and all mine.

Only problem was, by Tuesday night, I wanted out of that deal but did not know how to do it. I had not heard the song, yet to be written, "Fifty Ways to Leave Your Lover." I dragged around Wednesday, trying to keep up appearances without my heart being in it: jealous of John Henry, who had captured Doris deSha, and Grubb, who had cornered Martha Byles; both were from Hamilton County.

Thursday, I had regressed to hiding out, trying to avoid contact with Ms. Homegrown Blonde, missing some of the normal stuff going on. Sometimes, however, strange things happen.

Mid afternoon, probably back in the cabin, Kenneth Grubb informed me of some startling news: Doris deSha wanted to get together with me. "Yeah, sure." "No fooling"? "How can that be; what about her and John Henry"? Well, I was told, things change and somehow, that had not worked out. A little later, John Henry came by and agreed. "Yes," he said, "go for it." (whistling through his teeth on "yes")

This was uplifting news; however, I had to confess my dilemma to my buddies. I had to let them know I was betrothed and did not have the guts to get out of it. I had not discovered plain, straightforward English yet; fact is, this little problem plagued me more than a few times in this long and weary life.

But what are friends for? Grubb told me not to worry. He would check around and see what might be worked out. Do you believe in miracles?

In a very short time, with the clock ticking and dinner plus what might follow drawing near, Kenneth reported back: "Guess what" he said, "your problems are over; she has gone home." Just like that, order was restored to my life, the sun rose, and my future was promising.

I still have a picture somewhere of Ms. Homegrown Blonde, but even after reviewing name lists of camp, no one, I mean absolutely no one rings a bell. I remember all I have described, but just cannot, on threat of death, recall that woman's name. I am consoled only with the assurance (and hope) that she does not remember mine, either.

With that, I whipped on my favorite pull over shirt, applied the Vitalis, and charged down the hill toward the evening and whatever might follow.

The mating ritual of most animal species vary little: looks, moving closer, communication, sharing some happening, slight touching, all in some order or other. Such was the case this Thursday evening at Standing Stone State Park.

Doris deSha was, as I have said, from Hamilton County and, more specifically, from Chattanooga. Big city girls start off with an advantage: that is the assumption they have seen more, done more, know more, have more, and therefore, are more worthy. The special ones have the ability, perhaps God-given, to exhibit this aura without making it a moat, rarely to be crossed. She knows she has it, you know she has it, but if you have the courage to deal with it, it only enhances her worth, never detracts from it. The rest…..forget them! Big city Doris had that aura, but seemed within reach. She was average height, Leslie Caron face and eyes, full lips, and black hair kept simple and short. She was confident without being loud and reserved without being shy: a lovely smile…. heaven waiting beyond the gates.

Pre-arrangement always saves a lot of time and, as I said, the get-acquainted ritual was on a direct route as we moved through dinner and into the evening. As John Henry sang and preached a little for the group, I sensed some disdain on her part for his performance but, otherwise, this issue did not sidetrack us. I had observed her, been around her during the week, but had not gotten up close and personal.

There came a break in the square dancing, when partners usually stop to catch their breath and move outside for a little air (remember, this was June/July down south). I have never felt qualified to describe what followed. It was sweet, powerful, memorable and deserves considerate treatment. It also needs to be told at this point, so, to give depth and poignancy to these few moments, I hired an experienced "romance fiction writer," Ms. Allison Hartz (her pseudonym), for this purpose. I told her in my own words what happened, and she has given professional depth and feeling to this important event in my life. As she described it:

> *Outside the hall, catching their breaths from the fast, synchronized movements of the dance, they continued to hold hands as they strolled away from the building. Gradually, they left the fading light from the windows of the hall, moving into the growing light of a rising, almost full moon. Regaining his breath, Virgil said, "Would you like to go for a walk"?*
>
> *"Sure," she replied.*
>
> *"Can we go up toward your cabin? Don't guess they would like it if we walked toward mine."*
>
> *"Sure," she replied.*
>
> *At the fork, they turned right, up the gravel road, past the flag pole, and into the shadows of the overhanging trees as they neared the cluster of cabins that housed the girls. Nothing was said, but as they moved forward, from time to time, the pressure of their hands would increase, then relax, as they acknowledged this closeness. They approached the nearest cabin, a short distance from the road, and paused, listening to the sounds of the night: the music now resuming, but faint from the hall below, the crickets in the night air, a whip-o-will giving it's call from a distant tree, and their breathing, so close,…so near. They stood facing each other, the moon directing a soft, diffused light over Virgil's shoulder into Doris' eyes as she looked up at him expectantly. They drew closer.*
>
> *"Doris, isn't this your birthday"?*
>
> *"Yes, how did you know"?*
>
> *"Oh, a little birdie told me. I just heard some of you had a party, with cake and everything. Sixteen"?*
>
> *"Umhuh."*
>
> *"Sixteen all day, and haven't been kissed yet"?*
>
> *"Well.…"*
>
> *Awkwardly, but with determination, he moved to engulf her in his arms. He had never kissed a girl before and was acutely aware of it. A natural desire and sense of what was expected led him to wrap his right arm around her slender waist and place his left hand on the back of her head, as he gently moved*

her toward him. She looked at him, smiling, then, with a sudden urgency, joined him in passionate embrace. All the pent-up energy of their emotions fueled the strength of their closeness, as they clung to each other. Finally, slowly, they relaxed and moved back slightly.

"Whew!" he said. "That was nice."

"You were sucking on my nose," she replied, not harshly.

"Oh," he said. "Can I aim again"?

Her answer was muffled as he firmly pressed against her lush, ripe lips: hungrily, longingly, with determination to get it right, lost in the passion of the moment. Finally, when breathing became a more urgent necessity than kissing, they released from each other and slowly stepped back.

"Doris, I have never kissed anyone as delicious as you."

"You're not so bad yourself."

"What is that perfume you are wearing? I don't think I will ever forget it. It just makes me want to consume you."

"That's probably my Arid deodorant; got it at Woolworth's...two for sixty three cents."

"Think I'll get some."

"You should."

Again, they moved into each other's arms, emboldened by their increased familiarity with each other. They kissed with what seemed endless passion; they pulled back, to look into each other's eyes, only to move quickly forward into another, more urgent embrace. Finally, relaxing, Doris said:

"Guess we should get back. They are probably about ready to close."

"I know, although I could stay here forever. And to think, tomorrow is our last day."

"Yeah, and it's going to be busy. I've got to finish my needle-point."

"I've got to complete my belt."

They moved arm in arm down the hill, toward the hall and the lights streaming out of the propped-up, wooden, push out windows. As the sounds of music and laughter drew closer, Virgil said to himself:

"Hot Dang! Sixteen, I'm in love, and have already gone half the way! Life can't get any better than this."

Or something like that.

Friday was wind up day: finish the projects, complete the games, dance the last dance, and make promises that were intended to be kept a lifetime. This certainly happened when you were smitten seriously, as I was. Doris and I compared notes about what might be possible in the future, with Roundup in Knoxville seeming to be the nearest chance to cling to each other again. When you live 55 miles apart, with no car or telephone, you might as well live in Nepal for all the good it will do you. We promised to write.

This camp was also destined to end on a somber note. June 23, 1950, the North Korean Army crossed the 38th parallel into South Korea, engulfing our country and others into a protracted "police action." Since I do not have the exact date of our particular camp week, I am not sure if we received word of the outbreak of hostilities while we were there, or if it was just confirmed that reservist were to be called up. It did not matter. Russell was a Captain in the Army Reserves, having served in World War II. Before camp broke, we knew he was gone. He was recalled, spent time in Europe and, upon return, went to work for the Knoxville Fertilizer Company, leaving the Extension Service forever. To a man in McMinn County, we felt our 4-H days of fun and successes were over. We could not imagine anyone replacing Russell.

"Roundup," a fall affair held at the University of Tennessee in Knoxville, was like camp, only held in the city. Another difference was attendees were from every county in the state. It lasted a week and was designed to close out many state projects, announce winners, and cheer them on to national competition, including the national 4-H Club Congress in Chicago.

The activities were a structured mix of lectures, field trips, competition, free time, and recreation. The lectures and "business" part of the week would take place at the UT farm, in the College of Home Economics facilities, or in other UT buildings; meetings and evening recreation were in the old Alumni Memorial auditorium. The fun field trips were to Big Ridge State Park, north of Knoxville, and Clingman's Dome, in the Smoky Mountains, near Gatlinburg.

We stayed in various UT facilities: the boys usually in the dormitories located in the recently completed south addition to Shields-Watkins stadium. This, of course, was the home of the Tennessee Volunteers, our state football heroes, (unless your heroes were Vanderbilt, Memphis State, Mississippi or Arkansas, to name a few)

The clean, neat, sparsely furnished rooms in the stadium were nicer than anywhere I had lived: indoor plumbing down the hall, recreation rooms on each floor, and all the football heroes right around the corner in the "East" stadium dorms. This was good stuff.

The "All Stars," elite storm troopers of 4-Hdom, gathered in Knoxville on Saturday prior to Roundup week to be briefed by leaders on the week's activities and be assigned some responsibilities for that week. Almost all of these were friends of mine from camp or other meetings, including, of course, my true and only love, Doris.

John Henry had arranged a visit for the two of us to Chattanooga sometime between camp and Roundup in his (dad's) pickup truck. Doris had rounded up a friend to be his "date," and we went to Doris's home one Sunday to hang out. John Henry was not too impressed with his part of the deal; Doris's parents were there and, although we practiced the "Black Hawk Waltz" and visited, it was a blaah trip. Definitely no passionate kissing.

In Knoxville, Doris and I went to church Sunday morning, went somewhere with another couple Sunday afternoon, and she dumped me Sunday evening. As it turns out, John Henry had apparently been always on her mind, so she just tore out my heart and stomped that sucker flat; she made toothpicks of the timbers of my heart. She did not even send me a pillow to cry on. These last thoughts were courtesy of Corny Country Songs, Inc.

I survived the week, and some fine young women did their best to make me forget, but it took time. Three weeks give or take. What helped heal a broken heart included having my guitar with me and, after stumbling into conversations with some of the football players hanging out at the "E & E," I was invited over to the East stadium dorm to entertain them. Sure, they were two to four years older, but probably bored enough to find me amusing; I was in hog heaven just being there.

I also went to the "Alumni Gym" and pressed my nose against the window to watch eight or 10 football team members practice running those old single-wing plays. I remember (All-American) Hank Lauricella, Jimmy Hill, Ted Daffer, Dick Ernsberger, John Michaels, Herky Payne, and a few others. They would set up on the gym floor and run off tackle plays again and again and again, then again. This group and the rest of the team were Dunkel's pick as National Champions that year, going 11-1 and defeating Texas in the Cotton Bowl.

The extra-curricular activities around the university usually equaled the organized stuff when it came to the "plays of the day." The university then was primarily the buildings on the "hill," a few newer ones around the perimeter, and the farm, five miles south, across the Tennessee River. Cumberland Avenue, which ran in front of the University into downtown Knoxville, had a small town flavor and, even though the setting was impressive to a small town boy then, it bore no resemblance to the 25,000 student sprawl that is the university today.

The U.S. Department of Agriculture and the Extension Service of the University of Tennessee did replace Russell Humbred, of course. Soon after Russell departed for duty, we were introduced one day to Marvin Lowry. Marvin was a rather short, swarthy guy, with black wavy hair; he had some kind of accent that was different. It was not a lisp, not necessarily "southern," and really sounded sort of "Creole," although I believe he grew up in eastern North Carolina. He just sounded different. He was somewhat shy at first and did have the wisdom to acknowledge that he had big shoes to fill, asking that we be patient and give him a chance.

He did go to work, however, and soon was pushing us, practicing, taking us to farms all over, and trying to get us ready for the livestock judging competition. This takes us into the work portion of this story and nothing was more demanding than judging competition.

I had been a member of our dairy cattle judging team and, as indicated, we had finished fourth in the state. Judging dairy cattle was very basic; we primarily judged "Jerseys," the main breed of the dairy industry in Tennessee. We learned the important points of breed excellence, learned to recognize them, and learned to rank these points within the class used for the competition.

The procedure was quite simple: a class was shown (usually five or six cows), the official judges made their picks, and your judgments were measured against those of the official judges. The team with the highest total points won. Usually, a team had four members, and the highest three scores counted for the team's total score.

Livestock judging was another matter; the classes included sheep, hogs and beef cattle. In competition at the district and state, requirements included an oral presentation of your picks, explaining the rationale of your decisions. It was necessary to work "hands on" with the sheep and carefully scrutinize the hogs and beef cattle, as some of the essential points of the breed were not as apparent as with dairy cattle. It was hard work.

Traveling with Marvin, working, watching his enthusiasm every day helped us accept him; winning the district in 1951 sealed the bargain. Heading to the state finals, we were certainly a lighthearted, gung-ho team.

This event, in late October 1951, was one of the highlights of my 4-H days. We had worked hard, were confident, knew this would probably be our last chance to be in this competition, but knew, also, that all the other teams were good. That year, the state finals were in Franklin, Tennessee, with the competition staged on a farm nearby.

The stage was set for this drama as we left Athens for Franklin after school this particular day, in weather that was questionable, to say the least. In those days, before Interstate travel, it was at least a five-hour drive, in good weather. We started in rain, ran into some light snow in the Cumberland Range near Cookville and, later, freezing rain. Somewhere east of Nashville, as we were dozing along in Marvin's four-door 1951 Mercury, he lost it on a patch of ice, skidding off the road and into a ditch.

We took inventory, determined we were still alive and that the Mercury had only taken a shot to the mouth (a crushed grill). I really think I had a cracked rib, as I banged against the door armrest, but I could move, breathe, and did not want to be the team wimp. That said, we pushed the car out of the ditch, piled in, and headed for Franklin.

Arriving at an old hotel in downtown after midnight, tired, sore, hungry, and miserable, I do not think we gave ourselves much chance for later in the day. I distinctly remember being in a shared room with John Henry; rather than go down the hall to the common bath for the floor, he just looked at the "sink" in the room and made his decision; you can figure out the rest.

The next morning was clear and cold, with a light coat of ice and snow on the ground. Marvin treated us to a good breakfast and, looking at his tired, sore team, we probably gave him little reason for confidence. I remember, though, his giving us a pep talk, exhorting us to just go out, work, ignore the elements, and believe that we were better than the other teams. If we would just outwork them, we would win.

That is what we did. It was just brutal; even thought the sun was bright, it was cold, the sheep had ice all over their wool and our feet were freezing before we even got started. That day, we really invented the term "ice bowl" for our competition. As the classes were shown and we started the oral presentations, the training and practice started to pay dividends. With no knowledge of how we were doing, by the end of the day, to a man, we just felt we had won; we noticed we seemed to be "hanging in there" better than some of the other teams.

We cleaned up and went to dinner, where the winners were to be announced: the winner…(Drum roll) **MCMINN COUNTY!** Glory be! All that work was worth it. In addition to "hickory canes" for each winning team member, we won a trip to the national 4-H Club Congress in Chicago and a chance to compete in the nationals.

This saga, too, had a strange ending.

At the close of my junior year at McMinn, I wanted a job. Sounds simple, but did not seem so. I lived three miles from town, had no transportation, and the city guys always tied up all the usual stuff around town (store clerk, soda jerk, retail worker). Nothing against them, but that just seemed the way it was.

I noticed, however, that McMinn had a program called D.O. (diversified occupations), which was a co-op deal that involved going to class and working in a specific trade for high school credit during the senior year.

Usually, there were two classes in the morning and work in the afternoons, depending on the job. It occurred to me to give it a shot; maybe the coordinator could get *me* a *job*. It certainly never occurred to me that he might want students as badly as I wanted a job.

I signed up and, almost immediately, the coordinator, Lynn Bevins, contacted me to be convinced of my interest. I did my best to assure him and, presto, I had a job for that summer and for my senior year. Monday, after school was out, I went to work for the Athens Coal & Transfer Co., H.F. "Bo" McMillan, Prop.

Time moved on, I learned fast and, by late November, I was doing about all of Bo's chores in the coal, freight, scrap iron, ice, and, occasionally, friendly bootlegging businesses. After our big win in the state, Marvin planned to leave about a week ahead of the Congress in Chicago and the national competition. We were to work through the University of Kentucky, Indiana University, and Purdue University to practice our skills, including an introduction to "draft horses," which none of us had seen. Draft horses were included in the national competition.

Bo planned to go to the Tennessee-Kentucky football game November 24 and intended that I be at work to mind the store. That was it, period, no questions asked. It was a job, I was a hired hand, and he was depending on me.

Thus began a tug of war between the U.S. Dept. of Agriculture and the U.S. Department of Education, and I was in the middle, catching all the artillery. Lynn Bevins, the D.O. Department, and the high school side wanted, in fact insisted, I simply stay on the job and honor my school/work commitment, as if nothing had happened.

Marvin Lowry, my teammates, and the entire 4-H world beckoned me to Chicago, to the Super Bowl of Livestock Judging, and to sights never before seen. To make matters worse, it seemed my entire 4-H "class," i.e., all my close friends and girl friends had won in their categories that year and would be in Chicago. I had been our high point man in the state finals, and my presence would likely be missed. It was a position I should not have been in; however, Bo had made his plans and was not interested in compromise. I should have been complimented that Sam Queen and

Wash Martin, who had been with Bo 200 years, could not handle that half day on Saturday, but I, after five months and all of seventeen years old, could. It was awful.

I decided to stay. I guess I felt school and work had some balance of worth more than fun and games, but it hurt. Our team placed fourth nationally without me, and had I been there, who knows what we might have done. The crowning blow was some of my ex-team members telling me that, since I was not along, they just divided my share of the expense money and had a blast for two weeks.

Final: Tennessee 28—Kentucky 0

An epilogue to this tale is that Saturday, December 1, 1951, Lynn Bevins took me to Knoxville and treated me to my first Tennessee (football) game. It was the final game of their unbeaten season, against Vanderbilt, and Tennessee won, 35-27. It was certainly exciting but, again, I had to sit there and wonder: what were my friends doing in Chicago? Was John Henry with Doris? Had the team won?

I have for some reason always developed a strange, sad, and somewhat lonely feeling when the "fall look" arrives; leaves turn, days are shorter, and the sun is at a different angle. Thinking this through as I write, I believe it began during those days when I would be in that orange and green truck, delivering freight in Athens on a school afternoon, knowing my friends were in Chicago, and knowing what I was missing not being with them. I never really looked back, but that does not keep it from hurting a little, 50 years later.

There is a God in Heaven, though, in case anyone ever doubted it.

In 1952, I entered the Jr. Leadership contest again and did my best to give it a good shot. This was a county, district, and state competition and to win state, one had to make it through all the rest. Bottom line, it required putting together a "resume" of your 4-H "leadership" accomplishments and, truth to tell, perceptions probably counted as much as what you had done. At least your "resume" had to look good.

I attended my "last Roundup" (a little Roy Rogers, "I'm heading for the last roundup," if you please) in 1952, and it was memorable for several reasons. First, I was through high school, enrolled at Tennessee Wesleyan

College in Athens, and knew this would be my final fling. Several of my peers were there, but many had "won out" in '51 and/or had gone off to college that year.

Events actually started at a meeting in Chattanooga with our district "All Stars" a week or so before Roundup. During that meeting, I seemed to "lock eyes" with Carol Boyd from Soddy Daisy, and that lock seemed to be reciprocated. Before the meeting broke up, we commented that we would "see each other at Roundup."

At Roundup, as was the case previously, the All Stars went early to pave the way for the meeting; during this time, Carol and I talked a few times and seemed to hit it off. I had to return to Athens and work Monday, planning to return Tuesday. On Sunday night, I remember standing outside the small dorm, on the corner of what is now Cumberland and Stadium Drive, talking to Carol until they ran me off. The interest between us had stepped up a notch. I also remember hitching a ride to Athens on a truckload of green beans enroute to Chattanooga for Monday morning market. What trivia we seem to recall.

When I got back to Knoxville, Tuesday, one of the first people I ran into was the infamous John Henry, who advised me that "Carol was waiting." He confessed trying to spoil yet another of my dreams, but admitted being thwarted in this effort and quoted her as making it quite clear she was "waiting for me." Justice does indeed triumph, on occasions.

Oh, what a week we had. There were only two problems; I was "going steady" at home, and Carol indicated she was, too. I believe she told me she was actually engaged, or close to it. As a song-poet so aptly put it: "Three hearts in a tangle; one will have to break."

This is my last puppy love story, but I must alibi that I was not seeking this; it just happened on both our parts. In the end, I went back to Athens, my mood told the tale, I confessed, begged forgiveness, and cheated (if serious necking qualifies) no more during that 28-year relationship. I have always hoped Carol's life turned out as well.

I won the State Jr. Leadership contest and another shot at the National Congress. John Henry won the tractor maintenance competition, John L.

Baker won in his competition, and we would be going to Chicago, together.

I could write chapters about this Chicago experience and, in fact, kept a rough diary that I still have. Suffice it to say, it was worth the wait and the work.

I knew shortly after leaving Chattanooga, on the train for Chicago, that I had not won the national competition, which awarded a college scholarship to the winner. In fact, of the 44 members in the official party, I seemed to have been the only one not to have obtained a "physical," and I was almost kicked off the train. I know I was not told to get one; however, the officials were adamant and withheld my meal tickets until we reached Chicago and I obtained a medical certificate.

The disappointment of not winning had worn off before we arrived and events began. (John Henry Gilbert did win the national tractor maintenance competition that year, which included a scholarship; he used it for his first year at Tennessee Wesleyan, where we were the "horse" champions).

Just seeing Chicago, visiting places, and taking in the sights rivaled the scheduled programs. Yet, the events themselves seemed just one topping the other. Three times a day, at each meal, we filled the largest banquet hall at whatever hotel hosted the event and were treated to an extravagant show. It was celebrities, or bands, or inspirational speakers; at every occasion, the program was just a knockout.

We visited museums, planetariums, stage shows; it was almost too much to take in. On top of all that, I again lucked into an experience that has given me great memories and lots of fun over the years. I was selected by a Life Magazine photographer to be the subject of a story about the event.

Remember my comments about the distinctive sweaters the Tennessee delegation wore? At the first breakfast, I was pulled aside by a man, and I am quite sure the only thing causing me to be noticed was that sweater. He selected a girl from Arkansas, and I am equally sure it was because of *her distinct* sweater, but for a different reason. Shirley (sorry, cannot recall the last name) and I were his for the week. He took us to the head of the lines, to the front tables, took us to nice restaurants, and just smoothed out the rough edges of the week. In addition, mid-week, he had us pose for hours as he shot roll after roll, in preparation for a "cover" of Life. Big Time!

The story did not run. I still have the nice letter Wallace Kirkland, a long time staff photographer for the magazine, wrote me. That was the week President-elect Eisenhower made his promised trip to Korea. That, plus holiday competition, did our cover in. Mr.Kirkland split the proofs and sent Shirley and me equal numbers: literally, dozens of them, including the cover "mockup" that still hangs, framed, on my office wall.

I had mixed emotions about this story being in the magazine. When I got home and thought about the restaurants and night clubs he had taken us to, with the cocktail glasses and beer bottles showing in the background, I began to doubt my parents and church peers would understand my innocence. I breathed a sigh of relief when I sneaked a peek at the newsstand, looked at the cover, and saw it was not I. The magazine's choice of pictures would have been far different than mine, so all was well that ended well.

Everything I have described happened and more. In the end, most of my achievements happened on Marvin's watch and with his leadership. It could be said that Russell "racked the balls," and Marvin taught some of us how to "run the table." God bless them both and all the support personnel within the system; this includes the taxpayers who make it all possible.

While all this was happening, hundreds of equally deserving 4-H members back in McMinn County and a few thousand scattered across the state were worming their tobacco, plowing their corn, and staying home. I thought then and confess now my breaks came mostly by chance. I took advantage of them, however, and was blessed by the rewards that came. To the extent they were group efforts, I feel honored to have been part of those teams. Kenneth, Lane, John Henry, Clyde, John L.... I always considered you the real "stars." I was then and am yet grateful for these chances.

I was never Governor, but I got to introduce one.

I was never president of a major corporation, but was three-time president of the County Council; bet I had more fun.

I never played in a rock band, but I entertained the boys in the old East Stadium dorm. That counts for me.

I never made the cover of Rolling Stone, but I made the cover of *Life*; it is not my fault you did not see it.

With all due respect to the Packers and Cowboys, our team really played in the first "ice bowl" and won.

I never made it to the moon, but I remember my first kiss under it; I'm not sure I would trade the experience.

I was never famous…..but I sure had my days!

"Hail, Hail the Working Man..."

I am now retired, have punched out for the last time, and put all the service awards and company pictures away for good. Everything I say about work, working, where I worked, or what I did is with hindsight. While this distance from the action tends to create a little nostalgia from time to time, it also brings with it the blessing of understanding the difference between what was really important and what was less so.

Looking back, the most satisfaction came from being able to provide for those important to me. The drive to improve upon that capability usually carried with it a responsibility for added peripheral interests: employees, co-workers, the firm, or your boss. The ultimate driving force, and the subsequent high, was simply looking around at those depending on you and feeling that you had not let them down.

I know I did things that had an impact on the companies that employed me; I worked through a time of total change within the transportation industry. I have been part of a team that was the envy of others throughout our industry. I have managed facilities, territories, completed projects, succeeded, and failed. Work, productivity, improvement, and buying into the idea that your best can be better are worthy endeavors. I spent most of my life swimming in those streams.

In many instances, my actions or deeds affected other people's lives; when the final bell tolls, I hope the positives outweighed the negatives and those things having a negative effect on individuals and their families were for the greater good. In the real world, having to play Solomon occurs almost every day; playing the "divided baby," however, is never fun.

I have always felt the ultimate responsibility is to do your best, not to avoid the larceny of taking what was not earned, but to be honest with yourself. To look in the mirror each night and ask the question, "Did you do your best today, and are you prepared to do your best tomorrow?" is a sure invitation for some squirming.

No one can deny that success makes the juices flow, brings on accolades, helps make ladder climbing smoother, and gives cause for the family to gather round and cheer.

Yet, I believe—

No promotion I ever received created a feeling comparable to that of standing outside the delivery room and being told the baby and mom are fine.

Being told, "We are pleased to inform you that effective the first of the month, your salary will be increased," created no comparable emotion to that felt walking a daughter down the aisle, handing her over, and somewhat out of your life.

Absolutely no workplace occurrence rivals the raw emotions stirred looking down into a casket holding a parent or other close relative. Conversely, how could the best of factory news hold a candle to the words, "We are happy to tell you that the tests were negative?"

The news of a transfer to a bigger job in a larger city never matched the excitement of that first kiss, nor did much ever happen that rivaled the satisfaction of my last one.

One thing is for sure, however; my father and all fathers were dead on when they admonished us that, "If you do not work, you do not eat!"

Work, then, in addition to earning us our daily bread, tends to take on status, creates stress or satisfaction, becomes a source of social activity, and occupies some/most/all of our time. Too often, it becomes our identity; to be a doctor, to be a lawyer, to farm, to be a minister or, even lacking work, to be a failure.

With all this sorted out through the prism of that hindsight, I conclude what I did was certainly important, worthy, and of value. There are things that thought about, still stoke the fires; I would love to go back and do them again. However, talking about those successes (or failures) in detail would not be of much interest to anybody. It is with whom you did them and where, that remains important and of interest. It will be the events that involved interesting people and the times in which they occurred that will drive these work stories.

I turned professional when I was nine. That is the furthest back I remember seeking to earn some daily bread. The task probably belonged in the minor leagues of workdom, as it involved piling rocks in a field adjacent to the "down at Layman's" house. It was in a pasture field that ran from the road in front of our house for a considerable distance beside the house, widening out after a hundred yards or so, to contain the spring where we obtained our water. I do not remember the field rocky, in a "New England" or "old quarry" sense, but I guess it had enough to impede some type of progress. I just remember the opportunity to pick up rocks and place them in piles that would be gathered and hauled off later. My contract called for payment of one nickel. I do not remember whether that was for one pile, a dozen piles, a day, or all summer; just a nickel. I do remember doing it and being pleased at the opportunity. Earning that daily bread is a natural, powerful attraction.

There was always work from that time on at the Laymans. I was part of a work unit contracted for a specific responsibility. The pay went to our family, was never enough, and personal division was never a consideration. For instance, Homer and I may have milked 20 cows, plus or minus, twice daily, seven days a week, and received nothing other than room, board, and tuition to Mouse Creek for the effort. Definitely no allowance, as that was a mythical word used by comic strip characters such as Dagwood and Blondie. The rock pile, however, was my specific responsibility for my specific pay.

At the Gwinn place, when I was about eleven, I became yard boy and handy man for the Sam Elder family, who lived out the road next to Mouse Creek and its infamous bridge on Tennessee Route 30. Sam was manager of the local NAPA Auto Store, they had a nice little acreage and house, and were considered quite well to do by our standards. I mowed their yard, baby-sat, did projects, and was animal control officer for all the animals that seemed to be continually abandoned at the bridge, about three miles from Athens. This apparently was the distance it took to ease their conscience when the good Athenians would dump poor Fido or, for that matter, a paper bag of empty whiskey bottles, and drive back to the sanctity of West Madison. I will not go into my methods of elimination; suffice to say we did not run a kennel in my business.

Between mowing and dealing with the puppy problem, I recall a summer project moving a pile of dirt from beside the Elder's house to the back of the barn. This probably came from a septic tank being installed and was a big pile for a little man. A wheelbarrow load was more than I should have tackled but less than needed for my pride to permit me to quit. I worked most of the summer on this pile for the princely sum of five dollars.

4-H projects and family work are described elsewhere and, in most instances, did not help much toward my personal "daily bread." By the time I was in the last two years of high school, I became acutely aware of the difference between what I wanted and what my dear parents could afford to provide. A job, that is, a *REAL JOB*, seemed both the answer and a solution beyond possible achievement. The real jobs, particularly those allowing part time work during school and full time the remaining days, were in town and seemed to fall by divine right, or family connection, to town folks. What chance did I have?

A solution occurred during the latter part of my junior year when I considered the "D.O." program. I was quite thrilled with myself when I was accepted and started into what would become my career. (I guess that was, after all, the point of D.O).

Thus, the first Monday after school was out in June, 1951, I reported for work at the Athens Coal & Transfer Co. I was seventeen, thought I was a man, was dependable, had a driver's license, and was hot for that "bread."

Greeting me was another of those *most influential* adults in my life, Henry Francis (Bo) McMillan. To get the personals out of the way, he was about 47 at the time, average height, thinning hair combed straight back, bi-focal glasses, with a rather stern, serious demeanor. He actually was a very sociable and outgoing person, but when I was seventeen and he *father time,* owning half the town, I was a little intimidated. In addition, his wife, Mayme Jo, was moderately active in the business and, at times, became another boss.

Bo was involved in several ventures; he sold coal and had been very successful with this alone. With the advent of natural gas and electricity for industrial and home use, coal faded from the picture; however, it had been king. He also was in the scrap metal business, and this had been very strong during World War II. It was a fill in activity by 1951, but we still hauled off a truck piled high every now and then.

He was agent for a LTL truck line, and it was this part of his business that became my primary job. In a small office where everything went on, it just became difficult to separate out all the parts. Later, Bo went into the oil business, distributing gasoline and oil to "company" service stations. He also owned and operated an ice plant down the street, and I have no doubt he was involved in other ventures. He was a prosperous and well-respected man around town, and I am quite sure the Lions Club was proud to have him as a member.

On this Monday morning, Bo greeted me rather sternly and asked, "Do you have a driver's license?" He did not ask if I could drive, how many years experience I had, my driving records or references, but only if I had a license. Of course, I had! He then said, "Let's go down to my other garage and get the truck; you can take out a load of freight."

That I did. It is truly a wonder I did not kill half the town and myself. If I pondered about this in view of today's issues, I ought to go back and refuse to take the risk. Only because I had learned to drive on the "feed truck" Dad's employer let him drive home did I know how to drive and drive a truck, at that. However, that was only one of the issues. Using a hand truck, stacking freight, finding all the places around town, unloading (or loading) all the industrial products involved, and doing it "on the clock" was a challenge (the understatement of this page).

That first day, I handled 750-pound drums of glue, 600-pound wooden cases of yarn, iron castings, several-hundred-pound implement pieces, just to name a few. I had all the products that retail business uses around the Town Square and the challenge of placing every box where cranky store managers wanted them put. Help? Are you kidding? The only help I could draw upon was celestial, and while He may have cooled my fevered brow, He respectfully declined to lift any boxes.

I remember making it to the front porch, that first night, and stretching out; that was as far as I could go. I actually was in good shape then: good legs, about 170 pounds, reasonable strength; however, I ached all over. I felt as though I had been run through a sausage grinder and left in one piece. I did not want to go back.

Ah, but that daily bread——plus pride. My greatest work accomplishment in life was dragging out to Bo's torture chamber the next morning and taking another shot at my life's work.

There was one other motivating factor (in addition to my grade at school); there had been another student in this job the previous year who had flunked. He just could not handle it. From the first day, my adult co-workers called me "Parker" (his name), and I believe they made book on how long I would last. Thus, I had from day one Lynn Bevins (at McMinn High), Bo and Mayme Jo, of the Firm, my parents, all the industrial and retail entities around town, Sam Queen and Wash Martin, my fellow workers and mentors, to watch every move. They expected failure and withheld comment on any evidences of success.

I cannot offer any brilliant theory as to why I hacked it when Parker could not. I caught on to all the clerical stuff thrown at me. However, all the freight handling, driving, service around town, types of freight, and techniques of loading and unloading, that today require mechanical equipment, were and are a challenge to any adult, even after a formal training program. I had none and was expected to perform, starting at 7:00 A.M. the first day.

I guess this goes back to parental influence, whereby we always knew to "behave"; acting in a manner other than expected was just not acceptable. I formed a habit that has stood me well: never quit, never give in to a difficult situation, and always try to complete the task. Later, there were many times I would liked to have said, "Shove it," but 1) how could I face those depending on me, and 2) after that first week with "Bo," I felt almost anything could be handled.

In a few days, I could balance a hand truck, I knew where the docks and doors were at all the plants, I could back in square at the doors, I knew when help was really needed (and it was always given), and I was learning how we managed to load and unload freight that seemed impossible. I learned to rate the freight, cut the bills, do petty cash, teletype the other terminals, buy scrap from kids who came by, sell coal, and answer the telephone. By mid summer, Sam and Wash did not *call me* Parker; they just told tales *about* Parker. By then, we all shared in the joke.

I mentioned that I worked primarily with the freight; this was true. ET&WNC (East Tennessee & Western North Carolina Railroad Company) was a regional, LTL Motor Common Carrier serving the territory that its name implied. This company, as most others then and now, served the shipping and receiving public from "terminals"; freight from all directions was consolidated into "delivery" type vehicles for delivery (or pickup) to individual customers. The terminal would serve a geographical area to the extent practical. ET&WNC had large terminals in Knoxville and Chattanooga, one in Cleveland, a small terminal in Sweetwater, but no company terminal in Athens. Bo operated as a "commission agent" for the company; he owned the terminal, trucks, and supplied the labor and all other aspects of business in return for a fee: 10 cents per cwt. on all freight handled in and out. He was actually before his time, as commission agents serve most truckload carriers today.

Anyway, that was my start. By midsummer, I was an experienced hand. I did some stupid things, had some embarrassing moments, and had some corrective instructions along the way, but was pleased with my progress and myself.

One of the first things I bought was two pieces of living room furniture from Cherokee Hardware Company: a deep red/maroon vinyl sofa and chair. Orbel Erwin, the manager, gladly extended me credit, and Dad and I hauled it home on the back of the feed truck after work. That was something I wanted to do, and I was pleased that I could do it. I forgot to mention my salary was $30 per week for about 50 hour's work: five nine-hour days and one half day Saturday.

When school started, I reported to work at 1:00 P.M. and worked until closing time, continuing to work on Saturday. I had bread now, bought clothes, could afford cleaning, and had money in my pocket. My senior year at McMinn, we voted for "Superlatives." I know I was elected "best dressed." As editor of the annual (yearbook for you Northern people), I worked on the vote tabulation, and Don Smith, a large football player and BMOC, was helping tabulate votes. He was a sharp dresser, too, but out of the corner of my eyes and ears, I knew I was leading the votes. He had the tally, however, and when it was over, somehow, he won. I won a couple of others and thought it not worth a hassle to challenge this one. Hey, Don may have won, but, with my hard-earned bread and those store bought gabardines, I still believe deep down that I was the sharpest of the sharp that year.

I will always remember a couple of things from that time involving Dad. He worked almost next door and, during summer, we would meet occasionally at the Annex Hotel Coffee Shop for lunch. Remember, I was prohibited from smoking on threat of death and never did, growing up. However, after some of those lunches, I drifted into the habit of buying a couple of Tampa Jewel cigars for my afternoon pleasure. Dad never said a word. The fact that he was a chain smoker himself never deterred his curfew on all weed burning for the rest of us. By this time, however, I believe he accepted me as a man and thought it time I was allowed to make my own mistakes. I began to look forward to those little, wooden-tip Jewels. However, one day, I decided I did not like the habit I was drifting into; I have not smoked since. Dad, I owe you for trusting me enough to make an informed decision.

I usually rode to and from work with Dad. At night, after work, he often would let me drive; in fact, the route home usually involved his delivering an item or a truckload to some customer enroute. I would pitch in and help with the unloading. He would roll his window down, light up, and probably wind down from his day. Not a lot was said but we "bonded," man to man, worker to worker. Those were good days.

Schedule conflicts when I entered Tennessee Wesleyan College prohibited my continuing with Bo. During that last summer, I also got in his doghouse, and the reasons were more than I knew how to handle at that stage.

From time to time, Mayme Jo would drop by (in place of Bo, who might be out for some reason) and take over. She was a great person, and we got along fine; the problem was that during the morning, Bo would line things up for me to do during the balance of the day; Mayme Jo would come in and send me in some other direction. Bo, upon return, would ask why I had not done so and so, and I just had no good answer. I was too immature to face up to both of them and insist they get their act together; neither could I bring myself to rat on MJ. As a result, Bo thought, at times, I had lost interest. He at least confronted me on that a time or two.

In any event, one of our customers was the Williamson Hosiery Mill, located at the Southern Railroad viaduct on the way toward North Athens. It was a small mill, with a knitting and finishing plant that manufactured men's hosiery. The owner, John Williamson, was an up through the ranks guy from Englewood, who started in a small mill, worked, and expanded his way into moderate success. From time to time, when I had delivered freight to his mill, he had commented that, "I should talk with him, if I ever wanted to do something else." Entering college, I did, so I did.

John hired me as the assistant shipping clerk, starting September, 1952. With the head clerk, Billy Crittendon, I worked a flexible schedule: whatever time I had as long as there was work to do. This was from half time to full time, from the start.

Williamson Hosiery was the third largest men's hosiery plant in town, following the Athens Hosiery Mill and Vestals'. The knitting plant was run by Virgil Maupin, with the main office being there also. Initially, John ran the finishing plant, with supervisors for each department; Don Wattenbarger supervised the dye and boarding operations and two ladies (sisters), whose names have long escaped me, ran the production lines from boarding to shipping. Billy and I handled that end.

This was a natural for me; I set my hours with the only requirement being shipments had to be out each day. The task was rather simple: a stack of boxed (one dozen per box) hosiery came to shipping, with an order indicating where it was to go and who paid the freight. The order could be a dozen by parcel post or several hundred dozen, i.e., several cases, by motor carrier. We chose the appropriate packaging, put the individual boxes into shipping cartons, typed bills of lading, called the carrier, and made sure it was shipped. Parcel post was taken to the post office.

Our business was primarily with the chain stores of the day and other distributors, including some high-end retailers. I learned marketing, too, as we made the same socks for Woolworth that we made for Munsingwear or Wilson; the Woolworth would be in plainer packing and box; the mill price was $2.97 per doz. The Munsingwear or Wilson price, in a slightly fancier package, would be $3.00 per doz. At the store, a pair might cost 39 cents at Woolworth and 69 or 79 cents at Munsingwear.

Usually, I walked from school to work up the hill, through the bushes and kudzu vine, along my own shortcut, a distance of only a few hundred yards. Often, if I had a couple of hours between classes, I would work then go back to class. Billy and I got along well, and I remember sitting in his old car at lunch, listening to Hank Thompson and his Brazos Valley Boys' radio show, as we shot the bull about life's travails. Billy had a leg problem, probably from polio, and wore a brace, which caused him to limp with a pronounced hitch. I think this also caused him to over-react to relatively minor things, as he thought the world was somewhat against him.

This manifested itself toward the end of my first year at Wesleyan, when he became highly agitated at Mr. Williamson over something minor and quit. When asked, I told Williamson, "Yes, I could handle the job by myself" and he promptly gave me the opportunity to do just that. It meant more hours and sometimes having to stay later, but it was more money with the increased hours; it worked out well for me

During my second year in school and at Williamson, I began peddling socks on the side to guys at school and, in some instances, around town to some of the stores. John allowed and encouraged this; however, this and other instances caused him some grief later. In my case, I never got rich because I was a chicken salesman with my markup never being what it should have been. I was always the source of the "blue light special" to my customers. I made a buck or two, now and then and kept myself supplied with nice socks. My nickname to Wesleyan buddies became "the North Athens Jew," no offense intended.

John Williamson's business was rather simple; he was represented by a sales agent in New York City, a Mr. Goldberg, who would come to Athens once a year to work up the lines for the following year. They would design and agree on the patterns to be made, and Goldberg would go back into his world and sell them. He had an exclusive agreement to represent Williamson. The socks I peddled were only a drop in the bucket; Williamson sold irregulars, seconds and, in many instances, first quality socks on his own initiative. Goldberg sued John and, if not the primary reason, was a contributing factor to the company's going bankrupt a few years later.

About the same time I became the executive in charge of shipping, John brought in a relative, Bill Allen, to be General Manager. Bill was, I believe, a nephew of his (John's) wife. During my second year at Wesleyan, we also hired someone to back me up, with the idea of replacing me when I moved on. The chosen one was Claude Catron, from Wythville, Virginia. Cat played football and had a partial scholarship but, like most of us, had to hustle every way possible to make it through school. Cat and another friend of his, W.R. Kinzer, became good friends of mine through those days and beyond, as we double dated, hung out, and grew up.

A couple of lasting memories from Williamson included the time Mrs. Guthrie, standing at her position shaking socks into the trimmers to remove loose threads, said to me, "Virgil, you get you a good education so you will never have to work hard like us." That always comforted me, particularly when I felt near a stroke from pressure, frustration, work load, or responsibility; usually a combinations of all.

The other was during the summer after my second year at Wesleyan when, unexpectedly, Allen came up with a check and said something like, "I know you are going off to school; here's your check; good luck"! The jerk fired me without warning and with about six week left before I wanted to go. My protégé was given my job. We were slow that summer, but my warped logic had it that I was senior and, if there was a layoff, the junior man was out. Bill's logic was I was going anyway, so bye, Virgil.

In the big scheme of things, this was a non-event. At that time, when every penny counted, it was devastating, as I had decided to go on to the

University of Tennessee. That decision was based on a house of cards, financially, and this was a major blow.

I applied for unemployment and, surprisingly, got it. I got the scholarship I had applied for, too and, although only half of what had been the go-no-go cutoff, we decided to go. June, with help from her employer in Athens, The Farmer's Bank, got a job with the Hamilton National Bank in Knoxville, and all that was left as we moved forward was my finding something to do in Knoxville.

I must put in this plug; I was not magna cum laude at Wesleyan, but I graduated (this was a junior college during my tenure) in six quarters, passed every course, took enough work transferable to UT that I was accepted as a Junior in good standing, *and* worked from *half to full time every day* during this period. I get rather edgy with any of today's youth, including my own, who want to suggest that it cannot be done. Worse yet, that a full course load cannot be carried, *with no work performed on the outside. Yeah, I know; times are different!*

I went to Knoxville a couple of weeks before fall quarter, 1954, and called upon Professor William Way, head of the Transportation Department. Prof. Way was a well-known educator, who established the transportation curriculum (at UT) and nurtured it to become the premiere logistics study source nationally. I explained to him that I needed a job and asked if he could point me in a direction that might yield one.

He was a very sick man at that time and not a bundle of joy on his best days; however, he heard me out and told me whom to see on campus. That happened to be a Mr. Sams, who was to be in charge of the new student center being completed and set for opening when fall quarter began. Mr. Sams sent me to see Mr. DeFord who sent me to see June Baschler who gave me a job in the new center; my duties were to start the week before school started. I was a dishwasher/busboy and glad to be one.

Not much one can report about being a dishwasher; however, truth to tell, I washed the first dish in the (then) new Student Activity Center of the University of Tennessee on Cumberland Avenue in Knoxville, Tennessee in September of 1954. There was much confusion, finger pointing, and sharp words among the various levels of management as the Center opened and worked out the opening kinks. The ultimate fall-out was, in a few weeks, June Baschler was dispatched to the minor leagues, which for her was Old South College, on top of the hill, where she was to manage the snack bar in that facility. She asked that I help her, and her dying wish was granted. I climbed the hill each day and worked lunches, then, on a very irregular schedule, continued to work in the center. I worked days, nights, Saturdays, Sundays, holidays, and Football Saturdays; such is the life of a dishwasher, busboy and counter-man (for June Baschler). I worked nine months, carried a full class load, shared life with my wife, attended church, passed every class, and saw the Big Orange a time or two. It can be done!

Memories? This is a stretch but it is about my trying to stretch a privilege. Do not ask me how this actually happened but, *somehow*, I noticed employees of the University had Staff parking stickers on their cars and parked in nearby spots, when working. I applied and was given one; I doubt they asked if I was a student, and I know I did not volunteer to tell them.

With my sticker on the old Oldsmobile, I would pull into the faculty parking spaces below the College of Business Administration and usually study for an hour or so before class. I remember being eyed by Dr. Shaky Moore, of Economics Department fame, who ratted on me to the long arm of the law. That happened to be Officer Sam Lawhorn, of the University of Tennessee Security force, who, it turns out, knew my family. Some of his relatives had known Dad, when he was pastor of their church. Sam was a nice guy, and we became friends during my time at UT; he stalled as long as he could, but the pressure from Dr. Shaky became so intense that I had to find another spot for my merry Oldsmobile and me.

Another work-related memory that always stuck was that of a fellow worker in the dishwasher assembly line, one Nathan Tung. Nathan was from Mainland China, and, when the Communists took over from the Nationalists, Nathan's parents were lost in the shuffle. I can still see Nathan, beside me at the sink, smiling, as tears welled up in his eyes, saying, "I never expect to see my family again." I think Nathan was either a math or physics major, and this route was as foreign to me as his ethnic origin. I have always wondered what became of him.

Up at South College, a janitor, Sam, and I would talk a lot when we had a minute, although he stayed in the back during lunch hours unless he had to clean something. He was from Jamaica and would fiercely protest that he was, "Jamaican, not Negro" to little avail in segregated Knoxville. He was an artist and window dresser by profession and cynically told of being unable to get his foot in the door for any opportunities that might exist downtown. He did not seem bitter, just matter-of-fact, as we discussed many of life's issues. Sam was a man of great pride and knowledge, and I remember feeling sad regarding his plight; however, I could not change his status, and he seemed not to resent mine. I also have wondered what became of Sam.

After my junior year, we decided to return home for the delivery of our first child; Bo McMillan had contacted me and wanted me to work for him that summer. This was a Godsend, and I jumped at the chance.

The memorable thing about that summer (other than Pamela Gail arriving, August 6) was the fact Bo and I grew somewhat closer. He was often complimentary of my work and gave me a raise during the summer. I ran the office when he was out and enjoyed three months of good work experience. This is a fact: I learned more that had practical application from Bo McMillan than I did in school. This is not an indictment of college; to the contrary, I have always thought college, among other things, teaches you how to learn. At the Athens Coal and Transfer Co., and to some extent Williamson Hosiery, I gained experience "doing," and that was invaluable immediately following school.

A small footnote to Bo stories: my sister, Betty, worked for Bo following high school for two or three years and had to learn and endure all the same cast of characters and duties. At least, she did not have to deliver freight or coal.

My last year in school, I got a job at the ET&WNC terminal in Knoxville as a billing clerk and performed those duties until January, when, due to slow business, I was laid off. I tried selling pots and pans and hunted Knoxville for part time work, with little success. The last three months of college was the only time I did not work at least part time; that was only because I could not find anything.

The interview process began, and I talked with everybody; some jobs we drooled over and some we laughed at. I had decided I would chase all opportunities and go wherever the best opportunity led. This pre-ordained the possibility of leaving East Tennessee.

I will not wade through the job selection process; however, under some pressure from Professor Way, several other graduating Volunteers and I had agreed to go to work for the Interstate Commerce Commission. I had been accepted, fingerprinted, assigned a location (Louisville), and was resigned to doing this. Late in the year, I had interviewed with Burlington Industries, Inc., the world's largest textile company. The only notable remembrance of the interview is that I was relaxed (I had a job) but was sincerely interested in this company; I peppered the two interviewers with questions they could not answer. They kept saying, "If you get selected for an interview, I am sure they can answer your questions in Burlington."

Shortly before graduation, I was contacted by Burlington, who wanted me to come to Burlington (North Carolina) for an interview. I did and became excited about this possibility. They offered exactly what I wanted. I was interested in motor transportation, but did not want to work for a motor carrier. I was more interested in operations than traffic, and Burlington wanted me specifically for operations. I was impressed with their facilities in Burlington and thought this would be a great fit. The General Manager of Trucking & Warehousing, a pepper pot named J.B.Kennedy, interviewed me in Burlington, liked the fact I had a good handshake (from milking all those cows), and offered me a job. He told me about the progress other UT graduates, Garrett Woodward, Jim Shoffner, and Tom Stevens were making. He seemed to genuinely want me.

"*Better job at higher wages, ex-pens-es paid, and a car…*". It paid more; it excited me more; hello, Burlington, goodbye, Louisville! Sunday afternoon, June 10, 1956, I drove down Church Street in Burlington, North Carolina and found Mrs. Wilson's rooming house to begin what was to be a 21-year partial career.

There is, at this point, some housekeeping to get out of the way. Completing school, getting a job that was exciting after so much work, packing up, and heading for that report in date was like reaching the mountain top. It was every thrill and feeling of self-satisfaction that had been imagined for four years. In hindsight, I should have given graduate school or other careers some consideration but, then, there, that was impossible and inconceivable.

I also was not in this alone. To summarize one aspect of this, from the date June and I were married, we moved 10 times at my direction or at least in pursuit of my career. Never, ever, was she anything other than supportive, excited, cooperative, or whatever was required, to move the team forward. I am not now, nor was I then, so naïve as to believe this was without an emotional price. Worse, perhaps, she sought and quit at least seven jobs along that path, some with as little as a few hours notice.

I have had to deal with many employees and their spouses over the course of my career. Some of their reactions to experiences like mine have been about 180 degrees. I remember having my ears burned by a dear wife who had transferred from the South to the North and was bent out of shape because she could not find Dukes mayonnaise in the local stores. That, and other problems.

June, for keeping peace in the homeland (and working just as hard yourself) while I fought the foreign wars, I will be forever grateful.

Another little bit: I went to Burlington, by myself, for three weeks, leaving June and little Pamela Gail behind for only one reason; I had to draw *my* first check in order that June could make good those checks *she* was hiding in her cash drawer at the bank. It's called kiting, or similar ploys, and helped us make it through that last quarter at UT—another reason getting out and getting honest released such pent-up feelings of hope and satisfaction. It was just a milestone in our lives.

I reported to work for Burlington Industries, Inc. June 11, 1956, at the Burlington Terminal. My career was in the Transportation Division. Then, as now, this function was charged with managing the corporation's logistical activities. Of course, then, the word logistics had not been discovered; we just called it "traffic" or "freight."

My plan is this: I shall summarize my career path with Burlington and get that out of the way. Then, I shall relate some of the interesting things that occurred along the way.

In 1956, I began as a Management Trainee in Burlington and, three months later, was appointed Assistant Terminal Manager at the new Memphis terminal. I know my records state I was a dispatcher in Memphis, but J.B. Kennedy, explaining this move, very emphatically said, "Vugil, Ken Finley is going to be the number One man and every where we have a number One man we must have a number Two man. You are going to be the number Two man. You will be the Assistant Terminal Manager."

In 1957, I transferred to Rossville, Georgia, as Assistant Terminal Manager and, in September, 1957, to Columbus, Ohio, as the Terminal Manager. In one of a series of moves in August, 1958, I was promoted to Terminal Manager of the New Brunswick, New Jersey, terminal. During my stay in New Brunswick, terminals were grouped into Areas, and I became the first Eastern Area Manager, to complement the Southern, Central, and Western area managers.

In 1962, I transferred to Burlington, North Carolina, as manager of the Burlington Terminal. In 1968, I was promoted to Southern Area Manager, and in 1975, I became the Eastern/Central Area Manager. I have always described this period by saying that I managed the original "Thirteen Colonies," and Ben Tyler had the "Louisiana Purchase."

So, Monday morning, June 11, 1956, I showed up and reported to J.B. I shall try to avoid details on most of my cohorts whom I profile along the way; J.B. Kennedy must be explained. He was a Citadel graduate, who joined the Transportation Division in 1939. He had grown up with it, nurtured it, and was the driving force behind the operation in 1956. Bill Fayle had come aboard two years earlier from American Thread as General Traffic Manager and had taken some of the power J.B. previously enjoyed; however, operations were his, and he ruled with an iron fist.

He was a short, stout man, athletic, with a dissipated look that came from too much drinking. His trademarks were his temper, his absolute grip on his part of the pie, and his unique speech. He spoke with a grainy, raspy, high-pitched voice, dramatizing a combination accent and slight lisp: Virgil became "Vugil," Garrett became "Gariet," Curtiss became "Couteous," screening became "screaming," breakfast was "brefus," and so on. He was hell on wheels, then.

That first day, he arranged for my personnel data to be completed, then took me to the "Main Office" in Greensboro for a round of introductions: Lee McArthur, the Corporate Transportation Director, Jimmy Williams, the chief Human Resources (Union Buster) executive, and Spencer Love, himself, the founding father and legend of all Burlington lore. I was not kidding about the handshake; I did have a good one and, yes, it did come from years of milking cows and, yes, J.B. had taken notice. He prompted me on the way to meet Williams to give him one of those good handshakes. I had been set up. Jimmy Williams was an ex-boxer, about as wide as he was tall, and fully capable of crushing my poor paw in one of his off days, which he proceeded to do. I held my own, did not cry, but I sure hurt.

After my whirlwind journey hobnobbing with the big and powerful, I returned to Dave Jones, the local personnel manager. He told me, in not too tactful words, that now, "J.B. would not have much time to deal directly with me; I should just come to him (Dave) with any problems I had." I reported to Charlie Lewis, the Burlington Terminal Manager.

I must relate that I was hired by J.B. to be a freight-handling specialist. My title was "in freight handling." (Your guess now is as good as mine was then)[?] My training program was to get a hand truck and work each of the three shifts. They did not know how proficient I was with a hand truck; I denied all the onlookers the joy of watching me kill my self, as some trainees who followed usually did.

I worked those shifts, watched, scratched my head, and had no clue. I was not an engineering major and, although I knew of time and motion studies, I could not envision that 10 million different types of general freight could be measured, efficiency standards set, and the operation controlled. As I worked, I racked my brain, thought about cutting out breaks, watched who lagged behind and, in general, dreaded what was to come. When, in three months, I was called in and told that I was going to Memphis, no one knew the relief I felt. I considered this a reprieve from the guillotine. It would be eighteen years before a qualified and experienced engineer, familiar with methods and standards, would darken the doors of our division and lead us to genuine productivity improvements.

Burlington (the town) was an adjustment from college life. We moved into Brookwood Garden Apartments (in Burlington), employed a maid/baby sitter, and June and I went to work. No one rushed to greet us on the social front, however, and we were actually somewhat lonely. That short stay was a blessing; when we moved to Memphis, we had gotten over the shock of being away from home and school and commenced to create our own interests and friends.

I mentioned being directed to cut the cord from J.B., my benefactor, and I did. However, he would stroll out on the dock (his office was in the terminal building) every day or two to stretch his legs and would always come over and ask how I was doing. The interesting thing was, when he approached, it was like Moses parting the Red Sea; everyone scattered as no one, I mean no one, wanted to be face to face with J.B Kennedy or, horror of horrors, asked a question. Did not bother me. I always held my ground and told him how I enjoyed killing my feet pounding that dock. The minute he was gone, back from hiding everyone would come and sidle up to ask, "What did he want....what did he say?" John Dunn, Catfish King, Mr. Crabtree, Glenn Euliss, Joe Blalock, Shorty Morris; most of them dead and gone but not forgotten.

I will always remember being upstairs attending a safety meeting and Glenn Euliss sitting with me on the back row. Glenn was a successful Alamance County farmer, working this job on the dock as another "cash crop." He loan sharked on the side and had a country manner of speech, with one eye that did not trail exactly parallel with the other. This day, I noticed Glenn squirming and absolutely refusing to look at or focus on the program. About three-fourths through, he leaned over and whispered conspiratorially, "You know, Virgil, this ain't for guys like you and me; it's for those that ain't got no education."

Another memory from that August was Dave Jones coming out on the dock where I labored, accompanied by a lean, blond, dapper looking guy who Dave introduced as Ben Tyler. "He is going to join us. He is also from Tennessee so you guys ought to hit it off okay." I have often tried to imitate Ben at roasts or other civic occasions by attempting some of his known mannerisms; let's just say here that he sort of preened himself, eyed me coolly, put out his hand and simply said, "Whayee say." I have been to Eaton's Crossroads in Loudon County, Tennessee, and probably attended Sunday school with Ben when we were younger. I am from those Tennessee hills, so I understood. I probably replied with something equally cool; maybe, "Yo, bro." Neither of us could know nor even imagine that the path he started that day would lead to the President's office. Mine zigged in some other directions, but that is another story. What is for sure, a friendship started that has endured many rocks along that path and is most surely one that I have enjoyed.

I had completed my rotation of the shifts on the dock and moved into the dispatch office, when J.B. announced my move to Memphis. I had been welcomed into the office with a resounding thud of silence; Bobby Linens, the first shift supervisor, ignored me; Jack Stephens, the clerk, taking his cue from Linens, did the same; and when the shift changed, Jack Smith would look through me without seeing me. Seeing I was getting nowhere with this great training effort and knowing that number two men usually did the dirty work, I asked Charlie Lewis if I should learn to "switch" (drive); this was in case trucks had to be backed in/pulled out in Memphis when drivers would not be available. Thinking that a great idea, he held a conference with his brain trust to determine the type equipment most likely to be routed into Memphis and turned me loose with the switcher for a week or two before I left. They were 100% wrong on the equipment, but I foxed them on the switching as I had on the hand trucks; I could drive courtesy my experience with Bo McMillan. I did escape, however, from that frigid office and had fun driving around and around the terminal, the time I remained in Burlington.

Before leaving Burlington, I should point out this was 1956, in North Carolina. There was not a black driver, checker, clerk, secretary, supervisor, or employee in the progression chain of employment. This was a community with about 17 percent minority population. There were one or two lower grade helpers in the garage, who were subjected to "colored" drinking fountains and restrooms. It would be six-eight years before selling woolen blanket material to the government caused a little thing called EEOC to, I must confess, force change. More on that later.

In September, 1956, June, Pam, and I piled into our blue/white Belaire Chevrolet and, with a stop-off in Athens, headed to Memphis. This was not to see Graceland but to further our fortunes. I do remember our first night or two being in the Alamo-Plaza Motor Lodge, as we awaited Shamrock Van Lines' arrival with our meager possessions.

The first day at the "new" Memphis terminal was one I shall never forget. If we collectively had been in charge of D-Day, you, I, and Pvt. Ryan would have all been growing potatoes for the Fourth Reich. Bill Fayle, J.B.Kennedy, Ken Finley, a real estate person, Mr. Murphy (a cotton broker), four drivers with their trucks, and I were present. We all merged about the same time at the old warehouse that was to be our gateway to the West. The memory of those drivers, Bill Douglas, Thurman Terry, Joe Supthin, and I believe Saylor, all so professional looking and acting that first day, has never left me.

I do not believe anyone from Burlington had seen this facility before that Monday morning. It did not matter because, true or not, it was a poor choice. An old cotton warehouse south of downtown Memphis, it was not suitable for our use. It was in an alley, and it was difficult, almost impossible, for our tractor-trailer units to enter and back into the dock. The dock was a long, continuous affair, lower than the rear of the trailers, and not accompanied by matching doors into the warehouse. There was one door at the end of the dock leading onto a ramp into the warehouse, as the warehouse itself was "ground level." Nevertheless, this was our home.

Early job; Garn and Ruth Hayes' yard. Anyone recognize what I am pushing?

Downtown Pittsburgh; 1983

London, 1987

"Hail, Hail the Working Man..." 285

Alabama State Docks, Mobile, Alabama. Offloading aluminum billets from Puerto Ordaz, Venezuela 1987

Guy Arthur's Institute of Leadership; Burlington, NC 1966

Front row (left to right): Wade Shanklin, Bob Jenkins, Jack McNew, Guy Arthur, Tom Stevens, Fred Hoffman, Ben Tyler. Back row (left to right): Charlie Lewis, Bill Hunt, Ken Finley, Jim Bald, Tom Williams, Tom Nicholas, Virgil Mincy, Roger Padgett and Garland Marshall.

Everyone offered an opinion how to begin this operation, usually at the same time. I think Bill Fayle was the most vocal, as he had a "General Ike" quality that was impressive, regardless of the subject and regardless whether he had a clue what he was talking about. Finally, this hot, fall day, the drivers started getting the trucks backed into the dock; Bill Fayle and Ken took a handful of bills, and Fayle pulled out the "routing guide" our traffic department had prepared. They started "routing the freight." Guess who that left to start unloading the trucks? The number two man.

An interesting phenomenon occurred in this circus. The old warehouse was a rectangle inside with brick walls and high windows. As Mr. Fayle, with routing guide in hand, got organized, he took a piece of chalk and marked on the walls, purely at random, places where we would segregate the freight to be picked up by specific carriers: Western Carloading, Texas Motor Freight, Campbell's 66 Express ("Humping to Please You"), Preston, etc. Off the trucks, the drivers and I wheeled, calling out the destination, and Fayle would direct us to a spot along the wall or corner where we would stack it. Soon, we were humming.

Someone, probably Ken or J.B., then went somewhere to find a phone to call these carriers for pickup; however, by the time we got much off the trucks, I doubt we got any picked up that Monday. Nevertheless, we were in business.

The interesting point was that these chalk marks on the wall became the Bible. It did not matter that our heaviest volume, say for Western Carloading, was in the furthest corner and the lightest, perhaps Arkansas Truckers, was nearer to the door; we unloaded and loaded the freight in this manner as long as we operated out of that old building (six more months). Not the hot shot from the University of Tennessee, nor my Brackenridge, Pennsylvania boss, nor my crafty staff of Sparky Fields, J.D. Yopp and Jerry Luttrell, nor the occasional drivers who might help *ever caught on* that we should have changed those marks the second day. Bill Fayle had spoken!

A little background: Burlington Industries Inc. was the world's largest textile company. Consisting of perhaps 90 manufacturing plants at that time, Burlington manufactured almost everything needed in the textile world. With plants located primarily in the Southeast, they served the nation, with volume obviously flowing to population and manufacturing centers. Founded (in Burlington, North Carolina.) after World War I by Spencer Love, it had grown through expansion and acquisition to become what it was in 1956. The company brochures expounded on Love leaving World War I as a Major, traveling to Burlington and, with help from local businessmen and investors, starting a small mill and textile history. Not much was said about his Harvard degree or his Harvard professor father or other rather elitist advantages. However, on his own accomplishments, he had become legendary.

With Bill Fayle joining BI and bringing knowledge of industrial traffic practices and opportunities, the Transportation Division started a period of expansion and new ideas. This happened during the time of "regulated transportation," when all motor common carriers were regulated as to operating rights, territories, and rates. Burlington, a private carrier, was restricted to hauling their own products "…in furtherance of their primary business." Burlington had resorted to the courts to establish the right to haul *its own products from vendors* over the objections and dead bodies of the entire common carrier industry. In a landmark case, Burlington also established the right to deliver customer material on company trucks and add the price of the transportation service to the invoice (freight charge) under FOB Delivered terms.

The Columbus Terminal was opened in 1954 on the premise that truck loads of LTL (less-than-truckload) shipments could be moved from the Southeastern mills to some logical point (Columbus, Ohio), then reshipped by motor carrier to ultimate customers throughout the Midwest and Far West. A profit was realized on the difference between the existing "through rate" from the mill to the customer and the shorter, or "short-haul," rate from the reshipping point. This took into consideration the cost of operating the truck to that reshipping point.

With Columbus experience as a base, it followed that some point in the Southwest was more logical than Columbus for those shipments destined to the Southwest and Far West. Hence, Memphis in 1956. This same logic justified other terminals later in Texas and Los Angeles. Some of this was yet to play out when we opened those Memphis doors in 1956. When the traveling road show left town and the trucks slowed down, what was left was the Number One man and the Number Two man, i.e., Ken and me.

Ken Finley also deserves attention. Ken was 39 at this point, a "Pittsburgher" from Brackenridge, Pennsylvania, and an outsider from the then Burlington establishment. He had worked for Best Motor Lines, as had Bill Fayle, who provided the connection, and was rather skeptical of the traditional wisdom of the organization. He was about six-two and, at 20, probably weighed 145-50 pounds. He loved beer, however, and a rather sedentary lifestyle helped promote him to around 200 pounds by 1956; most of it was stomach, chin and chest.

I had been accustomed to taking charge and doing it or being told what to do and doing it; Ken's style was more subtle, so we went through a period of adjustment. He also had problems adjusting to Southern ways and hospitality. I remember his being quite upset and perplexed because his new neighbors came over, brought a pie or something and just asked if they "could do anything?" I can still see Ken with a deep, intense frown, pursing his lips and wanting to know, "What that was all about."

Ken was not nor ever became a doer; he did not like physical work or administrative details. Mix in some disdain for the reasons and a healthy dislike for the task and his reputation grew as something other than a team player. That was and is far from the complete story, however. He was a "people person." He loved to talk, debate, question, consider, weigh, evaluate and, given a little time, would set out or direct others to get done what *he deemed necessary* to be done. He was also a great coach and counselor; he seemed to have a knack for surrounding himself with capable people who could perform, and Ken would let them do just that. Several people blossomed under Ken's tutelage. If you "messed up," Ken had an ability to discuss the situation and lead you to discover a better way of getting it done, without any loss of face, ego, or self-esteem. He was not the typical company man. He was an extraordinary boss.

Memories from Memphis: First, we had to hire some help, and from the unemployment office, that first week, came the dynamic duo of Sparky Fields and J.D. Yopp. I interviewed them, quite sure Sparky had been on an all night toot before he came in. I brought them back to talk to Ken, and we hired them both, along with another buddy, Jerry Luttrell. To start on this crowd would be to never end. If Ben Tyler, Ken, Tom Stevens, Bob Jenkins, Fred Hoffman, Bill Roberson, and I could get together and our tales recorded, at least a book and a half would ensue; all hilarious and true. They (Sparky and his clan) were all from somewhere east of Memphis along the Tennessee border and entertained successive management at Memphis for their entire work careers.

I remember those Thursday (or whenever) nights at home, when Gunsmoke, Cheyenne, and/or Paladin came on. We opened the doors in our upstairs apartment as did our across the hall neighbors, the DeVilliers, shared Gunsmoke stew, family style, and took it all in. The Devilliers were old money folks from Mobile, with Ted being employed by the GM&O Railroad, in Memphis, enroute to a higher management role with the GM&O, following the steps of his father. Lucille was also of the manor born, but we were all in a similar boat at that time. With their two small girls, Lucille and Helen, we had a grand, if short, experience together.

Ted was crazy. I must share the story of our target practicing; the only problem was, we did it in the house.

He had a high-powered air pistol and together, we made a "target." It consisted of a box we constructed with an open face and sloping back. We stuffed it with cotton I had picked up at the warehouse and covered the face of the box with a paper "target," bull's-eye and all. The target was set on the kitchen counter-top, which offered a clear shot from the living room. The box being in front of the kitchen window heightened the risk factor. The safety net was to lower the Venetian blinds. Let's just end this story by confessing the blind tape was stretched by many an errant shot. May you rest in peace, Ted.

Then, there was young Elvis. He was just coming on and, yes, we did go by his house, but this was pre-Graceland. I remember it as a nice ranch (far above my means), with a wrought iron fence around it; musical notes adorned the fence in front. The traffic, even then, was picking up. June declares Elvis pulled up beside her on his motorcycle at a traffic light one day, and it is a fact that Vernon, Elvis' father, did his bidness at the bank where June worked. Our brush with fame.

I also remember driving across Memphis in a cab-over Mack, delivering freight, the afternoon Don Larson pitched his perfect game in the World Series. Charlie had lied about the type tractors that would reach Memphis, this not being one of them. Cab-over tractors posed a challenge shifting gears, because the shift lever was so long; I just could not find all the gears. I would go first, second, third and not being able to find fourth or fifth usually jammed it back into first. That was an embarrassing way to chase Elvis through Memphis.

Bo McMillan also visited me in Memphis. I believe this was business on his part, as Inter-City, headquartered in Memphis, had merged with ET&WNC, and he was there in some official capacity. He had called me in advance and wanted to talk.

Bo had a heart attack at the Rose Bowl about 1955 and seemed anxious to report to me that he "Had quit drinking and straightened up his act." I was flattered and touched that he made an effort to look me up and report in and just as important, was interested in what I was doing. Whether or not our paths crossed again, I cannot be sure. He died suddenly in 1966. I still have in my desk the note Mayme Jo wrote me (in response to my letter) about that event, along with other nice comments.

I am not sure all I learned from Bo has stood me well: the penchant for obsessive neatness, order, and compulsive re-arranging of things. Bo would come in, take the freight bills, put a stack on the edge of the stand up desk, and trim off every perforated "edge" remaining. He would take all the money, put it parallel and straight, press out all corners and wrinkles, make a neat stack or fold, and more. I can still see him subconsciously touching these things, as he would walk by. I coach myself to lighten up now and then, but I could have had a worse role model.

In April, 1957, I transferred to Rossville. Ken, as was his style, prompted me that this was in the wind. After some nudging by Ken, we finally got a commitment from J.B. on a Friday, with a directive I was to report to work in Rossville, Monday. June resigned, we left town to spend the weekend in Athens, and Monday, I was there. This is how things were done then; I always believed many moves came about to solve people problems that could have been prevented with some consideration before hand or other steps taken. Rossville was an example.

This facility existed to serve the Peerless Woolen Mill, in Rossville, Georgia. The assumption was that Trucking had to be on the spot to facilitate large shipping plants and this perhaps was true, to the extent that mill personnel were somewhat hostile to our operation, or at least not cooperative. "Couteous" Simpson was the manager. In brief, my going was part of the plan to move Curtiss out and move Frank Rudd in; Frank was being moved in to get him out of Burlington and J.B.'s hair. I am sure I was not told all of this before I arrived.

Curtiss was a short, "wired," ex-Marine; hard working, and loyal. He, at that specific time, was overworked, prone to mistakes, short with the drivers, unhappy at home, and could not get help in the way of authorized overtime or qualified backup. I was part of that solution, but he was not to be around to enjoy it.

Problems existed; however, I was able to resolve many of them *right now*. Curtiss was being worn into the ground by midnight calls most nights; I took an extra half hour making sure everything was correct before I left; after a thorough inventory of the yard to double check trailer numbers and such, I slept quite soundly most of the time. Curtiss soon left and Frank was in.

I must tell a Curtiss story; Curtiss was transferred to the new Altavista Terminal in Altavista, Virginia, and served well as the Assistant Terminal Manager for a few years. He died suddenly in the mid sixties of a heart attack, and Garland Marshall, Charlie Lewis, C.D. Jackson (the HR Manager), and I went from Burlington to the funeral. I was back in Burlington, then. I shall try to earn a PG rating for the following story.

On the way up, C.D. related an experience Curtiss had in the South Pacific during World War II, where he had been sick and near death. Curtiss had told of being in the hospital and in such poor condition, he had just given up; he had lost the will to live. One day, a pretty, young, nurse came in, sat down by the bed, and started talking with him. He noticed that, as she sat facing him, her short, white uniform worked its way over her knees and he could see she had nothing on "underneath." Well, Curtiss related, the more he looked at the sight of her untrimmed beauty, the better he started to feel. Remembering then and there all that life had to offer, he started his fight for recovery and won. He had been living testimony to the memory of that most fortuitous encounter.

We made it to Altavista and, in that beautiful church, the four of us were up front as the minister intoned the virtues of Curtiss' life. He was rolling along, and we were dozing along when, suddenly, we heard him say, "....And this fine man, in his brave service to our country, risking his life for us all, came within a *hair* of losing it...." Four pallbearers came within a *hair* of choking to death on that front pew, and no one would have ever understood.

The Rossville (GA) terminal was a change of pace in 1957; Memphis had been the "end of the line," a reshipping point, with no plants to serve or drivers to maintain. Rossville, on the other hand, was in the back yard of the mammoth Peerless Woolen Mill and also served Harriman Hosiery, Scottsboro Hosiery, and the Dothan, Alabama, plant. It domiciled drivers, had two "boards," (trip and local), and was a break-bulk terminal, combining loads from the Dublin, Virginia, and Gaston (Gastonia, North Carolina) terminals for forwarding to Memphis. On a smaller scale, this location did it all.

I mentioned earlier some symptoms that would prompt J.B. to make a management change. The pain was usually yelled by drivers who would voice displeasure over any of a host of issues; in those days, they usually would be heard. Now is a good time to point out that Burlington Industries, Inc. was a non-union company and intended to stay that way. The Transportation Division was no exception, with the dreaded "Teamsters" being a constant bogeyman, lurking and ready to devour women and children on sight. The Peerless plant *might* have complained, the City of Rossville *could* have complained, a secretary *may have* written a letter, and management would likely have authorized an "opinion survey." If drivers complained loudly enough, **management was changed**. Alongside those issues listed earlier, Curtiss' epitaph was written.

I arrived, Curtiss left, Frank came, and the show went on.

Frank Rudd was and is a genuinely fine person; he was always an appreciated friend who helped my family and me at needed and unforgettable times. That said, the brief Rossville experience was a mixed bag.

The reasons we both were there were soon non-issues, but one issue seemed to remain: costs. Frank had a reputation, deserved or not, of being a fiscal conservative. Frank, as a cost accountant in Burlington, had fostered this reputation by his attention to minute detail and his championing the art of non-spending. His presence in this function, I believe, prompted J.B. to put him in operations: he would be out of Burlington, and "I'll show him." How did all of this affect me?

We cleared up most of the petty problems, but the issue of costs remained. I do not know whether Frank, like Curtiss, just could not justify sufficient staffing to perform all the work necessary or, as I suspect, chose not to try. The alternative to having sufficient checkers in place or switching hours scheduled was to do those functions ourselves; i.e., Frank and me.

That summer I worked six-seven days a week, doing my share of the dispatching and administrative work, unloading and loading trucks, switching around the plant and, on occasions hitting the road to relay a tractor to a driver. The non-joy was multiplied by the fact we had miserable freight to handle: hosiery passed through in canvas bags that were too heavy to be fun and too light to complain. You just ruined your fingernails trying to grip them and you could not use gloves.

The Peerless product was a long roll just the right size to be a pain. One had to grab it as if he was lifting a tree out of the ground and carry it one at a time. Two on a hand truck were awkward but, another way. Sparky Fields would always carry two at a time to make a point to J.D.Yopp, but during the summer of '57, I was not into keeping score. Both the hosiery and woolen rolls ruined our chance to meet satisfactory productivity standards. So it went.

Frank seemed quite content to do the manual labor, keeping the "noticeable" cost down; managing seemed a secondary task. I did become a very proficient switcher that summer and, trust me, Peerless had some weird docks.

We had a good cast of characters at Rossville: drivers as well as checkers. Even though I may have disagreed with his choice of duties, Frank certainly pulled his weight, from a work standpoint. Tommy Cates, a dispatcher, was always there working his butt off with the rest of us. Pat Siniard lifted our morale just by walking by. There was "Worm," the switcher, who I must mention.

Worm was a small, scrawny character who was unique in that he could go about his business, appear to be in motion, move around, but just could not accomplish anything. He moved at a slow pace, stopped to gossip every other step, always checking and rechecking…just could not get a move on. He was neither obstinate nor insubordinate; actually, he was very pleasant. It was just necessary to stay after him all the time. He was the one who wrote the axiom that sometimes *it was just faster to do it yourself.* If you did, he just appreciated that.

Worm had a minor vehicular accident around the plant one day, and we were required to do a full-blown investigation: reports, questions and all. Ultimately, "avoidability" had to be decided so that "chargability" under our safe driving rules could be determined. A driver's bonus could be and was affected. Worm had to subject himself to our court, lost, and was charged.

His final assessment was, "Well, I guess that's just what I get for hurrying."

In early October, I transferred to the Columbus, Ohio, terminal. Again, it was one of those situations typical of our operation in those days.

When Memphis opened, a large portion of the volume that had flowed through Columbus was diverted to Memphis, reducing that terminal's activity. Ken Finley had been the manager at Columbus and among his crew of checkers/dock hands had been his brother-in-law, Mike Thompson. I actually never met Mike and have no basis upon which to judge his strengths or weaknesses. He was promoted from among his peers to be the manager when Ken left and, again, when "people" problems surfaced, the quick fix was to send in another body. The old World War I school of management. Problems had developed in Columbus, a band-aide was needed, and there was old Vugil in Rossville, developing into the designated mover.

Before I leave the warm and friendly confines of Rossville Terminal, I must relate the memory of meeting another new body passing through, one Robert E. Jenkins. In June, 1957, Bob arrived at Rossville on his way to Memphis to begin his career with Burlington. He also had graduated from those hallowed hills of Tennessee, and, of greater coincidence, had attended Tennessee Wesleyan. What made this stranger's connection stranger, he was from New Jersey and the victim of a reversal of the old "underground railroad." A year or so later, Bob, who became the Lenny Bruce of BI during his career, lamented: "What kind of planning results in Virgil Mincy from Tennessee being sent to New Jersey and Bob Jenkins from New Jersey wasting away in Tennessee"? It did tend to make one think.

Also to be reiterated is the fact I always considered Frank Rudd a special friend at Burlington; he had a long, productive and loyal career. If there was a small disagreement in management style at Rossville, it was just that; we had some great fun together.

There were several issues involved with my move to Columbus; at the time they were really of more importance than anything that happened while I was there.

First, June was sick. About the time I was leaving, she was having respiratory problems: the aftermath of years of allergies, a polypectomy while we were in Rossville, and a cold; all this turned into double pneumonia. Ruth Rudd literally found her at home, took her to a hospital, and cared for Pam a couple of weeks during this time. I was torn between what had to be done in Columbus and what was going on in Rossville. I remember one trip back to Rossville, spending the night with June, and sharing that little hospital bed. In these days when a "king" seems crowded at times, you might ask about that night; don't. It was the end of two weeks before she could join me in Columbus. Again, Rudds, thank you!

In addition, this (Columbus) was the first time I was the *Manager*. It had been easy enough watching Charlie Lewis, Ken Finley, Curtiss Simpson and Frank Rudd singing their songs, thinking I could do better. When my name was called and I had to "walk out on stage," my sweaty hands made finding those "F Chords" another matter. There always has to be a first time, the test; this was mine.

Finally, there was the matter of moving "North." Burlington's Transportation Division was a Southern operation, with the exception of the little operation in Columbus and the New Brunswick Terminal. The brief time I was in Burlington, I had been regaled with tales of the North, those operations, and experiences of those having been there. A year or so before I signed on, there had been some labor strife at a warehouse in New York City; a crew was assembled in Burlington to go up and "break the strike." Truth to tell, it was a bogus deal, and the crew did little but get drunk, circle around New York City a few times, and stand by while whatever the problem was faded away. That trip, however, was the most prevalent conversation at break-time for those who participated, for years. I can only compare the attitude of the average "Southerner" of that day to now, by suggesting a transfer to New Brunswick then would be like going to Somalia, now. Columbus rated, let us say, Germany. It was north of the line; I was game, but I was wary.

The Sunday night before I started, I met Ken Finley, Jim McNeil and Venice Smithers at the Deschler Hotel in downtown Columbus. Jim and Venice were from the Dublin (Virginia) terminal which was the origin point of trucks sent to Columbus. I was to report directly to J.B., also, nominally, to Jim, with the idea being Columbus would become a "subterminal." I am not sure I talked to Jim while I was in Columbus. I believe J.B. had come to Columbus the week before and wielded the axe; if not, Ken may have been delegated to do the deed. In any event, by Sunday night, it was done, and Mr. Thompson was history.

The conversation next morning was not about Vugil arriving to ascend to the throne, but about the Russians lobbing their first "sputnik" into space. In conversations I had, everyone struggled to understand what kept it up.

Columbus terminal was what remained of a reshipping point, with Memphis having stripped it of two-thirds of its volume. In 1957, the justification for it was questionable. After a few days, it was apparent to me that we had too much labor for what we were doing; I hit my first home run by terminating a part time secretary/clerk, a checker and one driver. Having done that and getting the petty irritants resolved that caused the demise of my predecessor, this was a smooth assignment. We would have busy Mondays, not much the rest of the week, and no reasons to screw up.

I fell in love with Columbus; the first weekend I was there, Ronnie Marshall, one of our drivers, invited me to his house for a cook out, and it was great. The leaves were just turning, the country was neat, and the city was impressive. If you drove 10 minutes North, South, East, or West you were through it; it all was to my liking. Someone gave me a ticket to see Ohio State play Indiana soon after I arrived. Ohio State was favored by about 40 points, yet, the stadium looked full. It was reported the crowd was the smallest in 19 consecutive games, and I believe there were 70 some thousand screaming fans present. In 1955, The University of Tennessee averaged 24,990 at its six home games. Think I did not notice this stuff? My first experience north of the "line" was totally pleasant, perhaps one of my best.

As things settled in and I became more familiar with the other Burlington locations and people, I could not help but contemplate what might be next. I thought I was the designated mover. Common sense told me, however, that any supervisor at one of the larger terminals seemed (to me) to have more to do and a more responsible job than mine, although I was a "manager." I put myself down the list, realistically, for promotion or change.

In August, 1958, all that reasoning was shuffled around. Lee McArthur, who was located in Greensboro and to whom our operation reported, died suddenly. In a most respectful manner, but totally in jest, I remarked to Dick Johnson, our one full-time checker, that I probably would be called any time to take over the Director position. My reasoning did not allow me the wildest hint I could be involved in any move. I had no clue how the company would fill that position, as he was removed by location and presence from the daily lives of us peons in the field.

However, I was. As it turned out, Bill Fayle was chosen to become Director of Transportation; Leon Goff, the New York Traffic Manager, was promoted to General Traffic Manager; Allan Cannon, the New Brunswick terminal manager, was moved into the New York Traffic office replacing Goff, and my phone rang. This is one of the few calls before yesterday, in my life, that I can remember, and yesterday is suspect.

J.B. called that week, probably waking me from my afternoon nap, and promptly told me he wanted to move me to become the New Brunswick Terminal Manager. Remember that this was to be likened as from Germany to Somalia. I know I was floored. The move itself, location and all, was not exciting, and I had brains enough to know the task was daunting, to say the least. Also, remember that I was a seasoned veteran of only 24.

I thought, however, since I was a manager, there should be some negotiation of terms; as I stalled to regain my composure and bide for a little time, I replied to J.B., "I will want to think this over, talk to my wife, and get back with you; what kind of an answer do you need right now?" I will never forget those 10 seconds or so of dead silence, then in a cryptic tone, these words: "Vugil, you are going to New Brunswick!" "Yes sir." And, I promptly did.

Leaving the best location and cushiest job I ever had with Burlington was not easy, especially going to, arguably, the worst and toughest; New Brunswick was no piece of cake. J.B. met me in New York, on Sunday night, before I was to hit New Brunswick, and I remember his having a big bandage on his forehead; he did not explain it quite this way, but he had been drunk in his living room and fallen into the corner of a coffee table. Before meeting him, as my first official act in New York City, I had gone up the Empire State Building for a look around.

My first Monday included a visit to the New York Traffic offices at 1400 Broadway for a briefing by Allan Cannon, my predecessor; then on to New Brunswick. For the sake of brevity, let me list some issues that faced me, day one:

1. The terminal/warehouse was a drab flat structure on a dirt yard full of potholes; it was across the highway (US 1) from a drabber, uglier truck stop.

2. The offices were cramped and messy, with one office for the manager staring into everyone else's space; they were crammed into an open area with no privacy or breathing room.

3. The office force was constantly yelling, cursing, mouthing, and was as unpleasant a crowd as I ever imagined in my worse nightmares.

4. The assistant terminal manager, Elmer Larson, had been demoted when Cannon came in, was passed over when I showed up, and was about as amicable as an angry hornet.

5. Allen gave me a briefing on how incapable everyone was, including the second shift supervisor, Walt Degree, who he said, "had to go." Among Walt's other transgressions, he had married a French woman and Allen confided in me, "You know, the French marry n———-s."

6. Dick Fletcher, the office manager, informed me my first day he was being transferred to Memphis as assistant terminal manager. J.B. had not told me this, and Dick was not going to be replaced.

7. I did not have enough money to pay the two month deposit on the apartment I selected to house my dear family.

8. Allen arranged temporary quarters for me in the truck stop across the street. In addition to the totally mangy room, every few minutes an air starter sounded off outside my window. *AND,*

9. The work force was *TEAMSTERS*, who, I had been trained to believe, ate women and children alive; these being a New Jersey Mafia controlled clan, they obviously ate fresh, young, inexperienced Southern types for breakfast, just to work up an appetite. I could go on.

This place was a challenge. This job presented many of those times when I would like to have said, "shove it" and moved on. I shall hit, briefly, how I faced some of the situations and talk about some of the positives.

First, I had to borrow some money from Tommy Quarado to get into the apartment.

Tommy was another of those characters who warrants his own book but a few things need to be understood: the setup at New Brunswick, on paper, was impossible. Burlington did not intend to have its name on a union contract, however, "in the beginning" "management" was convinced that union labor was necessary to operate in the New York City area. Warranted or not, the decision had been made to use Teamsters. A shell corporation was formed, K&K Transfer Co., to do the dirty deeds. K&K had no assets, just a revolving cash fund replenished by Burlington, as expenses were paid. K&K had the contract with Local 701 of the Brotherhood, and Tommy Quarado was the President of K&K. They (K. & K.) leased drivers to Burlington Industries Inc. Ostensibly, Tommy should have managed this leased labor and I guess indirectly did. The clerks and one dispatcher were paid through K&K, but the manager, assistant manager and office manager were Burlington employees; bottom line, any problem with labor and we, not Tommy, dealt with it on a day to day basis. We totally ran operations.

Tommy had a unique ability: he was the only person I have ever known who could always be depended upon to do the wrong thing every time, all the time, when it came to people. When we needed discipline, he would pussy foot, and when we needed diplomacy, he would rant, rave, and make everyone livid. A piece of work. He also owned our terminal building and the truck stop across the street. There were lots of intrigue and many different elements at work at New Brunswick.

Another issue beneath the surface: then, the I.C.C. (Interstate Commerce Commission, which regulated motor transportation) frowned upon private carriers leasing labor and frowned upon private carriers leasing trucks. They frothed at the mouth over the idea a firm might lease labor *and* trucks, and dropped dead in an epileptic seizure upon hearing a firm might lease labor and trucks from the *same source*. We leased the labor from K&K, trucks from "Guaranteed Truck Rental," and Tommy, by ignorantly running his mouth, convinced an I.C.C. inspector that we leased both from "him," starting a legal war with the government that lasted several years. That is another story, but one typical of Tom Quarado.

This terminal was another large reshipping point. It served the metropolitan New York area, New England, Philadelphia, and Western Pennsylvania; this area was not only a major textile market for our products but also a source of raw materials and supplies that we picked up for movement back to the mills. Several carriers and "agents" served these different geographical territories, supervised by New Brunswick management and reached by New Brunswick drivers, after loads had arrived from the South by non-union, Burlington drivers. J.B. would say, "New Brunswick is the 'noive' center for this area."

I was in this nerve center for four years, until September 1962. The demands of the job notwithstanding, this was a very productive and enjoyable "tour of duty." Somalia it was not, and it helped to reinforce a philosophy I had developed: "You take your happiness with you; you do not find it." I have seen many people relocate, convinced they would not like the new location, and usually did not.

We had New York City to explore; we visited New England and people living there. The cities of Philadelphia, Boston, and villages like Jewett City, Connecticut, were regular business calls. Broadway plays, Rockefeller Plaza, the Statue of Liberty, Yankee Stadium....anyone not taking advantage of all this is a few short of a dozen; take it all in, we did. We made friends and discovered again that people are much the same everywhere. We enjoyed a new learning experience: ethnicity.

With a little margin for error due to 43 years having passed, get this seniority roster: Garback (the shop steward), Notaro, Saunders, Carvello, Zunino, Marsh, Koropscak, Koller, Tinsman, Jaccoud, Schlosser, Duffala, Luizza, Cimino, and some I probably missed. These Italian, German, French, and Polish people were first or second generation, and who they were defined what they were and how they acted. That had to be understood and respected.

The agents we dealt with included Felson Carriers in New York City. Alfred Felson was the President and Norm Isenstein was a dispatcher with whom we dealt. This was a Jewish firm deep in the heart of the garment district. South Paterson Trucking Co. was in Paterson, New Jersey and, in addition to competing with Felson for New York City business, handled Northern and Central New Jersey. John Scala, his wife, two daughters and son-in-law, Johnny McKenna, were the principals and, except for Johnny, were Italian. The poor outsider was Otto Heintz (German), the operations manager and whipping boy for the rest of the family.

At Moon Carriers in Camden, New Jersey, was Henny LaBracio; 'nuff said. In Jewett City, Connecticut, Rapid Transit served us well and was headed by Richard (Dick) McCusker, who gave this mix an Irish-Catholic flavor. Two great people (at Rapid Transit) who worked closely with us were Flo and Art Dembinski; a weekend we spent with them at their home in the Connecticut countryside will always be treasured.

The big bad Teamsters could be a pain but, in actuality, we had a contract and, in some instances, it made managing easier to know clearly what you could or could not do. The work was done.

During this time, Spencer Love and Burlington were in a break-neck expansion mode: they gobbled up Hess Goldsmith (Scranton-Wilkes-Barre), Taylor Yarns (Taylor, Pennsylvania), Sidney Blumenthal (Watertown, Connecticut), Goodall-Sanford (Reading, Massachusetts), among others. Each of these operations had to be assimilated into ours, and often this was rather direct and bloody. Traffic managers or shipping supervisors were expected to become just clerks to our direction. James Lees (carpets) was acquired, although at times it seemed Lees had acquired us. The significance of the New Brunswick operation was that almost all those newly acquired companies, as well as the Division headquarters of most other Burlington operations, were in New York City. This was a major customer location. Service was closely monitored, necessitated by both volume and proximity. If something went wrong, we were near the complainer and had to provide tracing and expediting services, representing our entire operation, to the New York Divisions.

In 1959, the Transportation Division's growing terminal system was organized into Areas, with managers assigned to the Southern, Western and Central Areas. I was appointed the Eastern Area Manager. A funny (to me) sidebar: I know this happened because I saw it, although the originals seem to have disappeared. The first organization chart that came out was on one of those old, blue "dittos" and showed Tommy Quarado as the Eastern Manager, noting below that Virgil Mincy would be *most active*. No one (J.B.) ever said a word about that, and the next chart came out listing only me.

It was my responsibility to police and control service at our reshipping points and agents. The good news is this was interesting, required lots of travel, allowed me to meet and deal with great people, and was a great learning opportunity. The bad news is it could be likened to the person who juggles plates on top of sticks; something was always about to crash.

There were politics; J.B.Kennedy headed trucking and Leon Goff headed traffic. Each had his pet carriers or agents and, in some instances, had been responsible for establishing them. Those two people battling for supremacy (and they hated each other) made it tough being in the trenches. We survived it all.

Our division started piggyback service from the Carolinas; this was innovative and required an infinite amount of coordination on both ends. Ultimately, the service level was not satisfactory, but it was a tiger while it lasted.

Some other things: Elmer and I became friends, he settled into his role and, when I was made Area Manager, I appointed him Terminal Manager. Elmer was quirky and had his moments, but it worked for me. More on that later.

I named Walt DeGree Office Manager at New Brunswick. Walt was from Grosse Isle, Michigan, had gone to Washington & Lee, and into the service following college. He went directly from the military to the second shift supervisor job at New Brunswick without any training, indoctrination, or plan for success.

He blossomed in this (office manager) role; during this time, we (NBT) took on all freight bill payment for the area, expanded the tracing function, with Walt inheriting a little fiefdom of people he had to supervise. NBT (New Brunswick Terminal) also operated a small warehouse and Walt set this up on a perpetual inventory system, replacing the annual deal that would never balance. After a year or so, an "audit" of the facility was so successful and Walt had so impressed the auditors, that he was offered a position in the Internal Audit Dept; he took it and worked there successfully for years. Walt had to go, all right.....Up!

There were strange attitudes that prevailed in the division, overall. Generally, few wanted to move from the South to New Brunswick. This was less true as the numbers of young management increased and people like Bob Jenkins, Tom Nicholas, and others progressed and were interested in advancement, regardless of location. The funny thing, it was just assumed once you were there (at NBT), you wanted to get back South. Further, the general feeling was you had to manage in the South, preferably at the big, bad Burlington Terminal, if you were to get ahead.

After I had been at New Brunswick a couple of years, there would often be comments that "we have got to get you South, you need to work in the South," etc., and I recall telling Calvin Michaels (the HR Director), "Not to do me any favors....if it was not a good career move, I was happy where I was." I also recall his admonishing me, "Not to talk like that; some people might get the idea you are not interested in moving ahead and pursuing the big picture."

One thing was sure; Allen Cannon did not like living in the North. He was my neighbor and I heard his views on that and many things, regularly. In 1960, he was moved out of New York and became Western Area Manager. He held that position until September of 1961. I do not know what circumstances pressured the change from that position; however, I do know that in 1961 the heat was on to get me back South so I could re-learn grits and big time trucking. It was resolved that I would move to the Clarksville Terminal as Manager. On paper, I moved; was transferred. My record shows that. I never moved, however. Here is how it played out.

Allen had been appointed and announced as Eastern Area Manager (as I had been announced Manager of the Clarksville Terminal). He was going to do this from Burlington, as he was not going to move north, again. I aggressively looked for housing a month or so in the little village of Clarksville and could find nothing; also, June was pregnant with our third child (Debra, to be). I asked to delay the move until that was over. Another factor: Allen told me, "He was not going to have Elmer as terminal manager;

that was not going to happen." Whether I volunteered, whether Allen requested it (I doubt that), or whether J.B. or Bill Fayle intervened, I know I was asked if I would prefer staying in New Brunswick as Terminal Manager and I agreed. I much preferred that to Clarksville.

I told Elmer he was backing down again and, from me, he took it and went right on.

In January 1962, J.B. Kennedy died in a tragic fire that engulfed his home. His assistant, George Agamemnon, was promoted to be General Manager of Trucking, Charlie Lewis, who had been the Southern Area Manager, was promoted to Assistant General Manager, and Allen was named Southern Area Manager. Ken Finley, who had moved to New York City in a customer service capacity, became Eastern Area Manager. By September 1962, there was trouble in the big, bad Burlington terminal, and Vugil replaced the incumbent, George Southerland. I was back in the South where *real trucking* went on, at last.

Truthfully, this stage of my career could stop here; from 1962 until 1977, I ran trucks and operated terminals. In hindsight, after a year or two in Burlington, I should have pursued the traffic side of business with Burlington Industries, or elsewhere. The situation was like the Jerry Clower philosophy: "Once a tackle, always a tackle."

Our management was rather typecast. Very few switched from one discipline to another. Truth be told, we trucker types really thought we were the only ones who could *manage people* and that we were the stars. There was little desire to do anything else.

So, there I was at Burlington Terminal, which had more problems than those I described at New Brunswick: poor supervision, older drivers, many questions and no answers, and the scrutiny of the entire staff and management structure in Burlington looking over your shoulder every second. It was not much fun at first. Whether I did a poor job or whether I was poorly led, only God knows. I know Ben Tyler replaced Allen in August of 1965, and I believe George Agamemnon considered moving me out also. I have no doubt Ben interceded to some extent. Allen's last comment to me as he passed through the terminal was, "Well boy, you really let me down." Let him down? I felt like I was reprieved from being led into the swamp.

In 1968, I was promoted to Southern Area Manager; Ben told me I was the most qualified terminal manager at that time. Whether that was true or not is debatable. What is not is the fact I was the same old Vugil who was about to be thrown out before, just as Walt Degree was about to be deep-sixed, just as Elmer Larson was history back in history (when I left New Brunswick, Ken promoted Elmer back to Terminal Manager. He served there, then for 20 years as manager of the Lynchburg Terminal). Perception is a big part of reality, and a good leader can move average people to go great things. A poor leader will never accomplish much and can stifle the progress of everybody in his shadow.

In 1975, I replaced Ken Finley as Eastern/Central Area Manager, in a rather difficult move for everyone; Ken was my friend and much liked by most of his drivers. I move forward to that time just to discuss some of the things I remember during this period, "the Southern Years."

This is not in chronological order but, clearly, the most significant time for me was my involvement as we integrated our work force. When I was manager of the Burlington Terminal, our time as a division had come; we were mandated to produce some numbers. It would be nice to say someone stood up and said it was the right thing to do; I do not remember that being the case. Having been ordered, though, I am still happy to have been part of this and feeling that I, personally, affected some people's lives in a positive way.

It was more complicated than just "hiring some black people." We had policies in place regarding promotion that dictated a checker hired could progress through that job to switcher, then to driver. Hiring a checker determined that we would soon have black drivers. We had both the checkers and drivers to contend with as we prepared to hire that first checker. This pressure was no small thing. Much wringing of hands went on and, naturally, the Burlington Terminal was selected for this experience, as it usually was with controversial things. (Later, other locations had their day in the pickle barrel, as did Gaston with the SIS program)

Burlington's jobs were the second best in the area, behind only Associated Transport employees at their large Burlington terminal; they were

Teamsters. Anybody we hired would probably better themselves substantially from their existing job.

We took the easy way out with the first hire; we transferred Wallace Gant from Central Warehouse to become the first black checker in the trucking department. The first outside hire was Norman Hester; later his brother, Billy. We could absolutely pick the cream of the crop in Alamance County, and most of the original employees we hired were great workers and people; many enjoyed successful careers with Burlington.

I recall an old-time white driver approaching me on the dock during this time and saying, "You know, Norman is a good n——r; he don't smell like most of them do." Others swore they would quit when a black became a driver. Such was the thinking, but no one ever quit.

Later, at Lynchburg, the issue had progressed to our policy of allowing drivers to bid on "sleeper team" positions, which made possible/necessary matching a white/black team. Tempers flared and threats were made (serious ones, at that), as this issue wore itself out. I am pleased to have participated in some small way. My facility was first with the most, and I believe we did it well.

I was instrumental in the development of the (then, 1969) new Burlington Terminal. I know many of my ideas, some at a premium cost that were sold to upper management by Ben Tyler, have stood the test of time. That facility still stands in great condition and utility 32 years later, because it was designed to withstand wear and maintenance.

Trainees that passed through my watch include Bailey Tollison, Don Wall, Bill Roberson, and Jim Waddell, along with many others; I would like to feel I contributed.

Some great people associations were developed or continued during this time. Ben and I had a friendly, casual association before he became my boss; we suffered the same pains, the same bosses, endured the same stuff, and shared some common fun. He was a "good" boss, and we saw a lot of each other when he worked in Gastonia. When I was given the Eastern/Central assignment, Ben was transferred to Burlington, and we had offices next door to each other. I have known him since that August day in 1956, and we have shared a lot. I am appreciative of this friendship.

Earl Melton came into the division in the early seventies; I believe the first I heard of him were comments about that great golfer, Earl Melton, who was working on a project in the Garage. He had been asked for and was assigned to our division from the I.E. staff in Greensboro. The golf bit posed no threat to me as everyone was a better golfer than I, so, more power to him.

He started installing a "scheduling" system at Gastonia in 1974; it (S.I.S.) was a system of applying standards to the freight handling function and offered the possibility of significant efficiency gains. Remember 1956, when I was hired to "be in freight handling?" Eighteen years had passed, and little had been done of significance other than placebo treatments. Earl would, indeed, lead us to the Promised Land. This was tricky, however, as these improvements meant we soon had surplus labor. I believe the results speak for themselves, but of personal importance, Earl got in the boat and helped row as we "crossed into Jordan:" not just my locations, but everywhere. Earl was a good manager and friend.

In 1975, Earl started feeling symptoms of his first heart attack, in his office, and broke into my busy morning schedule to get him to the emergency room. I agreed, not wanting to create any further disturbance to the decorum of our work area, and we screeched off. There is debate to this day regarding the haste with which I did the deed. The fact is, I was the only rational and coherent one in the car, so I have always rested my case; I got him to the church on time. Earl and I have enjoyed work, picking, golf, weddings, funerals, soul bearing, and still do.

And on it goes. Tom Nicholas, Bob Jenkins....both were involved in various operations that interfaced with whatever I was doing for years. Personal stuff, work, Toastmasters. Both were men I respected and appreciated.

Don Henry, "General Patton"; we fought viscously when he was at Dublin and I was in New Brunswick. He was in my class at UT (and in several classes). He was my assistant at Burlington Terminal and the assistant to others for years. A more loyal person never existed. Like him or not, there was never any doubt where Don stood. Give him direction and he would move heaven or earth to complete the mission.

Tom Williams (and Dick Fletcher) was rooming with Mrs. Wilson when I drove in to town in June, 1956. He was working for me my last day. I could not express in words my appreciation for his friendship and professional cooperation for 21 years.

There were approximately 55 people attending our division meeting in 1960, and that represented only those I had worked with for four years; I have no idea what the count would be during the next seventeen years. I appreciate them all!

Not every thing was fun. Under my watch, the Clarksville and Fayetteville terminals were closed, affecting the lives of long time employees and their families. The company view demanded that when it is over, you should have retained the best. Not everyone always agreed with my choices, particularly when they did not have to make the decisions.

Burlington trained me, gave me opportunities to learn, and always provided in house career enhancements; I received, literally, a "Masters in Transportation."

In September, 1977, Burlington Industries also showed me the door.

Great things have happened to me since that time. Then, however, it shocked and it hurt. I was the head of the pack of about 25 management people caught in a down sizing before that term had been invented. In my case, three areas became two, and among Ben Tyler, Charlie Lewis and me, I was out. I was made an offer they knew I would refuse: terminal manager at Memphis. The age thing, I guess. I really did not consider it, as it would have involved backing down Carroll Craven and several others. It probably was my hangover from yo-yoing Elmer Larson all those times. I have sometimes wondered on a slow day what life would have been like had I taken it.

Charlie Lewis told me the news, and I will let the sands of time swallow the ruse developed to have me primed and ready for a "meeting" that Monday afternoon. Charlie was not well equipped by temperament or training to do this, but he gave it his best shot; he talked about, "selecting the best players for the team" and let me know I was to vacate the building, immediately.

I watched George Agamemnon and others affect their lives with bitterness and ill will over a lost job; I was not going to be victim to the same, even if it had been my nature to go that route. "If you live by the sword, you die by the sword," I often said, before and after this time. My opinions of those left did not change after I was gone. Most I respected and enjoyed greatly; a few, somewhat less. I wished them all well then and, in memory, even yet. In the final analysis, I never much missed the work; I did miss the people.

(Author's note: In February, 2003, the doors will close at the last facility of what had been the "Transportation Division." Burlington Industries Inc. is but a shadow of what I have known: "The Worlds Largest Textile Company." Another victim of human greed and stupidity)

It would be an understatement to say I was not prepared to look for a job in September, 1977. I remember when I joined Burlington fresh out of college and read all the company propaganda, I had counted that I would have 43 years of service when I reached 65, got the gold watch, and cashed in all my profit sharing for retirement. I was always proud of the company and pleased with my progress. I never seriously considered working anywhere else.

As commonly done today, I was not given out-placement assistance or anything to soften my shove into the afterlife. I had no resume and, by nature, was never much of a "net worker." I had a wife, five children, their college to consider, bills to pay, and the weight of all this on my mind every minute of every day. What I did not appreciate at the time was the fact my next position came in an almost textbook manner. Today, the rule of thumb is a month, for each $10,000 in salary, to find a new job. That, plus all the techniques of networking, cold calls, referrals, letters of introduction—whatever it takes. By January, 1978, I had no immediate prospects and was very down, to say the least.

My Toastmasters crowd had thrown me a roast, friends kept in contact, and I had actually talked to several people about potential jobs. It was interesting who came out of the woodwork, whom you might not have guessed, to keep your spirits up and, conversely, who disappeared, although you had worked together for years. I had gone on interviews and later been told, "You talked yourself out of a job," and had not pursued leads, for various reason, that might have proven beneficial. It was certainly new territory for me.

Networking did work for me, however. One of the first contacts I made, at Tom Williams' suggestion, was Gary Porterfield, with American Stevedoring, who supplied our labor at North Bergen. Gary said I should call a Bob Welch, with the Pepsi Cola Bottling Group, in Purchase, New York. I did, Bob discussed some opportunities that were possible, and invited me to come for an interview. During the interview, in early October, Bob discussed in detail a position in Pittsburgh and only mentioned other locations in passing, as he described the company. Bob was Corporate Fleet Manager; his function was "specing," buying, and maintaining all vehicles involved in the beverage business. Although that was not my specialty, it was a job, so I assured him of my interest. Pittsburgh was a stretch, but I was serious about this opportunity, if it was offered. I had not heard a word from Bob by January and had actually forgotten about it.

One gray Friday, the telephone did ring, and Bob, talking as if we had met the previous day, offered me a job in Dallas, Texas. Further, he wanted me in Dallas the following Monday to say "hi." I was to fly from Dallas to Purchase, New York, Tuesday, for a physical and the sign in stuff, and to Long Beach, California, by the end of the week, to participate in their annual meeting. Well, jangle my spurs! I did all this and moved into an apartment in early February, living there until all my gang could join me after school was out. The house I bought offered all my life's dreams: a basketball goal, an adjacent golf course, and a gas lighter in the fireplace. Under the blue skies of Texas, what more could a man want?

This job had its days. First, I was not technically qualified for it from some viewpoints; however, the immediate tasks did not require any wrench turning skills. I had four areas: Dallas, Houston, Phoenix, and Las Vegas. When I discuss those times, I try to keep a straight face talking about the travel, as it certainly was great territory. Within that territory, however, were more immediate problems than mechanical knowledge and great weather. In three of the areas, the managers were suspected crooks and known incompetents. At the same time, the company was installing a maintenance management system known as Mainstem, with the attendant vehicle numbering, inventorying and training that was involved.

I was located at Division Headquarters in the Frito-Lay Towers, near Love Field, in North Central Dallas. The Bottling Group was a functional organization, with a Sales Vice President, the Human Resource Manager, the Production Manager, the Controller, and the Division Fleet Manager (me) in the same office with a small staff. These were okay people, but pretty competitive and protective of their turf. Resolution of a problem sometimes had to reach the president of the company, the politics were fierce, and cooperation among functions rare.

My task was almost impossible. The manufacturing employees loaded and unloaded trucks and were the fork truck users. Sales employees drove the route trucks, fueled them, wrecked them, and abused them; both functions expected well-maintained vehicles available in the desired numbers at required times. One other tid bit: labor was tight, turnover high, experience nil, and abuse of equipment rampant. My people and I had no control over the use but were responsible for the results.

First things first; within three months, I had fired three of my four area managers: the ones in Dallas, Houston, and Phoenix. By mid summer, we were along the way with Mainstem installation and were beginning to get meaningful reports. We installed a fuel system to improve control of fuel usage and were also weathering a national fuel crisis that, at times, threatened to ground us. We were making progress.

In the two years I was with Pepsi, I attended three annual meetings: the one in Long Beach on the Queen Mary, in Las Vegas, and in Phoenix. These were great experiences, as Pepsi absolutely put on the greatest dog and pony shows I had ever seen. We previewed the new television ads for the following year, heard presentations by Pepsi executives, had fun and games throughout the time. and, at the last breakfast, saw a presentation of pictures taken at each event, including the previous dinner, set to music. I never could figure how they got it together that fast.

How it all may have worked out, I will never know. Things changed in Purchase. Bill Frye was removed from his job as the Sales Vice President for the Pittsburgh area and given the position of Vice President of Fleet

Operations. Bob Welch, then, had to report to him. This had no chance from the start. Bill Frye was the most obnoxious person with whom I ever worked closely. His style was to visit your location, travel with you all day, hover over every word, action, observation, and nuance, and offer critical comments along the way. It was a constant inspection. I can only imagine what it must have been like to be in an office next to him, when he was not out pestering the rest of us. About Bill was the term, "all form and no substance," first written.

Bob lasted a couple of months before Bill fired him. Of the four division managers, I was the third one he fired, so I should get some recognition for being first runner up. I will just close this chapter with a testimony to the measure of the man by relating that my last day, he followed me around all day, being petty and demeaning. He almost demanded that I go to dinner with him (where he blew cigar smoke my direction the entire time), suggested I go to his room about ten o'clock that evening, "to discuss a few things," then fired me. Some of my compatriots had warned me this was coming; this was one of the times in my life I greatly regretted being unable to beat him to the punch and say, "shove it," before he had his chance at me. Severance and such make cowards of us all.

At this same time, June and I had agreed to go separate ways, which was no small or trivial event. Dealing with the work front and home news was no easy task, however, as they say, "That too, did pass." I spent most of that summer around the pool in the apartment complex I had joined, not really being as diligent in the job search as circumstances required. It was an interesting lesson, however, as I observed my newfound friends and neighbors, younger than I, usually had far more troubles than mine. Let us just say I met no role models during this brief period.

I had answered all the ads, gone to the search firms, and done the easy stuff. What I had not done was work eight to 10 hours a day in a professional search. Who knows if the results would have been different, although I am willing to concede I was more lucky than good.

One Sunday night early in January, 1981, I received a call about midnight, Dallas time. It was from a Jim Nesbitt, in Cleveland, who said he worked for "CTS Transportation Co., a Division of the Sherwin-Williams

Co."; he discussed having a possible job in Dallas and wanted to meet me. When we met in Cleveland, he explained the job was at the Garland, Texas, manufacturing and distribution center and was Regional Transportation Manager for Sherwin-Williams. He did (truthfully) explain that Sherwin-Williams was terminating their Teamster drivers and replacing them with non-union drivers working for CTS, a wholly owned subsidiary of SW; because I would also head the CTS operation in Garland, I would wear "two hats." What he did not tell me was that the Garland operation already had a traffic manager and staff, who handled all their traffic functions. They made me an offer, I accepted, and reported to work one bright Monday morning.

Upon arrival at the Garland plant and being shown my "office," I saw evidence of the disdain greeting me: most supplies, including the office chair was piled on top of a desk, with everything in total disarray. Further, after some introductions, I immediately sensed the local drivers being fired that Friday seemed to be sons and husbands, if judged by the negative reception of Headquarters' plans. The local plant was totally hostile to me, why I was there, and whatever I might do.

The immediate task was to replace about 28 drivers by the following Monday. I had a stack of applications as a start.

I got 11 on the road the following Monday. I had to recruit, employ, test, indoctrinate, and shove out the gate with a load of paint, people who had never seen a load of paint. Further, and no small task, I had to create every rule, form, policy, pay procedure, and term with which "CTS" in Garland would run this little business. I soon learned that Cleveland was of no help, as no one there had any answers. The same thing was happening in Oakland, California, Chicago and Orlando, Florida. All this was under the cynical eye of my customer, the Garland Distribution Center.

Our primary function was to deliver paint to all the Sherwin-Williams stores in our region, which was roughly the Southwest. In addition, to make the operation viable, we were to solicit back-hauls for the trucks, although we were limited by having only contract carrier authority. This was during the infancy of "deregulation."

This period of time allowed me to accomplish some things that I found among the most satisfying of my career: I almost single handedly got the operation up and going in the face of tremendous odds, I assembled a small staff that worked well together, we "won over" the plant and became their most valuable tool, rather than an adversary, and we were soon the most profitable of the CTS regions. In 1982, I was "Manager of the Year." I have never been able to voice the precise analogy, but again, an observation: I was the same Vugil, Manager of the Year, as the one Bill Frye blew away with his cigar smoke eighteen months before. You go figure.

Again, who knows what might have been. I was reasonably content with this job, was considered successful, my family was in Dallas, I loved the area, I had a girl friend; life was good. One day, Tom Nicholas called me from Pittsburgh and inquired, "Would I be interested in a job?"

Tom, you will recall, was a peer from Burlington, who left the company about a year after I had. He had gone to work for National Aluminum Corporation, in Pittsburgh. Tom had called me since that time to touch base and see what was going on. He had always been skilled at keeping up with what every one was doing, and I give credit and thanks that it was his nature to do so. We were never particularly close at Burlington, as most of our common time was in different places; when he was in Burlington (city of), we were in different social circles. We did work together on projects, were in Toastmasters, and I certainly had the greatest respect for his abilities. I believe he left when he realized he probably would not be President of the Division, and he was very wise to have done so. His career flourished.

Tom reported that he was transferring from his position as Director of Traffic and Transportation into a manufacturing role and was involved in replacing himself. Was I interested? I had learned to enjoy and benefit from "job interviews," and, with nothing to lose, agreed to go to Pittsburgh for an interview. I really thought I would be another body passing through for review, while the real candidate in the lineup would be asked to step forward later. After lunch at Sgros, outside Pittsburgh, when Tom discussed the afternoon activities I asked him, "Who was the decision maker in this situation?" I was rather floored when he replied, "I am." I talked with a couple of Aluminum management people, some in the parent company, National Steel Corporation, then headed back to Dallas, having enjoyed the day. I still felt I was the "Judas Goat" in this deal. I knew I was *a* candidate, but had no reason to believe I was *the* candidate.

A week or so later, I went to the mailbox on a hot, Texas day and retrieved a thick letter from "National Aluminum Corp."; I applauded them for prompt payment of my expenses. When I opened the letter, which included an offer of employment, complete with all the goodies spelled out, I had to sit down on the curb to take all this in. *Pittsburgh Steelers? Cold weather? Leave my family? My girlfriend? What about all those Texas two-step places? Yippy Ti Yeh?*

In the end, I went. I have often referred to this as the "Godfather offer," although it was more than that. I concluded that to advance with Sherwin-Williams, I would have to move to Cleveland, and that prospect did not thrill me. The National position included overall traffic responsibilities, which I had not managed before. It seemed a great opportunity. This was actually the first time in my life I was faced with a decision that was not a transfer, order, or accepting a job because I did not have one. It was tough.

On August 11, 1982, I reported to the Grant Building, on Grant Street of course, in downtown Pittsburgh. I was flattered and somewhat surprised that Tom had replaced himself with me; this was a two-edged sword, however, because he was respected by the National people and was a tough act to follow. He was soon leaving town, as his new assignment was in Indianapolis, so everyone would be watching my initial progress.

A good thing about following Tom was that he was well organized, very literate, and left a good trail of the necessary actions in this function. Before any disaster struck, I had time to get familiar with the usual stuff and soon was settled in. This was a corporate staff position with oversight of transportation activities for six profit centers, including the trading function in Pittsburgh. Six different plants ran trucks, and I was responsible for truck leasing and operational reporting. Later, when the company got into international trading and importing, I selected ports, hired stevedores, did distribution, chartered vessels, and had a great time. I traveled, visited London and Caracas, and routinely contacted our plants, working with the plant traffic managers. I banged my head now and then, wondering why I had not done something like this long before. I met and married my present wife. More on that later.

After little more than a year, Tom moved back to Pittsburgh and took a position in the sales (trading) office. Later, in a company shake-up, he was named head of that department and along the way, became my boss. We worked together on many things, traveled together, commuted together, and enjoyed, for too short a time, a great professional and personal relationship.

Good things sometimes never last. The holding company of National Aluminum, National Intergroup, in what turned out to be a death march (for them), decided to divest itself of "its metal interests," which included our company. We were ultimately sold, and worse, sold piece meal. By 1989, Headquarters had been dismantled, and my life moved on.

I decided to go into consulting; I felt if I could not duplicate what I was doing in one company, I would divide myself among several. As it turned out, I rented a good piece of me almost at once to a Pittsburgh conglomerate, Ampco Pittsburgh, and became its contracted transportation manager. Between the public and private companies, I handled about sixteen plants from a corporate perspective. In addition, I did other interesting consulting assignments.

My wife, whom I married in 1986, worked for National Steel Corp., which had been the parent of National Aluminum when I joined it. We worked in the same building and met at the suggestion of mutual friends. Her company relocated its corporate headquarters to Mishawaka, Indiana, in 1992, and persuaded her to go. I begged and she agreed to let me go with her. I continued to work the Ampco assignment until late 1993, when the Berkman family sold a portion of the company, downsized corporate staff, and ended their use of me.

I piddled with a few assignments for awhile; however, the consulting business involves constant selling, and that is a career activity I have always liked less than a lot. I decided to get a day job like most people and wind up my career doing whatever made sense from Mishawaka, as Mouse (my main squeeze) pursued hers. I spent a few months with an "outplacement" firm, working all day, five days a week, doing all the things necessary to land a professional job. I was resigned to being a weekend warrior, as I doubted landing anything worthwhile close to home; I actually had several interviews in distant cities. In May 1995, I received a call one Saturday from Dave Lerman, President of Steel Warehouse Co. Inc. (in South Bend), who said he had just fired his traffic manager and guessed he needed one. I had sent him a brochure, following a social introduction a year or so back, when I was trolling for consulting work. I worked for months beating the bushes in a professional search, and an apple just fell off the tree, hitting me in the head. It goes that way sometimes.

I ended my work life in March of 2001, after working for Steel Warehouse since that 1995 date. I ran trucks, managed rail activities, handled imports, sold the services of our trucks "for-hire," and did whatever was needed in a steel service center. I actually retired in March, 2000, but was asked to come back toward the end of that year for another beating. This time served its purpose, and I am grateful that Dave Lerman kept that brochure.

I started this tale by stating that time tends to filter the important from the less so. When it is all said and done, the people, places and the memories of them remain,....not the statistics, the profit reports, the budgets, or the deadlines met. From it all, some superlatives:

- *Best Employer*: National Aluminum Corp.
- *Best Location*: Dallas, Texas
- *Most Satisfying Task*: (tie) Starting up CTS and First Ocean Vessel Charter
- *Lowest Moments*: Several third shift calls at New Brunswick and Burlington Terminal when operations were out of control and supervisors were incapable of handling them.
- *Best Boss*: (tie) Ben Tyler, Tom Nicholas and Ken Finley. Ben and Tom were similar, as both were leaders, excellent communicators, knew what they wanted and gave support while you worked to achieve results. They were willing to share the blame as well as the credit. Ken was certainly different; however, he

was a coach who let you play, corrected your mistakes in a constructive and non-confrontational way, and championed your advancement.

Earl Melton would have certainly fit the leadership role. He was never my boss, but I respected his management during projects we shared

Bob Welch (Pepsi) had some personal irritants, but was there for me when it counted a few times. I have not forgotten.

To those hundreds of others along the way who have supported, been part of, shared the times, suffered the set-backs, and enjoyed the victories....God bless you one and all! Many, if not all, could command your own chapter. At the very least, you are leading characters in re-runs of my old memory shows.

I reel them up all too often these days.

Picking, Grinning and Other Non-Essentials

It is, perhaps, only fair that you question the rationale for including personal, extra-curricular, and somewhat selfish activities in a story about family history. I do so for these few reasons: first, I have concentrated on family, work, relationships, other life-influencing activities, and shall soon get around to religion. While these subjects cover things of importance and necessity, they do not address fun, hobbies, interests or, we might say, the icing that holds this cake together. Further, while I have tried to be an adequate father, a capable employee, and an interested researcher, I want to present some evidence that I have "licked" that icing. Finally, I suggest that we are put here (or however you choose to phrase it) with a lot of ability we rarely use, and we miss much self satisfaction or many opportunities for service if we hide it all under that bushel.

Consistent with the purpose of this narrative, I do want my grandchildren, or theirs, to know that, in small ways, I tried; I have been more than a 4-H club member, transportation manager, seeker of family, or chronicler of family history. I have played a lot and tried to give a little back. I would urge everyone to do the same.

To begin on a high note (not to infer this is headed downhill), I "flew" for a short time. My description of life as an aviator will be as brief as my aviation career; however, I did achieve a personal goal and have always been proud of that fact. As early as I can remember, I wanted to fly; I read about planes, jumped on anything that resembled a plane at county fairs, and flirted with the idea of the military while in college; marriage, aptitude, and lack of science or math background nipped that idea in the bud.

In the mid-sixties, I befriended a guy working in my department who wanted to pursue a flying career. I helped him arrange a flexible work schedule, and he was able to continue with training for instructor and instrument ratings. When that was accomplished, he quit his "day job" and jumped into that flying career, going to work for a small, fixed-based operator at the Burlington (North Carolina) airport; he offered me free lessons if I would rent the plane.

I began taking lessons in 1967; I got my physical, completed "ground school," soloed, and was on my way. I have always been proud of the fact that, when I took the "written examination," I was the first one finished and scored 97 in a class where perhaps one third of the others flunked. I did the required cross-country, frightened myself a few times, did some stupid things, and survived. This was an enjoyable, yet brief, hobby.

I always envisioned owning or renting a plane and taking family or friends to Knoxville for the football games or to other exotic getaways. That was never a practical ambition. Relative to any time period, flying is expensive. I began to feel guilty soaring above Alamance County, circling my home, dipping the wings to my children below, and writing that check for the plane rental. Flying less and less caused my proficiency to plummet and gaining the skill needed to obtain a license seemed further and further away. By 1971, my ground school rating expired; I had not flown for months, so I retired. I was pleased to have done it, excited to have been up to the challenge, but, in the end, other priorities took precedence. This question occasionally comes up: "In the event the flight crew on a commercial jet became incapacitated, would you answer the call for help and bravely land the craft, saving scores of lives in the process?" No.

In a strange twist of fate, my flight instructor, Ken Marley, later worked for Burlington's corporate flight department; around 1976, he was chief pilot on a flight to a driver's meeting at a Virginia terminal location; the passengers included three or four other management members and me. When we started the return flight, Ken asked me if I wanted to take the controls for a few minutes. "Duh"? With approval of the senior executive on board, I jumped into the right seat and grabbed the wheel (yoke, I think, is the word); this was only a King Air, however, after a few minutes, Ken suggested he should perhaps take over. He expressed concern that the Atlanta control center would perhaps question why that King Air could not avoid fluctuating 200 feet up or down from the assigned altitude.

To clarify my answer to the trivia question about landing a commercial jet: if one has not experienced more than briefly flying a Piper Cherokee 140, don't attempt to mess up a good crash.

It may surprise many, but much of my life, I have been identified as often for attempting to "pick and sing" as any other tag I might claim. Having confessed, this allows me to segue into the broad subject of music, my enjoyment of it, and how it has affected my life...or at least several hours and days of it.

Music? Music means such different things to so many people that it is difficult, often impossible, to find common ground for discussion. Churches rise to battle over different styles; families war over generational differences or preferences; societies question mores or taste; commerce thrives or wanes because of changing public demand. There most certainly is a music industry, a Music City, and music teachers; sheets of all the music written could undoubtedly cover the world many times over. *The Hills are Alive to the Sound of Music.* I have always enjoyed music.

I have not always enjoyed being called upon to participate in it. You perhaps remember my embarrassment recalling the spectacle of being placed in front of a church and having to sing little choruses to the congregation, as Mom played the organ and my brother and sister all joined in. I have never ceased to be thankful, however, for having available to me the sounds of harmony, the science of music composition, the challenge of performing, and the opportunity to learn something about it. What gets intriguing is to contemplate why our souls are stirred by one sound and not another, or others.

As stated, I grew up hearing a piano or pump organ leading a congregation or individuals to sound out traditional hymns; early on, we did not even own a radio. My mother probably had some "piano lessons" and could play most simple hymns. I never remember hearing her play anything other than church music. In the back of my mind, she may have tried *When you and I Were Young, Maggie,* but I could not testify to that, under oath. She was not skilled but wanted her children to be.

Mom begged Homer to "take piano lessons," but I never recall the courtesy of his attempting to find middle C; my turn came next, and I was offered a bribe of 50 cents per week if I would buckle down and take those "lessons." Later, Betty took them for years (real lessons on a real piano), and…..she can write her progress report. We got the Sears Home Study Course, Mom set up a schedule, and, at the pump organ, I pumped.

It needs to be understood that one obstacle to musical progress was attitude: it just seemed to us Mincy children that to take piano lessons, one needed a piano. The keys were the same on the organ, of course, but I guess we likened it to picking up a date in a pickup truck; something just seemed to be missing. Pump I did, however, and those lessons began around the time I was 10 or11. I started, remember finding middle C, and learning *The Happy Sailor*. Further, when I had some understanding of sharps, flats, lines, and spaces, I ventured out into memorizing *Jesus Lover of My Soul*, *What a Friend*, and *Lilly of the Valley*; I always remembered it being rather easy.

With some regret, I have always been amazed that I did not have much interest in "learning music" or "studying piano." Further, I never remember my soul being stirred by the sounds of classical, pop, or most commercial music of that day, although I probably had not heard much, at that time. What I do remember catching my attention and competing with those organ sounds was the sound of guitar music: not the classics, not Segovia, not a gut stringed "classical guitar," but a plain old guitar played by someone singing awful sounding, hillbilly songs.

I have often wondered: if I had grown up in a big city, would I just naturally have heard more music of different types and just as naturally, learned to love those sounds? I will never know; I have enjoyed most types of musical entertainment, live and have usually appreciated it; I most certainly appreciate the skill, and work required to obtain that skill, of the performer. I have paid much to do so and shall again. But, stir the soul? It never has, to the extent a good country ballad, with distinctive rhythm guitar, steel, fiddle, drums, and bass does. I confess! I am branded! I am, also, addicted. I am a country music fan. I am proud of it.

This is not the place, nor am I inclined to enter into a debate over the merits of anyone's musical taste; further, there are tons of beautiful coffee table books extolling the virtues of every genre of musical sound. To each his own. Personally, I have wished I really were moved by Sinatra, Beethoven, The Rolling Stones or rap; how much greater would be my joy. I suggest that the lyrics of *New York, New York*.....are artistically no more soulful than, *hear that lonesome whippoorwill; he sounds too blue to fly...*(Hank Williams' *I'm so lonesome I could cry*). Most natives from Manhattan have no clue about whippoorwills, nor would Alabama citizens usually understand the romantic allure of the Big City. Different poetry usually meets different needs; I just came out of the closet early on and always understood what I am: a country music fan. (Country music, incidentally, is defined as any type music played on a station that identifies itself as country.)

I played piano on that old organ for a while, but wanted a guitar; I listened to the radio, (at neighbor's homes), identified those guitar sounds and, in my mind, just knew I could play it when it came....if it ever did. Problem was, I did not have the money to get one and Santa never obliged. So, I begged, whined, pleaded, and checked every semi-annual edition of the Sears Roebuck & Co. catalog for its good, better or best Silvertone models. Finally, in 1947, my parents gave in and sent in the order; few days were more exciting than when the package arrived with that arched top, F hole, Silvertone, with pick, neck cord, and instruction book (all for $14.95). Stand back!

Alas, when I picked it up, assumed a posture, and tried on the flat pick, the sound that came forth was not as I had imagined; there was the whole business of chords, calluses, tempo, and, in other words, musical technique; piano, all over again. My fingers started hurting, and the guitar was respectfully retired to the parlor in the house where we lived at that time. A humbling lesson.

I shall not belabor the next happening with detailed technicalities; however, my curiosity finally drew me back to the Silvertone, and I contemplated how I might move forward with my ambitions. I did not create a new style or break new ground; however, with no one to help me, I did experiment with "detuning" the strings into a natural chord; i.e., I could hit the strings and make a musical sound without knowing a single chord. From that, I began picking out, randomly, individual notes until I could play the notes of a complete song. I believe the first one was A.P. Carter's classic, *Wildwood Flower*. I had learned to (sort of) play a song before I knew the first chord. I was in business.

Soon, I developed modest calluses, which is vital to playing a guitar with steel strings; I then retuned the guitar, learned three chords, and was really in business. Trying to imitate Maybelle Carter, of the Carter family, who created the sound of that *Wildwood Flower*, I began my own style of beating out country tunes; I could play most melodies that I knew (if it was a simple "rhythm"), because that was the first thing I had learned: playing melodies. The rest is my history

I always knew I was not a singer; I could carry a tune, and, rather than ever take myself too seriously, I gravitated toward word songs: songs that either were clever, humorous, or simple; yet, so good, they just had to be sung. In the big scheme of things, this was a rather limited play list.

From the time I was sixteen, or so, my guitar traveled with me to pie suppers, camps, Boy's State, school affairs, Roundups, and to countless informal pickin' sessions. I never got much better; I just repeated that first year of experience for forty years and said I had been playing forty years, if asked. The songs followed the times: Little Jimmy Dickens, Eddy Arnold, Hank Snow, some Hank Williams; then, Buck Owens, Merle Haggard, Glen Campbell, Kris Kristofferson, Willie Nelson and Waylon Jennings. John Prine, Mike Cross, and others snuck in for several numbers on the Mincy play list. By 1980, I probably could knock off a couple of hundred songs, if pressed; if not pressed, I rarely volunteered as, remember, I rarely volunteer for anything. You will note I have not taken "a holt" of the latest stuff; it is arguably better and the artists, perhaps, more talented, but that is just arguably; most of it does not "move my soul."

I have turned many a tune for an audience of one; a couple of years, I headed a variety show in Graham, North Carolina, for our South Graham Elementary School PTA, before a packed auditorium at Graham High School. Much "strumming" was sort of in between.

In the early seventies, I was fortunate to become friends with Earl Melton, the industrial engineer for our Transportation Division (at Burlington Industries, Inc.). We soon found we had much in common; he enjoyed golf and country music and I did, also. Only problem, he was scratch at golf and I knew a few chords on the guitar; we each lacked the other's skill in a coveted area. We agreed to barter lessons, and Earl was a tireless and dedicated worker; he soon could play reasonable guitar and could always sing better than I; I was the better teacher, as I never became scratch at golf.

We worked and played extensively and, soon, we were the road act for meeting getaways or other gatherings where we worked. We never insisted, but usually got asked for a return engagement. Earl would always protest and claim he broke out in a big sweat, when asked to play, but he would always play; the power of applause is highly addictive, and, at times, I think we succumbed to it.

I play less, now; I have forgotten most of the songs, but not the memory of singing them. The moral I would suggest is that any hobby that brings personal satisfaction and, as a bonus, might bring joy to others is an opportunity worth pursuing.

I have owned many guitars; the loss of one led to another interest. At the time I was transferred from Rossville, Georgia, to Columbus, Ohio, in 1957, I possessed an arched top, Gibson, electric guitar (and amplifier). It had a reasonable sound, even without the amp but, in any event, was my guitar of the moment. During the summer of 1958, I was invited to play golf at an outing; I had never played golf and, further, had no equipment. Sadly, neither did I have any money to consider investing in another hobby. I was 24, not making much money, a parent, and golf clubs did not seem a prudent investment. However, the allure of hanging out with the movers and shakers of the Columbus transportation world, as well as my interest in golf, was a powerful draw; what could I do?

In my infinite wisdom, I decided to pawn my guitar and amplifier for $25, with which I promptly purchased a used set of golf clubs, consisting of three old woods, five beat up irons, a putter, and a vinyl carry bag; I was now in the golf business. Unfortunately, I was soon transferred to New Jersey, had no money to redeem my pledge, and left town without my

Some friends would claim I was "scratch" on guitar; I always knew I was about a 20 handicap.

The 18th at Pebble Beach

Some friends would claim I played like a 25 handicapper; I always knew I was better. I bogeyed this hole without touching the ball..

Daughter Debra wanted to know "what a principal figure was."

Principal Figures At Meetings

Dr. Craig Phillips, a candidate for state superintendent of public instruction, right, confers with Don McCorkle, left, and Virgil Mincy, who sponsored two meetings here yesterday to allow local voters the opportunity to hear the candidate's views on educational needs in the state. (Times-News Photo).

Alas, at the state level, a big, booming voice defeated the great story.

Mincy Is Contest Winner

Virgil Mincy of Burlington is the Area 6 Serious Speech contest winner.

Mincy defeated three other contestants in the Annual Toastmasters International Area 6, District 37 Speech Contest at Hilton Inn.

A member of Transportation Toastmasters Club, he will compete next month as the area's representative in the Central Division of District 37 contest.

Other participants in the contest were, first runner-up Ed Schuster of Durham, Everett Billingsley of Chapel Hill and Boyd Boswell of Burlington. Four weeks ago, these men advanced to the area event by winning their club's speech contests.

A manager in the Transportation Division of Burlington Industries, Mincy's speech title was "Some Questions About People".

The Central Division speech contest will be conducted in Greensboro April 19.

grand Gibson; I sent a couple of renewal payments back, however, I had not much more money in New Jersey so, alas, ultimately, that grand Gibson gravitated toward someone else's garden gate. I wrote a song about that: *"I hummed a sad line, as they hauled my strings away."*

I shall not belabor my golf life's story; I did play a little or a lot, intermittently, for the next 45 years. It has been a mixed blessing. I have enjoyed most rounds greatly and been frustrated greatly, at times, because of not playing better; nothing new there—so has Tiger.

What I can say is that I have been privileged to play with friendly people and great friends on many wonderful golf courses; those include Pebble Beach, Muirfield, Firestone, Bay Hill, Greyhawk, Pinehurst No. 2, Oakmont, and many others you never heard of that, in many ways, are just as enjoyable and beautiful. Golf, really, should not be embraced unless one is interested in working to improve or content to beat it around…usually by yourself. That said, handicapping systems and the tradition of the game permits people of all skills to compete and play together. By and large, however, skilled golfers prefer playing with other skilled golfers. I have been blessed by tolerant friends…and fawning vendors.

Golf would not be golf, of course, if we did not talk about it, ad nauseam; I have never understood the ritual of one's favorite professional entering the tent and reciting his round, blow by blow (I know, stroke by stroke) as the press respectfully takes note. One daydream I have harbored is to be star for a day; I would enter the tent, ask for a show of hands of those who had actually been on the course and seen me play, then, advise the assembled that only those having so ventured, could ask questions. Do you know any other profession (sports writers) where professionals can lounge in the shade, drink free beer, scarf up free grub, then have the stars stroll in and, basically, write their stories for them? I would not do it and, further, would not last in the business, as I would be labeled a trouble maker and probably fined by the Commissioner.

I did take to talking, however, but about other things. Yes, I know; I have been told many times that I talk too much; few have been kind enough to just tell me to shut up; rather, they wait until later and recite my excess. I was nudged into this habit at an early age.

During those early 4-H days, I was persuaded to enter the first "public speaking contest" held in McMinn County; I memorized some little talk and won. With no coaching or advice about how to proceed, I was called upon at an early age to hold meetings and conduct business in front of large crowds. I was always paralyzed by dry mouth and the shakes, but I was usually told no one noticed; I have always thought everyone was just being kind. During my senior year in high school, I entered the T & I Club (the state organization associated with the Diversified Occupations curriculum) public speaking competition and won at the state level. McMinn High seemed to feel my trophy was theirs and kept it; wonder if it still is carefully mounted and preserved. I began to believe winning was my divine right. Most gladiators, except Rocky Marciano, of course, ultimately come to know the agony of defeat. I think my string was broken in a state contest held in Nashville by the Young Farmers and Homemakers; I learned, sadly, that a big, booming voice with an average tale will take the day every time against a thin, nasal, little sound trying to sell the most cleverly crafted words. By the time I could shave, I was willing to get up in front of people and do whatever needed to be done.

Many years later, around 1972, George Agamemnon, Vice President of Trucking for Burlington Industries, initiated an in-house Toastmasters Club; training and development had always been emphasized and George, having been active in Toastmasters, thought this would be a good vehicle for improving our communication skills. I was selected to be the first president of our club; in time, our group excelled at being able to communicate on their feet, and many improved upon their beginning abilities. I have a box full of trophies claimed in various competitions, but others in this club surpassed any of my accomplishments. I claimed second in the state in 1974, but Nick Nichols won the national humorous speech competition a year or so later. Others, including my friend, Earl, have equaled or surpassed those honors.

Toastmasters, or other such opportunities, can offer a forum for great personal improvement; I learned to avoid those "uhs," but could never leave that East Tennessee twang behind; I was born to utter such sounds as nice, ice, right, tight, or night with great emphasis on the "long I" sound.

All men (or women) are not born equal when it comes to vocal chords or that innate ability to connect with another person or audience; humor cannot be manufactured if it cannot be conveyed in a humorous manner, and serious thoughts must be offered with the power of conviction. Technically, though, as we used to say in 4-H, with work, your "best can be better."

Actually, before Toastmasters, I had my little fling with politics and civic duties that forced me into facing sometimes friendly and, other times, hostile groups of people. It started in 1962, when we moved from New Jersey to Graham, North Carolina. Immediately, Pam entered the second grade at South Graham Elementary and, from that time until 1978, I think I had some daughter there continuously. (The principal, George Nall, spurred my interest in flying by taking me up several times in his Cessna 172.) I evolved into PTA president, for life. That led to holding those PTA meetings, being involved in school affairs, supporting various activities of the Alamance County school system, and associating with county educators. One such group was the Alamance County (NC) Better Schools Committee, a multi-racial group representing most schools in the county, along with various school administrators. In a segregated school system, this was lite salve applied to the separate but not-so-equal facilities and programs. I soon was elected president of this group.

About the same time, as unrest grew, in certain circles, with the county school administration (primarily the Superintendent), my next door neighbor decided to run for the County School Board. Dr. Robert McQueen was elected and soon, as the balance of power on the board shifted, the then-current superintendent was sent on his way and new blood was ushered in.

Because of the Better Schools group exposure and working with Dr. McQueen, and others who labored on his behalf, I became pretty well acquainted with the new administration. From time to time, I was called upon for minor, petty, little chores. The point of this background is twofold.

First, I labored with the Better Schools Group for a few months, but it appeared we did nothing but meet every month or so, have some little program, and go home, without accomplishing much but strained fellowship. Finally, one month, with absolutely no idea for a meaningful program, we just did not have a meeting. Nor the next month, or the next. I observed no one asked why we were not meeting or inquired about the "next meeting." The Better Schools Committee of Alamance County quietly fell upon its sword. I learned two valuable lessons for life: If something requiring time is not accomplishing anything of value, spend your time elsewhere, and, in any endeavor, do not take yourself too seriously; others usually do not miss you when you are gone.

Then, sometime in 1969, I was asked to attend a closed door meeting of a group including county commissioners, school board members, school administrators, and a few leading county citizens; the purpose was to discuss mounting a campaign supporting an increase in the county sales tax, to be directed to the county schools. North Carolina schools, then, were primarily state supported and, unless local "supplements" were available, existed on the funds the state provided. Generally, North Carolina ranked close to the bottom, nationally, in per-pupil expenditure. The (city of) Burlington school system had a supplement, but the county schools had to make do on the state dole.

The group was generally supportive of seeking the proposed tax increase but deemed it wise to make this a "grass roots citizen's effort"; before the night was over, I had been arm-twisted into co-chairing this effort with Roy Harris, a Western Electric executive, living in Burlington. I shall always remember the comforting words of R. Homer Andrews, chairman of the Alamance County Commissioners: "Virgil, we will be behind you all the way; just let us know what you need."

Roy and I went to work; he handled the City of Burlington and I spearheaded Alamance County. We gave speeches, wrote ads, granted interviews, and wore ourselves out in the endeavor; we sensed a lack of support from almost any direction, and I remember failing to even persuade most school principals to place "Please Vote" on their school signs. We were defeated by a six to one margin. Further, I never forgot R. Homer's comments to the press, the night our ship sank: "....the vote was ***just what I expected*** and I felt that none of the commissioners actually expected the tax measure to pass here. With no more effort in support of the tax and no more interest on the part of voters, what could we expect"? Further, "...residents who turned out to vote against the tax are fed up on taxes——they've had taxes and taxes from the federal government, from the state and from the county and they just don't understand it."

Virgil Mincy said, "....I was greatly impressed that so many people turned out to vote, indicating they are interested. Further, it vividly points out their feelings concerning any increase in taxes." He further said, "Those supporting the tax felt the one-cent sales tax was an approach to better meet the needs of counties and municipalities, but the vote here indicates this particular area doesn't want any increase in taxes." Mr. Mincy had a lot more to say.

Mr. Mincy also learned this lesson: when someone wraps his arm around you and promises to back you all the way, with the disclaimer that it is better that he stay in the background, do not walk, but run to the next county, turn off your phone, let the dogs loose, and shoot anyone trying to get you involved.

Another lesson, however, is that we have a responsibility to get involved. If "we" do not, who will? There is a huge vacuum and bottomless pit for free labor, however, since the beginning of this republic, citizens have contributed, taken charge and gained control over the affairs of others. Often, this is for the common good; sometimes it is not. Further, we must remember Alexander and Caesar conquered the known world; Hitler almost did. Only by those interested in the "common good," working to achieve common goals, do we thwart those whose intentions are less honorably motivated.

Some things did work out better; in 1968, I served as Alamance campaign chairman for an educator from Guilford County, Craig Phillips, when he ran for State Superintendent of Schools; he carried our county in a landslide, won the state election, and served with distinction for quite a while.

Today, I gain as much satisfaction teaching some frail senior lady to hold a computer mouse without strangling it, reading to a child in an attempt to reach grade level, mentoring a child in an attempt to add an adult presence to his life, or serving other volunteer needs. Why make the effort?

To honor a benefactor of many years ago, a short story, if you please:

During 4-H days and, later, in Young Farmer and Homemaker activities, an outstanding adult leader in McMinn County was Rex Moses; Rex was a successful farmer, an outgoing and interesting individual, and a person who greatly contributed to making possible many adolescent activities. He continued to serve throughout his life. I had not seen Rex or been in contact for perhaps 45-48 years, until I ran into him at a reunion of all Mouse Creek School classes. Rex had experienced a variety of health problems, did not appear comfortable, but after introducing myself to him and exchanging pleasantries, he looked at me with piercing blue eyes and asked what I was doing. I mentioned golf, substitute teaching, writing and, sensing my struggle to describe anything of substance, he asked again, "Virgil, what are you doing"? I mumbled whatever else came to mind and he interrupted, looked me directly in the eye and said, "You have got to give something back."

I still try; these few comments are not to suggest that any of the named activities changed the world or were worthy of great note. They were, however, a few of **my** efforts, and my conscience is just as clear for having tried to be of service as it is guilty for not having done more. I also had some fun along the way. My point for recalling these simple memories is to encourage my grandchildren, or anyone's grandchildren to attempt things they will want their grandchildren to know about; to jot those memories down, preserve them, and assure they will know you hunted, fished, swam, played softball, ran student governments, worked for senators, had fun, and later, contributed to society. After all, in the end, what else does one leave behind?

Family, Those Mincy Girls, Mouse and More

As you have noticed, I have dodged important issues as long as I could get away with it: emotion, feelings, love, regret,....all the juicy stuff that serves as the glue holding otherwise boring facts together. While not a pre-conceived, brilliant, writing hook, I stand guilty of just stating the facts, ma'am, the facts. I have confessed before to being stoic, reserved, perhaps "uptight," and controlling. That those traits have not always served me well is rather obvious, at least to those who have been affected. It is time, however, for me to face the music.

There have been many special people in my life; I have tried to describe some of them. It is others' turn now, but here is where it gets difficult for me. A word said or unsaid can offend; digging too deeply would probably cause visible tear stains on this text. When stories get personal, where is the truth, unless all witnesses are heard? Many times, the best of juries get the verdict wrong. Being human, I can only risk making human mistakes.

Since the Master of Creation's plan was to move us in a certain chronological order, I shall try to do the same. If I take some liberties shuffling things around, it is because my mere, human mind sometimes works that way; please understand. I had parents before I had a brother or sister; I have dealt with our parents. Homer and Betty were there before wives, children, or pets. They deserve some seniority, which they shall now receive.

My memory of Betty and Homer began at about the same time. I do not remember Betty's birth, being only three at the time; it just seems I always had a brother and sister. Homer is four years older and has always seemed more mature, wiser, bigger, and arguably, capable of "whipping" me. In my defense, I think we have fought to many a draw. I have conceded before that

I cannot do a "book" about my immediate family. What I hope to accomplish here is squeeze in a little of the boundless love and appreciation I do feel for those near and dear.

How could one not start life without an insurmountable debt of gratitude owed a brother, who has stood so tall, and been there when needed? Mouse asked Homer one time, "What did you do when Virgil was born?" Straightforward; direct. Such questions often invite answers from Homer similar to this one: "Well, I had been sent to stay with my grandparents, who lived around the bend of the highway. I had prayed for a little brother and hoped I might get one. When the time of delivery was nigh, I heard my mother's screams of pain, rushed home as fast as my little legs could carry me, and helped cut the cord." This, from Homer, is as straightforward and direct as one usually gets.

He was four years older, but graded, geniused, or smartalecked out of an elementary grade, therefore, was always five years ahead of me in school. We were together at Riceville; I knew he was there; I have related those death marches when we missed the bus; I do not share other school memories during that period. At Mouse Creek, we were together one year; he was in the big room and I, the little. We each may have been on the wrong side of cliques at times, but at others, we may have been with the mob against some other hapless victim. Such is the story of growing up. He was out of high school before I was in, so we never shared that. The same for college.

That is not the whole story, however. Homer always related things: events, feelings, ambitions. He wove them into conversations with me about his world. Sometimes, I think I can recall some of his happenings better than he can. Of course, I shall never know, because a "Mincy" trait we perhaps share is that of revealing what we choose to reveal and keeping what could be of interest, but is personal, for whatever reason or motive, to ourselves. While I think we almost share an extrasensory perception, I know there are areas of his life, or facts about it, I shall never know, and know not to ask; I would guess it is the same with me. Perhaps neither of us wishes it to be so, but it is.

I have always been proud of his exploits and achievements. His successes, professionally, in the field of education administration, are known nationwide; his influence upon those he has mentored, led, supervised, or inspired is immeasurable. I believe he has inwardly cheered any modest achievements I may have enjoyed....and equally, felt my pain when I hurt or was disappointed. We have never lived near, since the fifties, and really have shared little of the daily minutia of our lives; when we are together, we have seemed able to pick up where we left off and enjoy common vibes of those common interests.

Much of what I have described is shared by most siblings who enjoy healthy relationships. Memories I have, however, in my mind's eye, go beyond the norm. Beyond the gossip, the older brother stuff, the pride, the accomplishments, rest the simple facts of his contributions to my life. Many of them may seem trivial but, as we should always be aware, who knows what little deed plants a seedling that becomes someone's tree of life. I could recite many that Johnny Homerseed dropped along my way.

Around the stove, night after night when we lived at the Gwinn place, he read to me, and any others in the family who wanted to listen, the *Complete Sherlock Holmes*. I hung on to every word as he turned the pages of *The Hound of Baskerville, A Study in Scarlet, The Sign of Four,* and the dozens of short stories that make up this work of Sir Arthur Conan Doyle. I did not understand many of the terms of late nineteenth century prose describing London or the English countryside. It made no difference; those words, phrases, and descriptions that Homer read just became part of the story, to be taken at face value. Forty-three years later, I stayed at a hotel in London, around the corner from the "Baker Street" station of London's transit system. Each morning and evening, as I caught or exited the train, my mind could not help but recall those tales of Sherlock and Dr. Watson, woven into the fabric of that street. There was and is a Baker Street, of course. I was given and have read this work, again; in reprise, I must say it lacks the thrill of that enjoyed around the "warm morning" heater during those evenings, long ago, when he introduced me to literature and the joy and excitement that came from sharing the imagination of others.

Homer would write during his trips west, following high school, from such romantic sounding places as Muskogee, Amarillo, Denver

City....sometimes sharing adventure, sometimes sadness, sometimes optimism; but, always information. Then, letters came from Fort Jackson, from Japan, or from places in between. He would voice curiosity, approval, or disapproval of happening in my life. After that time in the service, he shared his school, girlfriends, or new car experiences. These were not always times of agreement. I always felt he cared enough to be interested.

In 1954, he brought Ila Ree Breazeale into the Mincy family, raising its level of respectability by a substantial amount. She has been like another sister; someone to pick on, share with, enjoy time together, observe growth, and feel love. They gave us John, the only "next" Mincy (with all my efforts being girls) until, in time, John's son, John Tyler came along. In the short time Homer, Ila, June and I lived in East Tennessee, I valued the experience of meeting and getting to know Ila's family. I can only explain it by saying they reminded me of the Hedgecocks, which would be the ultimate compliment I could bestow. Her parents were gracious, humorous, charming, and always hospitable. Her brothers were friendly, boisterous, accepting, and always good company. Mr. Breazeale worked in the (Southern Railroad) car shop in Lenoir City, and they also had a farm; they enjoyed the best of both worlds: city or country life, if and when they wished.

Homer and I have shared golf, travel, vacations with our families, UT football, bowl games, endless discussions about any or all of this, and have always wanted to do it again. What can I say, except that I love him like a brother.

Elizabeth Alice (Betty), my little sister, is a different matter; not with respect to feelings, but to circumstances. We were closer in age and perhaps closer in spirit than I was with Homer, during a certain stage of growing up. It may be an assumption but with Homer being seven years older, Betty may have gravitated more to me to participate in time killing little activities, during both our younger years.

I do remember our playing "store." We would find something to serve as a counter, bring out all the merchandise we could get our hands on, and set up shop. That much, of course, is a given. What seemed the most fun was "coining" our money. We had no monopoly or genuine looking play money, and had to make our own. Understand, making coins was more practical then, than printing big bills, as a half dollar would buy more than one may think. The best source I recall for this was empty, round, Quaker Oats cereal boxes. There was a lot of "yellow" showing and, cut into round pieces, made good gold coins. Trust me; the best scissors we could find were hardly adequate to cut through that cardboard, but, on the other hand, our coins would last. We would trade places as to who was the customer and who kept shop.

Often, Betty's friends were mine, too: Lucille Green, Mary Ladue,....whoever was around, as often, I might not have had a close friend of my own. Running in the rain, exploring the flooded "Spring Creek," keeping store, or just hanging out, Betty was my friend. Betty declares I blackmailed her into endlessly pushing me around the yard on a homemade wagon I had fashioned. Going through my present neighborhood and noticing the exact replicas of Hummers, Jeeps, cars....you name it...., all battery powered and zipping around like miniature Darlington Raceway participants, brings it all back. I once was fascinated by the comic strip, Tom Thumb, which was about "little people" and small things. It depicted miniature cars, planes, trains...., objects of my fantasies. I envisioned such creations, but they did not exist; at least, not in my world. With some boards, a few nails, the wheels off our worn out little red wagon, and Betty's tireless, blackmailed, sister power, I made do as best I could.

She may exaggerate but not about my desire for wheels; perhaps I did enlist her aid.

"Hey, Betty; I thank you."

The thing about my little sister, if there need be only one thing, is that I have felt she was always there for me; just loving, wanting to please, not asking for much, and perhaps all too often, not getting much. Although we shared four years together at Mouse Creek and one year at McMinn, I do not remember much that we shared emotionally during those times. She had her friends, and I had mine; the rides to and from school may have been our only point of contact. I will say this: I most certainly did not observe her metamorphous from caterpillar to butterfly.

Betty was a cute, perfectly blond, little girl. In the late elementary school grades, she put on a little weight. She was still cute and blond and, although not big, neither was she little. She was a freshman when I left high school and only a junior when I got married and left our home.

I remember very well the shock I felt when I saw some pictures June brought back from a beach trip she had taken with her Dad—one that Betty shared. These pictures were not of my little sister, but of an improved Marilyn Monroe or any doll of today you want to mention…who is naturally blond. I, shame on me, had been so wrapped up in my own world, I had not noticed.

But, June's first cousin, Ed Axley, did. He had returned from his stint in Korea about the time June and I were getting married, and I think he tried to make up for lost time with whomever he could woo into his new Dodge. At least, be brags about that now. But, he did notice Betty and seemed to be genuinely smitten. This presented somewhat of a problem in that he was about Homer's age, Betty was still in high school, and Mom and Dad were not overjoyed at the prospect of seeing their cradle robbed. In the final analysis, the compromise reached was Ed assuring Mom and Dad that Betty would finish high school, in return for her hand at the end of her junior year. He now claims he was the only husband to ever attend PTA meetings at McMinn High. This (marriage) presented such intertwining of family relationships that I shall not even attempt to explain them.

Betty will have to write her own book, as I do not know her inner feelings or the emotions of her lifetime. She surely did not date much; she never left Athens, and she gave immeasurably to two families as a faithful caregiver….to their very end. I hope she has never wished that it could have been otherwise, but, in many ways I have envied her: for friendships of a lifetime, for her contribution to families and to her church, for getting to remain close and know our families (at an acknowledged price), and for the totality of these circumstances that I have not shared. I made my choices and have enjoyed my experiences, but I just did not have those. Selfish, but we always want it all.

Did I say she was always there for me? Don't get me wrong; Betty will speak her piece and you know it, if your piece is running counter to her piece. However, rarely, if ever, will she end a conversation without saying "I love you." You know she means it. When June and I had finalized our divorce, I had not told either Betty or Mom. This is difficult to explain or understand, but I doubt Mother had ever heard of anyone in her family getting a divorce, and the idea that it could occur in her family was probably a thought she had never entertained. It (that idea) had elements of religious belief, wrong doing, faithfulness, (or lack thereof) that were just foreign to her character. I did not have the guts to broach the subject:

"Betty, how are you.......?"

Of course she agreed to talk to Mom; of course she (Betty) listened and of course she understood, even if she did not agree with the circumstances. And, she did not hard time me with one disparaging word. She has pushed that wagon around the yard all my life, and I miss not being able to repay that debt every day. I just try to let her know I love her a lot and wish we could be closer in fact; I think we are in spirit.

Now, how did all this work when we were together at home? This is a slippery slope, and I shall not stay too long on it, trying to maintain my balance. I shall use quotes, and, whatever I say, you may know it has been edited by all parties, or I felt so strongly about it, I just wrote the final word. In spite of our sometimes difficult circumstances, I always felt loved at home and at two, four, six or eighteen, would have described us as a happy family. We worked, worshipped, were taught right from wrong, and, for the most part, were influenced by those teachings and tried to comply.

Homer, in his teen years, always seemed to have an edge of hostility toward our parents; I have never understood why. He quotes Mom as saying that, "She always was proud of my grades and accomplishments, but just never understood me." What did he feel, deep down in those dungeons of emotion? He will have to say, someday, as I do not know and cannot say.

I always felt a love and affection from Mom that was, to me, demonstrated and obvious. As far back as I can remember, I thought she was physical, caring, giving to me, and I never questioned her feelings. She would hug me, pick imaginary ticks from my hair, scratch my itches, and heal my wounds of body and spirit. Neither did I question Dad's, although he, being quieter and slower of expression, could be misread unless one had the patience to turn the pages. I just never doubted their feelings toward me.

Betty has said, however, that she never felt Mom loved her as much as she did "the boys." She has mentioned talking to Mom about that and quotes Mom as saying, "She was told by a fortune teller, who came begging at her door in Roane County, that if she had a girl, she would show her special attention. She had thought this in the back of her mind, but never thought that she was different to me in our relationship." Betty has further observed that she could not remember ever seeing any affection between our parents; since she was seldom in other family situations, she did not realize it could be different. She acknowledges that they must have been content with their relationship, as she does not remember signs of disapproval of each other.

This gets to the heart of the matter: Mom and Dad did not show affection toward each other in our presence. They were respectful, pleasant (most of the time), cooperative and very supportive. They did not hug, kiss, hold hands or give evidence that they ever had. Betty has spoken, and only she knows how that may or may not have affected her own outward nature. I know and admit a long suffered hang up about public displays of affection (by me). I was probably void of the practice early on, and only gradually did I come to recognize that need in others. I try, one day at a time, to stay on the wagon. Again, Homer must speak for himself.

I do remember a few instances of friends' parents who were affectionate, flirted with each other, and who could hardly keep their hands to themselves, around each other. I noticed, because that seemed so different. I remember visiting J.R. Keylon's home when I attended Forest Hill; he had six brothers and sisters and their house was not large. I was just amazed at the joy, love, and affection that was evident. I mentioned that to him, recently, and he said, "You know, they all are still just the same way."

Mom and Dad: it is not your fault if we have ever been cold and indifferent, or if we have been incapable of always showing what we really felt. We should have known better. Children, if you are like me, because I was somewhat like my parents, it is not too late: *Your* children are watching. If you love someone special, show it; how else will they ever know?

Speaking of evidences of all-too important affection, my children cannot blame any lack of it on their mother. If blame is called for or in order, it must only be half blame. June certainly differed from me in being outwardly demonstrative with her feelings. Always did; always has. I often missed or ignored the signals she sent, by being rather stiff and unresponsive when it came to showing affection in public. Lack of feelings inside was not the issue, but I confess I came wired with a restraint buzzer that went off when it appeared I might be observed or noticed being anything other than behaving, puritan, or the model of decorum. And, sad to say, I expected the same of my "possessions," i.e., children, wives or slaves. I am sure that did not help the confidence of a wife nor foster the emotional growth of watching children. We shall lay this to rest. Unintended, perhaps unknowing, I have allowed too many of my life's special moments to tick off, without that time counting for much.

I earlier spoke of June: she was left, a while back, helping me through school, supporting me through large hunks of my career, and being around while we had our children. We were together 28 years, and that term in office deserves it own memoir; I will at least share some important and personal memories that deserve their space in these pages.

Yes, she kicked Leah out of the back seat of those high school cars and took over the vacated warm spot. Yes, from January, 1952, we dated steadily (for 28 years, actually) for the balance of our senior year, through my first year at Tennessee Wesleyan, and until we decided to get married in November, 1953. It was not that cut and dried.

June was my first serious relationship. If I say as serious as eighteen year old people are capable of experiencing, I am not belittling our place in that time; I am just acknowledging that most parents shudder at such a thought and, in general, ours did, too. But, from that first date, when I took her to a movie in McMinn Supply's big delivery truck, we were committed steadies. I loved her mom, Bess, her little sister, Kathy, and before long, knew all her family. Most Sunday afternoons were spent at her Aunt Nola's, with cousins Penny and "Euppie." Her grandmother lived with Nola, and many or most of June's aunts, uncles and cousins were Sunday regulars. They were, each and all, warm and gracious to me at that time and, for the rest of their lives, when we have had contact. If I describe the Farners as hard working people, I mean that as the kindest of compliments: most of them were knitters, fixers, or machinists in the hosiery industry, which was concentrated in three or four mills in "North Athens." I believe each family owned his or her home, was as "respectable" as I was, and on an asset scale, weighed more that the Mincys did; I felt comfortable and pleased to be part of this extended family.

As we closed out our high school years, our closest and regular friends were three or four couples who were also "going steady" and were either committed or heading toward marriage: Leah and Jim Key, Oran and Shorty Creasman, Bea and Charlie Gardner, and Jackie and Jequetia Hill. (These are the guy's last names, of course.) I think most were married by the time my first year in college was completed. This, to say the least, created considerable peer pressure to consider this step. I would be straying from the truth if I recounted much discussion on this subject between June and me; it was always there, as an issue, however. It was a very positive issue. We were in love. We, as did most kids, envisioned we could do better as a couple, than we were doing single: home, cars, furniture, and the whole nine yards. We watched our friends start, play house, do married people stuff, and it was a powerful attraction. Staring us in the face every date was the question: what's next?

As truthful as I can relate at this point, I think I was just straddling the fence, procrastinating, putting off a commitment because that was the very antithesis of "volunteering" or taking a position. Sadly, that is a personality trait I have been afflicted with that is difficult to overcome. At work, I always have tried to do what I had to do….sometimes hating every minute of it. Other times? Don't raise your hand and sit real low; maybe no one will call on you.

June "called on me." We had drifted along until the beginning of my second year at Wesleyan, and only she could say whether she was testing the waters or just testing me. Across the street from the Farmer's Bank, where she worked, was a Shell service station, owned and operated by Johnny Schultz. Johnnie was truly a good guy and, of course, crossed that street to make his deposits every day, getting his nice words in while my back was turned. She finally took him up on what I am sure had been many offers and went on a couple of dates with him.

I had an easy out; the perfect opportunity to slide off the fence and run in the other direction. I did not, and have never regretted that decision. I reviewed my situation, ran up to Wilson's Jewelry Store to see our classmate, Mary Belle Layman, who worked there, and bought that little .25 carat Artcarved diamond faster than Mr. Schultz could service a car.

I do recall the climatic moment when I went by June's house one afternoon (I remember the sun was still shining, it was after work, so it must have been early fall) and hid the little ring box under the seat of the sofa in the living room. I probably made small talk as I helped myself to another of Bess' great meals and sort of like saying "boo," simply handed her the ring. I doubt if I made much of a speech and certainly did not mess up the crease on the knees of my trousers. She seemed pleased. Goodbye, Johnny; hello, life!

Was that a good decision to have made? Every parent of every child in every county in the United States of American would almost universally shout, "NO," all things being equal. Fifty years later, each of the friends I mentioned are still together and, to look back, other than our personal failures, what would we have wanted to be different? Our successes? Our good times? Our children? Our many friends and neighbors in over half a dozen different cities? Most of our happy memories? I, ignorant of many things, immature and too young, most assuredly thought of myself as a man, thought my decisions sound, and thought I was working on a plan. I just went forward, happily, with it.

I did and still do consider that simple wedding at the North Athens Baptist Church a milestone; it was dignified, purposeful, and certainly meaningful to me. If was definitely a Mincy affair, as Homer was my best man, my father was the minister, my sister was maid of honor, and I had to go down before the ceremony and arrange the few plants we had ordered, as the "order" did not include "decorating." My old 4-H buddies, John Henry Gilbert and John Baker, were our ushers. A sister teller at the bank, Betty Greene, sang, and a young lady who had once pursued Homer, Vivian Taylor, played the piano. It was a nice affair.

"I present to you, Mr. and Mrs. Virgil Mincy." No, Dad did not say that, and I am not sure he even invited me to kiss the bride. You know that Mincy thing about affection in public.

He did pronounce us man and wife, and we met a few people at Bess' little house, a block up from the church on East Fisher Street, for what served as our reception. After a little while, I retrieved our 1947 Oldsmobile coupe from Reverend Hugh Ensminger's garage, and off to Atlanta we sped, toward whatever was next. Reverend Ensminger was the Pastor of North Athens Baptist and had been so generous as to give June's hand in marriage to mine. We started that trip so excited and full of spunk that we did not even consider the need to plan where we would stop or make reservations to assure we had a place to stop. Some would call our cavalier attitudes naive and immature; we just called ourselves brave and adventurous.

June and I continued that brave and adventurous journey for 27 more years; good years, productive years, happy years, and a few miles that were less so. This story has been segmented, including other periods of her life, and I shall not retell them. When I talk about our children, her character may re-appear, with speaking parts. Hers always was an important role. What happened? It would be pointless to tell my side and I cannot tell hers; remember, this is not a tell all. I only address the fact that our waves broke upon troubled shores, after a time, as a lesson point to anyone who may be interested in us, as people, or to anyone who can profit from other's mistakes.

I oft said, and still do, that for most of our time together, I thought we were happier than any other couple we knew or had known. We cared for each other, and there was no big scandal that broke us apart. My view and my lesson is simply this: little issues were never resolved and the scars that built up, in time, rendered me simply incapable of remaining loving, caring, happy and giving. I could see this in me, did not like it in me, but just seemed powerless to change. June is a Leo; she needed attention, reassurance and the security of knowing she was loved and wanted. She had only experienced that from her Mom and sister and strongly needed a continuation of that critical support from me. We failed each other. The point? Solve little problems before they grow into big tigers that devour you. That principle was not taught at McMinn County High, Tennessee Wesleyan or the great UT; sometimes it is taught at the school of hard knocks, but often, when you have served your time and been let out, it's too late to repay the victims. June and I have remained friends, and I hope we always will.

"And lo, the skies parted and children rained down upon the earth." Not just one, nor two; there came three, four, and five. All June's and mine. There were several factors, beginning with the fact I come from a long line of prolific progenitors. My great-great Grandfather, David Mincy, was the father of fifteen children, wearing out, understandably, two wives in the process. My Mother was one of 10 children. My forefathers just believed in the admonition to "go forth, and replenish the earth."

Yes, we were asked all the questions: Why so many? Did you plan for five children? How did you manage? The most direct answer, pure and simple, is: we liked each other. Next question?

I fondly remember going to Duke Indoor Stadium, back in the sixties, with Allan Cannon, to see a concert by Al Hirt, the renowned trumpet jazz artist. Either when he was introduced, or shortly into his set, it was mentioned he was the father of five children. The crowd went into it's obligatory frenzy and when it had quieted down, Al, with perfect timing, said in his raspy, seductive voice, "The pleasure.... was all mine!" Let's move on.

No, June and I did not attend Planned Parenthood sessions. We, irresponsible or not, did not set forth on paper our life's plan for the number of and sex of said number of children. We set out on our journey just assuming we would be parents and looked forward to that opportunity and challenge.

Pamela Gail did come along 21 months after we were married, in a seemingly normal and timely fashion. All our fans that just look at the total are not usually aware there was a five year gap from the time Pam was born until Tina blessed our home. During that time, we were eager for another child and were mildly concerned that there was a problem that prohibited number two from being on the census rolls. Truthfully, numbers three and four were rather close but, again, who would we throw back or what day would we not have wanted either of them to be a part of our lives?

Virgil and June's wedding, November 25, 1953

Front row (left to right): Rev. Hugh Ensminger, Betty, Virgil, June, Homer and Betty Green. Back row (left to right): John L. Baker, Vivian Taylor, John Henry Gilbert, Dad

We were warned not to smile; this was serious business.

Betty and Virgil 1982

My dear children: Christmas, North Carolina 1990

Left to right: JoAnn, Debra, Liz, Virgil, Pam and Tina

Magdalen Pundai Ciotti and Virgil

My last mother-in-law; I was blessed to have known, loved and been loved by two.

Dorothy Ciotti Mincy

My best friend
Granger, IN 1999

Peach Bowl 1988

Left to right: Buffy Wyrosdick, Ila Mincy, Jay Wyrosdick, Homer, Sam Wyrosdick, Mouse and Mike Wyrosdick. Some thought we were number 1; at least, we won: UT 27 Indiana 22

Again, there was a five year span from JoAnn's birth until Elizabeth's. Liz was unplanned and defied medical science by bypassing all barriers to struggle her way into this world. And what a blessing! Life has not always been an easy road for Liz, but no one is more fun to be around or loving (at least to me) than she is, and I am thankful she made it and is mine.

I must confess, when we had one child, in those early days, I looked somewhat askance at couples with large families, observing the difficulties, expense, sacrifices, and yes...sometimes the ridicule they perhaps endured (behind their backs). But in our case, our large family of lovely girls became a calling card, an identity, a source of pride that has been sustained. At times, as would any parent, we perhaps bemoaned what they may have done, but never ceased to be proud of whom they were. To lift and copy from New Testament theology, we, unmerited, have been blessed.

One other bit that needs to be understood is that Pam was an only child for five years; then, the pie started to get divided. It must always be this way: There is only so much time and parents just share what they have with whom there is to share. My mother, being one of 10, was never pampered as would have been an only child, but her stories were always rich and full of the joy of life among loving brothers and sisters and the amazement of discovering life pretty much on her own time. I hope my children each can feel they experienced some of that dose of life's medicine, in equal parts

I want to talk some about the girls; this can, at best, be only an overview, as they have each lived interesting and full lives. Neither they nor I am comfortable facing the fact they all are approaching middle age....and should write their own life's stories. I might recall some little tid-bit that could be of interest to their grandchildren down the road, and toward that end, I shall try to relate a few. Trying to do so causes me some sadness as, truth to tell, there are many happenings I simply do not remember. Let's see: Pam is 49, as of this typing session; add all the daughter-years and take away all the separated years, and that equals many lost or forgotten memories. But, I shall try and see where this leads; **don't count the words about** *any one, as the weight of my love and affection for them is not measured by the stories I can tell.*

Dr. Powell, at the Epperson Hospital in Athens, Tennessee, delivered Pamela Gail, August 6, 1955. She was a rather difficult delivery as many "first" children are or, at least, were. She was difficult in the sense once labor started, it was back and forth between home and the hospital until she made up her mind to join us. This was the summer between my junior and senior year at the University of Tennessee. We were living with June's mom, Bess; between Bess, and my parents, Pam was welcomed into this world by the hurrahs of a loving and supportive family (Pam was the first grandchild in both our families). When she was less than a month old, we returned to Knoxville for my last year. The program called for June to go back to work as soon as she could, as our budget, with both her and me working, was a shoestring and a thin one at that. We moved into an upstairs apartment on Tillery Road, off what is now I75, in North Knoxville. That was a lucky location because across the street lived a wonderful lady, Mrs. Whitaker, who became Pam's caretaker until I finished school. The routine was simple: drop her off on the way to school/work each morning, and whoever got home first picked her up each evening. The Whitakers loved her, cared for her in an excellent manner, and sort of became surrogate grandparents for Pam.

The tale has oft been told, but the routine each Friday was that I picked Pam up and went downtown to get June; she usually had to work later on Friday, as the bank was open longer. All you safety conscious people avert your eyes now. Heading downtown, I held Pam on my left shoulder and steered/shifted gears with my right hand through Knoxville traffic. No seat belt, either. I will never know or enjoy a warmer feeling than little Pam watching the lights and being as quiet as a doll all the way. This was a regular trip each week....sometimes more often, and Pam seemed to enjoy it.

Later in the school year, about the time Pam started to cut some teeth, I discovered too late she had found something other than lights with which to amuse herself: I had bought a new, 1956, Bel Aire Chevrolet two door, which had a painted, black panel next to the door glass on the front doors. I wondered why Pam was so quiet one trip, until I noticed next day that she had found it comforting to gnaw on that door panel, which probably soothed her little, emerging, front teeth. She had methodically scratched all across that panel, and her little fang marks remained as long as we had that car.

For five years, Pam was our primary toy. We played, enjoyed, and moved around the country during that period. She was living in her seventh home by the time her first sister arrived. If I had to identify a couple of character traits that emerged early on, they would be 1) she was accident prone; I believe I was in more emergency rooms with Pam, than all the other four combined—busted chins, lips, knees—wherever. It seemed she could find a way to get hurt more than her share. We tried to get our insurance provider to sell us stitching thread by the yard, at a discount, to no avail. 2) She was stubborn. In those early days, I learned in simple rough-house games that Pam would let someone choke her to death (if that had ever been the threat) before she would give up or yell "Uncle." Whether or not that trait carried over into adult life....I shall leave to the judgment of a jury of her peers. The up side of that characteristic has been her self-discipline, organization skills, devotion to her cause(s) and loyalty to her convictions.

Elizabeth, number five, on the other hand, arrived in an ordinary fashion, almost as if we had practiced it a few times: nine months, labor, go to hospital, and wait a little while until the doctor came out and said, "I am sorry Virgil; it is another girl." Sorry! If only Dr. A.J. Ellington could have known what a relief those words were. I will admit that our first opportunity caused me to think of my favorite male names: Steve Roper, Mike Nomad, and Clark Kent....all the famous cartoon characters of the day. Perhaps there were "boy thoughts" with the next couple, but by the time four and five came along, the logistical nightmare of mixing a boy or boys amongst all the girls would have been too much. No, JoAnn and Elizabeth, you are just what we ordered.

Elizabeth was certainly different than her sisters. I am not wise or learned enough to know whether it was genes or environment, but she certainly was not the quiet, reserved, and mannerly little infant that we had come to expect, know, and love. I have always said, and perhaps with justification, that she had to fight for her space and time and did so. She was active, loud and, yes, pretty, just as all our children had been. That active trait caused her to enjoy her share of bumps and bruises, too, as I suppose the quarterback is always hit more than the water boy. Liz was always on the move.

I wish I could pull up the memory files of intimate, personal, little bits of her childhood to embellish; the late sixties and seventies are sort of a fog of sleeping arrangements, adding on to our house, packing a car with five children for a beach trip, and the chatter of seven mouths all vying for air time. I do remember, at times, that unhappy little face. Six of us would be enjoying an occasional meal at the cafeteria in the mall, but Elizabeth would be voicing her dissent; posing for pictures at the church, her four sisters would jump into place, as they had been trained, but Elizabeth stubbornly refused to smile. All true but, equally true, I remember that when she did smile, it could and can just light up the room.

I shall always be saddened that her family separated when she was twelve; not necessarily more than for the other four, but there is a difference in the needs of a twelve year old and 25 year old child. She was thrust into a disruptive and uncertain growing up period that I know was not comforting. While provided with every material need and opportunity imaginable, mostly by her step-father, she sometimes struggled to realize the most potential from her use of that time. She did make it through school, and I am proud to say she has worked very hard to take her place in the world, be self-sufficient, and successful. She is and will be. That February 16th, 1968, at 12:10 P.M., when Dr. A.J. came out with the good news, he never knew what good news he, indeed, was delivering (in addition to "it being a daughter").

Debra Lynn, our middle child, arrived just as I described when I told about my Mom and her trip to New Jersey; what I have not revealed is how thankful I was that Debra did not mess up the seats of my new, four-door, Bonneville hard top as her first act of defiance, as we sped to the hospital that night.

Debra was the total opposite of Elizabeth; after she overcame some early formula adjustment times and started being a normal little baby, she was very quiet and made few sounds. I called her "Li'l Dropout," which was some kind of furry little cartoon character; not because of sounds she made or did not make, but because some of her early pictures just reminded me of "LD." I do recall our wondering if she ever would speak and, subsequently, talk. She was certainly alert and would watch us with those expressive, intent little eyes....just a sweet baby.

Early on, we noticed she would do weird things with her feet and legs; she would tuck her feet behind her at odd angles and sit on her knees/legs; we thought this appeared rather irregular and promptly took her to the Mayo Clinic of Graham for a diagnosis. Yes, we were told, her feet needed some correction, so she was prescribed and wore "Thomas Heels" for several months. What I do remember, as clearly as this morning, is an event whereby Debra (who was three or four by this time) for some reason had her shoes off and started to run from our yard toward our neighbors', the McQueen's, yard. It was just like Forest Gump; she flew! In the space of just a few weeks she started talking (more), started flying around with athletic moves, and started exploring everything on earth with a daredevil curiosity. She would walk up and jump into a swimming pool, as if to see what the bottom looked like. She would pick up anything moving, just to get a good look. She took on the boys in most games and held her own. She just blossomed.

She swam, she dove, she played baseball (with the boys), and she played basketball with the girls. She was pretty good at everything. She brought home ribbons by the basketful from her aquatic feats but, in the long run, gave that up. It became too enervating. She could stand at the foul line in a gym of screaming fans, with the game on the line, and do her job. She would throw up before having to get on the diving board in front of a few of her friends and their parents at a swim meet.

Debra started (basketball) her sophomore year at Graham High; we moved to Texas after her junior year, and by that time, she had begun to struggle with the competition in a school of 500 students. At R.L. Turner, in Farmers Branch, Texas, she started, and this school probably had an enrollment of 2,500. She was pretty competent, but basketball was better in North Carolina. Her team did win the District in Texas, and we followed the team to the Regional in Abilene, where it was one and out.

Debra and Tony (her husband) perhaps owe me for this: when Debra graduated from high school, among other considerations, she and some friends decided to attend Stephen F. Austin College. We (June and I) let her down, although not purposely. She was with a gang of people, and I foolishly thought she could settle in, handle it and, with the support of friends, all would be well. When she arrived, the room situation was unsettled, she was assigned to live in a motel, the discipline and routine of tackling college work was put aside, and in a short time, she was home. I did not foresee this coming and, had we stayed close enough to the situation, perhaps we could have helped. About the debt: A couple of years had passed, Debra had gone to Brookhaven Community College for a while and done well, but dropped out of that. She was working, had dated some and was, in time, dating a young man named Tony Hartnett. I had moved to Pittsburgh.

From the reports I received long distance, Tony seemed bad news; I have not the faintest idea what the issues were; I did know the "family," thought he was up to no good, and that he was definitely a bad influence on Debra or, at best, a bad choice. I made a trip to Texas to see what this was all about, and I can truthfully say I considered what alternatives I had at my disposal, including use of some Teamster friends, if it came to that. I met Debra in Dallas at a Bennigans restaurant (home of the great deep dish cobbler) to hear the low-down.

Debra told me about this guy and splattered big tears all over my cobbler from a seemingly bottomless well of grief. Yes, she loved him and yes, she wanted to be with him and yes, he was the man for her, if only we would give him a chance. What could I do? I ordered fresh cobbler and whussed out. It was just a few years until Mouse and I attended their wedding down in his home town of Cut-N-Shoot, Texas (or was it Gun Barrel City....I get them mixed up.)

Tina had to arrive with flair and style; almost an eleven month baby, she was large, fully developed, breech, broken collar bone, needed a pediatrician, and all the works. All my children were attractive, cute, pretty babies, and neat children. Tina was all that...not necessarily more or less. She was the most beautiful **infant** I have ever seen; she arrived with black, curly, hair, long fingernails, was alert, and I tell you truthfully, within a week was sleeping the night through. She forever owes a debt to her mom, who suffered her that long and endured the risk and pain of that delivery. She (Tina) just spent an extra month or two in a protected environment.

Tina's arrival caused a small-time precedent-setting incident in my company. When we filed our insurance claim, our company's carrier, Provident, denied any charges relating to Tina. After I pitched several fits, the next publication of our "insurance booklet" specified that a dependent had to be "fourteen days old" to be eligible for any benefits. I believe that was known world wide (in those days) as the Tina Mincy ruling.

JoAnn, number four on our depth charts but last in this briefing, also arrived by a more mundane route; in her case, Betty and Ed had visited us for a few days and the plan was that they be there to help us through June's first days after JoAnn was born. JoAnn just waited until, finally one Sunday, the Axleys had to go home. I recall, with no clue being given, June waving goodbye to them as her pains started. JoAnn arrived ("Sorry, Virgil, another girl") a few hours later.

Her calling card into life was and is perfectly blond, beautiful hair. I believe she let it grow for 26 years (not really) or so, but I do know it was waist/hip length in whatever time it took to get that long. June called JoAnn "her little armpit," as it seemed she was with June wherever they went. She was always the most pleasant, cheerful, and interesting company, as a child or adult, anyone would want. I do not remember scolding her, or needing to, until she was a senior in high school (in Texas), and I remember that, not for its reason, but that I did not handle it well. (My version) Whatever the issue, I took her to task, and she seemed so shocked to be crossed by her father that she clammed up on me for awhile. I took offense that she was not charmed by my advice and, also, pouted for a while; I was capable of better behavior and regret I did not display it. That little blip does not offset her exemplary behavior toward me her entire life. She got me back for my Texas talking, though.

I was visiting Dallas after I had moved to Pittsburgh; JoAnn and I were out in her little Chevet, looking for a Christmas tree; she was making a left turn at a busy intersection, and we both thought she had the light. An approaching car apparently thought otherwise and broadsided us, hitting my side and pushing us left, into a car entering the intersection from our left. I am still horrified by the memory of JoAnn being thrown around in that little car like a rag doll; I was probably behaving in a similar manner. We survived with bumps and bruises, but I always described that car as looking like the "Hilton H."

Thought I was through, did you? Of course, it is not possible to detail five lives in a few pages, but I shall try a little free association and see what comes up with random thoughts about my girls:

Tina was an accounting major at the University of Texas; Pam was a dance major at Appalachian State University and the University of North Carolina-Greensboro. Liz majored in interior design at East Carolina University, and JoAnn was a marketing major at North Texas State. Jo Ann's academic and activity achievements at both R.L. Turner High School and NTSU were outstanding; I always said that she could take over the world, if she set her mind to it. To my knowledge, few of these schools ever played each other in any sport; they all turn out great young ladies. Tina is a CPA and still works in public accounting; Liz works in sales/design for a tile distributor. JoAnn markets, manages, administers, and does about everything in their family's insurance agency. Pam married her boss and lived happily ever after.

But, there is more to it than that. Pam's finishing school coincided with our family moving to Texas; she soon went to work in a health club organization and, yes, she soon started dating her boss, Fred Clapp and, yes, in due time they were married. (*I recall a scene during that ceremony where, as Phyllis Ford (from Graham, North Carolina) and I played (flute/guitar) some music, Fred and his best man, Miguel, were sitting in the balcony in their suits, wearing "cowboy boots." Both propped those boots over the balcony rail, taking it all in; the guests could not see them, but Phyllis and I had a difficult time staying focused.*) They still are. Also in due time, Debra ended up working for the same company and for Fred; that is not the end of the story. One of Fred's other employees, a Wisconsin guy named Myles Goertz, met Tina and was impressed enough, or, they with each other, that they became man and woman together for life. Everybody has to be somewhere, and those health clubs in Dallas were the means that brought some of my family together; isn't that one of the main reasons single people go to health clubs? This story is a good endorsement.

I have talked about Debra's athletic achievements; however, in all fairness I think June and I attended more games to see Pam or JoAnn cheer than we did Debra dribble. Cheer leaders for life. Tina did not play basketball, but she blew away the competition with her smarts. And whether or not she realized it, she was and is one attractive woman. She also has taken up some of the reins as host, party give, and chef extraordinaire for family gatherings. She was always somewhat disdainful of normal family chores but took an interest in cooking before any of the others (that I remember).

Liz? In her early high school years, she had an opportunity to "ride" and spent a lot of time with horses….mostly walkers. In her riding habit, she made a dazzling picture posting up around the ring. She loved horses and mucked her share of stables as part of the price of gaining that experience. Some day I would not be surprised to see her hit the trail, again. She also "shows well" with her innate ability to visualize, arrange, decorate, place, and create visual beauty. East Carolina…or the school of hard knocks? Either one, she is Suma Cum.

Debra and Tony board and train dogs; Tony has achieved Master Trainer status through a lot of hard work and is recognized for his efforts. He works mostly with retrievers; it is quite a show to watch him communicate with the dogs using only a whistle, signals, and direction.

I have been blessed with grand grandchildren and, although I greatly miss not getting to see them cheer, bat, dribble or fish, I try to keep up with the results. The circle of life. These grandchildren are about eleven generations removed from original ancestors arriving in this country….and that is just an artificial starting point. That is what this narrative is about; stories of the journey from there to here, wherever there was and wherever here goes.

Let me share a little more of my story.

When June and I agreed that our lives should take a different direction, I moved into an apartment near where we lived (in Dallas); soon, June moved out of our house and I moved back in with the intent that we sell it in due time. I remained there for almost two years. As I describe happenings or relationships, it perhaps serves somewhat as a mask to cover the real emotions I was experiencing: disappointment, depression and a feeling of great sadness that life, as it had been, had ended. Immediately, I was also looking for another job, and that entailed some apprehension and concern. I had my plate full. I also felt that I had to move on and, after some sputtering, I remembered rationalizing that I had two choices with respect to my relationship, going forward, with June: war or peace. Peace seemed the more prudent option, and I resolved to try to get along, for everyone's sake. After a while, I also got out and tried to meet new people. At first, I was not a smashing success.

If you remember my high school tales and my lamenting that I had not dated much, try going forward 30-plus years and starting over. I was 46. I had forgotten all the "lines" that I had never known and, by nature, it was difficult for me to walk up to a stranger and say, "Hi, what's your sign?" or "Excuse me, is that your chair?" I hung around and waited to be discovered, often thinking I would still be in that pose when the grim reaper came a'calling. I was, to be honest, sort of disillusioned and discouraged. Similar to looking for a job, however, I knew it would not be easy and success was not a given, so I kept trying to meet new people.

I think my first date came about after going to a singles affair, and yes, I was sort of discovered and approached, and yes, I thought my ship had arrived and things were looking up. I found, just like looking for that job, that relationships seem easier to come by when one is in one. I am not sure what moral or psychological judgment I can make about this, but perhaps it goes back to the days of the gold rushes and the 49ers. Some people would rather jump someone else's claim than to find a new one on their own. Once started, I did work my way through a few friendships, most of which came to me.

A couple of years after my divorce I received the offer of a position in Pittsburgh; other than job considerations, I was very concerned about creating this distance from my family. I rationalized a move by concluding that in a short time, they would probably scatter, regardless of what I did, and if my chief reason for staying in Dallas were they, that reasoning was on shaky ground. On the other hand, I also had a girlfriend in Dallas and loved the city which, combined, made the decision difficult. In the end, to Pittsburgh I did go.

In Pittsburgh, it was starting over again. The friend I had left in Dallas was, indeed, a dear friend but, in the final analysis, it was destined to be no more than that. My new job entailed travel to several locations and, in time, I met people in some of those cities. By 1984, I did not have a girlfriend in every city, but had one in a few.

This is not to brag; in fact, I feel a little guilt and regret, particularly to the extent I hurt people's feelings. I relate this to describe where I was when love found me again. I was not looking to get married and tried to be honest with anyone I met. Some women I met were up front and described similar feelings; often, those feelings seemed to change and, in the end, some wanted more from me than I was willing to give. This, in general, describes me in the fall of 1984.

What I shall talk about now seems rather close to the way Mouse tells it, so I shall do it from both our viewpoints. I was not looking for a new friend; only male ego and selfishness provided the basis for any temptation to meet someone new. Dorothy Jean (Mouse) Ciotti Percy was working for National Steel Corporation in the same building in which I worked (for National Aluminum). She had been separated from her husband for some time and, selectively, was looking to meet a "quality" person.

Mouse, among other things, managed the car leasing program for National; her internal customers were employees who had an assigned vehicle, which included many top company officers and managers. One such person was Aluminum's Vice President of Metal Control, Joe Rheinhardt. Joe was pestering Mouse for some favor one day, when she asked him, "When are you going to do something for me?" She asked if he did not have a rolodex full of names of people he could introduce to her. He told her, anxious to get out of her office, that he had just the one: Virgil Mincy. Mouse says that she had heard about me, but what she had heard was that I had five children (supposedly living with me), a live-in girlfriend, was "older" and, therefore, told Joe, "No way."

Joe came straight back to my office and told me (Joe was a rather gruff, bluffing, and blunt personality, and he was a Vice President talking to me, a mere Director) that he knew someone who **really wanted to meet me**—Dorothy Percy. "Give her a call," he said. It was more an order than a friendly suggestion. Hmmm.

Then, this happened: the Director of Human Resources, Bill Baird, showed up the same day, saying, "Virgil, there is someone you should call; **she is interested in meeting you.** Her name is Dorothy Percy." Bill and Mouse knew each other, but it gets a little fuzzy why he was involved at that time; I suspect Rheinhardt may have suggested that Bill talk to me, in order to fulfill his obligation to Mouse and store up points for some future car consideration. However, talk to me they did and on the same day.

I knew Mouse by sight, but she claims she had never (knowingly) laid eyes on me. Flattered that **I was being sought out**, I considered this and thought, "Why not." I waited a day or so, called her, and gave her some corny line that I thought would make her day. I got "a less than having made her day" reception. I did ask her to have dinner with me and she did agree.

I pulled out all the stops. We caught the company van to Three Rivers Stadium, where I parked my Dallas Cowboy silver and blue Datsun 280ZX 2+2 hardtop; I whisked her north to my condo, where I showed her around, played my guitar, and sang some song. She let me know she was hungry. We ate at Maggie Mae's on McKnight Road, went back to her high rise on the Point, downtown, and chatted until she pushed me out the door. Driving back north that night, I truthfully did say, "I think…. she is the one."

For the record and for the ages, I shall just say she was attractive, professional, interesting, and challenging. For the record, she says she thought I was "okay," but that she was not bowled over.

She was leaving town for a week's vacation the next day, but I got her to agree to see me when she returned. I left her messages and let her know I had enjoyed meeting her and looked forward to seeing her again. The date was August 9th, 1984.

We have been together since. She was wary of me and my perceived baggage; her family thought I was too old (her sister claimed their mother wanted me for herself); and she actually was not divorced at the time and was more cautious of me than I was her. This may have been a blessing; had she jumped into my arms and sworn allegiance forever, I could have been scared off. Who knows? I took her to North Carolina in early October to meet all my girls at a big house warming June and Larry (her husband) were throwing. I had cautioned "the viscous ones" to be on good behavior, because this one "was special." Mouse was apprehensive, but they behaved and liked Mouse. She concedes meeting five children, an ex-wife, old friends, and a mob of strangers was rather trying, but she handled it fine.

When the dust of first meeting had settled, we, of course, had to get to know each other. I concede that, initially, I perhaps came on a little strongly, but I was interested in this relationship and wanted it to succeed. Though not a fun enterprise, I cut ties to other relationships I had scattered around; some were angry; others were hurt; and I wrote down the learned in life lesson that it is easier to get into many situations than it is to get out of them. In my six single years, I did enjoy friendships with some great people who were very nice to me; some are still speaking friends, and I hope the others have forgotten me, in peace.

Mouse and I have worked hard and endured the everyday stress of making a living and striving to get by. We have had some great times along the way. Some of our earliest adventures were finding and staying at country inns; often we mixed those with business trips. Frankly, I doubt we could name them all. I introduced her, kicking and screaming, to Tennessee football; after a while, I have sort of quit beating that horse. She introduced me to her family, which has been, indeed, a blessing. Her father, who died in 1980, was born in Italy and came to this country when he was four. He worked in coal mines in the little town of Yukon, Pennsylvania, (where Mouse grew up), until the mines played out. Mouse's mother, Magdalen (Madge) was a Pundai, which is, I believe, Hungarian.

Mouse took me to visit her Grandmother Pundai, in a rest home in Greensburg, on one of our early dates. She (Mouse) introduced me to her frail grandmother, who was bedridden, but alert, by saying, "Now, Grandmother, you can tell by his funny accent that he is from the South." As quick as a whip, she responded, "Now, Honey Bunch, he can't help that." For that, and for the fact Mouse says Mrs. Pundai made the best two-crust cherry pies the world has ever known, she warmed my heart.

All Mouse's family have been great to me: her sister, Mary Anne (Rho), her nephew, Brian and niece, Megan. Mouse has aunts, cousins, uncles…all who have shared their lives and been interested in mine. I finally negotiated a deal whereby Mouse would let me join that family and I did, May 17, 1986. We enjoyed a lovely, elegant, yet simple ceremony at Mary Anne's home, in Crafton, Pennsylvania, and one thing we all agree; it was hot! A friend from Burlington, North Carolina, and from Burlington Industries days, Everett Rumley, came up with some other friends and performed the service. Mouse claimed to have been nervous but, this time, the minister did say, "You may now kiss the bride," and I assure you she was up to the task.

We did take each other…. "in sickness and in health" and I know she has always been there, whatever my need; I hope she feels I try to do the same. We have shared family times, private times, vacation times, adventurous times, and this fairy tale continues. I can truthfully say that in 20 years, I do not recall an intended cross word. In war, or on the open seas, an occasional "shot across the bow" is used to signal a message, and we may have fired a few now and then. The secret is to not aim to hit. That my relationship with Mouse merits a fairer or more giving attitude than did others is not true; I have learned the hard way that, "it is more blessed to give than to receive" and that, in the end, the gift is returned. I have been blessed to have found Mouse and will never let her scurry away.

A book usually lists acknowledgements….people or sources who served to forward the work or the efforts of the author. This is my family acknowledgement space, and it should go on, but must end. I have known the love of family and have felt pride in the families of which I have been a part. Many, many never have any family; I have been blessed to be part of extended ones. The route has, on occasion, known bumps, but my destination has not been compromised. Homer, Betty, girls, "the little ones" and our large families; Mouse, and all your fine family; I thank you. I love you and treasure memories from this journey we travel together.

"My Faith Looks Up to Thee"

Put simply, this is about my "religious" beliefs. In some ways, this is a most difficult thing to do; in others, it will be quite easy. Difficult, because what I believe and why is foreign to billions of people in this world; easy, because what I believe and why *IS* what *I* believe. No one can refute or challenge the fact that my personal belief system is intact, that it was caused to be by specific events in my life, and, that remembering those events and the circumstances are important to me now and will be throughout eternity.

The challenge comes from those who have perhaps seen no evidence of what I am about to describe; who, in absence of that evidence and in absence of a similar faith-based belief, will simply deny such possibility. That concern I accept and understand. During my life, if or when I have failed to show evidence of my beliefs and what they mean to me or, worse, if I have acted in a manner that would deny their existence, I stand guilty of what is called sin. This I accept and understand, also. I confess to this, here, publicly, as I most certainly do privately to the One who matters.

The reason for including this in a story about the Mincys is quite simple: While there may have been ambiguity at times concerning my religious convictions and faith, I want no misunderstanding now as to what those convictions are and what my faith means to me. Let this serve as the record; accept this as what I know, believe, and feel regarding my relationship with God.

Broadly, I accept that "religion," "faith," "relationship with God," "eternity," "being saved," "being lost," and perhaps "Jesus," himself, are words that are out of favor and subject to a myriad of definitions by many, including those who identify themselves as "Christian." I am not literate enough nor inclined to challenge the belief system of the countless Protestant, Catholic, or other denominational groups, or individuals therein.

More people have probably been slaughtered in the name of God than for any other cause. I doubt that more literature has been produced proclaiming any cause than that of worship, "God", belief in a god, or the study thereof. I doubt there are any issues in which mankind is more likely to split hairs, argue ad infinitum, debate, part ways, or denounce beliefs once held, than the subject of "religion." It is highly unlikely, then, that my personal convictions will be likened to any doctrine worthy of being "nailed to the church door," or starting some new movement. To the contrary, they are quite simple, mostly Baptist, personal, and to me, very real.

What can be confusing is the fact thousands of churches are filled with millions of people who believe, or are being exhorted to believe, little shades of differences with respect to their relationship with God and, of equal importance, the eternal resting place of their souls. I would never attempt to enter into this debate or challenge the validity of their claims to paradise. I only know for sure of my experiences, and I know we are admonished to "judge not, lest we be judged…" therefore, I will do my best to make no comparisons between my worth and any other. To do so, would make me quiver in shame at my unworthiness. No, this is just a grand opportunity to explain myself; if this serves to encourage another or exhibit a "how to" that worked for me, I will have succeeded beyond my wildest expectations.

This story started long ago. As far back as I can remember, I was taken to church, exposed to a format designed to convince you that you were "lost," and to illustrate most graphically how to correct that situation. Those churches were usually Baptist, rural, small, and different in subtle ways from larger, urban churches of the same denomination. On that subject, I have always felt small, rural churches of any denomination usually have more in common than would any with a large, urban congregation. As I have well documented, my father was a minister, my mother wanted to be, and our home, with all its economic problems and challenges, could be correctly called "Christian." The main literature was the Bible and church literature; other than schoolbooks, these offered the main stimulus for learning. The music was hymns, and we all gathered 'round and sang them. One could cynically offer that we were simply brainwashed and, that any life-affecting views or decisions made were done so in an immature or, at least, premature circumstance.

I have never felt so. As far back as I can remember, I vividly recall observing young people and adults under the most emotional of worship situations, both accepting Christ into their lives and, equally important, rejecting that decision. I have witnessed adults who, though drawn to be in a worship service for whatever reason, refused opportunities to become Christ followers. I observed, also, no stigma attached to that refusal, other than the continued concern for that person's "condition" by the body of believers; therefore, I feel I left babyhood and approached manhood understanding not only the doctrine of "free will," but also the practical fact that I was free to take my own road. No one would shoot me if it was other than the way of the Cross. You have noticed by now my liberal use of "quotes" and other old time terms. They were the ones used then, still have meaning to me and, at times, I can think of no other. Journey with me now, and accept the fact this is my experience which, 50-plus years later, would be described perhaps differently, if at all.

I indicated my earliest memories of home included bible stories, singing hymns, and watching Dad or Mom study a sermon or Sunday school lesson. Please understand this in the context of proper place and time, as we worked, studied for school, slept, read the newspaper when we had one, and did what any other rural kids did; we were just directed to behave and were served a liberal dose of biblical teachings. When our parents went to worship, we were required to go also, until we were an age when we could say, no, and not get knocked down for our exercise of independence. This (going to worship) would be rather frequent, as church usually involved Sunday morning and Sunday evening, as well as a mid-week, usually Wednesday, prayer meeting. Mixed in were revivals, reunions, singings, and vacation bible schools, all directed toward the greater purpose of exposing us to God's teachings.

My brother, Homer, made a profession of faith at a very early age; I cannot remember when, and my memory bank lights up when he was probably eight or nine, so it must have been before then. Acknowledging our close brother relationship, and given the atmosphere described here regarding church and home, I can still say I remember no overt pressure or "altar calls" ever being applied at home or in church by my family. I was subjected to what everyone else heard, no more.... no less.

That was, for the most part, this: *Salvation is a gift from God to all people. Men and women can never make up for their sin by self-improvement or good works. Only by trusting in Jesus Christ as God's offer of forgiveness can a person be saved from sin's penalty. When God has begun a saving work in the heart of any person, he gives assurance in his word that he will continue performing it until the end of time.*

Further, that *"God so loved the world that he gave his only begotten son, that whosoever believeth in him should not perish, but have everlasting life."* (John 3:16.) Finally, *"That if thou shalt confess with thy mouth the Lord Jesus, and shalt believe in thine heart that God hath raised him from the dead, thou shalt be saved."* (ROM 10:9) I know there are many modern, more easily understood versions of the Bible; I quote from the King James, as that was what I grew up hearing. I do not want to insult anyone's intelligence by suggesting this is it; that memorizing and repeating these two verses is all that is required for eternal life. However, I suggest that an understanding of what you are "believing" and following the steps stated in Rom 10:9 is the path. I do not know another.

This, then, I absorbed, beginning as far back as I can remember. The circumstances of my adolescent days were no different from any other child who attended church regularly; I will concede that few young people had more exposure in the home than I, unless it was other "preachers' kids." I am trying to be careful in explaining that my religious experiences were not the result of an infant being dragged to the altar, nor the happening of other members gathering around and praying that I make a "decision" during the invitation hymn at church services. To the contrary, I just remember attending church, being involved in all the activities, soaking up the messages, being "urged" to get up in church and sing and, other than being made to behave, just doing what everyone else my age did.

Baptist often used a term to describe the time when a person is capable of making a decision regarding becoming a Christian; it was called reaching the age of accountability. This is self-explanatory. When you realize that you are lost and apart from God, you are; and, you are old enough to do something about it.

By the time I was about eleven, I deemed myself accountable. I do not recall a specific day when it occurred; rather, like fuzz on your cheek, different urges regarding girls, mischief stepping up a notch, and the math lessons getting more difficult, I just knew I was lost. When this fact was acknowledged, each worship service, each invitation, each question regarding, "Are you (or whoever) a Christian?" was cause for squirming and, in fact, a denial. I believed that I was "lost," I knew how to change that condition, but sometimes the decision to make that change is difficult; many never do in a lifetime.

The circumstance of my conversion was this: In 1945, my father and others were involved in establishing a new church in our immediate community. At the time, we were attending church at the McMahan Calvary Baptist Church, on the Clearwater Road in the Clearwater community. Dad, the Reverend Orlan Baker, Pastor at McMahan Calvary, and a few people active in this project held "Cottage Prayer Meetings" on an irregular basis in homes in the area where they envisioned the church being. These were regular worship services, with singing, a brief message, and perhaps a report on the progress of current activities. On one such night in July, of 1945, the meeting was to be held at the home of Mrs. Robert Lovingood, who lived along side the Decatur Highway (now Tennessee 30) about four miles west of Athens. Mrs. Lovingood was an active leader in the community in many respects and, in fact, served briefly as a substitute teacher at Mouse Creek when I was in the seventh grade, before the school closed and I ended up going to Forrest Hill.

The Reverend Baker delivered the message that particular night and, perhaps sensing my state, offered an invitation for "decisions" to anyone there in Mrs. Lovingood's living room. I do not recall any particular pressure from my parents up to that time; they may, in fact, have discussed the path to salvation with me, particularly Mother, but I do not remember being set up for any action that specific night. When the invitation was offered, I felt compelled to step forward and offer Reverend Baker my hand; we immediately knelt in prayer. He prayed that I could find a way to accept Jesus into my life and asked God to forgive me of my state of sinfulness. I will never forget the feeling of relief and satisfaction that came over me when I knew that I had been accepted by Christ into his Kingdom. Though I have not proven worthy many, many times, and have many times strayed from the direction I know my life should have taken, I have never felt that Christ has forsaken me, from that moment on my knees in that room, long ago. Two other memories have always lingered: one, as we crossed the yard toward the house that evening (we lived in the Guinn place at that time), I remember Dad having his arm on my shoulder. Nothing was said, but I knew how proud he was of me and the decision I had made. The other, I recall looking up at the stars about that same time and feeling I had never seen them so clear, so majestic. At eleven, I felt a nearness to God that has perhaps never been surpassed.

This description is, I concede, out of the old time revival handbook, both quaint and perhaps embarrassing to modern theologians; I could not describe it any other way, because that is what happened, how I felt, and what I believed then and now.

The following Sunday was baptism day at McMahan Calvary Church; baptism is the ritual followed by Baptist, whereby upon a profession of faith, a public expression of desire to become a member of a specific Baptist church and, upon the majority vote of those present at any regular church service, the prospective member is baptized by immersion. This action confirms his or her acceptance into that church body (and, symbolically, the family of Christ).

The baptism was to be held at Mouse Creek (the actual stream), below a bridge on Clearwater Road, which was about a half mile from the church. I knew that I could join the church, and thus become a candidate for baptism all in one move that morning, and went prepared. Again, knowing I would probably do so, Reverend Baker gave an invitation for church membership by the side of that creek. I stepped forward, and was voted in by those present; thus, I joined others being baptized that morning. The only problem was, it had stormed the day and night before, and this creek, which meandered through red clay farmland, was about the color of yellow/red paint. When raised from the water, the action may have been spiritually cleansing, but my white shirt and pants were never the same. The date was Sunday, July 29, 1945.

In the years since, I have performed about all the functions one can do in a Baptist church and, at times, not been involved at all in regular church attendance. My convictions have never weakened:

I believe in the existence of God, in the Trinity and in God's dominion over our world. We are endowed with a mind, the ability to learn, to reason, and are capable of discovering great truths about our origin and how all of nature works together. To many, it would seem that science refutes or, at least, trivializes religious belief; to the contrary, I find it only reveals. I cannot fathom astrophysics or studies about the origin of the universe. I fathom this, however: all I have ever read, heard, or seen that describes or attempts to describe the origin of the universe(s) never gets to that point of explaining the first spark of creation. Something, someOne greater than ourselves must have had a hand in this process, and that Someone, our ultimate Creator, God, is worthy of my worship. Further, someone capable of bringing into being this infinitely complex system of life, such as we know on earth alone, is certainly capable of sustaining that life, throughout eternity.

I believe in eternity. The scriptures describe heaven and hell, and describe heaven as a place with pearly gates and streets paved with gold. I am convinced that heaven is to be eternally with God, and hell is to be eternally apart from him. The writers who gave us the passages describing heaven, used descriptions and phrases to describe a place of ultimate magnificence, to the extent their imaginations were capable. Does it matter what it is really like? I have never been hung up on its appearance, whether or not I will know everyone, or what I will do. If our imagination, through faith, can grasp the concept of being with God, forever, we can surely trust him to assure it will be a condition of peace, joy, and well being.

Many, perhaps most, believe one dies, and that is it. Ignoring the fact that this view overlooks the entire chain of creation, nature, birth, and life itself, everyone will accept the reality of dreams. In dreams, we live scenes, vignettes of existence, experience fear, joy, frustration, all the emotions of "real life." We do not question that they occur, we cannot explain why they do or what they mean; we just accept that, for that time, we live in another realm that is as real as life, yet is not a part of it. These are but insignificant scenes in the big picture of existence. If we accept these small bits of surreal reality, why do we struggle so much with the concept of an "afterlife," in a form dictated by our Creator, after this all too brief form of "real life" is over? I believe I will be there, and I believe I will enjoy it, as will all others there. Any other questions I deem of no significance.

I believe in prayer. I cannot tell you how it works, or give you proof in each case, if it has "worked" in a demonstrative way. I know it has worked for me, and I will not belabor you with the examples. I believe the answers come in many forms and often from a most surprising direction….ourselves. We are endowed with powers that we all too infrequently use, or neglect to develop. It seems reasonable that, if and when we over come our egos, and admit to ourselves that we are fallible, and ask for help and direction from a source "outside ourselves," we often are surprised that we can see a clear direction or source for relief from our burden that was not apparent before. The answer, as oft stated, can be, no. The point is, however, to accept that we are not here alone, that we are promised an ever-present strength and comfort, and we have but to ask.

My knowledge is not deep, but my beliefs are real. I am not proud of many of my acts of commission and omission; however, I am comforted by that first step taken 57 years ago. My vision of the future is best stated by an old hymn; it is not used much any more, but is as poignant and inspiring in summarizing my testimony, as any other I know:

> *"When peace, like a river, attendth my way,*
> *when sorrows, like sea billows roll;*
> *whatever my lot, thou hath taught me to say,*
> *It is well, it is well, with my soul."…*
> *"And, Lord, haste the day when the faith I shall sight,*
> *though the clouds, be rolled back as a scroll.*
> *The trump shall resound and the Lord shall descend.*
> *Even so,…it is well…with…my soul."*

H.G.Spafford
B.T.Bliss
Copyright 1904
John Church Co.

Epilogue

....and the sands of time flow on.

There is, of course, much more that can, and perhaps should, be said. First, the gender issues: When my work began, it focused on finding the Mincys. While that search is ongoing, other families inserted themselves into the fabric of this yarn until it became a story about ancestors, descendents, parents, children, me, and all these relationships. The easy and perhaps ego driven out has been to follow the men. What about the Rausins, Ladds, Horns, Nicks, Staleys, Selvidges, Martins, Wrights, and Byrums? These families and the stories about them are arguably as worthy and entertaining as any other. With respect and admiration for these distant relatives, I will have to leave their tales to be told by someone else.

Then there are the Goertzs, Rileys, Hartnetts, and Clapps, whose gene pool is as important as mine to all of my grandchildren. These good German, Irish, and Mayflower Pilgrim families merit our attention. Their stories should inspire others to research and share them with us, while sources are still available and memories sharp.

To bring into perspective how many of these settings and events have turned out or what influence they may have on the present, let's look at the fields onto which the seeds of these stories were sown and see what has grown.

Lawnville community, now an exit off I-40 enroute to Nashville just before Kingston heading west, seems remarkably the same: peaceful, unhurried and, preserved. The road by Young's Chapel CP Church is paved now, as is Hedgecock Lane Road toward Merriwater Park. From the cutoff point to "Grandmother's" place, the hills and valleys look the same, with fields and appearances relatively unchanged. They are neither lush nor eroded; just cared for and well maintained. As Cousin Billie says, "We try to keep it that way."

Grandmother's place is occupied by its second owner since 1908. It has been restored and, with its neat white exterior, looks almost as I remembered it long ago. The huge maples still majestically shade the front lawn; they almost beg you to pull up a split bottomed straight chair, lean back, and remember the times before air conditioning, when rest, conversation, and thoughts of work well done restored the soul.

At the foot of the hill where the road curves to the left toward Merriwater Park and where the old "cannery" once stood, Billie and Hugh Evans Wyatt have restored the building, turning it into a museum. It contains hundreds of artifacts, bits of memorabilia, pictures and furniture: a record of the Hedgecock "home place." They have created a treasure, indeed to be appreciated and preserved.

The same could be said of the Cave Creek, Dogwood and Tennessee communities; the roads are paved, a few more houses or neat modular homes are noticed, but the overall area seems untouched, except for a little more kudzu vine here and there. The churches and cemeteries are well maintained. Other than knowing the TVA covered many acres of "bottom land" in use long ago and that developments exist on the lake, with a little imagination, you can envision these hills and fields as Dad saw them.

Alas, the house where I first saw the light of day stands no more; it burned within the last 15-16 years. Before then, having obviously been remodeled, it looked better than when we lived there. A flat spot on the hillside above U.S. Route 70 is the only reminder of where I once crawled in my little hand-me-down crib.

What of the "trail of tears"? At the Brown place, a nice, brick, ranch home was built on the spot where ours once stood. The area shows some change in roads and use of land, with many new houses replacing the old. It looks good.

"Up on the hill" can still be reached, but the field where our little abode dwelt has been planted over and harvested many times by Bowater. Although another small house sits nearby, the exact spot where we hit absolute bottom is covered in small undergrowth and is not visible. Just as well.

The Layman properties are another story. For whatever reasons, those 2,800 acres that were the prize of that area 60 years ago seem to have stopped living about that time. Cows are still in the field and some type of operation goes on. However, the barns have caved in, fields are eroded, and weeds are practically all that is visible. Fence rows are overgrown, showing years of neglect, with "rundown" the only description that comes to mind. The "down at Laymans" house burned long ago and, worse, the "up at Laymans" house is still standing and apparently in use. I remember it as no country manor 60 years ago, but this, too, is relative, as it appears to have gone down hill steadily since that time. This entire farm mirrors the main place.

The Gwinn home still stands and is occupied; however, the neat pastures and fields along the small creek that flowed from Craig's lake are overgrown. Some are completely obscured. The small cemetery, that aroused our curiosity as we played, has been fenced, kept in fair condition, and still contains some stones of Gen. James T. Lane, CSA, and his family. A flag flies on a well kept pole, the bottom of which is protected by carefully entwined barbed wire, perhaps sending a message not to tamper with the "Stars and Bars" that adorn its tip.

Robbie Ensminger, years ago, built a new house on the spot where we lived on the "Ensminger Place." On the West Side of the small hill along TN 30, her brother, Earl, lived, and the entire farm looks cared for and respected.

Athens was, of course, the square and a few blocks surrounding it, together with the core of industry that included the stove works, plow company, an implement company or two, and the two or three furniture manufacturing companies. There was also a full-fashion hosiery mill and a few half-hose plants, the largest of which was the Athens Hosiery Mill, in North Athens. All these are gone, replaced by new and varied businesses; some thrive and others are gone, or going. What has remained is the McMinn Supply Company, now, the Athens Supply Co., where Dad worked the last several years of his work life. In fact, Fred Robinson's daughter is president, and the firm has expanded into building materials and has grown and prospered. I believe their growth has included the property down the street, where I worked for "Bo," as that little warehouse building still stands. Of course, Mayfield, Goody's, and Proffitt's are national success stories.

Athens now is the strip from downtown to I-75, three miles west. It is made up of the usual commercial sprawl and is no better or worse than the spread of other cities that have grown toward roads, streams, malls, or whatever it is that gives wings to the flight from down town.

Alas, my employer for 21 years, Burlington Industries, Inc., shut the doors on its once mighty transportation division at the end of 2002; the company, itself, is but a shell of what was put together by Spencer Love long ago. This is the sad result of unmet competition, unimaginative leadership, individual greed and stupidity.

What are we to conclude?

Only this, I suppose: property, places, things or appearances mirror lives. Each is not static; rather, all change for the better or worse proportionate to choices made and directions taken. It is not God's will or fate that causes us to fail or succeed.

Instead, it is the abilities given each of us to use or neglect that turn opportunities into success. Those fields, hills and valleys still beautiful and preserved were caused to be and those sadly run-down were allowed to become so.

An interesting observation: The First Baptist Church in Athens still stands impressively at the "V" intersection heading east on Madison. This has been a bastion of conservative Baptist worship during the last century, with its parishioners including most of the town's professional and commercial leaders. The late Rev. F. M. Dowell Jr. set the tone during the forties and fifties, leading this church to become a staunch supporter of the Southern Baptist Convention's programs and recommended order of services.

Alas, in the past few years, the church has literally been split asunder by a variety of issues, including continuous battles with its minister, members leaving in droves, and bitter acrimony among those who stayed. The issues? Personalities, of course, but at the forefront were those old standards: type of music and style of worship; contemporary vs. traditional. I can just see F.M., Rev. Charles Runyon, Rev. Orlan Baker and Dad turning over in their graves. Remember our battle over these issues out at Lakeview? I am sure that First Baptist will continue to serve its mission, and serve it well; however, the more things change, the more they seem the same.

Remember the story of our family, in a desperate effort to "save the farm," digging for buried treasure? It turns out that during this period there was a robbery in the area. The "loot" (always imagined being gold, of course) was never recovered, and many thought it was buried in the area between New Midway and Cedar Grove, only a short distance west of our archeological efforts. A few years later a local farmer, Felty White, was often seen on the ridges above Cedar Grove road with a crude metal detector that he had fashioned, "looking for gold." We were not crazy, just digging in the wrong place. Who knows? I may just go back and find it; perhaps I already have.

And speaking of family and the old days, it is interesting to note that efforts continue by many people to trace roots, research family history, find old burial sites, and add to the known legacy of these many fine families; they do, indeed, live on.

Big city Doris and seventh grade Sybil? Alive and well; both emerged from childhood with their sense of humor intact; neither remember certain things that I do; both claim to remember things that I do not. Oh, the blessing of selective memory. Not surprising, their lives have been full and productive.

After attending Auburn University, Doris deSha Savage was one of the first females to be admitted to the Georgia Institute of Technology. Continuing to develop and use her innate skills and interests, she worked as a commercial artist in the newspaper and magazine industry and, at the same time, studied in preparation to teach art to children and young adults. Post graduate work at the Montclair School of Art and at Long Island University enhanced her development as a watercolor artist of wide renown. She continues to teach, create, lead and contribute.

Following high school, Sybil Wyner worked for the State of Israel, doing extensive travel throughout the Middle Atlantic area; over a period of time, she received degrees from Rutgers University and Seton Hall University. Later, she received certificates of continuing study from Temple University, Gratz College and Bowie State Teachers College. A recognized and awarded teacher, she has written and continues to write plays, religious instructional material, curriculum outlines, and is the author of many short stories for children, as well as a novel about second-generation survivors of the Holocaust.

I am proud that I can say, "I knew them (briefly) when." These two fine people, however, are but outstanding examples of the scores of family members, friends, co-workers and classmates, who have contributed to making this world a more worthwhile place to be during the last half of the twentieth century.

Finally, the "New" Lakeview Church, which sits a half mile or so from its original spot on TN 30, has commercial property to its rear that is at the intersection of I-75 and TN 30. This intersection covered the spot of the original church Dad helped start and was the cause of its relocation.

These businesses, for ecological or other reasons, have developed a small pond, a "lake" if you will, behind the church, which spews up fountain style at its center for aeration purposes.

It could be said that ***Lakeview*** Baptist Church, named (by Mom) after a ***lake*** it could not see, that was not much to ***view*** if it could, now sits in front of a "lake" it can see, if it chooses to look.

Mom, up there somewhere, observing with her smile that always conveyed, "I know something you don't….and I am going to tell you," is probably saying:

"The Lord works in mysterious ways, His wonders to perform."

Amen!

Index

Adkisson, Mary Jane, 32, 35
Adolphus, Tennessee, 68, 69, 72, 76
Agamemnon, George, 305, 310, 331
Alamance County, North Carolina, 322, 332, 333
Alden, John, 1
Allen, Bill, 273
Allen, Sally Hart, 75
Amburgey, L.M., 229
Ampco Pittsburgh Corporation, 317
Anderson, Clyde, 234, 241, 245
Anderson, Dallas, 222
Anderson, Mrs. Lucile, 213, 218
Andersonville Prison, the, 24
Andrews, R. Homer, 333
Antietam, the Battle of, 19
Arnold, Eddy, 326
Athens Coal & Transfer Co., 256, 266
Athens Hosiery Mill, 97, 100, 102, 107, 108, 271, 379
Athens, Tennessee, 26, 69, 77, 85, 86, 87, 88, 89, 91, 96, 97, 100, 102, 103, 104, 107, 108, 111, 112, 115, 134, 137, 139, 140, 142, 144, 145, 177, 180, 184, 186, 193, 198, 199, 204, 205, 208, 209, 213, 215, 216, 218, 220, 221, 222, 229, 231, 232, 233, 237, 240, 242, 243, 254, 256, 257, 258, 265, 266, 269, 271, 272, 273, 274, 276, 283, 290, 342, 348, 353, 371, 379, 380
Auburn University, 243, 381
Axley, Betty, 4, 167, 340
Axley, Ed, 11, 100, 102, 103, 104, 115, 179, 184, 185, 186, 214, 342, 358

Axley, Elizabeth Mincy, 4, 36, 41, 79, 80, 89, 97, 100, 101, 103, 104, 115, 143, 146, 159, 166, 168, 171, 174, 178, 179, 180, 184, 185, 186, 192, 194, 276, 324, 337, 340, 341, 342, 343, 344, 347, 358, 366
Axley, Grayson, 56, 57, 100, 105, 111
Axley, Jim, 100, 107
Axley, Monnie, 97, 100, 101, 102, 106, 108
Axley, Odine, 100
Axley, Winnie Hutsell, 105, 111

Baird, Bill, 363
Baker, Buenos, 77, 213, 214, 215, 235
Baker, John L., 211, 234, 243, 258
Baker, Kenzil, 215
Baker, Orlan Rev., 140, 380
Baptism, 59
Baptist, 52, 58, 68, 75, 85, 95, 97, 103, 119, 120, 123, 124, 132, 135, 138, 140, 141, 145, 147, 161, 163, 167, 169, 176, 177, 184, 186, 191, 195, 220, 347, 348, 368, 370, 371, 372, 373, 380, 381, 382
Barbourville, Kentucky, 24, 33
Battershell, Byron, 13
Belle Island, prisoner of war camp, 62
Benton, Bob, 218
Benton, Frankie, 103
Berry picking, 179
Bevins, Lynn, 218, 256, 257, 268
Bigham, Mrs. Effie, 199, 200, 201, 204, 206, 211
Black Dutch, 200
Blount County, Tennessee, 18, 25
Bowater Southern Paper Corporation, 109, 222, 223, 378

Boyd, Carol, 258
Boylston, Mabel Norwood, 71
Brabson place, 116
Brabson, J.M., 118
Brashear, Nancy, 1, 28, 32
Brashear, Robert Samuel, 31
Brasseur, Robert, 1, 4, 28
British, 14, 16, 17
Broadman Hymnal, the, 195
Brown Place, 132, 378
Browning, Gordon, 232, 233
Burlington Industries, Inc, 90, 278, 380
Burlington Industries, Inc., 90, 278, 287, 295, 380
Burlington Terminal, 278, 279, 280, 304, 305, 306, 308, 318
Burlington, North Carolina, 279, 287, 365
Byles, Martha, 234, 247
Byrums, 1, 377

Cagle, Beatrice, 346
Cairo, Ohio, 63, 66
Calvert County, Maryland, 10
Camp Dick Robinson, Kentucky, 20, 52
Camp Pine Knot, Kentucky, 21
Cannon, Allan, 298, 349
Cannon, Robert K., 21
Canup, Ester, 84
Canup, Thomas Sr.., 84
Canupp, David Amos, 85
Canupp, Elizabeth Wright, 85
Canupp, Elizabeth Yates, 85, 86
Canupp, Henry Jackson, 84
Canupp, Joseph T., 86, 87, 88, 89, 90, 91, 92, 93, 94, 97, 106, 107, 109, 187, 208, 281, 283, 362, 363
Canupp, June, 2, 4, 5, 26, 32, 51, 52, 58, 60, 72, 74, 83, 85, 86, 87, 88, 89, 90, 91, 95, 97, 101, 102, 103, 105, 106, 107, 108, 109, 110, 111, 179, 183, 216, 218, 219, 220, 222, 223, 224, 234, 240, 248, 251, 266, 274, 275, 277, 278, 279, 281, 283, 289, 290, 295, 304, 309, 313, 340, 342, 344, 345, 346, 347, 348, 349, 353, 357, 358, 360, 361, 364
Canupp, Mae, 34, 88, 89, 90, 91, 92, 93, 94, 177, 363

Canupp, Susan, 84
Canupp, William, 86
Canupps, 3, 83, 85, 87, 89, 91, 93, 95, 97, 99, 101, 103, 105, 107, 109, 111, 113
Carroll, Peter, 12
Carson-Newman College, 109, 120, 147
Carter, Maybelle, 326
Carthage, Tennessee, 24, 53
Casteel, William R., 212, 215
Cates, Tommy, 294
Catron, Claude, 273
Christ, 113, 142, 182, 369, 370, 372
Christian, 123, 163, 185, 200, 201, 367, 368, 370, 371
Ciotti, Dorothy Jean, 5
Ciotti, Magdalen Pundai, 365
Ciotti, Mary Ann, 365
Civil War Diary, 19
Clapp, Cristina Helen, 1
Clapp, Fred, 359
Clapp, Pamela Mincy, 2, 89, 90, 110, 183, 276, 278, 283, 295, 332, 349, 352, 353, 354, 359, 360
Clapps, 377
Clark, Julie Mincy, 67, 70
Clemens, Samuel L., 187
Clinch River, the, 20, 21, 32, 37, 74, 122, 156
Cloverine salve, 192
Clower, Jerry, 205, 305
Colquitt, Elizabeth Mincy, 48
Columbus Terminal, the, 60, 67, 91, 181, 279, 287, 294, 295, 296, 297, 327
Confederacy, the, 24, 53
Cooperative Extension Service, the, 228, 231
Creasman, Rev. Oran, 346
Crites, Patsy, 234
Crittendon, Billy, 271
Crox, Ann, 217
CTS Transportation Co, 313, 314, 315, 318
Cumberland Gap, Tennessee, 21, 24, 33, 53
Cumberland Presbyterian, 32, 40, 122, 124, 125, 157, 162, 177, 184

Dallas, Texas, 178, 222, 311, 312, 313, 314, 315, 316, 318, 357, 359, 360, 361, 362, 363
Daughtery, Mrs. Judson, 212

DeGree, Walt, 299, 303, 304, 306
desertion, charges of, 60, 62
deSha, Doris, 217, 234, 247, 248, 381
Devilliers, Ted, 253, 289
Diversified Occupations, 216, 255, 256, 266, 331
DNA, 44, 83
Dockins, Art, 105, 109, 110, 111, 112, 302, 381
Dockins, Bess, 86, 87, 88, 89, 91, 94, 95, 97, 101, 103, 104, 105, 106, 107, 108, 109, 110, 111, 112, 113, 214, 345, 347, 353
Dockins, Mary Jane, 18, 32, 35, 52, 110, 111
Dodson, James R., 215
Dogwood Community, the, 68, 76, 117, 119, 176, 378
Duckworth, Mrs. Clifford, 204

East Athens Baptist Church, 103, 185
East Tennessee, 18, 19, 26, 32, 37, 39, 45, 50, 51, 52, 61, 74, 85, 95, 117, 126, 133, 216, 269, 277, 331, 340
Elder, Sam, 265
Ellis, Nola, 101, 102, 110, 345
England, 8, 9, 10, 11, 28, 31, 44, 45, 46, 75, 265, 301
Ensminger, Reverend Hugh, 348
Erwin, Rev. George E., 207
ET&WNC, 269, 276, 290
Etowah, Tennessee, 57
Euliss, Glen, 281

Farmer's Bank, the, 274
Farner, Agnes, 95
Farner, Alvillia, 104
Farner, Eula Dean, 100
Farner, Harvey, 105
Farner, Hayden, 101
Farner, Hazel, 102, 105, 110, 111, 282
Farner, Jane Runion, 26, 49, 96, 97, 101, 105, 108
Farner, Lester, 41, 97, 100, 107
Farner, village, Tennessee, 95, 97
Farner, Violet Clayton, 105
Farner, Warren G., 104
Farner, William Issac, 14, 73, 95, 96, 97, 101, 106, 142

Farners, 3, 83, 84, 85, 87, 89, 91, 93, 95, 97, 99, 100, 101, 103, 104, 105, 107, 109, 111, 113, 345
Fayle, W.L., 283, 286, 287, 288, 297, 305
Felson Carriers, 301
Ferguson, Maggie, 103, 104, 323, 363
Ferguson, Ray, 103
Fields, Sparky, 286
5th Tennessee Infantry, 19, 24, 33, 53
Finley, K.B., 279, 283, 286, 288, 289, 290, 294, 295, 296, 305, 306, 318, 322
First Baptist Church, 380
fixer, textile, 87, 88, 104
Flannigan, William, 80, 82
Forest Hill School, the, 198
Forest Hill School, the, 198, 204, 205, 208, 210, 213, 344
Foster, J. Will, 211
4-H Club, 159, 212, 216, 217, 221, 227, 228, 229, 231, 232, 233, 234, 236, 237, 239, 240, 241, 243, 245, 247, 249, 251, 252, 253, 254, 255, 256, 257, 259, 260, 261, 266, 321, 331, 332, 335, 347
4-H project, 3, 17, 79, 118, 138, 177, 185, 192, 212, 219, 228, 230, 231, 232, 245, 266, 308, 371
4-H Roundup, 229, 233, 236, 241, 251, 252, 257, 258
Fox, Margaret J., 18
Frazier, automobile, 88

Gardner, Charles, 346
Gastonia Terminal, the, 292, 306, 307, 308
Gerves, Mary, 10
Gettysburg, the Battle of, 19
Gibson, 84, 327, 330
Gilbert, John Henry, 234, 235, 236, 241, 247, 248, 252, 255, 258, 259, 260, 347
God, 120, 147, 163, 169, 174, 175, 181, 182, 185, 193, 222, 235, 248, 257, 260, 305, 319, 367, 368, 369, 370, 371, 372, 373, 380
Goertz, Tina Mincy, 183, 349, 357, 358, 359, 360
Goertzs, 377
Goff, Leon, 297, 303
golf, 240, 308, 311, 327, 330, 335, 340

Graham, Mary Ola, 34
Grainger County, Tennessee, 45, 46, 47, 48, 49, 50, 51, 52
Grand Old Opry, 204, 237
Green County, North Carolina, 45
Green, General Nathaniel, 17
Green, Lucille, 341
Grubb, Kenneth, 195, 225, 234, 236, 247
Guilford County, North Carolina, 14
Gwinn, Mrs. Bennett, 177

Hamilton County, Tennessee, 217, 234, 247, 248
Happy Top, 107
Harrod, Ross, 212
Hart, Elizabeth, 117
Hart, John Sawyer, 1
Hart, Letitia Marney, 1, 75
Hartnett, Debra Mincy, 181, 184, 304, 355, 356, 357, 359, 360
Hartnett, Joseph Michael, 1
Hartnett, Tony, 357
Hartnetts, 377
Harts, 1, 43, 45, 47, 49, 51, 53, 55, 57, 59, 61, 63, 65, 67, 69, 71, 72, 73, 75, 77, 79, 80, 81, 118
Hedgcock, Robert E., 8
Hedgecock, Ada, 38, 39, 125, 151, 159, 160, 184
Hedgecock, Burton, 37, 38, 41, 154
Hedgecock, David, 25
Hedgecock, Frank, 38, 39, 40, 152, 160, 184
Hedgecock, Henry Marion, 25, 26, 28, 35, 36, 41, 42, 150
Hedgecock, Minter, 15, 24, 25
Hedgecock, Sara Alice, 1, 102, 105, 151, 154, 162, 169
Hedgecock, Thomas, 25, 28
Hedgecock, Virgil, 40, 104
Hedgecock, Willis, 15, 18
Hedgecock, Willis E., 19
Hedgecocks, 1, 7, 8, 9, 11, 13, 15, 17, 19, 21, 23, 25, 27, 29, 30, 31, 33, 35, 37, 39, 40, 41, 151, 157, 159, 340
Hengert, 9
Hengist, 9
Henry Donal, 308

Higgins, Kenneth D., 221
High Rock Lake, 90
Hill, Jack, 217
Hill, Jequetia, 346
Hitchcock, Christopher, 10, 13
Hitchcock, Isaac, 9, 12, 13, 14
Hitchcock, John, 12
Hitchcock, Phillis Anna, 12
Hitchcock, Thomas, 15
Hitchcock, William I, 10
Hitchcock, William II, 10
Hitchcock, William III, 12
Horsa, 9
Huguenot, 1
Humbred, Russell, 232, 233, 241, 243, 244, 251, 253, 260
Hutsell, Evelyn, 103, 193
Hutsell, Floyd, 193
Hutsell, Frank, 192
Hutsell, Jimmy, 201

Idlewild School, the, 204
Interstate Commerce Commission, 277, 300
Ireland, 1, 44, 45, 72

Jackson, Levi, 69
Jenkins, Robert E., 289, 295, 304, 308
Jones, Mary, 11, 12
Jones, William Sr., 10, 11
Joppa, Maryland, 10, 11, 12

Kennedy, J.B., 277, 279, 280, 281, 282, 283, 286, 290, 291, 292, 293, 296, 298, 299, 301, 303, 305
Kent, England, 8, 9, 10, 354
Key, Jim, 346
Kidwell, Annie, 160
Kimbrough, Mary Ellen, 196, 197
Kingston, Tennessee, 2, 4, 8, 10, 12, 14, 16, 18, 20, 22, 24, 26, 28, 30, 32, 34, 36, 38, 39, 40, 42, 44, 46, 48, 50, 52, 53, 54, 56, 58, 60, 62, 64, 66, 68, 70, 72, 74, 76, 77, 78, 80, 82, 84, 86, 88, 90, 92, 94, 96, 98, 100, 102, 104, 106, 108, 110, 112, 116, 118, 120, 122, 124, 126, 128, 130, 132, 133, 134, 136, 138, 140, 142, 143, 144, 146, 150, 152, 154, 156, 158, 160, 162,

163, 164, 166, 167, 168, 170, 172, 174, 176, 178, 180, 182, 184, 186, 188, 190, 192, 194, 196, 198, 200, 202, 204, 206, 208, 210, 212, 214, 216, 218, 220, 222, 224, 228, 230, 232, 234, 236, 238, 240, 242, 244, 246, 248, 250, 252, 254, 256, 258, 260, 264, 266, 268, 270, 272, 274, 276, 278, 280, 282, 284, 286, 288, 290, 292, 294, 296, 298, 300, 302, 304, 306, 308, 310, 312, 314, 316, 318, 322, 324, 326, 328, 330, 332, 334, 338, 340, 342, 344, 346, 348, 350, 352, 354, 356, 358, 360, 362, 364, 366, 368, 370, 372, 374, 377, 378, 380, 382
Kirk, David, 224
Knupp, Jacob, 4, 83
Kreis, Almeda S., 26

Ladd, Martha, 26, 35
Ladds, 1, 377
Lakeview Baptist Church, 140, 141, 142, 145, 174, 177, 381, 382
Larson, Elmer, 106, 299, 303, 304, 305, 306, 309
Lawnville Cemetery, 27, 78, 81, 159
Lawnville Road, 26
Lawnville School, 41, 157, 158
Layman, Guilford, 135, 136, 137, 138, 175, 197, 201, 265, 379
Layman, Mary Belle, 347
Lenoir City, Tennessee, 75, 214
Lerman, Dave, 318
Lewis, C.W., 280, 282, 291, 295, 305, 309
Life Magazine, 120, 188, 237, 250, 259, 260, 261, 352
Lincoln, Abraham, 15, 18, 19, 67, 84, 132, 182, 187
Littleton, Henry, 76, 80, 123
Littleton, Henry M., 80, 81
Littleton, Sophia Mincy, 76, 80, 81, 82, 123, 164, 169
Livestock judging, 256
Long, Mrs. Peggy, 211
Lord Baltimore, 11
Love, Spencer, 280, 287, 302, 380
Lovern, Joyce, 211, 212, 216

Lovingood, Mrs. Robert, 204, 371
Lowry, Marvin, 214, 253, 254, 255, 256, 260

machinist, textile, 87, 88, 100
Marietta, Georgia, 53, 55
Marion, General Francis, 16, 17
Marley, Ken, 322
Marney, Amos, 1, 4, 72, 74
Marney, Amos I, 1, 4, 72, 74
Marney, Letitia, 1, 75
Marney, Polly, 74
Marney, Robert, 72, 73
Marney, Sarah Vance, 72, 73
Marshall, Garland, 291
Martin, Dr. LeRoy A., 220
Martin, Wash, 257, 268
Martins, 1, 377
Mary Washington College, 1
Mason, Leatrice, 217, 218, 345, 346
Matthews, Joffery, 104
Mayfield Dairy, 229
Mayfield ice cream, 210
Mayfield, Mrs. Regina, 205
McArthur, Lee, 280, 297
McCaslin, Carrie Ann, 110
McCaslin, Dewain, 110
McKinney, Emma Lou, 231, 234
McMillan, H.F., 256, 257, 266, 267, 268, 269, 270, 271, 276, 282, 290, 380
McMillan, Mayme Jo, 266, 268, 270, 271, 290
McMinn County High School, 88, 208, 211, 213, 232, 331, 342
McMinn County, Tennessee, 35, 47, 50, 69, 71, 86, 128, 129, 133, 136, 137, 145, 165, 168, 208, 209, 211, 231, 232, 247, 260, 331, 335, 348
McMinn Supply Co., 139, 167
Melton, Earl, 142, 144, 308, 319, 327, 331, 379
Melton, Marvin, 214
Millikin, Mary Ruth, 14
Millikin, Will, 14
Minchew, 46
Mincy, Cora Clark, 70

Mincy, David, 15, 16, 24, 25, 47, 49, 51, 52, 53, 54, 55, 56, 57, 58, 59, 60, 68, 69, 77, 78, 85, 103, 107, 349

Mincy, Dorothy Ciotti, 362

Mincy, Dorothy Ciottia, 5, 103, 133, 136, 137, 138, 149, 197, 198, 200, 204, 205, 207, 208, 213, 229, 231, 265, 317, 335, 337, 338, 339, 341, 343, 345, 347, 349, 351, 353, 355, 357, 359, 361, 362, 363, 364, 365, 366, 371, 372

Mincy, Elizabeth, 1, 4, 12, 15, 17, 18, 47, 48, 49, 50, 52, 72, 75, 76, 84, 85, 86, 117, 128, 167, 340, 352, 354, 355, 359, 360

Mincy, Eva Hedgecock, 1, 7, 8, 17, 18, 36, 38, 40, 42, 79, 95, 115, 119, 122, 123, 124, 125, 128, 133, 134, 135, 137, 138, 139, 140, 144, 145, 146, 147, 149, 150, 151, 152, 153, 154, 155, 156, 157, 158, 159, 160, 161, 162, 163, 164, 165, 166, 167, 168, 169, 170, 171, 173, 174, 175, 176, 177, 178, 179, 180, 181, 182, 183, 184, 185, 186, 188, 189, 190, 191, 194, 195, 196, 206, 207, 209, 214, 222, 245, 323, 324, 342, 343, 344, 348, 349, 355, 369, 371, 382

Mincy, George L., 71, 77, 78, 79, 80, 81, 82, 118, 119, 121, 123, 125, 127, 128, 129, 134, 138, 146, 162, 163, 166, 167, 224

Mincy, Henry Major Merideth, 47

Mincy, Homer F. Jr, 1, 4, 36, 76, 79, 80, 81, 82, 115, 117, 118, 119, 122, 123, 124, 125, 127, 128, 129, 131, 132, 133, 134, 135, 136, 137, 138, 139, 141, 142, 143, 145, 146, 147, 159, 161, 166, 167, 168, 170, 171, 174, 175, 178, 179, 180, 188, 191, 192, 194, 195, 197, 199, 200, 207, 209, 211, 213, 214, 218, 219, 222, 245, 265, 324, 333, 337, 338, 339, 340, 342, 343, 344, 347, 366, 369

Mincy, Homer F. Jr., 1, 4, 36, 76, 79, 80, 81, 82, 115, 117, 118, 119, 122, 123, 124, 125, 127, 128, 129, 131, 132, 133, 134, 135, 136, 137, 138, 139, 141, 142, 143, 145, 146, 147, 159, 161, 166, 167, 168, 170, 171, 174, 175, 178, 179, 180, 188, 191, 192, 194, 195, 197, 199, 200, 207, 209, 211, 213, 214, 218, 219, 222, 245, 265, 324, 333, 337, 338, 339, 340, 342, 343, 344, 347, 366, 369

Mincy, Homer F. Sr., 38, 75, 82, 91, 115, 116, 117, 118, 119, 120, 121, 122, 123, 124, 125, 127, 128, 129, 131, 132, 133, 134, 135, 136, 137, 138, 139, 140, 141, 142, 143, 144, 145, 146, 147, 161, 162, 163, 164, 165, 166, 167, 168, 174, 175, 176, 177, 178, 179, 181, 184, 185, 189, 190, 191, 194, 195, 197, 201, 204, 208, 210, 214, 230, 267, 269, 270, 275, 342, 343, 344, 347, 369, 371, 372, 378, 379, 380, 382

Mincy, Ila Breazeale, 340

Mincy, John Tyler, 340

Mincy, John W., 1, 51, 118, 119, 120, 123, 125, 135, 168

Mincy, John Wesley, 1

Mincy, Margaret Byrum, 56

Mincy, Martha Martin, 47, 49, 51

Mincy, Martha Selvedge, 58

Mincy, Octavia Lancaster, 80

Mincy, Olive, 77, 78, 79, 80, 81, 82, 119, 123, 125, 128, 162, 163, 164, 166, 168, 169

Mincy, Robert, 58, 59, 67, 69

Mincy, Samuel, 45, 46, 48

Mincy, Sara Elizabeth Hart, 105, 119, 128, 209

Mincy, Sara Josie, 67, 71

Mincy, Sarah Tennessee, 56, 57

Mincy, Sophronia Jackson, 68, 69, 70, 77, 84

Mincy, Susan Hart, 72, 105, 119, 128, 209

Mincy, Virgil, 225, 295, 303, 334, 347

Minshew, 45, 46

Mississippi River, the, 63, 67

Mix, Tom, 192, 206, 207

Moon Carriers, 302

Moon Pie, 210, 214

Morrill Act, the, 227

Moses, Rex, 335

Moss, Marion, 231

Mouse Creek School, 103, 133, 136, 137, 138, 149, 197, 198, 200, 204, 205, 207, 208, 213, 229, 231, 265, 335, 338, 341, 371, 372

Music, 323

National 4-H Club Congress, 228
National Aluminum Corporation, 315, 316, 317, 318, 362
National Geographic, 44
National Honor Society, the, 211, 212
National Steel Corporation, 317
New Brunswick Terminal, the, 303, 304
New Hopewell Baptist Church, the, 71, 135
New Midway Church, 123
Nicholas, Tom D., 304, 308, 315, 318
Nicks, 1, 377
Nicks, Phoebe, 32
Norman, Pearl Hedgecock, 40, 103
Norman, Roy, 40
North Athens School, the, 85, 97, 100, 101, 102, 103, 145, 212, 271, 346, 347, 379
North Bergen Terminal, the, 311

Orange County, North Carolina, 14, 31, 275

Parkinson, Lane, 234
Parks, Blan, 231, 234
Patterson Creek, 25
peaches, 37, 124, 126, 189
Pepsi Cola Bottling Group, 311
Petit, Junior, 207
Philadelphia cemetery, the, 50
Philadelphia, Tennessee, 26, 48, 50, 52, 54, 56, 58, 60, 61, 62, 77, 78, 79, 84, 301
Pittsburgh, Pennsylvania, 115, 181, 311, 312, 315, 316, 317, 357, 359, 362
Porterfield, Gary, 311
Presley, Elvis, 289, 290
prisoner exchanges, 62
PTA, 198, 326, 332, 342
Puett , Mrs. Anna, 195
Puett, Mrs. Anna, 196
Pundai, Grandmother, 365
Pyott, John W., 25

Quaker, 13, 14, 341
Quarado, Tommy, 242, 243, 294, 300, 303

Rausin, Mary Ann, 18, 25
Rausins, 1, 377
Rayburn, Samuel T., 74

Rebels, 21, 151
Republican, 19, 230
Resaca, Battle of, 33
Resaca, the Battle of, 53
Revolutionary War, 14, 15, 28, 73
Reynolds, Riley, 86, 109
Rheinhardt, Joe, 362
Riceville School, the, 136, 191, 197, 222
Riceville, Tennessee, 26, 109, 111, 129, 132, 134, 136, 168, 169, 190, 191, 195, 197, 198, 208, 209, 213, 222, 338
Richmond, Miser, 160
Riddle, Jean, 215, 216
Riggs, Cliston, 245
Riley, JoAnn Mincy, 352, 354, 358, 359, 360
Rileys, 377
Roane County, Tennessee, 25, 26, 27, 28, 32, 41, 48, 50, 51, 52, 54, 56, 58, 67, 68, 72, 73, 74, 75, 81, 117, 124, 127, 166, 179, 344
Roberts, Brashears, 1, 26, 32
Roberts, Edwards, 27
Roberts, Nancy Brashears, 32
Roberts, Sara Alice, 35, 150
Roberts, Thomas, 26, 151
Roberts, Thomas L., 33
Roberts, Zaccheus, 27, 32
Robinson, Nellie, 232, 242
Rockholt, Paul, 207
Roderick, Franklin, 234
Rodrigue, Sheila, 50
Rogers, Peggy, 32
Rossiter, Dr. Dudley, 8
Rossville Terminal, the, 295
Rowan County, North Carolina, 14, 15, 17
Rudd, Frank, 291, 293, 295
Rumley, Everett, 365
Runion, George, 96
Runion, Maru, 95, 96
Runion, Nancy Jane, 96
Runion, Rachel Kirkland, 96

Sale Creek, Tennessee, 53, 61
Scotland, 1, 72
Selvidges, 1, 377
Sherman, General, 55, 56, 63, 216, 241
Sherwin-Williams Co., 314

Shirley, 259, 260
Shoffner, Jim, 277
Silvertone, 325
Simpson, Curtiss, 280, 291, 292, 293, 295
Skinner, Linda, 51
Skinner, Linda Mincy, 51
Smith Walton, 38
Smith, Don, 270
Smith, Ruby Hedgecock, 41, 119, 153, 158, 160, 184
Smith, Tom, 41
Smith-Lever Act, the, 227
South Bend, Indiana, 243
South Paterson Trucking Co., 302
Spurlin, Tommy, 242, 243, 294, 300, 303
Staleys, 1, 377
Stallings, Richard, 10
Standing Stone State Park, 240, 243
Stanfield, Kathy, 86, 107, 108, 109, 110, 111, 345
Steel Warehouse Co. Inc, 318
Stephens, Jack, 282
Stevens, Tom, 289
Studebaker, 242, 243
Sultana, the, 60, 63, 66
Sunday, 41, 102, 121, 135, 139, 140, 142, 146, 154, 169, 171, 174, 178, 185, 191, 252, 258, 277, 282, 296, 298, 313, 345, 358, 369, 372, 373

Tarleton, Colonel Banastre, 17
Tate, Mrs. James, 199
Taylor, Vivian, 347
Tennessee 4-H Club Congress, 229
Tennessee 5th Infantry Regiment, Company B, 33
Tennessee Baptist Church, the, 74
Tennessee River, the, 58, 68, 74, 76, 253
Tennessee Volunteers, 48, 252
Tennessee Wesleyan College, 208, 219, 220, 221, 222, 224, 235, 257, 259, 270, 272, 273, 274, 295, 345, 346, 348
Toastmasters, International, 308, 310, 315, 331, 332
tobacco, 11, 18, 39, 79, 109, 118, 121, 126, 132, 136, 143, 144, 171, 190, 244, 245, 260

Torbett, Anna Ruth, 207
Torbett, Bobby, 199, 201
Tories, 15, 16
Trott, Master James, 51
Trotter, Dorothy, 217
Tyler, Ben J., 139, 177, 279, 282, 289, 305, 306, 307, 309, 318

Union Chapel Methodist Church, 135, 136, 171, 174, 176, 221
Union, the, 19, 21, 26, 33, 48, 49, 52, 53, 54, 59, 61, 62, 63, 69, 77, 135, 136, 151, 171, 174, 176, 221, 280
University of Tennessee, 80, 89, 222, 223, 224, 241, 244, 251, 252, 253, 274, 275, 277, 278, 286, 297, 308, 340, 348, 353
US 70, 119

Vance, Samuel, 73
Vestal Hosiery Mill, 87
Vicksburg, Mississippi, 60, 62
Vortigern', 9

W.L.A.R., 204, 206
Waggoner, Larry, 111, 364
Walker, Laura, 34, 216
Walnut G rove Church, the, 191
Watkins Products, 38, 128, 129, 132, 133, 134, 168, 189, 252
Way, Professor William, 225, 274
Way, William, 225, 274
Webb, Ms, Mrytle, 229
Webb, Ms. Mrytle, 231
Welch, 27
Welch, Bob, 311, 313, 319
whipping, 195, 197, 199, 302, 337
Wilkes County, North Carolina, 45
Williams, Tom, 309, 311
Williamson Hosiery Mill, 271
Williamson, John, 223, 271, 273
Wilson, Pete, 222
Winder, Jessie, 102
Winder, Wayne, 102
Wolford, Colonel Frank G., 77
Wood, Elizabeth, 15, 17
Woodward, Garrett, 277

World War II, 88, 100, 104, 137, 196, 228, 251, 267, 291
Wyatt, Billie Hedgecock, 41
Wyner, Sybil, 205, 217, 381

Yopp, J.D., 286, 288

978-0-595-40474-2
0-595-40474-X

Printed in the United States
67406LVS00008B/45